HOLY RAMBLINGS

HOLY RAMBLINGS

Travelogues, Commentaries, and Meditations
on
Pilgrimages Far and Near

KENT G. HARE

CONTINUANDUM

Copyright © 2020 by Kent G. Hare

All rights reserved. This book or any portion thereof may not be reproduced or used in any manner whatsoever without the express written permission of the publisher except for the use of brief quotations in a book review or scholarly journal.

Scriptural quotations from The Catholic Edition of the Revised Standard Version of the Bible, copyright 1965, 1966 by the Division of Christian Education of the National Council of the Churches of Christ in the United States of America. Used by permission. All rights reserved.

All maps and diagrams drawn by the author. Base Maps for Assisi, Orvieto, Florence, Rome, Mexico City, and Jerusalem obtained via CADmapper.com using data © OpenStreetMaps contributors, cartography licensed as CC BA-SA.

Maps and diagrams are for orientation purposes only and are not to be considered of navigational quality. The author and the publisher assume no liability for damages arising from such use.

All information contained herein is believed to be accurate at the time of publication. The author and publisher assume responsibility for neither information that might change nor any liability for damages that may result from the use of information contained herein.

First Edition: 2020

ISBN 978-0-578-22950-8 (hc)
ISBN 978-0-578-22951-5 (pbk)
ISBN 978-1-79488-157-0 (ebook)

CONTINUANDUM
P.O. Box 7377
Natchitoches, Louisiana 71457

www.continuandum.com

Front Cover: The Rotunda and Edicule of the Basilica of the Holy Sepulcher, Jerusalem, Israel. Photograph taken by the author, 20 August 2018.

Back Cover: The author at the Lowest Bar in the World, Kalia Beach on the Dead Sea, Kalia, Israel/The West Bank. Photograph taken by a fellow pilgrim, 19 August 2018.

Pro certo autem dico, quod non tantum laborem habui de loco ad locum peregrinando, quantum habui de libro ad librum discurrendo, quae rendo, legendo, et scribendo, scripta corrigendo et concordando.

However, I say for certain, that I did not have so much labour in making my pilgrimage from place to place, as I had in running from book to book, in thinking, reading, and writing, correcting and correlating what I have written.

– Felix Fabri, *Evagatorium*
(quoted by Kathryne Beebe, *Pilgrim and Preacher,*
"Note to the Reader," n.p.n.)

Dedications

Anne
Father Humphries
Doctors Ingram and Britten

See the Acknowledgments

CONTENTS

List of Figures   ix

Acknowledgments   xi

Preface   xiii

Introduction
What is a "Pilgrimage"? The Power of Place   1

PART ONE
Pilgrimages Past

Chapter One
The Eternal City
Pilgrimage to Rome and Italy   13

Chapter Two
¿No estoy yo aquí que soy tu madre?
Pilgrimage to Our Lady of Guadalupe and Mexico City   71

Chapter Three
It was here! In this place!
Pilgrimage to the Holy Land   123

PART TWO

Pilgrimages Future and Present

Chapter Four

Pilgrimages Far ... 255

Chapter Five

... Pilgrimages Near ... 273

Chapter Six

... and Pilgrimages Here 309

Chapter Seven

Concluding Thoughts and Advice for Pilgrims 333

Appendix One

Itineraries: Ideal and Reality 351

Appendix Two

A Regional List of the Painted Churches of Texas 353

References 359

LIST OF FIGURES

Figure 1: Pilgrimage to Italy with the Minor Basilica of the Immaculate Conception, October 2014.. 12
Figure 2: Map of Italy 64
Figure 3: Map of Assisi 65
Figure 4: Map of Orvieto 65
Figure 5: Map of Florence 66
Figure 6: Map of Rome.. 66
Figure 7: Layout of St. Peter's Basilica 67
Figure 8: Map of the Vatican City. 68
Figure 9: Mass in the Extraordinary Form, St. Peter's Basilica......... 68
Figure 10: The Basilica of St. Paul Outside the Walls..................... 69
Figure 11: Our Leaders in Rome 69
Figure 12: Pilgrimage to Our Lady of Guadalupe with Dr. Taylor Marshall, February 2016.. 70
Figure 13: Map of Mexico.. 116
Figure 14: Map of Mexico City.. 117
Figure 15: The Image of Our Lady of Guadalupe, New Basilica.... 118
Figure 16: The Spanish *Virgen de Guadalupe*............................... 118
Figure 17: Layout of the Shrine of Our Lady of Guadalupe, Mexico City. 119
Figure 18: The Old Basilica of Our Lady of Guadalupe,. 119
Figure 19: The Hares and the Marshalls, New Basilica. 120
Figure 20: Our Mexican guides: (L) Roberto; (R) Anne and Pablo.120
Figure 21: Father Juan Diego, our Spiritual Director..................... 120
Figure 22: Templo de Santo Domingo, Puebla – Capilla del Rosario. 121
Figure 23: Radio Maria Pilgrimage to the Holy Land, August 2018. 122
Figure 24: Brother Miguel, Father Emilio, and the author. 122
Figure 25: Map of Israel... 244
Figure 26: Map of the Galilee.. 245
Figure 27: Layout of the Sanctuary of the Annunciation, Nazareth 245
Figure 28: The Grotto of the Annunciation, Nazareth. 246
Figure 29: Derelict trucks from 1948 Israeli attempt to relieve besieged Jerusalem... 246

Figure 30: Brother Miguel and Tony, our Israeli guide................... 247
Figure 31: Map of Jerusalem, Bethlehem, and the Dead Sea ..... **Error! Bookmark not defined.**
Figure 32: Restored Byzantine murals inside the Church of the Nativity.. 247
Figure 33: Layout of the Basilica of the Nativity 248
Figure 34: Map of Jerusalem: The Old City and the Mount of Olives 249
Figure 35: Praying at the VIII. Station of the Via Dolorosa............ 249
Figure 36: Map of The Via Dolorosa.. 250
Figure 37: Layout of the Holy Sepulcher... 251
Figure 38: Golgotha or Calvary Chapel, Church of the Holy Sepulcher. 252
Figure 39: The California Mission Trail... 308
Figure 40: The Painted Churches of Texas 357
Figure 41: Inside St. John the Baptist Church, Ammannsville, Texas – "The Pink Church."... 357

ACKNOWLEDGMENTS

There are four persons whom I must thank above all others:

Anne, my wife: For 35 years – half a lifetime, well more than half *our* lifetimes – she has stuck by me through thick and thin, bearing patiently with my mercurial temperament (which manifests at no time worse than when I am obsessed with some project such as this), supporting me faithfully but calling me down firmly when necessary. She lives the ideal of Proverbs 31: 10-31, and I thank God for her every day. Any words I write here beyond these would be woefully inadequate: Thank you, and I love you.

Reverend Ryan Humphries of the Catholic Diocese of Alexandria in Louisiana: Leading my first pilgrimage, as recounted in Chapter One, and sage advice given at the outset are only the beginning of what I owe him. During his all too brief three years as Rector of the Minor Basilica of the Immaculate Conception in Natchitoches (2013-2016), his spiritual direction and example probably had a deeper impact on me than any other priest I have known. Priests come and go in any parish, but I will always look back on those years as being when I turned from being neither cold nor hot in my Faith (Rev. 3: 15). Finally, before I ever considered authoring this book, Fr. Humphries provided valuable feedback on my evolving ideas about "pilgrimage" that ultimately became the Introduction.

Christopher Ingram, M.D., Cardiologist, and Dennis Britten, M.D., Cardiac Surgeon, partners in the Regional Cardiology Clinic at Natchitoches Regional Medical Center: The story appears briefly at the beginning of Chapter Three, but the even more concise version is that without their joint efforts and accommodations less than a week before departure, I would not have gone on the pilgrimage to the Holy Land ... perhaps ever.

Beyond those four to whom I owe debts of gratitude that I can never repay and to whom I dedicate this book, there are others whose understanding permitted my accompanying the pilgrimages to Italy and the Holy Land. Particularly for the former, which meant two full weeks out of the classroom at mid-semester, either William Housel, Ph.D., then-Coordinator of History and Social Sciences at Northwestern State University, or Joseph Morris, M.S., then-Head of the

Department of Criminal Justice, History, and Social Sciences, could have vetoed my absence outright. Contrary to the movies, not all academics are like Indiana Jones, able to dump our teaching duties on graduate assistants at will and chase adventure around the world. More recently, when the dates of the pilgrimage to the Holy Land shifted into the first week of classes for the fall semester, Mark Melder, Ph.D., present Head of CJHSS, calmly rumbled, "You have a plan to cover it? I don't see a problem." I am grateful beyond measure.

As I have drafted this book over the past few months, I have discussed various aspects of it with colleagues and friends who encouraged me where appropriate and discouraged me from heading off in utterly wrong-headed directions when necessary. That would include especially my former student, now colleague in History at NSU, Christopher Gilson, Ph.D. Once written, Ingrid Cannella-Newell rendered valuable criticism; her close reading of portions of the draft helped transform my overly convoluted prose into something at least resembling Standard English. The resemblance would undoubtedly be closer had I incorporated more of her thoughtful suggestions.

I also wish to acknowledge the members of the Monday Night Bible Study at my and my wife's house, now in its *twelfth year*, as well as the members of the *Nova Schola Cantorum Natchitochensis* (New Chant Schola of Natchitoches) whom I have had the pleasure of leading at Sunday Vespers and Mass in the Extraordinary Form at the Minor Basilica for several years now. While the members of these two latter groups have, for the most part, had no direct role in the production of this book, their friendship, encouragement, and indulgence have been an enormous blessing and support for which I am incredibly grateful. Some ideas presented herein were, furthermore, first explicitly developed in the context of that Bible Study group. *Docendo discimus* - It is by teaching that we learn. None of those mentioned bear any responsibility, of course, for what are doubtless a great many mistakes, lapses in judgment, and oddball ideas. Those are all mine.

Finally, the organizers, guides, and various fellow travelers in the pilgrimages to Italy, Mexico City, and the Holy Land, *did* have, without knowing it at all, a direct role in the production of this book. Thank you all for the incredible experiences we shared and for all you did for me - which goes double for my companions in the Holy Land. Among those latter I thank especially my wife's sister-in-law, Kristal Granger, whose presence was a blessing.

Natchitoches, Louisiana
08 January 2020 - Solemnity of Our Lady of Prompt Succor

PREFACE

This book grew out of a longstanding desire to share the wonderful experiences of several pilgrimages over the past five years. Beginning with Italy in October 2014, continuing with Mexico City in February 2016 and the Holy Land in August 2018, and other, shorter trips in between and after, I have maintained a blog[1] where I recorded our – my own, my wife's, and our fellow pilgrims' – preparations and travels, our adventures and misadventures, impressions and insights, and so forth, with plenty of pictures and maps, and generally anything I could think of that might help convey to the reader who might discover it the wonder of the sites and sights we beheld. Being a historian, I included a good deal of research on each destination. Soon after each pilgrimage was completed, I had produced a fair amount of verbiage to complement hundreds of pictures between my own, my wife's, and those of fellow pilgrims who graciously shared them with me.

At first, I thought I would simply edit the blog narratives into a reasonably cohesive form, beef up the historical and descriptive content, slam them together between two covers, and be done with it. In some ways, the core of this book – Chapters One, Two, and Three – could be considered just that. Nevertheless, the deeper I got into the writing, the more I felt something to be missing. I realized that I must consider some fundamental questions: What exactly *is* a "pilgrimage"? What is it *not*? As explored more fully in the Introduction, a "pilgrimage" is not merely a "trip." It is not merely "tourism," even "religious tourism." That term is woefully inadequate to describe the unique spiritual quality inherent in "pilgrimage."

In retrospect, I believe I have known instinctively that there is a difference between "pilgrimage" and "tourism" for years, although not for all my life and not completely or even consciously until recently. The perception that pilgrimage is more than just a special kind of tourism is founded in my shifting worldview as a young adult experiencing what my family and former "church friends" would consider a radical conversion. It remained unformed in my subconscious for a long time, however, even as my scholarly interests centered on related ideas in

---

[1] *The Absent-Minded Professor's Travels* [https://www.theprofstravels.blogspot.com].

medieval studies. It only surfaced into consciousness in the context of the three major international pilgrimages mentioned above, between 2013 and 2018. But it really came into focus only recently, in early 2019, when I contemplated why I instinctively called a fourth excursion, a much shorter trip close to home, to south-central Texas, a "pilgrimage." The answers I discovered transformed the purpose of this book into something I hope will be of interest and use to the reader beyond simply sharing my travelogues. My intention became to put those pilgrimages into a broader perspective as a series of case studies of one type of pilgrimage among the variety that are possible, to a variety of destinations, both far (halfway around the world) and near (just a state or two away), even (arguably) so near as one's laptop sitting in one's easy chair in the comfort of one's home. I consider different forms of "Pilgrimages Far and Near" in Chapters Four, Five, and Six.

Besides the narratives of my three "big" pilgrimages and quick surveys of pilgrimage sites from the international to the local level, therefore, a unifying thread runs through this book. "What is a pilgrimage?" There are related questions weaved in with it, of course. Given my developing conception of what it is, perhaps as important is the question, "What does pilgrimage mean to me?" Directly related to the very definition of pilgrimage is a curious fact I perceived as well and confront directly in the introduction: "What is the significance that 'pilgrimage' is a distinctively 'Catholic' word among modern Christians?"

None of those questions can I honestly say I understood or considered to *be* issues in the summer of 2013 when the prospect of a parish pilgrimage to Italy presented itself. Of course, as a historian of the Middle Ages, I was familiar with pilgrimage as a historical phenomenon. But I thought of it, as I dare say most people do, merely as a journey to some destination having religious significance. The source of the significance varied by locale. The Holy Land was the most obvious, being the stage upon which the momentous events of the Bible had played themselves out. Other destinations took their importance from association with some saint, most often his or her death or martyrdom, perhaps by possession of the saint's relics. Or maybe some extraordinary event or revelation had occurred there such as an appearance by the Blessed Virgin Mary. I knew that pilgrims sought out those locations for many reasons: to pray to God or the saints; to obtain the saints' intercession; to fulfill a vow; to satisfy a penance. I also knew that, around the turn of the first millennium, the last of these –

penitential pilgrimage – came to be regarded as the most effective way to get right with God. The inherent difficulty of travel in the Middle Ages rendered such a journey extremely hazardous, making it a profound sacrifice of great spiritual benefit.

Medieval pilgrimage was critical in my specific areas of doctoral research, the origin of the idea of Crusade as it suddenly came together in Pope Urban II's epochal address at the Council of Clermont, 27 November 1095, giving birth to the First Crusade (1096-1099). From the perspective of western Europeans, the inherent danger of travel to the most important pilgrimage destination, distant Jerusalem at the far end of the Mediterranean Sea, was compounded by the unfortunate fact that the entire Holy Land had languished under Muslim rule for the past four hundred years. For the latter half of the intervening period, moreover, Christian western Europe had endured constant attacks from pagan Vikings and Magyars as well as Muslims. This perfect storm created an existential threat which drove the rise of a new armigerous nobility of feudal knights in defense of Christendom. Then, ca. 1000, the coincident (and temporary) decline of those non-Christian assaults simultaneously left no outlet for the Christian knighthood's military energy except bloody internecine conflict and seemed to render their reason for existence, the defense of Christendom, increasingly irrelevant. The violence of their vocation was judged increasingly incompatible with the Christian life. Not surprisingly, the knighthood developed a profound sense of unease about their prospects for salvation. When they sought absolution, a frequent penance (whether imposed or willingly undertaken) was to make a simple, unarmed, pilgrimage to Jerusalem. Such a dramatic demonstration of devotion to God was deemed to offer the best chance to win His mercy on Judgment Day. Hence the dismay when the rise of the Turks at mid-eleventh century effectively closed the pilgrimage routes to Jerusalem, and the enthusiasm when Pope Urban II offered the spiritual benefits of pilgrimage to Christian knights who vowed to *fight* their way to Jerusalem and win it back from the Muslims. This wedding of the ideas of penitential pilgrimage and holy war gave birth to the First Crusade, which accomplished that task on 15 July 1099.

Although my own research focused on the developing idea of Christian holy war,[2] I was necessarily aware of the medieval practice of

---

[2] Kent Gregory Hare, "Religion, Warfare, and the *Gens Anglorum*: Aspects of Holy War and its Development in Anglo-Saxon England," M.A. Thesis, Louisiana State University (1992), followed by "Christian Heroism and Holy War in Anglo-Saxon England," Ph.D.

penitential pilgrimage. But I did *not* know, nor did I really ask, the more fundamental question of what might set pilgrimage itself *apart* from mere "religious tourism." The goals seemed the same, to visit a place where something religious had taken place. How was that fundamentally different than visiting, for instance, where the Declaration of Independence was signed or Vicksburg National Military Park, except that the intense religiosity of the Middle Ages provided the motivation? Nor did I consider whether pilgrimage might have any relevance to the modern world. I thought of it as a fundamentally medieval phenomenon even though I knew that Catholic friends occasionally "went on pilgrimage" to such places as Medjugorje or Fatima. From my perspective, their trips appeared little different from any other type of tourism or even from the occasional "visit to the Holy Land" taken by members of my family's church during my youth. I never gave pilgrimage in the modern context any more profound thought than that.

... Until that announcement of a potential pilgrimage to Italy, my and my wife's enthusiastic response, and the experience itself began a personal journey that forced me to consider those questions. How clueless I was and how my understanding developed form a thread weaving in and out of mainly the first three chapters but also impacting on my subsequent consideration of various other pilgrimage destinations as well as the multiple types of pilgrimage proposed as available to the modern world.

The result is this book, which I offer to readers in hopes that they find it at least interesting and perhaps even useful in their own understanding of what pilgrimage is and what relevance it might have for them. Especially those first three chapters are intensely personal, based as they are on my own experiences. One might question the amount of detail I include, much of it incidental and arguably of little interest to anyone but myself and my various companions. Even more questionable are the many unsolicited and self-indulgent digressions (some, but not all, relegated to footnotes) in which I offer my idiosyncratic views on subjects at best peripheral to that of pilgrimage. A content editor would doubtless have suggested – more likely demanded – that

---

Dissertation, Louisiana State University (1997) [Abstract: https://digitalcommons.lsu.edu/gradschool_disstheses/6485/]. Both use the Anglo-Saxon experience and evidence to explore the ideological origins of the Crusade in Christian holy war; any such study begins with Carl Erdmann's *Die Enstehung des Kreuzzugsgedanken*, (Stuttgart, 1935). trans. M. W. Baldwin and Walter Goffart as *The Origin of the Idea of Crusade* (Princeton, 1977). Much has also been written on the role of penitential pilgrimage in the origin of the Crusade, although the best starting point remains Jonathan Riley-Smith, *The First Crusade and the Idea of Crusading* (1986; repr. London: Continuum Press, 2003).

these things be cut. No doubt, he would be right to do so. But this would be a quite different book had I done that. The details are what separate the travelogues from being a mere gazetteer or guidebook, of which there are many and better than I can provide. Similarly, one fruit of pilgrimage is reflection, and ideas and insights that came to me before, during, and after the events, even during the writing of this book, are to my mind integral to the experience. Moreover, as I conclude in Chapter Seven, practical considerations can be drawn from my experiences and ruminations, which I pray will enhance the readers' own encounters with the Divine in what I call "the Power of Place."

INTRODUCTION

WHAT IS A "PILGRIMAGE"?
The Power of Place

　want to begin this book by saying that, "Making a pilgrimage to the Holy Land had long been on my mind when the opportunity to do just that presented itself in early 2018." But I cannot. Although the thought had occurred to me a few years earlier after my first explicitly termed "pilgrimage," to Italy in 2014, I had only started thinking seriously about it in 2016 when the subject came up during my *second* pilgrimage, to the Shrine of Our Lady of Guadalupe in Mexico City. While we were conversing during our "farewell supper," the last night we were there, the organizer of that pilgrimage, Catholic philosopher and podcaster Taylor Marshall, expressed his hope to lead a group of pilgrims to the Holy Land … "someday," "maybe next year." At the time, he had another pilgrimage already planned for later that same year, to Italy. Afterward, I started paying closer attention to his blog and podcasts, expecting to hear an announcement of a pilgrimage to the Holy Land in 2017. But 2017 came and went with no word of such – another pilgrimage to Rome, but no Holy Land. Exchanging text messages with him in early 2018 about something else entirely, I brought the subject up again and received the same answer – "maybe next year."

I understood. A pilgrimage – any kind of international group travel – is a significant undertaking, far more to organize and lead than simply to accompany. In the meantime, however, my brother Michael had announced late in 2017 that he and his wife were planning a "visit" to the Holy Land with their pastor for 2018. That is what really whetted my appetite; indeed, it was partly what prompted me to sound out Taylor when I had the chance. I always intended to go with him, but his noncommittal answer made me very receptive when another opportunity arose just a few weeks later, on Good Friday of that same year 2018.

Once our respective trips were planned, mine ironically coming up quickly in August to precede Michael's in October 2018, I perceived something interesting in our occasional conversations.

Specifically, I noticed we spoke differently about our upcoming trips. While I consistently referred to my forthcoming "pilgrimage," Michael spoke variously of their "tour" or "visit." Eventually, I asked him, "Do you ever call your trip a 'pilgrimage'?" His answer was what I expected, "No. Why?" Which, of course, started me thinking: What *is* the difference? What makes a "tour" a "pilgrimage"?

Although some may dispute what follows and consider the distinction merely one of terminology or semantics, no more than a splitting of hairs (if you'll pardon the pun), I believe the difference is profound and signifies something fundamental to the Catholic Faith that I profess and that my brother does not. I am a convert to Roman Catholicism of more than thirty years. My brother remains Southern Baptist as we were raised.

On a certain level, to be sure, pilgrimage is indeed a form of tourism. In either case, the journey arises from a natural human desire to visit places out of the personal ordinary, whether it be merely to see unique or unusual sights or to experience on a deeper level places associated with significant events or individuals – to walk the land, to breathe the air. The latter (which includes the former, of course) I call the Power of Place. I gained that insight during my first – belated – excursion to England and Scotland in 2008. After well over a decade as a medieval historian with a particular interest in those areas, during which time I "lived" there through the medium of the written word, physically walking the battlefield at Hastings or strolling atop Hadrian's Wall (and I could multiply examples) gave me a sense of connection to events that hitherto had been, I realized, little more than stories. I suddenly felt a closeness to persons a thousand or fifteen hundred years gone. That was true for the events and figures of English and Scottish history I had long studied; it was nothing, however, compared to experiencing places important in the history of my Faith as I did a few years later. In Italy, I walked in the footsteps of St. Francis and participated in the Mass of the Ages in the "capital" of our Church, surrounded by the treasures of near two thousand years of Catholic history. At the Shrine of Guadalupe, I gazed on the *tilma* bearing the miraculous image of Our Lady from almost five hundred years ago. In Nazareth, I stood within feet of the place where the angel announced to the maiden that she would conceive and bear a son who would be God Himself. In Bethlehem, I touched the spot where He was born, and in Jerusalem, I touched the very peak of Calvary where He suffered and died for me (and I could multiply examples). In all these places, I felt something more than just the Power of Place, something powerfully and profoundly religious, the presence of the divine.[3]

That perception is, I believe, key to understanding the fundamental difference between tourism and pilgrimage. Whereas tourism most typically has as its goal pleasure or personal enrichment, pilgrimage is an expression of devotion seeking encounters with the divine. The impulse to pilgrimage can be found in virtually every religion from antiquity to today. The pagan Mesopotamians, Greeks, and Romans all visited, paid respect to, sacrificed at, requested favors at places associated with and important to heroes and gods – Eridu, Delphi, Cumae, among many others. Old Testament Jews heeded the mandate to go up to Jerusalem for the major "Pilgrimage Feasts" because only in the Temple could sacrifice be made (Exod. 34: 18-23; Deut. 16: 1, 9-10, 13, 16-17). In the modern world, Buddhists visit Benares, where the Buddha claimed enlightenment, and Muslims must, as one of the Five Pillars of Islam, make the *hajj* to Mecca and worship at the *Kaaba* at least once during their lifetime. Both of these are called "pilgrimages." Pilgrimage seems to be a near-universal impulse within religion.

Christian pilgrims journeyed to the Holy Land as early as the second century, when a churchman in western Asia Minor, Bishop Melito of Sardis, determined to visit the holy places where the events described in Holy Scripture had occurred. Pilgrimage to many different locales besides the Holy Land – Rome, Santiago de Compostela, Mount Athos, Canterbury – was a primary motivation for what long-distance travel existed in the Middle Ages. As I mentioned in the preface, disruption of the pilgrimage routes to Jerusalem by the eleventh-century advent of the Turks helped provoke the Crusades, whose warriors the Church explicitly defined as armed pilgrims. Then, after the sixteenth-century Reformation sundered western Christendom between Protestants and Catholics, the term "pilgrimage" as a real-world journey became largely confined to the latter, while the former tended to allegorize it as in John Bunyan's *Pilgrim's Progress* (1678).[4]

---

[3] In retrospect, I experienced something of the specifically "*Pilgrimage* Power of Place" in those 2008 and 2010 excursions to England and Scotland, especially on the Holy Islands of Lindisfarne off the coast of northern England and Iona in the Inner Hebrides off western Scotland – and at the tombs of Sts. Bede the Venerable and Cuthbert of Lindisfarne at the opposite ends of Durham Cathedral. Those were merely a foretaste, however, and play little role in this book.

[4] The allegorical or spiritual understanding of pilgrimage is in fact quite in line with the Catholic tradition, rooted in several New Testament passages (e.g., Hebrews 11: 13 and 1 Peter 2: 11 per the traditional Catholic English Douay-Rheims translation of the Latin

After my exchange with my brother, examination of two articles on Wikipedia confirmed my impression in that neither under "Pilgrimage" nor under "Christian pilgrimage" does the word "Protestant" appear. Besides the Holy Land, the sites mentioned as pilgrimage destinations are distinctively Catholic – Rome, shrines associated with Catholic saints, with apparitions of the Virgin Mary, and so forth. That cursory investigation brought me to a question I pondered for some time: Why, among western Christians, does one hear of "pilgrimage" only from the lips of Catholics? Even in visiting the Holy Land and doing the very same things, and seeing themselves as engaged in a religious exercise (as my brother and his wife surely did – and as my wife's Baptist sister-in-law avowedly did when she joined in my trip; see Chapter Three), Protestants, by and large, refer to their journey only as a "trip" or a "tour," while Catholics call it a "pilgrimage." Why do Protestants avoid using the term "pilgrimage" even when walking in the footsteps of Jesus? Does that fact signify anything? Why do Catholics so readily use the word in that and many other contexts? For instance, as a minor basilica, my church in Natchitoches (Immaculate Conception) promotes itself as a pilgrimage destination for special graces and indulgences available to those who visit it.

Before I press onward, I acknowledge that, like most generalizations, there are counterexamples. It does seem that in recent years, some Protestants may be reclaiming the term "pilgrimage." For instance, Christian Pilgrimage Journeys appears to be a Protestant pilgrimage broker; their web site is not explicit, and, being based in Athens, they may well be Orthodox, but the overall tenor of their material seems more Protestant than Orthodox to me. It is not exclusive of Catholic content, however.[5] Similarly, Journeys Unlimited makes free use of the term "pilgrimage" in referring to its tours of the Holy Land and other destinations yet seems clearly Protestant or at least generically Christian.[6] Against those examples, however, stands the

---

Vulgate). It is, moreover, the prevailing sense of the term in the modern *Catechism of the Catholic Church* (e.g., §§ 352, 657, 769, 853, 972, 1013, 1198, 1392, 1419, etc.); only in § 2696, referring to "places of pilgrimage," does the Catechism employ the more literal sense of the term. My perception is, however, that the theological perspective of the Catechism does not align with the actual usage which is of concern here, i.e. the disparity in meaning between Catholics and Protestants.

[5] https://www.christian-pilgrimage-journeys.com, accessed 30 September 2019.

[6] http://www.journeys-unlimited.com/index.aspx, accessed 30 September 2019. Journeys Unlimited does have a partnership agreement with the Catholic travel agency Regina Tours as well as several other cultural tourism brokers: ET African Journeys; Group IST (International Specialty Travel); and Variety Cruises (http://www.journeys-unlimited.com/partners.aspx).

blunt self-acknowledgment opening what is a fascinating look at the Catholic practice of pilgrimage from a Southern Baptist perspective, entitled "Holy Ground: Catholic Pilgrimages to Rome" – "'I'm going on a pilgrimage,' said no Baptist ever."[7]

Perhaps not "no Baptist ever" – but certainly not *many* Baptists nor Protestants in general, ever. And I suspect that in those instances where Protestants do avail themselves of the term, they do so as, e.g., Journeys Unlimited seems to, virtually as a synonym for "tour," with perhaps a bit of a religious flair to it. In my judgment, however, the difference between "tour" and "pilgrimage" signifies much and arises from a fundamentally different worldview.[8]

In what follows, I consciously limit myself to the question of Catholic vs. Protestant usage, specifically to that of Catholic vs. modern "Evangelical" or "Bible Protestant," with which background I have more familiarity. Some Reformed and Liturgical Mainline Protestants may lay more stress on an incarnational worldview closer to what I describe for Catholics. Orthodox Christians do so for sure. Nevertheless, there exists a significant difference between what Catholics call a "sacramental worldview," which Protestants mostly do not possess, and a general tendency among Protestants to see a sharp division between the material and the spiritual.

Foundational to Catholic theology, grounded in the Mystery of the Incarnation, is recognition of the goodness of – and even a potential sacrality inherent to – the material world. God reveals Himself and comes to us through His Creation. Consider the classic definition of a Sacrament, e.g., in the Baltimore Catechism (Q. 574): "A Sacrament is an outward sign instituted by Christ to give grace." Fundamental to the "outward sign" of the Sacraments is matter or physical action of some kind – things we can see and touch: water for baptism, bread and wine for the Eucharist, the laying on of hands for confirmation and ordination, to name but a few. Catholics envision a far closer relationship between the spiritual and the material than do Protestants, one in which the spiritual (Grace) can infuse and be conveyed through the

---

[7] Madeline Arthington, "Holy Ground: Catholic Pilgrimages to Rome," *International Mission Board (IMB)* (09 November 2018) [https://www.imb.org/2018/11/09/catholic-pilgrimages-to-rome/].

[8] Although I did not make specific use of it in composing this chapter, *Fish Eaters* hosts an excellent overview of "Fundamental Differences Between Catholics' and Other Christians' Worldviews" [https://www.fisheaters.com/differences.html], accessed 01 May 2019. Also, Catholic evangelist and pilgrimage guide (and former Baptist) Steve Ray considers the issues in a YouTube video posted on 04 January 2019, "Why Do Catholics Go On Pilgrimages?" [https://www.YouTube.com/watch?v=3gu0HJ5Yxo0].

material (the matter of a Sacrament). The invisible, transcendent, spiritual God created the material world and saw that it was good. He hallowed it by deigning to enter it Himself, becoming Incarnate as Man while remaining God, one Being Who is both. The hesitance – most often refusal – by Protestants to acknowledge that Mary is indeed the Blessed Mother of God betrays their incomprehension of this central fact of the Incarnation in all its consequence.

In the same fundamentally non-sacramental worldview originates Protestants' rejection of Catholic veneration of the saints and their relics. God's holy ones (those who die in a state of Grace and thence live with Him in heaven) will, we believe, one day be reunited with glorified bodies in the General Resurrection. These will not be *new* bodies; these will be *our own* glorified bodies, the *same* bodies we left behind at death, which God will raise to eternal life in heaven. Until that time, a mysterious connection endures between the soul of the saint in heaven and his body here on earth, forming a locus of intersection between heaven and earth. The inscription once adorning the tomb of the fourth-century St. Martin of Tours attests to the antiquity of this belief:

> Here lies Martin the bishop, of holy memory, whose soul is in the hand of God; but he is fully here, present and made plain in miracles of every kind.[9]

Touch a relic, and you touch heaven, just as in receiving and eating the Consecrated Host you receive and eat the Flesh of the Son of Man – the glorified Body of Christ. I do not, of course, equate relics with the Blessed Sacrament, but I do draw an analogy. Catholic teaching furthermore recognizes as relics not just the bodily remains of the saints (First Class Relics) but also objects they used or with which they were associated in life (Second Class Relics) or which can be related to them even indirectly by contact with either of the first two types of relics (Third Class Relics). What "object" could be more closely associated with a saint than the place where he lived, where he worked, where he taught, where he died? The Holy Land is holy not simply because of geography but because Our Lord graced it with His presence during His life, death, and Resurrection here on earth. Just so, the altar of every Catholic church is hallowed by the Eucharistic Sacrifice that is enacted upon it in the Holy Mass, which is, in fact, the very same

---

[9] E. Le Blant, *Les inscriptions chrétienne de la Gaule* (Paris, 1856), 1: 240, quoted by P. Brown, *The Cult of the Saints* (Chicago, 1981), p. 4.

Sacrifice Our Lord accomplished on Calvary. Every time a Catholic attends Holy Mass - indeed, every time a Catholic enters a Catholic church - he makes a pilgrimage to a Place hallowed by the presence of God Himself in the Flesh.

The spiritualized Christianity of Protestantism admits none of these enduring physical realities consequent to the Incarnation. Instead, Protestants characterize as all-important a vague "personal relationship" with Jesus as a Christ they cannot touch, as a God they cannot see. Christ's divinity is unmediated through the material, which they dismiss as nothing more than symbolic. The "invisible" Church founded by Christ is, at most, signified by individual congregations. Baptism is a symbolic act of obedience effecting no change in the believer's spiritual state. "The Lord's Supper" is a merely symbolic remembrance of the Body and Blood of Christ, no more effective than as a reminder of His Sacrifice. As central as it is to Protestants' identity, the Bible has meaning solely in the words it contains and the Word they signify.[10] Similarly, Protestants see nothing inherently religious in the Holy Land as a place. For them, it is just a place - a place, yes, where the Savior was born, lived, died, and rose again - but just a place, nonetheless. There is no spiritual power inherent *in that place as a place*. For Protestants, whatever their usage of the term, I would go so far as to say that the *Holy* Land is *not*, really, at least not in the same way it is for Catholics. It rather serves Protestants as a memorial, a reminder, something that turns their hearts and minds toward God. For Catholics, the Holy Land is so much more. It is the greatest of relics, and pilgrimage there brings us into contact with the divine.

To say all this is not to belittle the Protestant world view as such nor to derogate any individual's authentic encounter with the divine. It is to acknowledge how profoundly different are the respective Protestant and Catholic outlooks and the corresponding implications for the relationship of divine to human as well as for interpretations of pilgrimage and the power of place.

There are, admittedly, other explanations for Protestants' avoidance of the term "pilgrimage." The association of pilgrimage with visiting shrines dedicated to Roman Catholic saints, such as is the context for Chaucer's *Canterbury Tales* everyone learns about in High School, perhaps sets up a conscious avoidance of the term as simply

---

[10] *Catechism of the Catholic Church* § 103: "[T]he [Catholic] Church has always venerated the Scriptures as she venerates the Lord's Body." The entirety of §§ 101-104, on "Christ - The Unique Word of Sacred Scripture," is relevant here.

too "Catholic." Or, what I consider to be a prominent and unfortunate use of the term "Pilgrim Fathers" to identify the radical Puritan Separatist passengers on the *Mayflower* who landed at Plymouth in 1620. These did not call themselves "pilgrims," nor would they be called such for over 170 years, until the discovery of a manuscript written by Plymouth colony governor William Bradford in which he referred to the group as "saints" and "pilgrims," invoking the imagery of Hebrews 11: 13-16:

> **These all died in faith, not having received the promises, but having seen them afar off, and were persuaded of them, and embraced them, and confessed that they were strangers and pilgrims on the earth. For they that say such things declare plainly that they seek a country. And truly, if they had been mindful of that country from whence they came out, they might have had opportunity to have returned. But now they desire a better country, that is, an heavenly: wherefore God is not ashamed to be called their God: for he hath prepared for them a city.** (King James Version)

The term "Pilgrim Fathers" first appeared decades later, in a speech by famed orator Daniel Webster during the 1820 bicentennial of the founding of the Plymouth Colony,[11] but quickly took hold in the popular consciousness. In reality, the *Mayflower* "pilgrims" were religious refugees from the Established Church of England seeking a new home where they could live and worship in freedom. That reality, I would suggest, creates a subconscious association in the American Protestant mind between "pilgrim" and "refugee," or at least, "immigrant," that, absent the Catholic tradition of pilgrimage, dissuades their usage of the term.

The other iconic usage of the term "pilgrim" does not capture the essence of its true meaning either but instead contributes to the misunderstanding. In the popular consciousness, the term is especially associated with actor John Wayne. It is a staple phrase deployed by impressionists mimicking "The Duke" - "Howdy, Pilgrim!" The ubiquitous association of the man with the phrase far exceeds his actual usage, however. In reality, Wayne appears to have used it in only two films, John Ford's *The Man Who Shot Liberty Valance* (1962) and

---

[11] History.com Editors, "The Pilgrims," *History.com* (02 December 2009; updated 04 October 2018) [https://www.history.com/topics/colonial-america/pilgrims].

Andrew V. McLaglen's *McLintock!* (1963). Self-proclaimed "cinephile and movie blogger" Robert Frost sums up the former movie: "Wayne's character (Tom Doniphon) uses the term as a nickname for Jimmy Stewart's character (Ransom Stoddard) because Stoddard is new to the west, having traveled from the East coast. He uses the term around twenty times."[12] I contend that the association of the word "pilgrim" with the newcomer to the west Ransom Stoddard, simply as a stranger in a strange land, by an icon of classic American cinema, contributes to the widespread dissociation of the word from its proper connotation of a journey undertaken for religious devotion.

Regardless of its origin, the reticence among Protestants to embrace the term "pilgrimage" signifies most of all their impoverished understanding of the sacramental world of God's physical Creation. Beyond the power of place as an accident of geography, a coincident of event and location, in the Catholic sacramental worldview place gains power through the presence of the holy – the eventually-to-be-glorified bodies of the saints, the presence of those bodies in life and in death; the presence of Our Lord in His Incarnation and in His Blessed Sacrament. In the Catholic mind, going to such a place with religious intention, to venerate or to worship as the case may be, makes such a journey far more than a "trip." It makes it a pilgrimage.

---

[12]Robert Frost, "When did John Wayne first use the word 'pilgrim' in his movies?" *Quora* (answered 02 August 2015) [https://www.quora.com/When-did-John-Wayne-first-use-the-word-pilgrim-in-his-movies]. Frost embeds "a YouTube video someone made capturing them all," "Pilgrim.." [sic] (uploaded by "ICLAIMTHISNAME" on 13 December 2007) [https://www.youtube.com/watch?v=9O8oLqY2sxo]. The same YouTube contributor also posts the scene from *McLintock!* containing the word – incidentally, perhaps my favorite John Wayne scene ever: "But Pilgrim...!" (uploaded 24 December 2007) [https://www.YouTube.com/watch?v=qrqlP6hzofE].

PART ONE

PILGRIMAGES PAST

Figure 1: Pilgrimage to Italy with the Minor Basilica of the Immaculate Conception, October 2014. Photo courtesy Magnificat Travels, LLC.

CHAPTER ONE

THE ETERNAL CITY

Pilgrimage to Rome and Italy

From my very first pilgrimage, I have kept thorough records not just of the travels, but of preparations and developments before departure. As one purpose here is to provide complete accounts of the trips as models of the pilgrimage experience in a variety of situations, I will be including much of that preparatory information in detail. With expected variations depending on trip and broker, I think the result, taken together, is a typical overview of what to expect. Such has been my experience. Much of my personal "prep" work for these trips was the same as I undertake for almost any type of travel, different mainly in that the logistics of arranging travel and lodging was out of my hands. The main thing to remember in this account is that the trip to Italy in 2014 was my first pilgrimage conceived as such, as opposed to mere travel, even for historical purposes. The realization of how fundamentally different the experiences are – and should be – was something that came slowly to me, over time.

Quite soon after arriving in Natchitoches as Rector of the Minor Basilica of the Immaculate Conception at the end of June 2013, Fr. Ryan Humphries and his newly hired Director of Evangelization, Ashley Hebert, began canvassing for interest in a parish pilgrimage to Rome. So I discovered on Sunday 11 August when I, as per my custom, sat in our vehicle reading the parish bulletin immediately after Mass while my wife made a few purchases in our local pharmacy. When she returned, my big grin told her something was up. I showed her what I had just read – and watched her eyes light up. Anne had wanted to go to Italy for years. The time (and, frankly, the money) had never been right. We could justify our trips to the United Kingdom in 2008 and 2010 in terms of my scholarly interest and research in early medieval Anglo-Saxon England. Moreover, I found working up a trip to an Anglophone country all by myself much less daunting (but daunting enough!, especially the first time) than the prospect of doing the same for a country where, despite the prevalence of

English these days, the language and culture are quite a bit more different. I knew it could be done, but the language barrier would add another level of complexity to an already stressful process. We had toyed with the idea of joining a package tour but had never gotten beyond contemplation. Another factor in our hesitation was the generally uncertain financial situation at the University where I teach. Such concerns are never far from our minds at a small state University in Louisiana, where higher education funding frequently seems dead last in priority, but the period from ca. 2009 to 2013 was especially precarious due to an extended state budget crisis. Nevertheless, when this opportunity presented itself – to go to Italy, on a package tour with people we knew; the chance to see sights that may not be in my primary area of expertise but are well within my wider area of historical interest – how could we say "No"? It took us about two seconds' consideration to say, "*Yes!*" Within minutes of arriving back home, I had shot off an email to Fr. Humphries that Anne and I were "in." I added that, in consideration of interested members of the University community (hint-hint), the summer would be the best time to plan the pilgrimage. I also mentioned that our son, Tristan, might be able to join us if it were in the summer.

A week later, Sunday 18 August, Fr. Humphries mentioned the pilgrimage from the pulpit – and I found out that the timeframe would be October, right in the middle of the fall Semester. After Mass, Fr. Humphries explained to me that a fall date rather than the summer was preferable overall because it would be after the typical "tourist season" and therefore more affordable (I'm all for "more affordable"!); the weather would be quite a bit more moderate as well (not yet having direct experience of a Mediterranean summer, I could not argue with that[13]). Luckily, I easily cleared with my immediate supervisor as well as the department head the prospect of being absent from the University for two weeks right in the middle of the semester, with the understanding that I would plan my classes around my absence and leave assignments for the students, thus maintaining the instructional time. More than a year would be ample time to plan for that! The most natural solution was, I already knew, to schedule all my classes for fall 2014 as Internet classes, which I did. I typically teach two to three of my five class sections each semester online anyway, so that would not be too far out-of-line.

---

[13] Although now, having had that experience, I could. Would it have been worse than Israel in August?

Of course, the date knocked our son Tristan out of the pilgrimage altogether. The fall of 2014 would be his first term at University. He did not take it awfully hard. He had been only mildly interested, being convinced that he would probably be the only young person going with a bunch of "old people," and that such a rigidly scheduled tour as this would allow no possibility of doing anything of specific interest to him, as we made sure to do during our 2010 trip to the UK. He was right on that latter score.

A few weeks later, we received tentative dates for the pilgrimage – the last two weeks in October 2014. About the same time, however, my department head dropped by my office and informed me that even though I would be teaching all online courses and not in the classroom that semester, such an extended absence from the University would require me to take Leave Without Pay unless I could relate my absence to my University duties. He expressed no doubt that I could do so, but I would need to formalize it. So, I started thinking about specific ways to justify my absence in terms of the University's identity and mission as a small, state-funded institution of higher education and my role as a faculty member within that mission. A few days after our conversation, I submitted a document focusing on four key points: the University's primary mission of teaching; its encouragement of continuing professional development among its faculty; its emphasis on innovative use of technology in the classroom; and its requirement that faculty engage in some form of community service.

Taking those points in order, I first addressed the question of how I would fulfil my teaching duties *in absentia* by reiterating my already-approved plan to schedule all my courses that semester as online sections that I could manage from anywhere having Internet access. I argued that this present opportunity should count as professional development by noting my developing conviction, since the trips to the United Kingdom a few years before, that experiencing the physical environment in which historical events occurred is essential to understanding those events – what I would later call the "power of place." Rome, from its beginnings through the Renaissance, is integral to almost every course that I teach, but I had never had the opportunity to go there. Moreover, I stated my intention to accumulate an archive of photographs and video clips for use in my classes later as well as to share with my students in real time by means of a daily blog documenting my travels, allowing them to participate in the trip in a virtual manner. Finally, although I did not have a formal leadership role in the trip, I argued that my historical knowledge of the places we would be visiting could enhance my fellow travelers' experiences and constitute a form of community service.

My proposal was immediately accepted and my two-week absence cleared by the administration – with one modification. The plan that all my courses be online had been approved at the department level, but the higher-ups insisted that there must be at least one face-to-face section of my freshman-level *Early World Civilization* survey. Forming part of the University's core curriculum, that course had to be available for entering freshmen that fall semester. I therefore scheduled my customary one section of History 1010 face-to-face, with the understanding I would cover my two-weeks' absence by making audio recordings available to the students during that period.

The first organizational and informational meeting for the pilgrimage took place on the evening of Tuesday, 29 October 2013. Fr. Humphries opened by outlining for about thirty interested parties the spiritual purpose of a pilgrimage as opposed to a "sight-seeing tour" in the context of the broader mission of a minor basilica such as our parish and its special canonical relationship with Rome and the Holy Father. Next, representatives from Magnificat Travel, the pilgrimage broker out of Lafayette, Louisiana, showed a promotional video about their company, what it does, and how it is different from a typical travel agency in being exclusively devoted to Catholic pilgrimages and missions. They provided us with a general itinerary listing the important places and activities we would be attending in Assisi, Florence, Orvieto, and Rome. Finally, we received pricing information and a description of various payment options. In the end, Anne and I opted to register immediately and pay in full, taking advantage of a discount offered for doing so:

$2799 base price per person
+ 225 insurance
3014
- 150 discount for paying in full by check
2874
x 2 persons
$5748 total paid

There would also be an additional $400-$750 per person, "taxes and fees" imposed by the airlines, the exact amount of which would not be known for sure until a few weeks before departure. Not an unreasonable price by any standard, given all it included: flights, transportation, hotels, two meals a day, and all admissions. Not an *inconsiderable* amount either, on the other hand. It would mean some belt-tightening and sacrifice over the next year, especially with a son headed off to college. But, we recalled, Fr. Humphries had just gotten through emphasizing that sacrifice is part of the essence of holy pilgrimage. The rewards would be well worth it.

Of course, all that happened a year out from the pilgrimage itself. Frankly, it seemed a bit unreal for a long time. It was something looming in the distant future. It got a bit more real, however, with the coming of summer 2014. Sometime in June, Magnificat Travel announced the "final" meeting – of two – with our group of pilgrims. That second meeting was still distant, however, on Tuesday 09 September at 18:00. What *really* snapped things into focus was each getting an email that together revealed the final toll for the trip. As mentioned previously, even though we had paid "in full" the previous October, it was with the understanding that there was still a $400-$750 "airline fees and taxes" assessment to be made. Per person, of course. Well, as I figured, it ended up being at the high end of that range, $728.47. So, we owed just shy of another $1500.

Here, therefore, is the total pilgrimage cost for myself and my wife:

$5748 total paid in October 2013
+
$728.47 taxes and fees, per person
x 2 persons
$1456.94 to be paid by 15 August 2014
==========
$7204.94 GRAND TOTAL

Still a good deal for two persons, I knew ... but ... *owww!* It would be worth it, of course. In truth, what we would be getting was priceless. Only with time would I come to realize how priceless.

The Final Pilgrimage Meeting finally came. We finally received hard information about our anticipated itinerary, which was the chief information my wife and I were both wanting, at that point, for slightly different reasons. I am not going to bore the reader with all the necessary administrivia that we received as well (baggage allotments, etc.), although it was at that meeting that we also met the Magnificat Travels representative who would accompany us, Alexis Darbonne.

As soon as we got home that evening, my wife and I both started working with the information we had received. In Anne's case, with breakfast and dinner included in the package, we knew we would be "on our own" for lunches, and she wanted to start making specific plans for those. The Rick Steves travel guide we had purchased some months back was about to get some heavy use scouting out recommended eateries. She had great success in the past, during our UK trips, finding some real treasures.[14]

I set about expanding the itinerary with parenthetical notes including driving distance and anticipated travel times derived from Google Maps. It is something I do for every trip I take. I am an obsessive planner. For both of our previous trips to the UK, I planned things out virtually to the minute, and it paid off. Even my wife, who does not naturally do things that way, readily admits that there is no way we could have accomplished as much as we did in the time we had if I had not planned things out in such painstaking detail. Of course, things do not always go according to plan – but the extensive research and thought I had put into those plans usually meant I had some kind of backup plan in mind even if it were not on paper. I would do it again. I do it for just about every trip I take, if the trip itself has a purpose other than just "getting away." That type of vacation, or one that I am basically tagging along with my wife, doing what she wants to do, I can just relax and go with the flow.

In the case of a packaged trip such as this pilgrimage was, you are doubtless still wondering, "Why?" Even in such a case, it is part of the anticipation, familiarizing myself with every aspect of the trip. I call it "prepping" or "modeling" the trip, especially when it comes to working out such things as travel times and the like. It is just who I am. But it also gives me a ready reference for such information when I need it later, such as during the process of writing blog entries. It also gave me a basic outline into which I started plugging information I had been accumulating for the past several months. By that time, especially over the summer, I had done a good amount of research so that I would have a lot of useful historical information pre-written that I could quickly import into my daily blog of the trip and not have to waste time writing it on the fly. I also wanted to be more thorough than a quick Internet search would allow. I envisioned my students reading

---

[14] The way things developed, however, we used none of what she had found once we were in Italy. It was a hugely different experience from the UK, where we were on our own. In Italy we were not. The only meals for which we were on our own in Italy were lunch, and for all our guide's assurances that we had plenty of time, we usually did not. Either the two of us alone or with a small group would find something fast wherever we were when we were released for lunch. We did have good luck with that, however. Follow the locals. They know where the good food is.

along as I traveled, remember; that had been one of my "selling points" getting permission to be out of the classroom for two weeks during the middle of the semester. I knew, moreover, that I would have better things to do than to labor over a laptop computer ... fine wine, fine Italian cuisine, *limoncello*, Tuscan sunsets, fine wine, and so forth!

Yes, I was really getting into this "pilgrimage" thing, and for all the right reasons!

Monday 20 October – Italy 2014 Day One: *Embarkation*

The long-awaited day finally came ... very early. Actually, with packing and preparing for the trip, my wife and I barely got any sleep that Sunday night. I had not really intended to sleep, hoping that would help me sleep on the plane, but I could not sleep as late as I wanted to Sunday morning. By this time, we typically attended the Extraordinary Form Latin Mass which Fr. Humphries had implemented the previous Advent, celebrated at 17:00 on Sunday. So, Sunday had become our usual morning to sleep in. This particular Sunday, it did not happen for various reasons including sheer anticipation, and after about 18 hours with my contact lenses in, I could not take it anymore. By about 01:30 Monday morning, we were both pretty much done, anyway, after a full day of travel preparation, packing, repacking, cleaning the house, confirming with my wife's cat-sitter, and so forth. Out my contacts went, and out we went ... sort of. My mind continued to race until my alarm went off at 02:30, when up we came, in my contacts went again, and by about 02:50 we were in the car headed for St. Mary's School, where the Natchitoches group of pilgrims would gather and our journey would begin with Holy Mass.

To make a long story short, we got to the school, stowed our luggage on the bus, participated in Mass in the chapel promptly at 03:15, and were rolling out of Natchitoches right on time at 04:00 and arrived at the Dallas-Fort Worth Airport almost precisely on time at 08:00. We met up with our Magnificat travel companion, Alexis, who gave us our e-tickets. TSA was typically brusque, but by approximately 10:00, we were sitting at the gate, waiting for a 10:50 flight to Atlanta.

To make a much *longer* story short because it was kind of a blur by the time I was next able to make notes, on Tuesday evening, our flights to Atlanta, where the non-Natchitoches pilgrims joined us, and thence to Rome both went great. That did not keep me from being exhausted through the day on Tuesday, however ....

There were many other pilgrim groups on the flight from Atlanta to Rome besides our own, and at least a dozen priests and religious. Among those, we as we deplaned in Italy, was Fr. John Zuhlsdorf, who, besides having some notoriety via his eponymous blog ("Fr. Z's Blog"), had given an outstanding Lenten mission at the Minor Basilica only a few months before, culminating with the first Solemn High Mass in the Extraordinary Form to be celebrated in Natchitoches in over fifty years. We felt very safe on that flight.

Tuesday 21 October 2014 – Italy Day Two: *Arrival; to Assisi*

We landed at the Rome airport – actually, Leonardo da Vinci International Airport at Fiumicino, down on the coast near Ostia at the mouth of the Tiber River, ten or twelve miles from Rome itself – at about 07:10 local time. By 08:40, we had proceeded through passport control, claimed our baggage, and met our "escort," Debra Mallinson, a British expatriate married to an Italian who works with Magnificat Tours. She had us on the bus and headed to our first destination, Assisi, home of Saints Francis and Clare, by 09:30. Our bus driver for the entire trip would be one Luigi. We were a total of 46 pilgrims, mostly from the Minor Basilica in Natchitoches as well as a few from neighboring parishes in the Diocese of Alexandria. Additionally, a group from Vacherie, Louisiana, accompanied Fr. Humphries' brother priest, Fr. Chris Decker of the Diocese of Baton Rouge. There were also a few outliers from Lafayette, New Orleans, and even a father and his adolescent son from Little Rock, Arkansas. And Alexis, the representative from Magnificat.

Among the Natchitoches group were friends whom Anne and I had known for years as well as parishioners we had never met. Our parish is relatively large for the area, with several distinct Mass communities. We even had family – my wife's cousin, a local pediatrician, and her husband, along with two of their granddaughters, aged about twelve and sixteen. Between those two cousins (albeit somewhat distant, second-once-removed[15]) and the young man from Little Rock, our son Tristan's expectation that there would be no other young people on that "old-people" trip turned out to be unfounded. We had

---

[15] My wife and "Doctor Chris" being first cousins, Tristan and Chris' pediatrician son "Doctor Brett" are second cousins, making Tristan and Brett's daughters second cousins once-removed, i.e., a generation apart although they were roughly the same age. Contrary to popular conception, especially here in the southern United States, that is how consanguinity is reckoned.

discovered that only late, however, and it would not have mattered in any case. He could not be absent for such an extended period from his first term at college.

The trip from Rome to Assisi took about three hours, punctuated by a "comfort stop" along the way. Debra pretty much talked the whole time, which we would find to be the case for the entire trip. I found the countryside to be stunning and much hillier than I imagined it. From years of reading, study, watching movies, and so forth, I had an image of Italy that was not entirely accurate. I show my students pictures of and describe the broad rolling hills of the plains of western Italy, where Roman Civilization was born, and pictures are indeed worth a thousand words – but seeing it for yourself is worth a thousand pictures. By Louisiana standards, western Italy seemed downright mountainous, although there are extensive flatlands too. Even in October, it was very green. The fertile landscape made the Romans' conception of themselves as simple Italian farmers easy to understand.

We crossed and re-crossed the Tiber River several times along the way. Each time I thought how puny it seemed in comparison to the rivers I am accustomed to seeing. It was, again, something I knew intellectually but needed to see to really comprehend. I have long shown my students a side-by-side same-scale comparison of the Tiber River at Rome and the Cane River Lake at Natchitoches, which are roughly the same width. Specifically, the Cane River Lake is about 225 feet wide while the Tiber River is about 250 feet wide at Rome. Once the bed of the Red River flowing through Louisiana, the "Cane River" ("Lake" is usually omitted in everyday parlance) was left as a long, winding lake after the Red River shifted several miles to the east in the early-mid nineteenth century. Although not technically correct, "oxbow" is the best way to describe it. In any case, it is relatively narrow, fifty to a hundred yards in width, insignificant compared to such as the Mississippi River (2,700 feet wide at Baton Rouge), the Ouachita River (750 feet wide at Monroe, Louisiana), the Red River (600 feet wide at Alexandria), or any other of a number of rivers flowing through Louisiana. Yet, the little Cane River is comparable in width to the Tiber River, the great river of Rome, the principal river of west-central Italy. Each time I saw it, I was astounded.[16]

---

[16] A few days later, we would find the other great river of western Italy, the Arno River in the north, to be only slightly wider, about 300 feet where it flows through Florence. Incidentally, had I seen the Jordan River several years later when I traveled to Israel (Chapter Four), which is only about fifty or sixty feet wide. I would have been even more impressed at how such a small thing can loom so large in our cultural heritage

On the other hand, although I knew that by the time we got to Assisi we were in what are effectively the western foothills of the Apennine Mountains, the "spine" of Italy running its length from north to south, and that the town itself is multi-tiered, I still was not quite prepared for the reality. The bus park is at the bottom of the western end of the city. We had to walk quite a distance, making a big loop up a steep incline to get to our hotel. Although Debra said it was "not too steep," and we would "take it slow," I do not think those words mean the same thing to her as they do to me! It was quite taxing. But we made it and checked into our hotel, the Hotel Giotto, by about 12:30.

Magnificat had booked us into an excellent hotel. Anne and I received a top-floor room on the corner, giving us spectacular views out two directions, to the south and the west. Unfortunately, it was two flights of stairs, really three floors, up from the lobby. The small elevator only went part of the way, so it was more climbing. We made it, settled in, reorganized our luggage from travel mode to daily mode, and had time to rest for just a few minutes before we had to be back down to the lobby for 14:45 to be taken out to the Basilica of Santa Maria degli Angeli, on the plain below Assisi. There we heard our first Mass in Italy, said by Fr. Decker (assisted by Fr. Humphries), in a small chapel devoted to St. Clare. The religious component of the pilgrimage began, with plenty of tourism blended in.

Like about everything else we would see, St. Mary of the Angels is of immense historical significance. It is a huge church, built around the small church of the Portiuncula (modern Italian *Porziuncola*) – literally. The latter stands intact within the nave of the former. The Portiuncula is a little ninth-century chapel that by the time of St. Francis in the early thirteenth century was in dilapidated condition. Francis restored it and essentially "rented" it for a basket of fish each year from the Benedictines of nearby Mt. Subasio (*not* to be confused with Subiaco, where Benedictine monasticism began, I found). The modern Franciscans still pay this rent for their first motherhouse, because it was here that Francis gathered with his followers and founded the "Franciscans," in 1208. It is where Francis received Clare into the religious life four years later, in 1212, and thus began the "Poor Clares." Finally, it is where Francis died in 1226, having requested to be carried there by his followers when he knew his end was near.

Inevitably, visiting the sites around any particular locale must be done in some logistically reasonable manner that seldom bears any resemblance to a coherent narrative. That was the case at Assisi, as can be seen from the facts related to the Portiuncula given above, which are scattered across much of the life of St. Francis. To put our experiences at Assisi into better context, here is a brief narrative of the life of St. Francis. He was born into a wealthy merchant family as Francesco Bernardone, probably in 1182. As a worldly young man, the romance of the troubadours, love, and war, fascinated him. Fighting in one of the many petty wars between Assisi and its rivals, he was captured and held prisoner for a year in Perugia. He emerged from captivity a changed man. He renounced his inheritance and became a beggar, embracing an ideal that he called "Lady Poverty." Praying at a small, ruined country church dedicated to St. Damian, he claimed a vision of the icon of the Crucified Christ speaking to him: "Francis, rebuild my church which has fallen into ruin." Taking those words literally, he set about begging for stones to do just that. Restoring San Damiano, Francis proceeded to other abandoned chapels, including the Portiuncula. His example drew other young men to his following, and in 1208 he formulated a simple rule of religious life for his "little brothers" (Friars Minor). Pope Innocent III approved this new religious order in 1210. Based at the Portiuncula, the Order of Friars Minor (or simply "Franciscans") took as its vocation preaching and service to the poor. With Papal approbation, Francis' following grew, attracting a group of young noblewomen, led by Chiara Offreduccio. Francis received Clare's vows at the Portiuncula in 1212 and soon afterward established her and her companions as a Second Order of Franciscans, popularly known as the "Poor Clares," living in community at San Damiano. Francis would later respond to the desire of married men and women to live a life of Franciscan spirituality by creating a Third Order.

Francis' zeal to spread the gospel eventually took him to Egypt, to preach even to the Sultan of Egypt. This attempt to convert the current leader of the Muslim world failed. The Sultan was, however, sufficiently taken by Francis himself that he commanded his people not to molest the friar and his companions and gave them safe passage to Jerusalem. So began the Franciscan presence in the Holy Land that would prove critical in preserving Catholic interests in that hotly contested part of the world. Returned to Italy, Francis embarked on a life of increasing asceticism which culminated in 1224 during a private retreat on Mt. Alverna. There, on the 14 September Feast of the Exaltation of the Cross, Francis became the first documented recipient of the stigmata, the wounds of Christ Crucified. Suffering greatly from these and other ailments, he requested his followers to bring him to the Portiuncula, where his Order began and where he died in 1226. Less than two years later, Pope Gregory IX declared him a saint.

Although Francis did have a great love for all God's nature, many of the stories about him (including his preaching to the forest animals) are clearly apocryphal. They usually overlook the most important aspects of his life – his great love for the Eucharist and his profound respect for the priesthood which he considered himself unworthy to possess. He never said, "Preach the Gospel at all times. When necessary, use words." All such are merely superficial embellishments that pale beside the life of heroic sacrifice he lived and the profound witness he offered. Through his example, Francis of Assisi saved the Church in an age when escalating wealth and scandalous behavior among the priesthood and hierarchy threatened to alienate the laity – truly heeding the voice he heard from the San Damiano Cross: "Francis, rebuild my church which has fallen into ruin."

After a tour of the basilica and a trip through the gift shop, where I was incredibly proud of myself for managing a transaction in Italian, we made a quick trip across the street for my first taste of *gelato* (Italian ice cream, or so they say. I say gelato is to ice cream as Guinness is to Miller Lite. Gelato has a higher proportion of whole milk to cream, with much less or even no egg yolk, about half the fat-content and as little as half the air-content produced by a slower churn. It is *exceptionally smooth*! There would be more!). We then boarded back up for a short trip back to the bus park. Anne and I took the walk from the bus park slower this time, hitting a few shops along the way. In my earlier travels, I had grown accustomed to seeking out three items as souvenirs from each destination – a T-shirt, a necktie, and a coffee-mug. I found two of those three, the shirt and the mug, right off the bat; a tie is always the hardest to find. Then, back at the hotel, I started recording the events of the day and my impressions. I felt quite pressured to get the blog up and going for my students.

A three-course dinner began at 19:00, early by Italian standards. It consisted of pasta, chicken, then a dessert, and was all excellent. Wine and good company made it even more so. Afterward, Anne went back to the room while I sought out a marginally better Wi-Fi signal in the lobby to check in on my courses and finish the day's account. I accomplished only the first of those tasks. At 20:58 Italy time, I noted that "Bed is looking *really* attractive...." Consider that 20:58 Italy time on Tuesday, equating to 14:58 Louisiana time, meant that it had been more than 36 hours since 02:30 Louisiana time the previous day,

Monday, when my alarm had gone off to get up and head out for the beginning of this journey. There had been little sleep since early Sunday morning, and there had been little sleep on the plane. I never really sleep well on planes. I was, and am, surprised at how I was still going. I was not for long.

Wednesday 22 October 2014 – Italy, Day Three, Assisi

Our wake-up call came at 06:30, to be ready for breakfast at 07:30 and departure from the lobby at 08:30. Breakfast was meats, cheese, and bread, in addition to more American staples like scrambled eggs, bacon, and cereal. Plus, a coffee machine, juices, and fruits. From the lobby, we walked uphill (everything seems to be uphill in Assisi!) along the Via Frate Elia to the Basilica of San Francesco, the present mother church of the Franciscan order.

Built into the side of a hill at the western end of Assisi, overlooking the plain below, the basilica contains two churches, the Upper Church and the Lower Church, in addition to the actual tomb of St. Francis in a crypt below. Because of the danger that the saint's relics would be stolen by a rival town (such as Assisi's traditional enemy, Perugia), the Lower Church was ostensibly built specifically to house them more securely. That was not considered sufficient, however; the Lower Church was in fact a deception, with the relics being secreted further below in the crypt. But they were hidden so well that their location was forgotten. It was not until the nineteenth century that the relics were rediscovered. The magnificent shrine housing them today dates from that later period.

This fascinating tale illustrates something that is, to the modern mind, one of the *weirder* aspects of medieval piety. By the early Middle Ages, the original practice of building churches over the tombs of the saints had changed. Being moveable, relics of whatever class (as discussed in the Introduction) provided "portable holiness" that could be incorporated into altars anywhere. Even today, a consecrated altar must typically contain relics. Many medieval churches and monasteries assembled huge collections of relics for the spiritual power they held, but also to tap into the "pilgrimage industry." The pilgrims in Chaucer's *Canterbury Tales* were going there because of the relics of St. Thomas Becket. Relics – and the pilgrims they brought – were highly prized assets of any church or monastery. Competition for relics ran fierce, sometimes crossing the line to what we would consider entirely unethical tactics. The buying and selling of putative relics were the least of it; there was a vigorous "black market" for relics taken legitimately or illegitimately from the tombs of saints. When all else failed, there was always "*furta sacra*," "sacred theft."[17] There are many, many examples, perhaps the most infamous being the theft of the relics of St. Foy. The monastery at Agen possessed the relics and benefited from a brisk pilgrimage business; the monastery at Conques did not, and languished. So, Conques infiltrated one of its monks into the community at Agen. He worked his way up to Keeper of the Relics – at which point he absconded with the relics of St. Foy. A stern chase followed across the countryside, the outraged monks of Agen in hot pursuit of the culprit. The thief barely outraced his pursuers, passing through the gates of Conques barely ahead of them. The gates slammed shut behind him, barring the monks of Agen. The community of Conques then proclaimed that the success of the theft demonstrated the will of the saint to be moved from Agen! The elaborate measures in the Basilica of St. Francis show that the friars of Assisi took very seriously the possibility that *their* saint might similarly decide to "up and move"! As a result, the saint was lost to them for centuries, and his basilica is in fact three churches stacked one atop the other!

We heard Mass in the Franciscan brothers' chapel, also known as the "Peace Chapel," said this time by Fr. Humphries assisted by Fr. Decker – our first time ever hearing the Mass celebrating the new Feast of St. John Paul II.

Our Italian guide for the day, Marco, was late coming from Perugia because of traffic related to the chocolate festival going on there that day. Anne asked me how far Perugia was from Assisi; I answered, "Close enough to hurt!" (Perugia seems to be the Hershey, Pennsylvania, of Italy. Eurochocolate, begun in 1993, is the largest chocolate festival in Europe.) While we awaited Marco's arrival, we went down to the crypt and saw the real tomb of St. Francis, and I got a few pictures there and in the Lower Church before I was rebuked and told that photos were forbidden! Respecting their rules, I took no more ... but I did not delete the ones I already had! I was later (after the trip was over) told by someone who should know that the docents do not have the authority to stop you from taking pictures, but my rule of thumb is to follow the posted rules, for the most part. As I see it, I am a guest in their country, and I am going to show them the same respect that I hope they show us if and when the situation is reversed. Occasionally the temptation is too great, of course, and I have grabbed

---

[17] Patrick J. Geary, *Furta Sacra: Thefts of Relics in the Central Middle Ages* (Princeton: Princeton University Pres, 1978; rev. ed. 1991).

furtive shots on the fly, but by and large, I refrain even from that. Mostly.

Anyway, once Marco got there, he led us on a tour of the Lower Church, then the Upper Church, then out to the plaza in front of the basilica, then up the Via San Francesco, which gave way to the Via Portica, through the lower town into the upper town. We continued past an old Roman temple to Minerva via the Corso Mazzini to the plaza in front of the Basilica of St. Clare (Santa Chiara), where Marco left us about 12:45. Marco was an excellent guide – enthusiastic, informative, if a bit over-the-top in his enthusiasm for Pope Francis. Already by late 2014, barely a year and a half into his pontificate, the Pontiff had shown himself to be a divisive figure. Most recently, just a month or so before, he had performed a mass wedding "legitimizing" a couple of dozen couples hitherto cohabiting without the benefit of marriage, without properly catechizing them; more recently, just a couple of days before we were in Assisi, the first "Synod on the Family" had concluded amid rumors of coming relaxations in the Church's stance toward civilly-divorced and remarried Catholics as well as practicing homosexuals. It was too much for Fr. Humphries. As Marco effused about the great compassion and mercy of this present Holy Father, Father grew more and more visibly agitated until he could no longer restrain himself, He had to jump in and set forth what was, is, and will continue to be the official teaching of the Church. It was an awkward – but absolutely necessary – interruption to Marco's brief departure from his top-notch job of explaining the various frescoes in the basilica, by Cimabue, Giotto, and so forth. Thanks be to God we do have good priests willing to stand up for the truth!

With Marco's departure, our group scattered to the four winds. Anne and I wandered back the way we had come, looking for a good lunch and an ATM to get some cash. We found both, then hit various shops (including me finding a new T-shirt – XL/XG in Italy is smaller than XL at home, as I found with the shirt which I had bought the day before! In fact, I ended up getting two T-shirts, one just for Assisi, a second for St. Francis, with his Canticle of the Creatures on it in Italian). We also got gelato – twice – on our way back up the Via San Gabriele and other narrow streets to the Basilica of St. Clare, which had been closed from 12:00-14:00. It is an active convent of Poor Clares, which fact would impress itself on us in a beautiful way, as you shall see.

Inside the Basilica of St. Clare, we saw the actual cross from the Church of San Damiano that originally "spoke" to St. Francis in 1205, imploring him to "Rebuild my Church!" (Why here? We would find out shortly.) We also went down into the crypt to view the incorrupt body of St. Clare. While we were peering through a window at the saint, a nun approached the window, smiled, and signaled to Anne that she was closing the curtain ... and within a few moments, we heard beautiful chanting begin from behind the curtain. The nuns were singing the afternoon office of None around the body of the saint! That only lasted five to seven minutes, and then the curtain opened again for pilgrims to view the body. For those few minutes, however, we seemed to have been transported into heaven. It was an awesome experience, the grace of being in the right place at the right time.

We continued wandering through the town, generally back toward our hotel along the Via Fontebella, occasionally encountering others of our group, arriving about 16:15. Anne and I then sat out on the balcony outside the lobby with a few others who had returned, drinking coffee and water, respectively. At 16:45, taxis arrived to take those of our group who wanted to go to San Damiano, the original little church restored by Francis. We had to go up in taxis because they do not allow tour buses or indeed tour *groups*, so we had to go through as individuals, unguided. In some ways, that was better than some other rushed tour experiences we had!

Before we entered, however, we found out why we saw the Cross of San Damiano at the Basilica of St. Clare. Although it was kept at San Damiano for a long time, eventually the vulnerability of that church outside the walls of Assisi compelled both the community of Poor Clares and the Cross to be moved into the city and eventually to the present Basilica. A group of male canons took over custody of San Damiano.

We were at San Damiano for about an hour, then back to the hotel about 18:00. Anne and I rested for a few minutes - and called our son, Tristan, for a very few minutes - then went down to supper for 19:00. It was another three-course meal, but by the time I got a chance to make notes, I could not remember any specifics - so much blurred together before I found time to record it! However, I did note that at 20:30, Alexis gathered us all in the hotel lounge for about an hour of prayer and "sharing," a Magnificat tradition. We had been "warned" to expect such an exercise, and for some groups, I am sure it is a valuable experience. Some individuals thrive on this. Others, such as I, do not, and we seemed in the majority, to Alexis' evident disappointment. One problem was that this attempt at "caring and sharing" came at the end of a very full day, after a large meal including wine. By the end, I for one was barely staying awake. Although Anne and a group (including the priests) went out for *another* gelato immediately upon the Prayer and Sharing session petering out, I went back up to the room, showered, and headed for bed only a little after 22:00. There was no way I could get any blogging done that night. I barely managed to deal with some NSU course work and emails and was beginning to realize that the "live-blogging" thing was not working out as I planned. We were so rushed all day; then, in the evening, I was so tired I could barely focus on the screen. I knew I would just have to get to it when I could, but I found myself getting further and further behind during the coming days.

In the end, my ambition of "live-blogging" the trip for my students, with daily updates, ended up being a bust. One of the trade-offs of being part of a packaged trip and thus not having to worry about arrangements and so forth, just be where they say when they say, is being on someone else's schedule, just be where they say when they say – and they drove us pretty hard. I understand – it had to be that way for us to get in all the things we wanted to do. But by the end of each day, mental as well as bodily weariness made it difficult to think coherent thoughts much less compose an extended narrative. As with the sharing sessions planned for the end of each day, a substantial three-course dinner with wine did not help the cause of blogging. To my disappointment, I also discovered that little of my pre-written material was usable without considerable rewriting; it was all too dry and impersonal, with none of the "life" and "character" that comes from experiencing the moment-by-moment events as they unfolded. But I was in no shape to fix it then. In the end, I did well to get notes jotted down in my pocket journal so that I would have a reliable record to work from when I eventually got around to "back-writing" the blog. After a valiant attempt the next morning, trying to type into my laptop while on the bus to Orvieto, a combination of the difficulty of typing in a moving vehicle plus the constant distraction of the ever-changing Italian countryside (and Debra's incessant commentary), caused me to just give in. While I did snatch time here and there to make some progress along the way, I composed much of what was essentially the first draft account of the Pilgrimage to Italy during the flight home, on the morning of Wednesday 29 October, just out of Italian airspace over the Mediterranean Sea and the south of France.

At one point, a flight attendant asked me if I were writing a book....

Little did I know.

Thursday 23 October 2014 – Italy Day Four: *Orvieto*

Our second morning waking up in Italy began with what Debra called "Six-Seven-Eight": wake-up at 06:00, breakfast at 07:00, assembly in the lobby at 08:00 to head down to the bus park for our drive to Orvieto, about an hour and a half away from Assisi. As mentioned, I tried to get some work done on the bus, but typing was next to impossible. So, I just put the laptop away and enjoyed the scenery since I also found it impossible to nap. As we drove, the terrain became even more mountainous than around Assisi. My inexperienced mental image of Italy, with the Apennines down the eastern spine of the peninsula and "broad, rolling plains" to the west, was not all that accurate, I increasingly realized!

Located in southwestern Umbria, Orvieto presents a magnificent sight as you approach. The town center sits atop the flat (more or less) summit of a volcanic butte. Although cars may now ascend to the top via a steep road at the southern end of the bluff, busses cannot negotiate the sharp turn back that is involved. We therefore had to disembark and transfer to a *funicular*, an inclined cable car at the northern end, for our ascent.

The name of the city, "Orvieto," comes from the Latin *Urbs Vetus*, "The Old City," and old it is, being the site of one of the major Etruscan cities. A wealth of ruins in the immediate vicinity give evidence of that mysterious people who flourished in western Italy from about 900 to 400 BC. Tuscany takes its name from them. For a critical century, from about 600 to 509 BC, the Etruscans extended their dominion southward across Latium, the core of modern Lazio, the central-western plain of Italy. They found a close grouping of Latin villages on seven hills overlooking the Tiber River to be the perfect location for dominating Latium. They unified the villages, enclosed them within a wall, drained the swampy area between the hills and paved it over, and gave the new city its name – *Roma* is an Etruscan word probably meaning "Rivertown." By all accounts – later *Roman* accounts – the Etruscan kings were nonetheless cruel despots whom the Romans eventually overthrew. Although the Etruscan domination of Rome had followed rule by native Latin kings, the Romans now swore, "*Never again!*" Roman antipathy to kingship would be one of their defining cultural imperatives. Instead, they set up the Republic and embarked on their own rise to Empire.

Nevertheless, Etruscan influence is visible in every facet of Roman life. The "Roman" alphabet we use today is in fact the Etruscan alphabet, although the language that they represented with that alphabet still eludes translation. The distinctive form of Roman names derives from the Etruscans. Etruscan religious practices such as divination and gladiatorial combat - a form of human sacrifice to dark gods who imparted to the Etruscans a macabre obsession with death - endured in Roman ritual until the triumph of Christianity almost a thousand years later. Etruscan engineering skill that built monumental walled cities, roads, and aqueducts served as the foundation for Rome's great accomplishments in those areas. Orvieto has proven to be an archaeological treasure trove. Unfortunately, although it was one of my ambitions, our limited time here did not allow me to go through the Etruscan museum at Orvieto. There was much more to see and do, more in line with the spiritual focus of a pilgrimage that I was tardily embracing. Anyway, the expanding Roman Republic annexed Etruscan Orvieto in the third century BC, and the city became something of a backwater. We just do not know that much about Orvieto during the centuries to either side of the BC-AD divide when Rome evolved from Republic to Empire. Our guide for the city attributed that to the fact that since the Romans more or less dominated all of Italy by that time, they did not put such a premium on the easy defensibility of the plateau and built their main settlement down on the plain below. But that security did not last, and as the Empire melted away into the early Middle Ages security became much more of a consideration, and the height flourished once again. Medieval Orvieto was an early episcopal city with close ties to the Papacy. It eventually became part of the Papal States and remained so until 1861, when all of Italy but Rome itself was united into a kingdom. The importance of Orvieto to the Papacy as well as the fact that St. Thomas Aquinas was teaching there before he became Papal theologian to Clement IV are both important in the story explaining Orvieto's attraction for pilgrims.

After a short shuttle trip from the upper end of the *funicular* to the cathedral square of Orvieto, we found our breath taken away by the sudden sight of the Duomo. The generic Italian word for "cathedral" is, it turns out, unrelated to the dome or cupola that usually surmounts it. The word derives instead from the Latin word for "house," *domus*. The Duomo of Orvieto is one of the finest in Italy, presenting a magnificent façade covered with bas-reliefs of Biblical scenes, mosaics inlaid with gold, and carved statues of the four evangelists. Even on that grey, overcast day, it was brilliant; I can only imagine how it would dazzle in sunlight.

After only a few minutes gazing in awe, we walked around to the back of the cathedral for an 11:00 Mass in the crypt beneath the eastern end of the church. As we did so, we noted that we were treading on a sidewalk of old gravestones; then, entering the crypt, we were greeted by the sight of bones visible through a window in the front of the altar as well as through several windows inset into the floor. The latter gave us a view down into the catacombs carved in the porous volcanic tufa below the Duomo – much like the Etruscans' elaborate underground tombs, dubbed "Cities of the Dead." I do not believe we were told whose bones those were over which Fr. Decker said Mass with Fr. Humphries assisting, but their presence combined with cooler temperatures – especially in that crypt – to bring our own mortality very much to mind. It was incredibly eerie but very Etruscan. Their obsession with the dead, with an afterlife that seems to have held no promise, gave birth across hundreds, even thousands, of years to literary Descents to the Underworld envisioned by the greatest Italian poets. Both the Roman Virgil, author of *The Aeneid*, and the Florentine Dante, who wrote *The Divine Comedy* – thirteen hundred years apart – were natives of Tuscany, the land of the Etruscans. The macabre outlook of the Etruscans seems to have impressed itself deeply upon the medieval Christians of the region; it certainly did so on me

After Mass concluded about 11:45, our group scattered as usual for lunch. Anne and I ended up at a little restaurant called L'Altro Vissani, sharing a margarita pizza and prosciutto. We tasted the peculiarly saltless bread of the region around Orvieto. Legend has it that this culinary oddity resulted from the imposition of a tax on the use of salt during the period that the Holy See ruled Orvieto (and much of Italy) as part of the Papal States. Neither of us found it really to our taste.

We reassembled in the Piazza del Duomo at 13:30, meeting our guide for the day, Manuela. She began by taking us through the Duomo, where the highlight was that previously mentioned reason that Orvieto became a pilgrimage center: The Corporal of Bolsena, a material relic of a Eucharistic Miracle that occurred in 1263. A priest in Bolsena, a smaller town about twelve miles to the southwest of Orvieto, found his growing skepticism about the Real Presence of Our Lord in the Eucharist rebuked by an astounding confirmation of that Truth. The Host that he doubtfully consecrated began to bleed onto the Corporal, the square linen cloth upon which rests the Host during Mass. The priest's disbelief was not unique during that period of intense controversy regarding the doctrine of Transubstantiation, which would soon be formally enunciated and named as such by St. Thomas Aquinas in the *Summa Theologiae*. Pope Urban IV investigated the claimed miracle, consulted with Thomas, who was currently teaching at Orvieto, validated it, and commissioned the theologian to compose the liturgy for the new Feast of Corpus Christi, established in the next year, 1264. The Pope also, of course, translated the Corporal bearing the Blood of Jesus from Bolsena to the Papal city of Orvieto, where it would eventually be enshrined in the northern transept of the Duomo whose construction was begun in 1290 and would be dedicated to the Assumption of the Blessed Virgin Mary.

Allowing us a few minutes to venerate the Corporal, Manuela then continued our tour. In the southern transept, we beheld another awe-inspiring sight, the great frescoes depicting the Apocalypse as envisioned by Luca Signorelli in the late fifteenth century. The famous image of the Antichrist, painted to look at first glance like Jesus Himself with Satan whispering in His ear, occasioned a short impromptu teaching moment by the Fathers about the seductive attraction of sin.[18]

Leaving the Duomo, Manuela walked us through a couple of sections of the town, all the way to the Plaza of the People, the main civic square. We were then free once more for a little less than an hour, which afforded Anne and me a chance for gelato and shopping as we made our way back to the Plaza of the Duomo for 16:00. I took time to revisit and pray before the miraculous Corporal as well as to catch a quick look across the Umbrian countryside off the cliff just south of the Duomo.

Here I will insert an observation regarding something that would be with us from that day on, basically everywhere except Assisi – beggars. Some were simply that, begging, and either horribly deformed or faking it very effectively. Many were obviously the latter. In Orvieto, we saw the first of many individuals whose feet seemed stunted or twisted all in the same manner. It appeared to be an extremely common affliction, a horrible congenital deformity, I thought, and one could not help throwing them a couple of coins at least, especially when it seemed genuine. But it very quickly became plain that many (most? all?) were *not* genuine, were indeed faking, and our hearts (or at least mine) hardened. We are to see Jesus in the poor, but are we to see Him in the con artist? And then there were the people trying to push cheap merchandise off on us. "No, *Grazie*," especially when

---

[18]Talk about timing! Just the week before I had started reading a book urged on me by Fr. Humphries, Michael D. O'Brien's *Father Elijah: An Apocalypse*. In addition to the settings thus far in my reading, which was only a third or so of the way into the novel and already included Rome and Assisi, these frescoes in Orvieto had formed a major aside in the narrative.

followed by "*signore*" or "*signora*," only encouraged them more. I started barking a firm "*NO!*" when first approached, which worked ... most of the time. It became quite annoying. I eventually learned a new, more forceful refusal - "*Basta!*"

I believe that Orvieto was where we also first experienced how aggressive the street vendors could be, and how ugly they could get if their attempts to press their cheap wares on "tourists" were rebuffed. One of our group was a young African American woman who had the English racial slur spat in her face by one of those vendors. As it happened, one of the men in our group was a former marine. He stepped in and barked the appropriate response. The desired result was attained as said vendor slunk away as fast as he could.

In any case, a quick shuttle ride and the *funicular* back down to the bus park, and we were headed back to Assisi, arriving about 18:00. Along the way, we watched perhaps the first half of a subtitled Italian movie about Saints Francis and Clare.[19] It seemed quite good, but I was kind of in and out of it with little catnaps. Back in Assisi, Anne and I hit a gift shop across from the bus park and made it back to the hotel with just enough time to freshen up in time for dinner at 19:00. As usual, it was three courses, pork steaks for the middle course. After dinner, I stayed down in the lounge for better Wi-Fi reception. I tried to get some work done on the blog but what I said before plus being distracted by other pilgrims' talking about the trip thus far kept that from happening. I also had to get back to the room to make our suitcases ready to be picked up outside our rooms quite early the next morning.

Friday 24 October 2014 - Italy Day Five: *To Florence*

We were up no earlier, at 06:00, but more rushed as we had to set our suitcases outside the rooms by 06:45. Then it was down to breakfast for 07:00 and assembling in the lobby to leave the Hotel Giotto at 08:00 to walk down to the bus park. And so, our time in Assisi ended. I think everyone on the pilgrimage agreed that it was a high point of the trip - quieter, less crowded, not a bit less rushed but altogether more enjoyable than the rest of our time in Italy. That sentiment extended from the religious sights we beheld to the hotel itself, which possessed a quaint character that our lodgings in Florence and Rome lacked. Especially regarding the meals that we enjoyed in

---

[19] *Chiara e Francesco* (a.k.a. *Clara e Francesco*, a.k.a. *Clare and Francis*), directed by Fabrizio Costa (Rome: Lux Vide and Rai Fiction, 2007).

the hotels' respective restaurants, Giotto far outstripped either the Croce di Malta in Florence or the Hotel Cicerone in Rome in both food and hospitality. But we could not stay in Assisi forever.

The drive from Assisi to Florence was a bit more than two hours. Even the Tuscan countryside sported extensively rugged hills, really mountains, that I had not expected. On the other hand, Florence itself is flat, on an alluvial plain deposited by the Arno River, surrounded by highlands. I do not know where to start regarding Florence. It is such a historically and culturally significant city! So, I will confine myself to a few random and general facts and observations. The Italian form of the name is *Firenze*, so it is a bit more different from the English form than is the Italian name of Rome, *Roma*. The meaning of either form is, however, the same, "the City of Flowers," for which the symbol is one familiar to all from Louisiana – the "Florentine lily" that the French call *fleur-de-lys*. Founded as a Roman *colonia* for his discharged veterans by Julius Caesar in 59 BC, the city's rise to prominence began a thousand years later, when it became a center of medieval cloth manufacture, trade, and finance. Its importance became incalculable as the birthplace and epicenter of the Italian Renaissance in the fifteenth century, coincident with the rise of the Medici family of clothiers-become-bankers to political and cultural dominance which they would maintain for about three hundred years. The city would eventually serve a brief stint as one of several successive capitals of the Kingdom of Italy during its first decade, the 1860s, until Rome was taken and became the only possible choice. The cultural importance of Florence is highlighted by the fact that the Tuscan dialect became the standard for modern Italian, as much as anything because Dante Alighieri, the writer of *The Divine Comedy* and the greatest poet in Italian history, was a son of Florence. Said to have the greatest concentration of artistic masterpieces in the world, the city also gains renown for its jewelry and fashion, especially leatherwork.

Busses may not enter the city center, so Luigi pulled into a bus park right by the river, where we debarked and set forth walking again. We trekked several blocks to enter the Piazza Santa Croce in the shadow of a huge statue of Dante. The Basilica of the Holy Cross at the eastern end of the plaza contains the tombs of many famous and important Italians – Michelangelo, Galileo, and so forth, and one for Dante himself – although that tomb is empty. The Poet's body is not there because Florence's great rival Ravenna, where he died in political exile, has obstinately refused to return his remains!

Shops and restaurants lined the other three sides of the plaza, which teemed with people. We spent some time there, beginning with Misuri's, a fine gold and leather shop which treated us to a show of how they make their products and how to distinguish fine gold and leather from lower quality wares. They also offered a considerable discount for members of our tour group (not uniquely to ours, of course – the same show and deal was clearly being offered to other groups while we were there). It worked; most of our group came out of there with something either for themselves or as gifts for friends and family back home. Anne bought a leather purse; we bought Tristan a wallet (and I got one just like it). The purchases included free gold monogramming. By the time we exited, Misuri's had taken most of our time as well as a fair amount of our money!

We grabbed a quick lunch of *panini* (flat toasted sandwiches on Italian bread). While Anne got the food from a small café and I held one of the small tables outside, I had a pleasant conversation with an English gentleman from the Cotswolds. Sadly, by the time we finished eating, there was not enough time to do a self-guided tour of the basilica, which others who had foregone lunch or the leather shops said took about thirty minutes.

There in Piazza Santa Croce we met our guide for Florence, Isabella. She led us on a brisk walk that first took us to the Piazza della Signoria, where we marveled at various monuments, including a replica of Michelangelo's *David* and the marble Fountain of Neptune at the terminus of a still-active Roman aqueduct. I was a bit dismayed that Isabella glossed over in favor of those works of art and engineering the many noteworthy events in Florentine history that took place on that square. Those included the 1497 "Bonfire of the Vanities" presided over by the Dominican friar Girolamo Savonarola during his brief time as dictator of Florence, followed the very next year by the Dominican's own execution when the Florentines tired of his fire and brimstone preaching. Savonarola and two of his followers were first hanged, then their bodies were burned; the ashes were cast into the Arno River to prevent the recovery of any relics. But onward we marched, passing by the Duomo of Florence, the Cathedral of Santa Maria del Fiore (St. Mary of the Flowers), with virtually no comment. We reached the Galleria dell'Accademia di Firenze, or Gallery of the Academy of Florence.

Over the next hour or so, we viewed the *real* statue of *David* by Michelangelo and much, much more. Then we backtracked to the

Duomo, which landmark of Florence we finally entered for a similarly quick tour before taking up the march again.

If this feels rushed, then I have succeeded in conveying how we felt that day, when the inherent drawback of this type of "packaged" guided tour became irksome. In an hour or so, we viewed the *real* statue of *David* by Michelangelo and much, much more in the Academy. But we spent hardly enough time in any *given* gallery before being shuffled through to the next. It was impossible to properly *see* anything, much less everything. I know we passed by many, many artistic masterpieces familiar to me from my studies or just general knowledge – but they all blur together. And it was pretty much the same in the Duomo. Again, our guide saw fit to say nothing regarding the significance of Filippo Brunelleschi's dome, the largest brick-and-mortar dome in the world, the iconic image of the Florentine skyline. We did get to behold the magnificently painted interior, Giorgio Vasari's *Last Judgment*, however – and then we were out.

We proceeded from the Duomo to the Basilica of San Lorenzo, where Fr. Humphries said Mass in the Canons' Chapel. St. Lawrence was the special patron saint of the Medici family and namesake of its most famous son, "Lorenzo *Il Magnifico*." This was pretty much the "family church." Although we did not see it, many of the Medici rest in the mausoleum. We did not tour the church proper at all, but this first Renaissance chapel in we heard Mass was, as might be doubly expected given it was the Medicis' own, exquisitely ornate. After Mass we continued onward, passing by the Basilica of Santa Maria Novella, finally arriving at our hotel, the Croce di Malta.

After dinner at 19:00, some of us went across the street to get some gelato. Anne continued with the group as they walked back up to the square in front of Santa Maria Novella while I came back to the room and managed to get Tuesday's blog entry posted (!), as well as performing some Internet course maintenance.

Saturday 25 October 2014 – Italy Day Six: *Florence, then to Rome*

We spent only one night in Florence. Wake-up was slightly later – 06:30 – with our bags to be out in the hallway for 07:30, the same time as breakfast.

At 08:30, we walked the short distance from the hotel to Santa Maria Novella, where Fr. Decker said Mass in the Chapel of the Blessed Sacrament, after which Isabella met up with us again and we walked to the Uffizi Gallery, just off the Piazza della Signoria. Built in the sixteenth century to be offices (*uffizi*) for Florentine city officials, the gallery very early became a show-house for artistic treasures accumulated by the Medici family who dominated those offices. The last Medici heiress bequeathed it all to the city in the seventeenth century. Our group of 46 then split up into two smaller groups to tour the repository of some of the most famous paintings and statues in the world. Anne and I followed Isabella. Once again, a couple of hours were not nearly enough. The lack of time was downright frustrating, in fact, the one constant albeit inevitable annoyance of this journey. Anne and I both desperately took pictures, as much to capture something of what we were seeing with barely enough time to register it as to post on my blog.

Far too soon, our two groups reunited for a walk back to the Piazza Santa Croce, where we could have had another chance to tour the church and see the tombs of so many outstanding Italians. Anne and I opted instead to eat lunch and rest. Lunch was pizza on the *piazza* near the statue of Dante. The food was good, although the service was lousy. I made a quick sweep through the many gift shops, mainly seeking a necktie. I had glimpsed many in passing but could not break away from the group to check them out. Here my efforts were rewarded with a nice rose-colored tie with a print of Florentine lilies. I also returned with various other items, including a Pinocchio Christmas ornament (Carlo Collodi was Florentine). Having accomplished all that, I just sat outside the pizzeria and enjoyed a beer and good company. Then another walk back the way we had initially come the day before brought us back to the bus park.

Before we left Florence completely, Luigi made a quick stop at an overlook across the river at the Piazza Michelangelo, affording us an excellent view of the city center from a familiar perspective. As countless photographers, painters, and – yes – tourists have, we found it the perfect backdrop for a slew of photographs. Then we were on the road again for the four-hour drive to Rome, broken only by a brief "coffee in, coffee out" (another of Debra's many memorable phrases). We also viewed the remainder of the movie about Saints Clare and Francis.

We arrived at the Hotel Cicerone, on the Vatican side of the River Tiber, about 19:15, just in time for our scheduled 19:30 dinner. After dinner, I came back up to our room, intending to work but being too beat by several days' relentless touring to do anything but fall into bed. I was so tired I worried myself, wondering briefly if I was coming down with something.

I fell asleep quickly, not realizing I was missing out on what several others of our group would look back on as one of the highlights of their whole trip.

Sunday 26 October 2014 – Italy Day Seven: *Rome*

Oh, blessed day! A week earlier than in the US, Italian clocks "fell back" overnight. So, we got an extra hour of sleep! I generally disapprove of "Daylight Savings Time," which puts our internal clocks an hour out of sync with the sun for about two-thirds of the year, but – *man!* – I do like "Fall Back Weekend"![20] For a second morning, as well, the wake-up call came a little later by the clock than the usual 06:00 – 06:15 for a 07:15-ish breakfast. I woke up refreshed and relieved that my worries the night before, that I might be coming down with something, proved groundless.[21]

Although the breakfast spread was every bit as good as we had enjoyed before (and the bacon was, well, *infinitely* better), I cannot say I liked the regimented way the Hotel Cicerone did things. The dining room attendants had to confirm our room numbers and directed us toward specific tables, seeming to follow no pattern. I guess it is related to something said by one of the padres a few days before. The main rule in Italy is that the rules do not make any sense, and they change daily for no apparent reason. Anyway, we started assembling about 08:00 for the bus to depart at 08:15.

By that time, I believe I had discovered what I had missed the night before. A couple of our good friends, Burley and Cindy, along with Frs. Humphries and Decker had taken a stroll through the evening streets to the Piazza San Pietro – St. Peter's Square – only a few blocks away from our hotel. They gushed about how beautiful it was, seeing it at night and practically deserted. I was very jealous. We tentatively planned to make the excursion one evening before we departed for home, but to my disappointment, the opportunity never presented itself. It is one more thing to add to my "Maybe next time!" list.

In contrast to the private Masses just for our group that was the norm for this pilgrimage, said in turn by Fr. Humphries or Fr. Decker,

---

[20] I did not like it nearly so much when the shift from Daylight Savings Time actually came the next weekend back in the United States, and the two back-to-back time-shifts compounded with our return trip's jet lag threw me for a loop.

[21] As a good night's sleep seemed to snap me out of it, I assume that it was indeed simply exhaustion. There is a chance that I dodged a bullet, however. One of our pilgrims did, about the same time, come down with some kind of malady that kept her down and out for at least a couple of our days in Rome. Her husband was a model of marital devotion in staying with and caring for her. These things happen, unfortunately and likely unavoidably.

this Sunday in Rome we attended a regular 09:00 Mass in Italian at one of the four major basilicas of the Catholic Church, the one of most direct significance to our group because it is our "Mother Basilica" – the Basilica of Santa Maria Maggiore (St. Mary Major). What that means requires a brief explanation.

A basilica was originally a style of public building in Rome, generally rectangular with a central nave and aisles separated by colonnades. Beginning with the Christianization of the Roman Empire in the fourth century, at first through gift, then through appropriation as Roman government melted away in the fifth-century "Fall of the Roman Empire," many basilicas became churches. Over time, the term came to mean new constructions built according to the same general pattern, then gradually came to denote certain churches of major importance granted special ceremonial rights by the Papacy regardless of their layout.

There are two ranks of basilica. Our "Basilica of the Immaculate Conception" in Natchitoches is, properly speaking, a "minor basilica." Despite common reference to our church as "The Minor Basilica,"[22] the diminutive is less important than one might think. All but four basilicas throughout the world share that "minor" status. Only four churches, all in Rome, enjoy the status of "major basilica" – St. Peter's in Vatican City, of course, as well as St. John Lateran, St. Paul Outside the Walls, and St. Mary Major. Every other basilica is "minor." Every minor basilica is, moreover, affiliated with one of the four major basilicas, deriving from that relationship certain rights and indulgences. The Minor Basilica of the Immaculate Conception, Natchitoches, Louisiana, enjoys such a special relationship with the Major Basilica of Santa Maria Maggiore, Rome, Italy. Hence, Mary Major is our "Mother Basilica."

Saint Mary Major is the largest Marian church in Rome and one of the most ancient churches dedicated to Our Lady. It dates from the fifth century, immediately after the 431 Council of Ephesus confirmed Mary's status as *Theotokos*, "God-Bearer," affirming that she is more than just the "mother of Jesus," she is indeed the "Mother of God." Despite being damaged, repaired, and repeatedly reconstructed through the centuries, the edifice retains its core of original classical Roman structure and houses many historically important fifth-century mosaics and some of the oldest representations of the Blessed Virgin. The left transept, the Borghese Chapel, for instance, enshrines the

---

[22] Which includes holding the Internet address, http://www.minorbasilica.org/.

ancient icon of the *Salus Populi Romani*, "Salvation of the Roman People," one of a number of images of Our Lady traditionally "written"[23] from life by St. Luke the Evangelist on wood from the table of the Holy Family's home in Nazareth as he listened to her account of the life of her Son – especially the wonderful and mysterious events surrounding his birth, which he would eventually and uniquely record in his Gospel. Even if this legend is not based in fact, this icon is of great antiquity, dating from the very earliest centuries of the Church.

Also associated with the Nativity, the crypt below the high altar includes the Chapel of the Nativity and the Manger in which Our Lady laid the newborn Christ child on that first Christmas night.[24]

A popular alternative name for the Basilica of St. Mary Major is "Our Lady of the Snows," which makes for a charming story. Per the 1911 Catholic Encyclopedia,

> During the pontificate of Liberius, the Roman patrician John and his wife, who were without heirs, made a vow to donate their possessions to the Virgin Mary. They prayed that she might make known to them how they were to dispose of their property in her honour. On 5 August, at the height of the Roman summer, snow fell during the night on the summit of the Esquiline Hill. In obedience to a vision of the Virgin Mary which they had the same night, the couple built a basilica in honour of Mary on the very spot which was covered with snow. From the fact that no mention whatever is made of this alleged miracle until a few hundred years later, not even by Sixtus III in his eight-line dedicatory inscription ... it would seem that the legend has no historical basis.[25]

---

[23] Conventional terminology has icons "written" rather than "painted."

[24] The widely reported return of this relic to Bethlehem in November 2019 was exaggerated. Pope Francis sent only a tiny portion of the Manger from St. Mary Major to the Basilica of the Nativity; the majority remained exactly where it has resided for over a thousand years. – "Jesus manger: Relic returns to Bethlehem in time for Christmas," *BBC News* (30 November 2019) [https://www.bbc.com/news/world-middle-east-50600025].

[25] Michael Ott, "Our Lady of the Snow," *The Catholic Encyclopedia*, vol. 1 (New York: Robert Appleton Company, 1911) [http://www.newadvent.org/cathen/11361c.html], accessed 02 October 2019. The air of skepticism with which this *Catholic Encyclopedia* entry ends puts me in mind of two quotations which adorn my office door: "This is the West, sir. When the legend becomes fact, print the legend!" (John Ford, dir., *The Man Who Shot Liberty Valance* [1962; Paramount Home Video, DVD, 2001]); and "It is quite easy to see why a legend is treated, and ought to be treated, more respectfully than a book of history. The legend is generally made by the majority of people in the village, who are sane. The book is

We entered the basilica shortly before 09:00, wandered around a bit in awe, seeing the aforementioned relics, and then assembled in the nave before the main altar, awaiting the beginning of Mass. We only realized that we were in the wrong place when the celebrants (including Fr. Decker, who is fluent enough in Italian to concelebrate the Mass) processed in via the side aisle and entered the Borghese Chapel – which explained why that side chapel had been slowly filling up. We ended up having to stand in the rear of the area, some even outside the gate dividing that chapel from the nave! Later, Fr. Decker revealed that he was as startled as we were when the procession took a left turn and entered the chapel, and Debra apologized profusely for the failure in communication, but the sacristan with whom she had confirmed the Mass earlier apparently did not consider it important that we know the precise location of the 09:00 Mass within the vast basilica!

Mass in Italian was interesting. Based on my familiarity with Latin, I could pick out words here and there, but could not make much sense of it otherwise. This seems to me to support the argument that in a "universal" – *catholic* – Church, there should be one common language of worship (Latin, of course), but frankly the structure of the Holy Mass, even in its Ordinary "Novus Ordo" form, is the same no matter what the language, and I got the gist of the critically important parts.[26] Anyone who maintains that they "cannot follow" the Mass in another language, particularly Latin, has a bigger problem than just language. Communion was, however, an experience in itself. Debra had already impressed on us that Italians do not know the concept of a queue. We got a perfect example of that here, as communicants pressed forward without any order whatsoever, practically elbowing others aside to

---

generally written by the one man in the village who is mad" (G. K. Chesterton, *Orthodoxy* [1908], in *The Collected Works of G. K. Chesterton*, vol. I: *Heretics, Orthodoxy, The Blatchford Controversies*, ed. David Dooley [San Francisco: Ignatius Press, 1986]).

[26] The *structure* is the same, but "the devil is in the details" – or the lack thereof. Within the structure of the post-Vatican II Mass, many "details" were cast aside, watering down a theological depth that had evolved organically over the course of many centuries. It is too much to go through here but lining the order of the 1962 Roman Missal up beside that of the 1970 "New Mass" clearly demonstrates that to be the case. They are the same rite – but the expression of the latter is incredibly impoverished. To give but one relatively minor example off the top of my head, the new formula of the *Confiteor* ("I confess...") dismisses some of our most powerful saintly intercessors – no longer are "blessed Michael the Archangel, blessed John the Baptist, the holy Apostles Peter and Paul" invoked by name; they are simply demoted to inclusion in "all the angels and saints." Less is not more. This is but one of many examples. Devotees of the Traditional Latin Mass such as I are often accused of being fixated on the language (and I do love Latin and consider it superior as a liturgical language), but the vernacularization of the Mass is of far less concern than the theological hatchet-job inflicted by Annibale Bugnini and associates.

make their way forward toward the priests distributing the Sacrament. It was wild.

Once Mass ended, it was back to the bus as quickly as possible to drive to St. Peter's Square, where crowds were already assembling for the Pope's weekly Angelus Address at 12:00 on Sunday. We were let loose to find our spots in the plaza, with only a predetermined meeting time and place for afterward, late enough to allow us time to find lunch after the Angelus. That time was to be 14:00; the place was to be in front of the Domus Artis gift shop just outside the square. Having a little while before it got *too* crowded in the square, most of us engaged in a bit of shopping there in Domus Artis, purchasing various religious items to be taken home with the Pope's blessing bestowed at the end of the Angelus. And so, after we left Domus Artis about 11:30, Anne and I did not see anyone from our group as we pressed our way through the crowds to what we figured would be a good vantage point. It turned out to be excellent, up near the right where Bernini's four-column-deep colonnade flares out into the arcs encircling the Egyptian obelisk that once adorned the Emperor Nero's Circus on the Vatican Hill across the Tiber River from the Seven Hills of the city itself. That obelisk may well have been the last thing St. Peter saw with his mortal eyes – inverted, from where he was crucified upside-down at his own request.

Pope Francis appeared right on schedule, delivering his address in Italian and acknowledging one group of pilgrims from Peru, I believe, who were there with a big procession, banners, even a big Rosary made of helium balloons that they released into the air – we would see it again. Of course, I had no idea what he was saying. An English translation is posted weekly, by which I later learned that he gave an extended meditation on the Gospel reading of the day, from Matthew 22: 34-40 on "The Greatest Commandment."[27] The one part that I *could* follow was the Angelus, which he led in Latin, further confirming the value of a common, universal liturgical language. Pope Francis may not have been my favorite Pope even then, and he has become less so as time has passed, but he is the Pope, the Vicar of Christ, the 265th successor of St. Peter, the Prince of the Apostles, and I will give him the respect that he is due on that account. I pray for him every day.

Afterward, Anne and I made our way out of St. Peter's Square, stopping at a couple of shops along the way. I went into the Pope

---

[27] Pope Francis, *Angelus*, Saint Peter's Square, Sunday, 26 October 2014 [http://www.vatican.va/content/francesco/en/angelus/2014/documents/papa-francesco_angelus_20141026.html].

Benedict XVI Bookstore, where I was somewhat surprised to find a small selection of merchandise in English, including a Bible which has ever since been my reading Bible of choice.[28] Then we found a little café on a side street to the north of St. Peter's. There seemed to be a respectable number of locals there, including priests, and for a good reason. The pizzas and the wine were excellent. We followed them with gelato from one of the omnipresent street vendors before meeting the others in front of Domus Artis at 14:00.

After walking back to meet Luigi waiting with our bus, we passed through the ancient city walls of Rome, following the Appian Way southward to the Catacombs of St. Callixtus. (Along the way, several miles from the Vatican, we caught sight of the Peruvian Balloon Rosary high up in the sky, floating merrily away.)

The catacombs are man-made tunnels built during the earliest days of Christianity, while the faith was still outlawed, to serve as burial chambers rather than the more stereotypical places of refuge and worship. Undoubtedly during the worst persecutions, they served the latter purposes as well. The particular group of catacombs we visited carries the name of the deacon and future Pope St. Callixtus (r. ca. 217-222), who created and administered them in the early third century under Pope Zephyrinus (r. ca. 199-217). They once housed the tombs of a number of second- to fourth-century Popes, although by the ninth century all such relics had been translated to the various churches of Rome, leaving the catacombs empty but for a wealth of early Christian iconography. For ages they were forgotten only to be rediscovered in the nineteenth century. Under the direction of a priest of the Salesian order now overseeing them, we toured these catacombs where our earliest Fathers in the Faith once reposed.

By 16:00, we were back on the way into the city, headed for an evening "out on the town" in one of the centers of Roman night-life, the Piazza Navona, each carrying twenty Euros given back to us by Magnificat to buy our own dinners. But first, we took a short side-trip to the Pantheon, one of the most ancient buildings in Rome. On the walk from the bus park to the Pantheon, Anne risked getting scolded for leaving the group to fulfill one of her goals for the trip, to procure for

---

[28] Published by the London-based Catholic Truth Society, *The CTS New Catholic Bible* couples the text of the Jerusalem Bible (1966), albeit rendering the Divine Name "Yahweh" more traditionally as "the Lord," with the Grail Psalter as used in the Liturgy of the Hours. Attractively bound in a soft "leatherette" cover, it is moreover chock full of extensive tables and charts detailing how extensively Scripture is used in the liturgy. Because it is not a strict "formal equivalence" translation, I do not use this Bible for intensive Scripture study – but for sheer readability, I consider its moderate "dynamic equivalence" hands down the best.

Tristan a scarf for the soccer team A[ssociazione] S[portiva] Roma, which she spied in a shop as we passed. I stood look-out, keeping my eyes on Fr. Humphries's little bald spot receding into the distance as she concluded the transaction in record time. Then we dashed to rejoin the group where they had stopped in the plaza in front of the Pantheon. We were back with them so quickly that no one even knew we had left.

The Pantheon was originally built by the first Emperor Augustus Caesar's friend and right-hand man Marcus Agrippa just before the BC-AD divide. It was rebuilt by Emperor Hadrian in the second century after suffering significant damage due to an earthquake, but has undergone little change since that time, except for being repurposed from being a pagan temple to the Roman gods – *all* the gods, which is what "pantheon" means – into a Christian church dedicated to the One God through St. Mary and the Martyrs. Its most distinctive architectural feature is the largest free-standing concrete dome in the world and the large circular hole or "oculus" at the very top of that dome, supplying the only natural light to the interior. It holds the tombs of two of Italy's modern (late nineteenth-century) kings.

After a short self-guided tour of the Pantheon, I let myself get snookered. Here's how I treated it when I posted a picture on Facebook: "*Learn from my mistake – What not to do as a tourist/pilgrim/etc.: They want money, of course ... I knew that. But I'm in Rome, outside the Pantheon, they are Roman soldiers. It was like catnip to me! All reason fled! Along with a number of Euros! Merda!*" Enough said. It happens.

We then walked to the Piazza Navona and went our separate ways with just a time and place to meet up. After marveling at the Fountain of the Four Rivers at the center of the plaza, several of us went through the Church of St. Agnes in Agony, which included a secluded shrine displaying the skull of that young martyr. St. Agnes was only about thirteen years of age when she refused to give up her purity despite the Roman authorities escalating attempts to humiliate and torture her into renouncing her Faith. The name of the church comes, however, from the Latinized Greek *in Agone*, referring to its and the piazza's location on the site of Diocletian's Circus, where games would take place as well as persecutions – the Greek *agon* means "competition." But I think the English gloss with the modern connotation works tragically well. Afterward, a group of about ten of us had dinner at an open-air restaurant named Tucci's. It was excellent. We enjoyed a jazz band playing in the piazza near our restaurant. Followed, of course, by a dash to a gelato shop.

At 20:30, we all gathered and made our way back to the bus, and Luigi drove us back to the Hotel Cicerone after the longest day out yet since we arrived in Italy. I was barely able to get the pictures off my phone and Anne's memory card to my computer before conking out, although we did also call and chat with Tristan for a few minutes.

Monday 27 October 2014 – Italy Day Eight: *Rome*

The wake-up call came early – 05:30, for 06:30 breakfast and 07:15 bus departure for the Vatican City, the temporal center of the Holy Roman Catholic Church. The Vatican is like Florence – where to start? Well, here is the gist:

Vatican City is a walled, independent city-state found entirely within the city of Rome. It covers an area of about 110 acres, with a population under a thousand, ruled by the Pope as its sovereign. It takes its name from the Vatican Hill, west of the Tiber River, across from the Seven Hills of Ancient Rome on the east and includes once-marshy fields abutting the Janiculum Hill. This walled area is all that is left of over a thousand years when, in addition to being the spiritual leaders of western Christendom, the Popes were temporal rulers of central Italy, the so-called "Papal States." In 1861, the King of Sardinia united all of Italy save Rome into the modern Kingdom of Italy; the Popes lost all except the city itself. Then, when the Franco-Prussian War in 1870 required France to withdraw its troops which had been protecting Rome's independence, the Popes lost Rome as well. They retreated within the walls of the Vatican, not to emerge for almost sixty years until the 1929 Lateran Treaty between Pope Pius XI and Benito Mussolini secured the status of the Vatican as an independent state. St. Peter's Basilica, the most important of the four major basilicas of Rome, fronted by the great Square with the sweeping colonnades, is only a small part of the complex, which contains much more – residences for the functionaries of the Holy See, offices, chapels, museums, libraries, gardens – only a fraction of which were we able to see in our day there.

The day began with Holy Mass in St. Peter's Basilica – and started so early because, while the basilica is set aside for liturgical activities until 09:30, there is a typically Roman lack of order in allocation of altars. Priests wishing to say Mass in the basilica receive assignments first-come, first-serve, with no prior reservation, and it is best – really, imperative – to get there early. We arrived well before our "scheduled" time of 08:00 (was it really "scheduled"? I am convinced that was just a fiction, at best a *target*), with the following plan: Fr. Decker would take the majority of our group of pilgrims for Mass in English, in the Ordinary Form, while Fr. Humphries would take the small number of us (about a dozen) who wanted to experience a Traditional Latin Mass in the Extraordinary Form in St. Peter's. I was, of course, first in line for the latter! The priests received their altar assignments in the sacristy, then we simply trailed them as they followed a sacristan to their respective altars. Fr. Decker was directed to the Altar of the Crucifixion of St. Peter; Fr. Humphries said Mass at the Altar of St. Peter Healing the Lame Man, although he made mention of this being the Chapel of St. Philip Neri in a short commentary at the end of the Mass, emphasizing how the very same Mass, with the very same words – not different words in different languages saying more or less the same thing, but *the very same words* – has been said in this church for *centuries*: "St. Philip Neri [sixteenth century] said the same Mass at this very altar." Its precise identification matters not, however. It was in St. Peter's Basilica, within a few yards of the Pope's high altar! It was moving beyond words. This Mass was the highlight of my entire pilgrimage to Italy. The often-overlooked transcendent reality is that every Mass ever said, no matter how magnificent or how humble it is, whether in a great and ancient basilica or on a portable altar on the hood of a jeep (as in times of war), is one and the same Holy Sacrifice made by Our Lord at Calvary. Father's point brought that home. And yet this one was indescribably special. My understanding of that supernatural dimension of pilgrimage grew a little deeper.

One mild disappointment followed, however, when in the press for altars to accommodate the many priests wanting to say Mass in St. Peter's we were allowed no time to pray quietly before that altar once the Mass was over, to ponder the profound reality we had just witnessed. A sacristan immediately appeared and shooed us away, back into the nave, to make way for the next group. But we then had time to wander around, soaking it all in – although many of the increasing crowds of people were not observing the requested "Silence and No Photographs" in the period before 09:30.

Our group gathered by Michelangelo's *Pietà* just inside the Holy Door just before 09:30. We gazed on one of the most famous sculptures in the world, Mother Mary holding her son in death. We could only gaze at it from a distance, however. Ever since an infamous hammer attack in 1972 severely damaged the masterpiece, requiring extensive reconstruction, the *Pietà* has been visible only through a large pane of bulletproof glass keeping visitors several yards away. The Holy Door is opened only by the Pope during Jubilee Years such as would begin, although we did not know it at the time, a little more than a year later, on the Solemnity of the Immaculate Conception, 08 December 2015, for the Extraordinary Jubilee Year of Mercy 2016.

There by the Holy Door, we met our Roman guide for the next two days, Roberta. She was quite good, a perfect balance of knowledge and piety, better on that count than our earlier guides. And our tour began. Once more, it was overwhelming, and the press of time dictated that there was no time to linger and take it all in – the constant refrain of this and, I find, every guided pilgrimage. We generally followed a question-mark path beginning with the Holy Door at the right rear of the vast church, past various shrines, chapels, and altars – St. Sebastian's Chapel which now contains the Tomb of St. John Paul II; the Chapel of the Blessed Sacrament; the Altar of St. Jerome, beneath which can be seen the incorrupt body of Pope St. John XXIII; to the Statue of St. Peter Enthroned, one of the few pieces preserved from the Old Basilica.

"Old Basilica"? – The "Modern" St. Peter's Basilica is *not* the first church on this site. It is a mere five hundred years old, begun during the later days of the Italian Renaissance on orders from Pope Julius II (whose name we would hear a lot that day) to replace the original basilica, which was by then over a thousand years old. The quick history lesson here is that the bulk of the Vatican is on the Vatican Hill, but St. Peter's is largely built on the old cemetery next to it. The Vatican Hill was the site of Nero's Circus, where many Christians suffered martyrdom in the immediate aftermath of the Great Fire of Rome, AD 64, which Nero blamed on the Christians. Among those martyrs was St. Peter, famously crucified upside-down in that Circus and afterward buried in that cemetery, which is why Emperor Constantine almost three hundred years later built the first St. Peter's Basilica in that spot, with its altar directly over the saint's tomb. The presence of St. Peter's mortal remains have been confirmed archaeologically in recent decades, which means that when Pope Francis says Mass at the Papal Altar, he does so directly over the remains of his 265th predecessor, a point made by Fr. Decker. That first basilica stood for over a thousand years until it was razed to make way for Pope Julius' great project, the New St. Peter's, built between 1506 and 1626. The historian and traditionalist in me is appalled at the destruction of the first "capital church" of Christendom, but the result is by all accounts near infinitely more majestic, the summit of Renaissance architecture.

In any case, we continued from the traditional rubbing of the well-worn foot of St. Peter counter-clockwise around the back of the Papal

Altar – the one with the tremendous spiral-shaped columns, also designed by Bernini – with a side trip up before the Tomb of Pope Alexander VII; and back around to the Statue of St. Andrew, bearing the X-shaped cross upon which the brother of St. Peter was crucified in Greece. Behind that statue we entered a narrow stairway down into the Holy Grottoes beneath the church, where we were asked to stop taking pictures, which had been allowed freely hitherto. In the main church we were even allowed to use flashes, which were generally prohibited because of their long-term effects on paints and pigmentation; contrary to appearances there are hardly any paintings or frescoes in St. Peter's to be faded by cumulative exposure to light – all of the images are finely crafted mosaics! Nevertheless, we were asked to take *no* pictures in the crypt. I am not certain exactly why, but I abided by their rules. We saw the tombs and sarcophagi of many of the Popes buried beneath St. Peter's, although not (as I understand it) that of St. Peter himself, which is located deeper still. The grottoes are actually at ground level beneath much of the present basilica; the older tombs including St. Peter's are below ground level and can be seen by prior and limited arrangement only, in what is known as the "Scavi Tour" (from the archaeological excavation carried out in the mid-twentieth century). We did not do that, however. Instead we ascended back to the main body of the church and made our way toward the front and out, I believe, mainly along the left aisle, although my memories are blurred. There was so much to see, and although I was snapping pictures furiously, I look at many of them now and think, "I don't even remember that!" I am particularly unsure about that route because it also seems we emerged from the basilica somewhere on the right side!

Once out of the basilica, however, we made our way through the steadily lengthening lines of people waiting to get inside. It pays to be part of a defined tour group like ours, and even better to be classified as "pilgrims," as we would see later. A photographer awaited us just outside the Square. It was for this official group photograph that Alexis had asked that we all wear the Magnificat Travel T-shirt we received on the very first day.

The photograph took only a few moments, then we were off once again, trekking by foot out and around the walls of Vatican City for a quarter-hour or so, to re-enter through the street entrance of the Vatican Museums.

It was now about 12:00, so we took a short break in the cafeteria just inside the entrance. Then began a sprinting dash through gallery after gallery of artistic masterpieces and archaeological treasures, both sacred and profane, culminating in the Sistine Chapel. Pictures were allowed until that point, without flash – but once we entered the Sistine Chapel, they were not allowed at all, and here the guards enforced that rigorously – "*No pho-tos!*" They attempted to enforce the rule of *silenzio* as well, but with lesser success. I later quipped that their admonitions to silence were about as well heeded as Fr. Humphries's to the congregants at Immaculate Conception after 09:00 Sunday Mass! I am proud to say that here, once again, it was not our group flouting the rules.

Very quickly (as was our tour), the Vatican Museums were founded by the same Pope Julius II who began the modern St. Peter's Basilica to display an ancient sculpture of the Trojan priest Laocoön and his Sons that was unearthed near the Basilica of St. Mary Major in 1506. It now hosts the vast and ever-expanding collection of treasures held by the Vatican. It is one of the most visited museums in the world. Its 54 galleries (we saw only a fraction) culminate in the Sistine Chapel, famous for two reasons: 1) The magnificent frescoes and paintings which cover all the walls as well as the ceiling – the side walls, fifteenth-century frescoes by Botticelli and others, illustrating the lives of Moses and Christ; the ceiling, Michelangelo's early-sixteenth-century depiction of the Creation (painted before 1527); and the wall behind the altar, by Michelangelo again, showing the Last Judgment (painted after 1527 the year in which Lutheran troops in the Imperial Army of Charles V sacked Rome, a truly apocalyptic event acknowledged even by secular historians as bringing down the curtain on the age of the Italian Renaissance. It is likewise considered by most to have inspired Michelangelo's depiction of the Last Judgment); and 2) This is where the College of Cardinals meets in conclave to elect each new Pope.

Our tour of the Vatican ended about 14:00 – just *two hours* in the Museums – and we scattered for a late lunch. A group of us ended up at the Café de San Pietro, right beside Domus Artis, which served cafeteria-style. Anne and I shared a vegetable lasagna with mushrooms and a chicken salad; I liked both, but she cared for neither. Then there was a little bit of time for more shopping outside Vatican City before we met in the same location as before, outside Domus Artis, at 15:15, to make our way to where faithful Luigi waited with the bus to take us to another of the major basilicas of Rome.

I must say that, among those four major basilicas, I found something particularly enchanting about the Basilica Papale di San Paolo fuori le Mura (Papal Basilica of St. Paul Outside the Walls), so named because it was for much of its history outside the walls of Rome. The recent discovery of first-century remains including a sarcophagus directly beneath the main altar, as can be seen through a small window into the crypt, seems to confirm that it was here that the early Roman Christians interred Paul of Tarsus after his execution about two miles away.

The elaborately descriptive name is only the beginning. Even at first glance, St. Paul Outside the Walls presents a decidedly un-churchlike impression. With the palm trees in the front courtyard and the golden shimmer of mosaics on the western façade, it put me in mind of something out of the Caribbean. The statue of the Apostle at the center of the courtyard does not contribute to any churchlike mien, depicting him brandishing the sword as it does. The whole looks distinctly out of place among the churches we saw in such rapid succession that memory blurs most of them together. This one stands out.

Inside St. Paul Outside the Walls is as magnificent as the outside and just as distinctive. One of the most notable features is several ranks of circular medallions high around the periphery, bearing the visages of all 266 Popes – and room for perhaps five more. The dwindling space is important if you believe the legend, which says that the Second Coming of Christ will occur when all the Papal medallions have been occupied. Besides those Papal images, the iconography in this basilica is a marvelous mix of styles from Byzantine to Baroque. I cannot in any way agree with the assessment of the *DK Eyewitness Travel: Italy 2014* that it is "soulless" (p. 446). The author would have done better not to qualify their framing statement that the Basilica of St. Paul "is a faithful ... reconstruction of the great fourth-century basilica destroyed by fire in 1823." Granted, what we saw was mostly a modern construction, but most of the ancient buildings in Rome have suffered severe damage and reconstruction over the centuries. In this case, my understanding is that the fire destroyed mainly the nave of the fourth-century church founded by Constantine above the tomb of St. Paul, with the eastern end suffering much less damage. Even with the rebuilding, this magnificent church best represents the model of an ancient Roman basilica.

St. Paul Outside the Walls has seen much history since its foundation. It came into the care of Benedictine monks in the sixth century and was fortified against Saracens raiding up the Tiber River in the ninth century. It became a daughter house of Cluny, the center of Church reform in the tenth century, and saw its prior, Cardinal

Hildebrand, bring that reforming impulse to the Papacy in the eleventh century as Pope St. Gregory VII. It served as the seat of the Latin Patriarch of Alexandria (Egypt) from 1215 to 1964 and continues to function as a Benedictine monastery.

Again, our time was all too short, especially for those of us who like to try to pick up guidebooks and the like in the gift-shops that (almost) inevitably serve as the terminus of these tours. But by 17:30 we were loaded up and headed back to the hotel. That did give us a little time in the locale of one of the prime shopping districts in Rome, just a couple of streets from our own Via Cicerone, the Via Cola di Rienzo, and we put it to use exploring that area. Dinner was at 19:30, once again followed by no sharing session; apparently, the hotel was not that cooperative in providing a room for us to engage in that, to the disappointment of no one to whom I talked. We instead put the time after dinner to use in a ... you guessed it ... gelato run. We all felt somewhat liberated, knowing that the wake-up call the next morning would not come until a luxurious 07:00![29]

Tuesday 28 October 2014 – Italy Day Nine: *Rome*

Our last full day in Rome – and it was packed! It began with a relatively late wake-up at 07:00, 08:00 breakfast, to be met by Roberta in the lobby, thence immediately onto the bus for the drive to St. John Lateran, the last of the four major basilicas of Rome we would visit on our pilgrimage. It is the oldest of the basilicas, the first in rank (thus formally called the "A*rch*basilica of St. John Lateran"), indeed, the oldest surviving church in the West. It, moreover – *not* St. Peter's – serves as the Pope's cathedral in his role as Bishop of Rome.

The archbasilica's life as a church goes back to the early fourth century, when Constantine the Great gave it to Pope Miltiades, but the structure is in fact much more ancient than that, being part of the complex making up the extensive Palace of the Lateran branch of the Sextian family, one of the most ancient families in Rome. (Among early notables was Lucius Sextius Lateranus, of Licinian-Sextian Law fame and first plebeian Consul of Rome in the fourth century BC). Emperor Constantine had inherited the Lateran Palace by his marriage to his second wife, Fausta, but from the early fourth century AD

---

[29] In retrospect, this would have been Anne's and my only chance to walk down to St. Peter's Square in the evening. Perhaps we considered it and rejected it; perhaps not. Several years later, I do not remember. My suspicion is that we considered a little less than two hours not enough time to do so before dinner, and if the later evenings on every other night is any indication, our stamina was flagging quickly after dinner.

through most of the Middle Ages it would serve as the usual Papal residence. It had undergone periodic restorations to repair damage by fire or earthquake, such as in the tenth century, before being magnificently embellished by Pope Innocent III in the early thirteenth century. It hosted several Ecumenical Councils, including one of the most important gatherings in the history of the Church, the fourth council bearing that name, presided over in 1215 by that same Pope Innocent III, which defined doctrines and established norms that would stand unchanged for eight hundred years. Then an extended period of vacancy during the Avignon Papacy in the fourteenth century (1305-1378) left both palace and basilica in near ruins. Nevertheless, once the Avignon Papacy and the subsequent Great Western Schism between competing claims to the Papal office were resolved, by 1417, with one Pope, in Rome, the early Renaissance Popes rebuilt and embellished them grander than ever. Architect Allessandro Galilei (kinsman to Galileo Galilei, but a century later) designed the modern (eighteenth-century) façade, "remov[ing] all vestiges of the ancient basilica architecture, and impart[ing] a new-classical façade."[30] Nevertheless, some elements of the most ancient structures were preserved throughout, including the *Scala Sancta* ... but we will get to that.

Our tour of the church itself went pretty normally, Roberta giving us a running commentary as we examined the exterior and made our way around the interior. Late during our time inside, however, we started noticing an increasing number of people taking places up around the altar. Then attendants started shooing sightseers out of the area around the main altar and the forward part of the nave. It turned out that a Cardinal whose name I never caught was to say a special Mass, which began with a procession from the right transept a little past 11:00. I had earlier noticed a guy entering the church with a guitar strapped to his back, which was not what I had seen so far as typical tourist attire. I must say it suddenly became a bit surreal to be standing there in that majestic, ancient basilica hearing the beginnings of a *guitar Mass!* – with a *Cardinal!*

Soon after that Mass began, we moved out of the basilica and across the street to another part of the Lateran complex, which today houses more museum space as well as pastoral offices for the diocese of Rome. The most renowned feature is, however, the *Scala Sancta* (Holy Steps) which are, according to tradition, the very steps that Our Lord ascended, wounded and bleeding after being scourged, to face

---

[30] Wikipedia, s.v. "Archbasilica of St. John Lateran," accessed 21 November 2014

Pontius Pilate again. The Holy Steps are among the many relics brought from the Holy Land to Rome by Emperor Constantine's mother, St. Helena, in the early fourth century. The original marble is covered by wooden planking, but there are narrow frontal openings through which the marble can be seen, as well as several very small (4"x4"?) glass windows in the tops of several wooden steps, revealing dark stains on the marble – drops of the Precious Blood from Our Lord's stripes, by which we were healed (Is. 53: 5).

Indulgenced custom is that pilgrims ascend the Holy Steps on their knees, praying an Our Father, a Hail Mary, and a Glory Be each for the intentions of the Holy Father. A considerable number were doing so as we arrived. Most of our group joined them, including myself. It is harder than you might think. Ascending the 28 steps, takes about half an hour as pilgrims prayerfully (and painfully) make their way from step to step. But all who started persevered to the end. Roberta had cautioned that once you begin, there is no turning back; I consider that to be more a practical consideration than anything else, given the press of pilgrims around you as you ascend. Several of our group afterward called the experience the most moving part of their pilgrimage. For myself, it is indeed right up there with hearing the Traditional Latin Mass in St. Peter's Basilica, which I previously identified as the high point of my time in Rome and will stand by – but I must admit ascending the Holy Steps is a very close second.

Standing up with great relief once the ordeal ended, wondering whether my knees would ever be the same and considering with some shame how much crueler was Our Lord's suffering, I could look into but not enter the *Sancta Sanctorum* of the Pope's private chapel at the Lateran. The Chapel of St. Lawrence contains a wealth of relics. Front and center, there is another icon said to have been started by St. Luke and finished by angels. Called the Uronica, the image is that of Christ in majesty. (Latinists: "*Sancta Sanctorum*" is indeed correct in this case, referring to the plurality of relics present there.)

As I made my way down the exit stairs to the left, I heard a voice call my name from behind. I turned and found, to my immense pleasure, Fr. Luke Melcher. He is one of our priests of the Diocese of Alexandria, who was at the time assigned to Rome, earning a Doctorate in Liturgy. My wife and I have very fond memories of him from the year he served as an assistant at Immaculate Conception in the mid-2000s. He is also friends with Frs. Humphries and Decker, had come to meet up with them at the Lateran, and had scaled the Holy Steps along with us. It is a small world.

After a few minutes reassembling our group outside the Holy Steps, we made our way back to the bus for a short trip (short enough that Luigi chided Debra that we could have walked and saved him finding a new parking space) to an "off-the-books" church. By that I mean that the Basilica of Santa Croce in Gerusalemme was not part of our formal itinerary. Our "itinerary" was getting somewhat scrambled by then anyway when compared with the "final" itinerary provided at the meeting in September, but with more pilgrimages under my belt, I know that is not at all unusual. This one was well worth seeing.

The Basilica of the Holy Cross in Jerusalem is sometimes called the "Basilica Heleniana," after St. Helena, because she dedicated it to host the most precious relics that she brought back from Jerusalem - fragments of the True Cross itself. "In Jerusalem"? - She transported soil from the Holy City to Rome and incorporated into the foundation so that when you are in this basilica, you are literally walking on the earth of the Holy Land. There were various other relics of the Passion there, as well as a full-size facsimile of the Shroud of Turin donated to the basilica by Turin and a life-size crucifix with a Corpus accurately depicting Our Lord's wounds as shown on the Shroud. The latter impresses the observer mainly with the savagery inflicted on Him during the Passion - most crucifixes you ever see are quite sanitized, "clean" as one of our number commented as she beheld it. Incidentally, this was the main instance I think of where being pilgrims cut us a break. Technically, the basilica closed for lunch while we were there, but Roberta explained our status to the porter and got us the few minutes we needed to finish our tour.

From there, we drove to the Trevi Fountain, one of the most popular tourist attractions in Rome and the site of countless movie scenes, most notably in the Audrey Hepburn and Gregory Peck movie, *Roman Holiday*. It is near where Princess Ann got her hair cut. It was, unfortunately, out of commission, with scaffolding erected all around it as it underwent a major restoration and cleaning. We could see little of its Baroque/Rococo magnificence. Nonetheless, we broke away for an hour or so for lunch in the immediate vicinity and, yes, some more shopping. We and Burley and Cindy took this opportunity to grab up gifts for our tour guides and driver: Alexis from Magnificat; Debra, our overall guide in Italy; and Luigi, our driver.

After lunch, we traveled out to another "off-the-books" site, the Colosseum. It had always been mentioned as a possibility for individuals to break off and see it during our "free time" (?!), but it had never been part of the official itinerary. That fact was the main thing that garnered protests at the September meeting when we received the official itinerary. The explanation given at that time was that this *pilgrimage* was meant to concentrate on religious and spiritual sites rather than *tourist* spots. That is true – but the site where so many early Christians suffered martyrdom certainly qualifies as a "religious and spiritual site"! It is, ultimately, a testament to the adaptability of our leaders that they responded to the considerable demand for at least some time at one of the iconic monuments of imperial Rome. Debra even tried to procure a last-minute opportunity for a tour of the interior, with no success. Nevertheless, we did get to walk around the outside and view the immediately adjacent Arch of Constantine as well as the Roman Forum – the center of the civilized world for most of a thousand years – from a bit further distance.[31]

The final church we visited in Rome was the Basilica of San Pietro in Vincoli, St. Peter in Chains, only a short walk from the Colosseum. According to legend, the mid-fifth century Pope St. Leo I the Great acquired the chains that had bound St. Peter in Jerusalem until the intervention of an angel (Acts 12:1-10); when they touched the chains that had bound St. Peter in the Roman Mamertine Prison before his upside-down crucifixion, the two chains miraculously fused together into one, whence Pope Leo built the basilica on the Oppian Hill. The Chains of St. Peter are not, however, what most people best know at the basilica today, although they may not make the association. Even those who have no idea in what church to find it are familiar with Michelangelo's famous statue of "horned" *Moses*.

"Horned?" you say…? Michelangelo is sometimes ridiculed today for this seemingly bizarre design feature. In reality, he was working within an established medieval and renaissance tradition. Ever since the late fourth century, when St. Jerome had translated the Hebrew Scriptures into Latin to create the Vulgate, the official Bible of the Catholic Church, Moses had been depicted artistically with horns. In translating the Hebrew of Exodus 34: 29 that "the skin of [Moses'] face shown [*keren*] because he had been talking to God," Jerome construed *keren* in an alternate meaning – "was horned" rather than "shown." Just like English, Hebrew contains homonyms, two words that sound alike but mean very different things. Such a translation, moreover, was

---

[31] In a disappointing lapse, our pilgrimage's resident historian (err… that would be me!) did not connect the dots until later and realize the significance of the date when we stood at the Arch of Constantine. That monument commemorates Constantine's victory in the Battle of the Milvian Bridge, just north of Rome – on *28 October* 312! – the victory which led directly to his legalization of Christianity early the next year. Argh!.

not so far-fetched as one might think. Symbolically, horns meant wisdom and rule to the ancient world, attributes that fit Moses very well. Jerome was aware of the double meaning as well as the symbolism and acknowledged them in his commentary accompanying the Vulgate translation.[32]

Fr. Humphries celebrated our last pilgrimage Mass in Italy there at St. Peter in Chains, in an ornate Blessed Sacrament Chapel dedicated to the Assumption and Queenship of Our Lady. Fr. Decker beautifully chanted an extended Communion Antiphon to conclude the Mass. It was all quite moving.

Another quick walk down and across several blocks brought us to our Farewell Dinner, about which Debra had been teasing us as a "surprise" for several days. And it was. The venue was Le Terme del Colosseo (The Baths of the Colosseum), an expansive arched hall that once formed part of the water system for a set of Roman Baths adjacent to the Colosseum. That was cool enough in itself. But then, after we had time to settle ourselves at the tables for a few minutes, the fun *really* began. It was signaled by the onset of very loud music, which made me think, "*Oh, no! – So much for conversation!*" There followed, however, a trio of singers, two men and a woman, sweeping out and serenading us before the first and every other course of the best Italian dinner we had, with plenty of wine to go around. Everyone had a fun time, including Fr. Decker who ended up joining the show, receiving a close shave from the Barber of Seville!

Unfortunately, it had to end. As our bus took us back to our hotel we found out the "bad news" we had all been expecting. The next day would be an *early* day, with wake-up coming ... well, *early*.... Since this would be virtually the last time we would see them all together, Burley, Cindy, Anne, and I caught our guides all together at the end of disembarking from the bus and presented them with their gifts, a bottle of *limoncello* each, as a small token of our appreciation.

ednesday 29 October 2014 – Italy Day Ten: *Departure*

This full day of good-byes began earlier than ever. Wake-

---

[32] Art Levine, "Ki Tissa: Moses' Horns: Not a Mistranslation," *Yerushatenu: Our Heritage* (08 March 2012) [http://rabbiartlevine.com/Home/tabid/2652/ID/840/Ki-Tissa-Moses-Horns-Not-a-Mistranslation.aspx], referencing Bena Elisha Medjuck, "Exodus 34:29-35 : Moses' "horns" in early Bible translations and interpretations," M.A. Thesis, McGill University (1988) [Abstract: http://digitool.library.mcgill.ca/R/-?func=dbin-jump-full&current_base=GEN01&object_id=20 449].

up was at 04:30. We assembled in the lobby and departed the Hotel Cicerone at 05:30, each carrying a "brown bag" breakfast. Luigi drove us down to the Da Vinci Airport, and for all that what followed was a *long, long* day, there is not much to say about it. The flights went off without a hitch, from Rome to Atlanta (along the way I caught my first-ever glimpses of the "wine-dark" Mediterranean Sea and the snow-covered Alps as I worked on drafting my account of the pilgrimage), thence to Dallas, with various groups and individuals peeling off along the way toward their particular destinations, and then the final long bus-ride home. We arrived back in Natchitoches at about 01:30 on what was by then properly Thursday 30 October. By that time, it was about 07:30 Thursday morning in Rome, and we had been traveling for over 26 hours!

The MBIC Pilgrimage to Italy 2014 ended. *Deo Gratias!*

I am proud to say that, exhausted though I was, I went into my office on that Thursday. Luckily, I did not, however, have to teach, as my face-to-face class only met on Mondays and Wednesdays. *There,* I might have been. *Coherent,* I probably was not.

Addendum 1: The *Real* Final Toll

As best as I can figure based on credit card charges (the majority of our transactions were either via credit card or cash that we withdrew in Euros from ATMs once we were in Italy (we took very little cash with us), Anne and I spent approximately $1,950 while we were on this trip. Added to the "grand total" of $7,205 paid to Magnificat Travels, the ultimate final cost was $9,155. And well worth it.

Addendum 2: *Assessment*

Overall, our pilgrimage to Italy was a wonderful experience. As I concluded that entry to my blog account more than a week after the trip ended, "Speaking only for myself, I will treasure the memories of Italy 2014 all my life."

Nevertheless, as I have considered it from the perspective of several years later and in light of a deeper understanding of the nature of pilgrimage as well as my experience of two more pilgrimages, I reluctantly must assess it the least satisfying as a religious experience. In part that resulted from factors I had no control over: Debra's nearly incessant talking; the near absence of any religious devotions beyond daily Mass (Alexis' attempt notwithstanding; "Kumbaya" was not really in line with that group's religious sensibilities), the two-day diversion to Florence (which is undeniably culturally and historically – and artistically – crucial; spiritually? ... Partly because of the local guide who emphasized the artistic heritage at the expense of religion, it seemed more like a secular tour than a pilgrimage). I bear responsibility as well. I have mentioned my desultory preparation through prayer and fasting (hardly any). When the opportunity first arose, Anne and I signed onto the pilgrimage with nary a prayer of "discernment." While I do not doubt that God did want us on that trip, my focus was less on Him than it was on the chance to go to Rome. Only with Fr. Humphries' admonition during that first meeting of potential pilgrims did I begin to realize there is something more to pilgrimage than sightseeing. Sadly, I did not take his advice to heart.

I also suffered along the way from a sense of distraction that was detrimental to my pilgrimage experience. In part, this, too, was beyond my control. Given the unfortunate timing of the trip, in the middle of the semester, if I were to go, I had to devise some arrangement with my University to allow me to fulfill my contractual obligations from a third of the way around the world. The Internet is a wonderful thing! But it also meant that the need to manage my online courses from afar, daily, was never far from my mind. That was unavoidable, and I would do it again in a heartbeat (with additional prayers for God's grace and guidance in handling it better). In part, however, the distraction was very much of my own making. My ambitious, well-prepared, and well-announced plans to blog the pilgrimage in real-time for the benefit of my students proved unrealistic given the intense pace we were keeping throughout those ten days. Even my attempt to pre-write bits proved to be unusable in the context of actual events, changes in the itinerary, and the like. The resulting disappointment and guilt added to my distraction, along with apprehension whether there would be fallout from my not following through on that part of my justification for being away. (Luckily, there was not.)

These issues particular to me in the context of that trip are, I believe, significant of a profound difference between modern pilgrims and our historical counterparts. Distraction by the world we leave behind is inevitable in today's "wired" world where instant contact between any two geographic points is possible. Most of us are never far from our smartphones. Anne and I used ours, most notably to check in with our son, Tristan. Although he had indeed started college only a couple of months before, mom and dad were still adjusting to the empty nest. All our pilgrims on this trip were regularly getting news from back home. We all regularly checked the Internet, sent emails, updated Facebook, as if we were at home. The long and short is that, for all our distance from home, we had not left our homes behind.

The premodern world had none of those distractions. When a medieval pilgrim left home to set forth on pilgrimage, he did so knowing that for months or even years he would be entirely out of contact with those he left behind, in a new, strange, and many ways frightening world. But he was able to focus on the road he traveled. He was never entirely free from distraction, of course; being in constant danger from brigands, wild animals, the elements – Muslim slavers if headed for Jerusalem – those threats could be pretty distracting as well, I imagine! But it was altogether slower paced. The travel, usually afoot, gave much time to commune with God free of the distractions of home that inevitably turn our minds from Him. Even if he accompanied a group – then as now usually the case – a medieval pilgrim became part of a new community with a collective, dedicated purpose, and mutual support.

Think of it in these terms: Pilgrimage is like a retreat. A retreat is a period in which an individual leaves behind his everyday life, withdrawing from the world into a period of prayer and time with God. The purpose may be spiritual renewal, discernment, penance, or any number of individual motivations. In seeking communion with God through a retreat, we follow the example of Jesus on numerous occasions in the Gospels (Matt. 14: 13, 23; 15: 29; Mark 1: 35-37, 45; 6: 30-32; 9: 2; Luke 6: 12-13; etc.). In particular, a communal retreat – or even an individual retreat at a monastery, sharing for a brief time in the religious life of solitude and prayer – bears a number of points of correspondence with a "pilgrimage in place." Conversely, a pilgrimage is like a "mobile retreat." This is by no means a unique idea. It may be likened to historian Jonathan Riley-Smith's perception, based on his considering the pilgrimage origins and nature of the First Crusade, that eleventh- and twelfth-century contemporaries conceptualized that "armed pilgrimage" as a "monastery on the move."[33]

Taking first the essential elements of a retreat (adapted from Steven John Lichtman's online article on "Catholic Retreats"[34]):

> *A time apart*: Although there are one-day and overnight retreats, more common are three-day weekend retreats up to

---

[33] Jonathan Riley-Smith, *The First Crusade and the Idea of Crusading* (1986; repr. London: Continuum Press, 2003), pp. 2, 84.

[34] Steven John Lichtman, "Catholic Retreats," *Body Theology* (a section of the website, *Institute for Traditional Medicine*) [http://www.itmonline.org/bodytheology/part1.html], accessed 03 October 2019

a practical maximum of a week. The idea is to get away for some time apart from the distractions of everyday life.

A place apart: Whether at a monastery or convent (a popular option for Catholics) or at a retreat center sponsored by a diocese, a tranquil setting, distraction-free, is essential. Most places of retreat have expansive grounds for meditative walking, areas for group conferences as well as ...

A place for privacy: ... individual accommodations for private prayer and contemplation. Even in a group retreat, retreatants need time to themselves.

Dedicated prayer: Time and place set aside for prayer and contemplation – individual, but also liturgical: Holy Mass, the Divine Office. Sometimes group retreats are built around talks and programs, but solitary time for prayer is essential.

Meals: One might question including this, but the retreatant should not be compelled to leave the site of the retreat for meals; provision of meals avoids the disruption of the retreat mentality. Meals taken in common, even if in silence, can be an integral part of a retreat.

Spiritual direction: Most retreats, individual or communal, are under the direction of someone with training and experience to offer personal guidance. For Catholics, that may well be a priest, who offers the Mass as well as Confession.

Consider pilgrimage in those same terms – especially a group pilgrimage:

A time apart: A pilgrimage should be, as discussed above, a time apart, away from the distractions of the world.

A place apart: A pilgrimage is definitely "a place apart." But ...

A place for privacy: ... not so much! By its nature, especially a group pilgrimage is hectic. Like any guided tour, there is an imperative to get in as much as possible in minimal time. Self-guided or individual pilgrimages are a different story, of course, and most pilgrimage destinations are inherently quiet and peaceful settings. The popular ones are not necessarily so, however, and the most important, the places where the most momentous events in salvation history occurred, are definitely not. They are instead crowded with a lot of activity that you must get past – St. Peter's in Rome, the Shrine of Our Lady of Guadalupe, the Basilicas of the Annunciation and the

Nativity, the Church of the Holy Sepulcher. In the latter two, especially, everything focusses around specific spots, and at any given time there are hundreds of people trying to make their way to and through a tiny little door for their thirty to sixty seconds trying to say a prayer in spots hallowed by the Birth, Death, and Resurrection of Our Lord. And as far as personal space, there is not much to be had except maybe in lodging – which is, on a typical pilgrimage, pretty much all it is – a place to wind down at the end of too long a day, get too little sleep, and try to be ready for the next day's sprint....

Dedicated prayer: Mass in spiritually significant locations, perhaps other liturgies as well as devotions like the Rosary, the Divine Mercy chaplet, and so forth. In my experience, there is overall not much time set aside for individual prayer. On the other hand, inevitably when in one of the pilgrimage churches or shrines, especially when in the presence of relics or miraculous objects, everyone with any religious sensibility at all instinctively pauses in a pew or at a kneeler, and prays, if only for a few moments. It all adds up.

Meals: Group pilgrimages usually provide the meals, at least breakfast and dinner. Of course, the reason is not the same, being born mainly in practicality – but the effect is that those common meals are integral to the group's experience

Spiritual direction: Almost every Catholic group pilgrimage has a spiritual director, usually a priest even if it is organized and sponsored by a lay individual or group. How engaged they are as "spiritual director" *vs.* as "just another pilgrim" is, it seems, dependent on personality and circumstance, including the dynamic between the priest, the organizer, and the guide (who is usually separate, at least in my experience typically a native or at least a long-time resident intimately familiar with the destination). Of the three pilgrimages which I have made, easily the best (by which I mean most diligent) spiritual direction was provided by Fr. Juan Diego in Mexico (see the next chapter); besides Masses, he explicitly set aside times for Confession and any other consultation we might need. It is just another reason that of those three pilgrimages, although Italy was first and will always have that special place in my memories, and the Holy Land is – *well, it is the Holy Land* with its inherently profound attraction – I assess the pilgrimage to Mexico City as the most spiritually rewarding.

As a meaningful retreat will, by its nature, be undercut by any more than necessary contact or excursions back into the world, so will a pilgrimage be undermined by too frequent calls back home or self-imposed pressure to "share" the experience on social media in real-time. Better to stay focused. Savor the experience. The world will likely still be there when you return....

None of which is meant to denigrate the experience of my first pilgrimage, to Italy. It was wonderful. And even if it had not been, if nothing else, I would benefit greatly from that experience – from my own mistakes – going forward.

Figure 2: Map of Italy

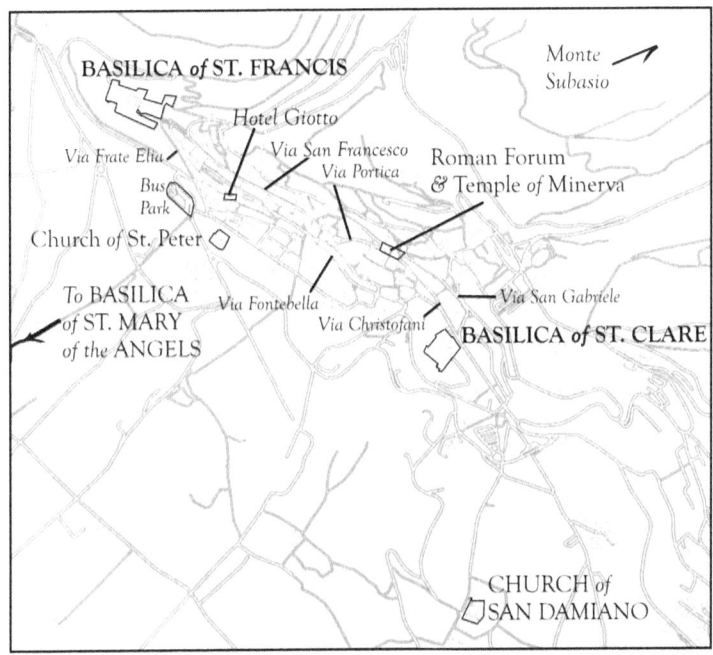

Figure 3: Map of Assisi

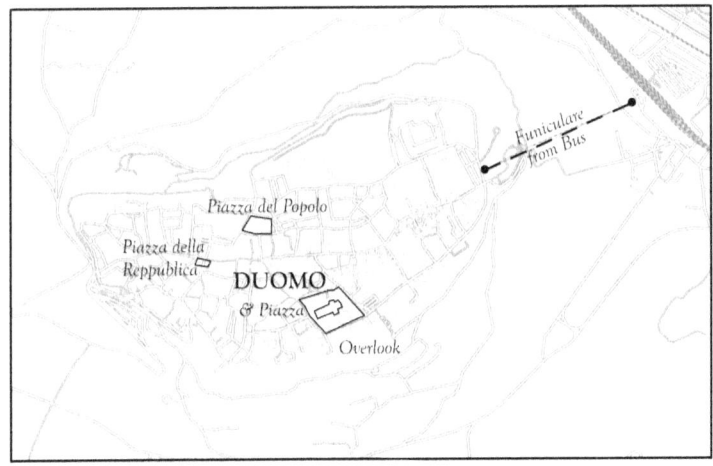

Figure 4: Map of Orvieto

Figure 5: Map of Florence

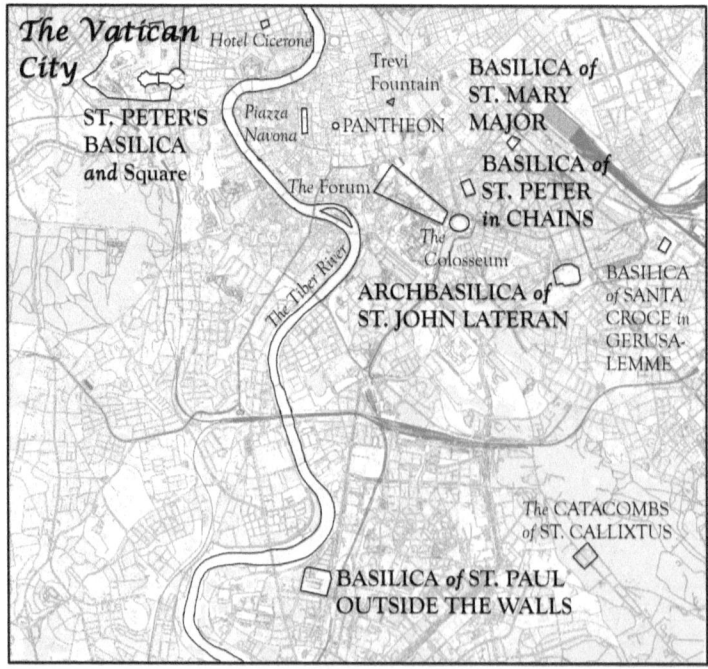

Figure 6: Map of Rome

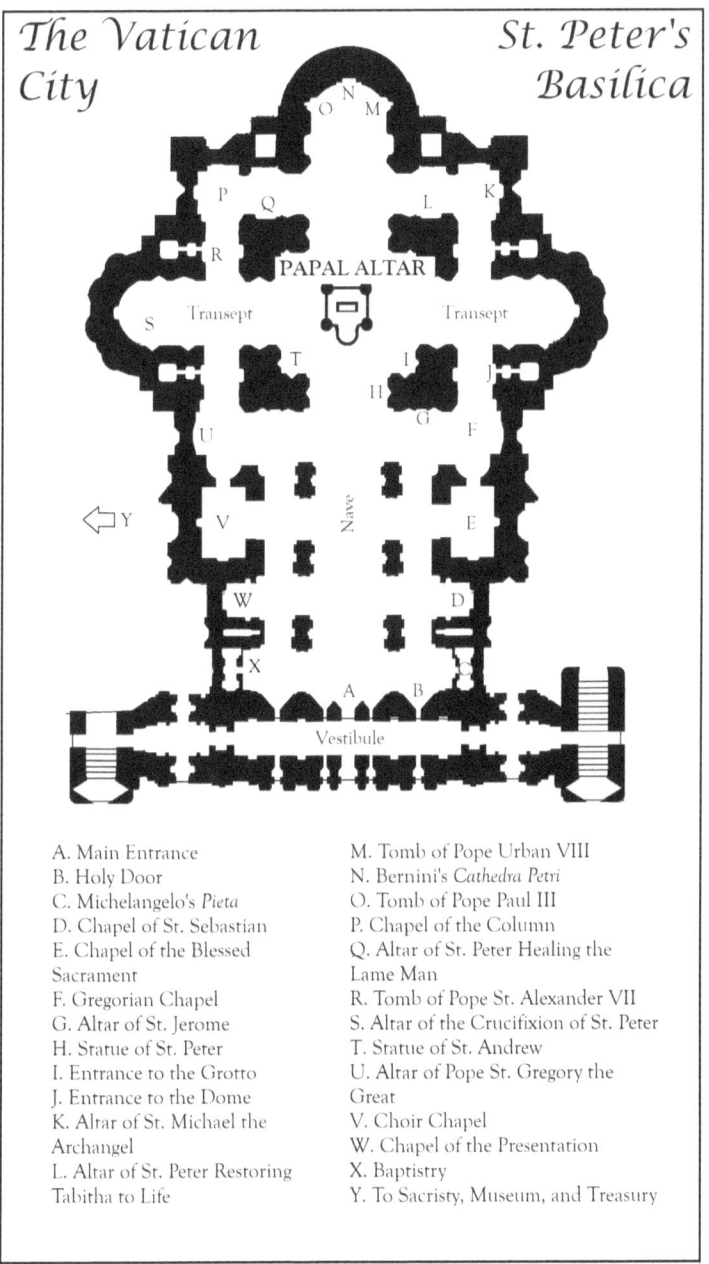

A. Main Entrance
B. Holy Door
C. Michelangelo's *Pieta*
D. Chapel of St. Sebastian
E. Chapel of the Blessed Sacrament
F. Gregorian Chapel
G. Altar of St. Jerome
H. Statue of St. Peter
I. Entrance to the Grotto
J. Entrance to the Dome
K. Altar of St. Michael the Archangel
L. Altar of St. Peter Restoring Tabitha to Life
M. Tomb of Pope Urban VIII
N. Bernini's *Cathedra Petri*
O. Tomb of Pope Paul III
P. Chapel of the Column
Q. Altar of St. Peter Healing the Lame Man
R. Tomb of Pope St. Alexander VII
S. Altar of the Crucifixion of St. Peter
T. Statue of St. Andrew
U. Altar of Pope St. Gregory the Great
V. Choir Chapel
W. Chapel of the Presentation
X. Baptistry
Y. To Sacristy, Museum, and Treasury

Figure 7: Layout of St. Peter's Basilica

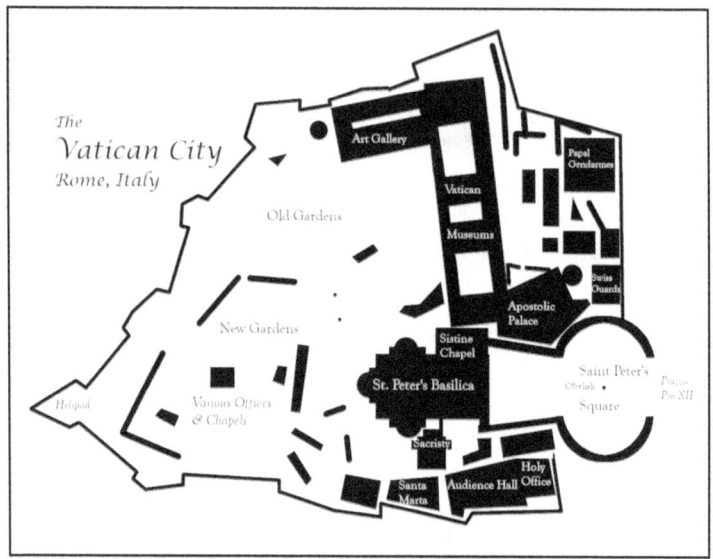

Figure 8: Map of the Vatican City.

Figure 9: Fr. Humphries offering Mass in the Extraordinary Form, St. Peter's Basilica. Photo courtesy of Ashley Hebert Ducote.

Figure 10: The Basilica of St. Paul Outside the Walls. Photo by the author.

Figure 11: Our Leaders: Fr. Humphries; Roberta, our guide in Rome; Alexis, Magnificat Travels; Debra, our guide in Italy; Ashley, MBIC Director of Evangelization; Fr. Decker. Photo courtesy of Anne Hare.

Figure 12: Pilgrimage to Our Lady of Guadalupe with Dr. Taylor Marshall, February 2016. Photo courtesy 206 Tours.

CHAPTER TWO

¿NO ESTOY YO AQUÍ QUE SOY TU MADRE?
Pilgrimage to Our Lady of Guadalupe and Mexico City

The pilgrimage to Italy having concluded, I considered it a once-in-a-lifetime event. Anne and I both came away from it with a deeper understanding of our Catholic Faith, especially the special place of Rome and Italy in it. We looked back on that time fondly. We reminisced with fellow travelers in our home parish, some of whom we barely if at all knew before, whom we now count as friends. Little did we know that in only a little over a year, we would be planning another such excursion.

By the fall of 2015, I had been a member of the New Saint Thomas Institute, an innovative endeavor in online Catholic theological and spiritual formation founded by Dr. Taylor Marshall, for over a year. I had followed Marshall, a lay Catholic philosopher, for some time before that via his podcast, *The Taylor Marshall Catholic Show*.[35] Through the Institute, Marshall offers multimedia tutelage toward certificates in such subjects as Catholic Philosophy and Thomistic Studies, Theology and Apologetics, History, Scripture, and Patristics. In addition to short HD video presentations of the critical points of each unit's subject matter, with lively Internet discussion among a membership spanning the globe, Marshall also presents periodic YouTube seminars elaborating on specific points or questions that arise among the members.

Listening to one of his podcasts as I drove home from the University one afternoon in October 2015, I discovered that Marshall's response to long-standing online discussion among the members desiring some kind of conference where we could meet him as well as each other was to offer two guided pilgrimages in the next year. One he announced to be to various sites in Italy including, of course, Rome and the Vatican; the other would be to the Shrine of Our Lady of Guadalupe in Mexico City. Having only a year before made the pilgrimage to Rome, I naturally focused on the latter, to Mexico City,

---

[35] The New Saint Thomas Institute [https://newsaintthomas.com/]; *The Taylor Marshall Catholic Show* [https://taylormarshall.com/].

although with that one scheduled for February, just a few weeks into the spring semester, I figured there was no chance I could go. Taking off two weeks during the fall semester to go to Italy was a one-time opportunity, justifiable because of the specific importance of Rome in just about every history course that I teach. Mexico, on the other hand, is not especially relevant to any of those courses beyond tangentially to my *Early World Civ* survey and a couple of lectures in my *Renaissance-Reformation* course.

As soon as I got home, I went online to the web page he referenced to find out more specific information. I also grabbed a calendar, just to see ... and discovered what I had fleetingly hoped to be the case: Despite how early in February the pilgrimage was to be, it was around about Mardi Gras – ending, in fact, on that very day, Tuesday 09 February 2016. Suddenly the timing got a lot better. Here in Louisiana, Mardi Gras is a BIG THING, closing the University from Monday until noon on Ash Wednesday. And with my schedule that spring semester having no face-to-face classes or office hours on Fridays, departing on Thursday 04 February and coming back on Tuesday 09 February would mean missing (or rather, having to otherwise cover) only one day's class-meeting, that Thursday. That was, I considered, easily arranged.

So, I proceeded to the video embedded in the web page and found it even more compelling than Marshall's audio pitch. I had never really felt more than a mild interest in the miraculous image of Our Lady of Guadalupe. It had been many years, nigh on thirty, since I had spent any time delving into the subject, and that consisted of reading only a couple of books – Jody Brant Smith's *The Image of Guadalupe: Myth or Miracle?*, and Warren Carroll's *Our Lady of Guadalupe and the Conquest of Darkness*. Nevertheless, I suddenly had an intense desire to join this pilgrimage. The NSTI connection, the opportunity to meet Marshall and other members of the Institute and to benefit from his instruction live, was part of the attraction, to be sure, but I furthermore found myself overwhelmed with the conviction that the image of Guadalupe is precisely what it purports to be, a holy artifact of Our Lady reaching down from heaven to interact with this world at a critical juncture in history. I found myself overwhelmed with the urge to be in its presence.

The package price given on the page did not include airfare, but links were provided to determine the cost with airfare from a variety of airports. In my case, the nearest listed was Shreveport, Louisiana, a little more than an hour's drive from Natchitoches. From there, a short flight would connect through Dallas with a longer flight directly to Mexico City, at a total price that was not too bad. I figured that for myself and my wife, the total cost, flights and pilgrimage, could be about $5000. Not inconsiderable, but manageable, I told myself.

As soon as my wife got home from work, I showed her the video. She is not a member of NSTI but has often been in the room when I was viewing the certificate modules, and I have shared with her some of the material as well as episodes of Marshall's free podcast, so she was already familiar enough with him. To my delight, she was at once enthusiastic, as well. Considering the reputation that Mexico has as dangerous and crime-ridden, with considerable drug-related violence, I had worried that her reaction would be otherwise. It was a concern that Marshall addressed directly in the video. Not only had he made the pilgrimage to Our Lady of Guadalupe before – alone, albeit part of a pilgrimage group – this time he was bringing his wife and newborn daughter. And when I say "newborn," I mean "newborn." I knew that she had been born only days before I heard that podcast.

Anne and I went through the web page, which already had a detailed itinerary. There was the standard information about what was and was not included. "Included" was something that would set this pilgrimage apart:

> Dr. Taylor Marshall will teach 4 classes on the coaches or in the evenings during the Guadalupe pilgrimage:
> > History of Marian Dogma and Doctrine
> > How to Explain Mary as Mediatrix
> > How to Explain Mary to Protestants
> > The Story and History of Our Lady of Guadalupe

I did not pull the trigger and commit to the pilgrimage at once, however. I wrestled with it for a couple of days, with the sticking point being the cost more than anything else. "Manageable," yes, but also "not inconsiderable," and we had recently had a few unexpected expenses come our way. I did not yet realize the magnitude of some of those unexpected expenses. But – and this is key, considering how I had *not* done so before Italy, I prayed about it and found my feeling that we must go on this pilgrimage to remain undiminished. Within a couple of days, I was moved to take a leap of faith and commit, registering for the pilgrimage and making a down payment of one-third of the total cost, including travel and cancellation insurance, just in case.

…

And then those "unexpected expenses" started manifesting themselves. Believe me, I had second thoughts, but with the down payment in it was going to take something compelling and catastrophic to make me back out, and nothing like that occurred. Furthermore, I called it a "leap of faith." Faith is going to be tested. So, we remained committed and looking forward to the experience.

As I did in the months preceding the pilgrimage to Italy a little more than a year before, I started "prepping" via study and "modeling" of the trip. That included rereading Warren Carroll's book mentioned above, *Our Lady of Guadalupe and the Conquest of Darkness*, putting the Guadalupe Event into the overall context of the Spanish *conquistadores'* encounter with the Aztec Empire. Then, a couple of days before the feast day of Our Lady of Guadalupe, 12 December, Marshall hosted a YouTube seminar that I attended. For an hour or so, he presented the general history of the miracle and its devotion, during which he made a recommendation for what he indicated to be the best single book he has ever read on the phenomenon, Paul Badde's *Maria of Guadalupe: Shaper of History, Shaper of Hearts*. I immediately ordered it, read it, and must concur. I found it a perfect complement to Carroll's book. In his typical manner, the historian Carroll looks at the big picture and incorporates the overall context into a straightforward yet gripping narrative. Badde, on the other hand, is a journalist and writes in a more personal, conversational manner recounting his own discovery and encounter with the miracle while including valuable source material and linking it to the larger world of Marian devotions and apparitions through history.

Reading books, assembling data on our various destinations according to the published itinerary, "modeling," and the like: I had done that kind of "intellectual prepping" before Italy. This time I did something else, more deliberate "spiritual prepping." I was more aware of the spiritual dimension of pilgrimage, and I wanted to better prepare myself in that respect. So, beginning on the first day of the year, I undertook the full Montfortian Total Consecration to Jesus through Mary, as described in St. Louis de Montfort's book, *True Devotion to Mary*, a 33-day regimen of prayers culminating in the consecration itself. It is customary to begin the preparation on such a date that the consecration takes place on a Marian feast day. Starting from 01 January, the Solemnity of Mary, the Mother of God, put Day 33 on Tuesday 02 February, the Feast of the Presentation in the Modern Liturgical Calendar, but according to the Traditional Liturgical Calendar

Candlemas, the Feast of the Purification of Mary, forty days after the Nativity. On that Tuesday, just two days before we headed out for Mexico, I read aloud my handwritten consecration at Our Lady's Altar in the Minor Basilica, which Fr. Humphries witnessed, and I placed it in my lockbox for safekeeping. Perhaps it has no meaning for anyone else, but it does for me.

Overall, I feel that I was much better prepared for my second pilgrimage, and it made a difference.

Thursday 04 February 2016 – Mexico Day One: *Arrival*

Anne and I were up shortly after 03:00 and left Natchitoches about 04:30, arriving at the Shreveport airport at about 06:00 for our 08:04 flight to Dallas. We had breakfast and passed through security. As we waited to board, I finished transcribing various friends' prayer intentions into my pilgrimage notebook. In an email a week or so before our departure, Marshall had suggested that we collect such intentions to present to Our Lady before her image. That exercise was one way that, from the beginning, there was more of a spiritual focus to this pilgrimage than the others.

After a short and uneventful flight to Dallas, we exchanged $600 US for Mexican pesos ... which I would later learn also uses the "$" sign.[36] I am not sure what the exact exchange rate was in the airport. It is notoriously poor in such places, but we were paying for the convenience since neither our bank, nor any other that I know of in Natchitoches, does currency exchanges at all. It is one of the drawbacks of living in a small town. In general, we found the rate to be $18 (pesos) per $1 (US); I just used twenty as a rough on-the-fly estimate. We also grabbed a bite to eat then boarded the plane for Mexico City.

We had another uneventful flight. The only difficulty was an immigration form that they only provided in Spanish. Luckily, a young lady seated next to Anne was able to talk us through it. The US-born daughter of immigrants, she was visiting Mexico for the first time in her life – against the wishes of her Mexican-born parents. They considered the country too dangerous, especially for a young, attractive, twenty-something traveling alone. That gave us pause, despite

---

[36] Sometimes the most diligent research overlooks the most obvious information. In this case, I believe the identical symbols masked the difference. The symbol for peso was literally hiding in plain sight.

Marshall's reassurances in the original video. Just what were we getting into?

The pilot announced early in the flight that there was turbulence at the normal cruising altitude of 36,000 ft., so he kept us low at about 28,000 ft. for the duration of the flight. As a result, our view of the changing landscape was unusually striking as we crossed into the rugged mountainous area around Mexico City.

We landed a little after 13:50. One thing that struck both Anne and me was how short the flight really was. We have flown several times to New York City. In quite a bit less time than that took, however, we were in a different country, which because of that fact was conceptually – in our "mental geography" – much further away. Such worldview-altering realizations are one of the great benefits of any kind of travel, not just pilgrimage. Deplaning, we made our way through customs, baggage claim, and so forth, finally spying a sign for "206 Tours," the broker for our group. It seemed that our pilgrims were trickling in, however, because while about a dozen of us ended up shuttled to the hotel in two vans at midafternoon, others would not arrive until late in the evening.

The ride to the hotel was not very pleasant. The van was uncomfortably warm; it might have been February, but the weather in Mexico City felt more like April in Louisiana.

We finally arrived at the Galeria Plaza Reforma Hotel, about 15:30 or so. Then Anne and I had another unpleasant surprise. The hotel staff would not have our room ready for another hour. It was during that debacle that we met the Mexican guide representing 206 Tours, Roberto, who was as irritated as we were.

To be fair, the first impression that mishap gave us proved to be a *mis*impression of the Galeria Plaza. Aside from the delay in gaining access to our room, which was, as far as I know, unique to us among our group, the hotel and its staff were nothing but helpful and gracious through our entire stay. At the time, added to other unpleasantnesses through the day – confusion over baggage allowances in the Shreveport airport; the realization that even some native Mexicans consider their country "dangerous"; the uncomfortable shuttle ride – this pilgrimage seemed to be getting off to a bad beginning. That was a misimpression as well, because after the inconvenience of having to sit around for an hour waiting for our room to be prepared left us only about half an hour to freshen up before returning to the lobby where the group were to assemble at 17:00, everything else on this trip seemed to work out perfectly. It was as if everything "bad" was pulled to the beginning and was then out of the way.

Returning to the lobby as directed, we introduced ourselves to members of our pilgrimage group who had already gathered by a large banner welcoming our group with the image of Our Lady of Guadalupe. One of our fellow pilgrims, a lady from Houston, recognized Joy Marshall as she walked by carrying the "newborn" mentioned previously, now about four months old; a few minutes later, I spied Taylor Marshall and briefly introduced myself. I was a bit gratified that he "recognized" me, although we had never met in person. We had, however, exchanged occasional messages and emails through NSTI, which was apparently enough for him to dub me "Professor," which seemed to stick; for my part, on the other hand, as with everyone else, he quickly became simply "Taylor"; the formality of "Dr. Marshall" just did not fit his easy-going Texas persona.

There followed a short round of formal introductions. We discovered that not only was Taylor accompanied by his wife, Joy, along with their baby Maggie, but one of their sons was with us as well, a lad of nine years named Jude. There are six other Marshall children; the others stayed at home with grandparents, although they would all be joining their parents on the upcoming pilgrimage to Italy. We were formally introduced to Roberto as well, and then probably about two-thirds of what would eventually be our total group of about 45 walked several blocks, past a large traffic circle with a magnificent monument at the center, a pillar surmounted by an angel commemorating Mexican Independence, to a little church, the Parroquia de Nuestra Señora del Sagrada Corazón y Capilla del Santisimo, where we had our first pilgrimage Mass in Mexico.

That Mass was celebrated by Fr. Juan Diego Sutherland, whom we discovered that Taylor had invited along as spiritual director. Fr. Juan Diego is a big, ruddy, blue-eyed Canadian – and if you are thinking that the name "Juan Diego" does not seem to fit that description, you are having the same reaction we did. "Juan Diego" is the name he took upon his entry to religious life as a member of the Franciscan Friars of the Renewal. He came to Mexico City from Nicaragua, where he was serving in prison ministry. His introduction engendered some confusion, at least on the part of Anne and me, as we had spied another priest among our number and assumed that *he* was our spiritual director. We would soon learn, however, that this latter priest was Fr. Peter Mangum, the Rector of St. John Berchmans Cathedral in Shreveport. He was "just" a pilgrim, i.e., paying his own way (or having it paid for him; there were a few parishioners with him. Fr. Juan Diego was, as spiritual director, there *gratis*, I presume).[37] As it happened, Fr. Mangam said at least a couple of the Masses.

After Mass, we were able to walk around the church. For just the first of many times during these few days we were virtually overwhelmed by outstanding beauty. Ornate gold-leafed dark wood carving served as a backdrop for an abundance of statues and iconography devoted to a host of saints. These included the familiar and expected as well as the unfamiliar or unexpected. The familiar and expected included, for instance, familiar scenes from Biblical and Church history, the Sacred Heart of Jesus and His Divine Mercy, the Immaculate Heart of Mary and Our Lady under many different titles, always including at least one rendition of the image of Our Lady of Guadalupe that was the primary object of our pilgrimage and the central fact of the national identity of Mexico. As for the unexpected or unfamiliar, two stand out in my memory, both of which we first encountered here. I never would have expected the nineteenth-century Lebanese holy man St. Sharbel Maklouf to have been featured prominently in every Mexican church we entered, but there he was, a testament to heavy migration of Lebanese Catholics to Mexico during the twentieth century. Also common, we found, were transparent glass sarcophagi with a life-size and life-*like* effigy of the crucified Christ, as if just taken down from the Cross, a portrayal which was unfamiliar and perhaps a bit disturbing in its realism to most of our pilgrimage group.

As we exited the church, Roberto took us around the corner to see the Adoration Chapel attached to the church, which offers Perpetual Adoration in what he described as a somewhat less than reputable area of Mexico City filled with clubs and the like. It was open at that hour, about 19:00 or so, by which I mean one could walk into the small chapel area and be in the direct presence of Our Lord, but the doors to the chapel would later be locked, closing off such access from the street while leaving the Blessed Sacrament secure but visible through a large plate glass window. It is a novel arrangement. I have never heard of such in the United States and can only imagine the indifference with which it would be met – or worse; in Mexico City, for all its rough reputation, however, a still-pervasive Catholic identity, despite more than a century of varying degrees of governmental

---

[37] Interestingly, Anne's cousin from the Italy trip, Dr. Chris, had attended Mass at the Cathedral in Shreveport just the previous weekend, heard the priest talking about going to Mexico City during the coming week, and wondered if he were going to be with our group. He was.

hostility that we would learn more about, resulted in most passersby at least recognizing and giving some small reverence to their Lord and Savior.

As darkness descended, we walked back to the hotel, again passing the Angel monument which was now lit up in pink for Breast Cancer Awareness Day as we were told, and directly into dinner in the hotel dining room, presented as a buffet with a host of different offerings. We had been worried about Anne's options, as she was trying to adhere to as gluten-free a diet as possible due to mild non-celiac gluten intolerance that makes it better if she avoids it altogether. The variety of foods available, however, meant that she was always able to find something suitable. And the food was always excellent as well as plentiful for both breakfast and dinner. The pilgrimage package included lunch as well, but in a local restaurant wherever we happened to be each day.

This first night, Anne and I shared a table for four with a Filipino couple now living in Boston, Arsenio and Gemma. We would share a couple more meals with them over the next few days and found them very engaging. Overall, the experience was different from Italy, where the evening meals were typically a set menu, and the tables were larger, usually accommodating eight to ten individuals. Both arrangements had their advantages; both had their disadvantages.

After supper, Anne and I availed ourselves of a Circle K convenience store a block away from our hotel (I kid you not – a Circle K!) to buy a couple of bottles of drinking water. Even today, it is considered prudent not to drink tap water in Mexico, even in a high-end hotel in the capital, such as was the Galeria Plaza. We would do the same most of the evenings we were in Mexico City.

Later in the evening, Anne and I took advantage of a coupon for free margaritas our first night only. In the hotel bar, we found Fr. Juan Diego, along with a pair of ladies from Houston, Molly and Kate. They were blue – the margaritas, I mean, not the padre nor the Houstonians. They were anything but blue – and we sat and had a jovial visit before we retired to our room.

Friday 05 February 2016 – Mexico Day Two: *Guadalupe and Teotihuacan*

Our first full day in Mexico City began with breakfast in the dining room at 06:30, to be on the bus by 08:00. Anne and I again dined with Arsenio and Gemma, enjoying another spread of a variety of foods, both familiar and unfamiliar. I had fried cactus leaf for the first and only time in my life. I also had a "tamale" filled with a sort of pasty white cheese; it was not really to my liking either and there was never a "real" tamale on the buffet. There was, in fact, little if any of what we Americans consider "Mexican" food (which is really, of course, "Tex-Mex"). But there were plenty of other good things to eat – egg dishes, pastries, sliced meats,[38] and abundant desserts. We did not go hungry. Some veterans of cruises likened it to the experience there.

In any case, once everyone assembled at the bus, we set off. I have not yet mentioned our other Mexican guide, Pablo. We may not have met him until that first full day in Mexico. He may well have been there before; I just do not remember and could not find him in any of the pictures I have from the first evening (which includes some posted by other pilgrims to a shared Dropbox folder). Just as was Roberto, Pablo was ideally suited to his role – knowledgeable, eager to help, with a hilarious sense of humor that made him our "resident comedian." We grew very fond of them both very quickly. On the other hand, I know for sure that we first met our driver, Mario, at that time. He spoke no English that we could tell, and we did not get to know him, but he grew to be a familiar face to us.

Mexico City is a huge city, both in area and population. Regarding the latter, depending on how it's counted, I have seen figures ranging from nine million to the seventeen million quoted by Roberto; consistently it appears in lists of the five or ten most populated cities in the world; as for the area, suffice it to say you get nowhere fast! In this case, the couple of miles to the Plaza of the Three Cultures took us twenty to thirty minutes. The "three cultures" are the Pre-Columbian Aztec, the Colonial Spanish, and the "Mestizo" nation of independent Mexico, all three represented by buildings on the site. The ruins of an Aztec temple complex stand flanked by the Church of Santiago de Tlatelolco and modern buildings once housing Mexican governmental offices as well as, more recently, upscale residential housing. Within

---

[38] I do not remember specifically if we availed ourselves of these that first morning – or through the rest of the day. Anne and I both try to maintain Friday abstinence throughout the year, not just during Lent. See 1983 Code of Canon Law, canons 1250-1251 [http://www.vatican.va/archive/cod-iuris-canonici/eng/documents/cic_lib4-cann1244-1253_en.html#CHAPTER_II.], and the United States Conference of Catholic Bishops' 1966 Pastoral Statement on Penance and Abstinence (still in effect), nos. 19-24 [http://www.usccb.org/prayer-and-worship/liturgical-year/lent/us-bishops-pastoral-statement-on-penance-and-abstinence.cfm], as discussed by canon lawyer Cathy Caridi, J.C.L., "Are Catholics Supposed to Abstain from Meat Every Friday?," *Canon Law Made Easy* (05 March 2009) [http://canonlawmadeeasy.com/2009/03/05/are-catholics-supposed-to-abstain-from-meat-every-friday/].

the church, although the current building was built about a century later, can be seen the massive baptismal font in which the visionary of Guadalupe, St. Juan Diego, was received into the Catholic Church only a couple of years before Our Lady appeared to him and changed the world. Tlatelolco is also where, in earlier Church buildings erected hastily during the first decade after the Spanish conquest, Juan Diego met with Bishop Zumárraga and presented to the prelate the miraculous sign he had requested. More on all that momentarily....

If Roberto mentioned the most tragic event to happen on this site in recent memory, however, the Tlatelolco Massacre of 1968 as part of the Mexican government's brutal suppression of political opposition on the eve of the 1968 Summer Olympics, I do not remember it. There was so much to take in, and at times the "Whisper" radio units through which the guides could communicate with us while keeping their voices appropriately low did not work that well (especially before I switched out the cheap earbuds provided with my own higher-quality pair).

We walked around the plaza and the church for perhaps an hour before getting back on the bus and continuing to our first visit to the primary destination of our pilgrimage, the great Shrine of Our Lady of Guadalupe. Along the way, I believe, Taylor began the teaching that was an integral part of this pilgrimage, giving us an historical timeline of the events in and surrounding December 1531. I did not take notes, nor did I record his or any other presentations, which I now regret. The story of Our Lady of Guadalupe is well-enough known, however, that I can summarize the substance of Taylor's talks for Friday and Saturday into one narrative, although I cannot remember what he talked about specifically on which day.

> It all began with a small statue of the Blessed Mother allegedly carved and painted from life by St. Luke the Evangelist before the year 50, a figure to which many miracles were attributed and which ultimately (through several intermediaries including Pope Gregory the Great) made its way to Spain in about the year 600, only a century or so before the catastrophic Muslim invasion between 711 and 719. Owing to the Muslims' practice of desecrating and destroying Christian images, the miraculous statue needed to be hidden away. So well was it hidden that it vanished from history ... until ca. 1300, when, at the height of the Reconquista (ca. 1000-1492), the 500-year Reconquest driving the Moors back out of Spain, a

humble cowherd named Gil Cordero claimed to have been led to a specific site along the Guadalupe River in Extremadura by an apparition of the Virgin, who commanded that priests should dig there. Initially skeptical of Cordero's story, when the local priests nevertheless did as he said, they discovered the statue and built a shrine around it, which became the focus of a royal monastery named for the river, Our Lady of Guadalupe. It so happens that many of the conquistadors of the sixteenth century, including Hernan Cortes, were from Extremadura and had a great devotion to this earlier Our Lady of Guadalupe; Christopher Columbus had received his royal commission from Ferdinand and Isabel at that monastery before setting out in his three ships, the *Santa Maria*, the *Niña*, and the *Pinta* (which may be rearranged as "*pinta niña Santa Maria*" or "the little painted lady holy Mary"), and upon his eventual return made pilgrimage there to offer thanks to God for a safe voyage.

The Spanish conquest of the central part of the great New World, which Columbus unwittingly discovered understandably left bitter feelings on the part of the native American Indians. When Hernan Cortes encountered the Aztecs in 1519, he found a local empire across central Mexico that was built upon brutality and human sacrifice on a scale the Spaniards could not comprehend and could only attribute to the devil himself, and which drove the Spaniards' brutal efforts to rid the earth of the darkness. Compounded with the diseases that the so-called "Columbian Exchange" brought, which proved far more devastating to the Indians than even the manifest military superiority of the Europeans, the Aztec Empire collapsed almost overnight. Given that experience, it is understandable that the survivors were not very receptive to efforts by the first Franciscan missionaries accompanying Cortes, nor their successors, to preach to them the Good News of the God of Love and Mercy and to convert them to Christianity. Only a bare handful had accepted baptism in the first dozen years after the conquest.

Among those who did were a fifty-odd-year-old nondescript Indian named Cuauhtlatoatzin, baptized Juan Diego; his wife, baptized Maria Lucia; as well as his aged uncle, who was baptized Juan Bernardino. Maria Lucia had died a couple of years later, before her husband became one of the most important individuals in early Spanish American history.

On Saturday 09 December 1531, Juan Diego was traveling afoot the ten or so miles from his home southward toward Tlatelolco for his customary religious instruction. Passing Tepeyac Hill just before entering the five-mile causeway from the northern shore of what was then a great lake surrounding the island-city of Tenochtitlan, Juan Diego heard beautiful birdsong. Intrigued, he climbed the hill, only to encounter a young maiden who identified herself as the Ever-virgin Mother of God and requested that the Bishop erect a chapel in her honor on that spot. Continuing onward to his destination, Juan Diego requested and ultimately received a brief meeting with Fray Juan Zumárraga, Bishop-elect, who was skeptical but asked that Juan Diego return in a day or so. The next day (Sunday 10 December), Juan Diego met the Virgin again. Reporting his failure and begging that she choose a more worthy messenger, he was told that he must be the one to carry the request to the Bishop. Having had time to reflect prayerfully on the tale Juan Diego had told him the previous day, Zumárraga was less skeptical when the peasant begged his audience again, although this time, he requested a specific sign which Juan Diego hastened to pass on to the Virgin. She consented to give him such a sign on the morrow.

But by Monday morning, 11 December, his uncle Juan Bernardino had fallen gravely ill, compelling Juan Diego to care for him through the day and night as his condition worsened to the point that death was imminent. Early on Tuesday, the twelfth, Juan Diego set out to bring a priest to administer the Last Rites. He tried to avoid the Virgin and the delay that such an encounter would entail by taking a different route around Tepeyac, but she intercepted him and asked where he was bound. Juan Diego explained and received her mild rebuke for having doubted her: *"¿No estoy yo aquí que soy tu madre?* – Am I not here who am your mother?"

The Virgin assured Juan Diego that his uncle was well and directed him to go to the top of Tepeyac hill and gather the flowers he would find there – on its bare summit near mid-winter where nothing normally grew except a few cacti and shrubs. Juan Diego did indeed find an abundance of roses, which he gathered into his open *tilma*, a sort of poncho woven of maguey cactus fiber, two ends tied around his neck, the others gathered in each hand to make a sort of sack. The Virgin arranged the flowers in the *tilma* and told him to present them to the Bishop. Eventually gaining entrance to the prelate a third time despite the efforts of minor clerics who considered the Indian's tale a fraud, Juan Diego let drop the ends of the *tilma* so that the roses poured onto the floor and beheld the Bishop and his aides at once fall to their knees before him – before the image of the Virgin herself which was revealed by the fall of roses.

Returning to his uncle the next day, escorted in honor by the Bishop and his men, Juan Diego found Juan Bernardino cured, just as the Virgin had said. In fact, at the very instant she had spoken to the distraught nephew, she had appeared to the dying uncle – and he was healed. She had, moreover, told Juan Bernardino that she wished to be known as the Lady of … Coatlaxopeuh. In the Aztec language, this was pronounced something like "Quatlasupe" and meant "one who crushed the head of the stone serpent." But it was heard by – and resonated with – the Spaniards as "Guadalupe."

And so began a miraculously quick reconciliation of the two hostile peoples, conquered and conqueror, with the conversion of nine million Aztecs to Catholicism within seven years – less than a generation after a comparable number of northern Europeans had separated themselves from Holy Mother Church in the early years of the Protestant Reformation. The image became the unofficial banner uniting the new Mexican people that would evolve from the merging of the Spanish and Aztec. The *tilma* itself, in addition to its wondrous origin, exhibits a host of characteristics beyond rational explanation. It has endured for almost 500 years, when comparable maguey-fiber cloth typically disintegrates after a mere decade or so – and has survived at least two incidents that should have destroyed it outright, an accidental acid-spill in the eighteenth century and a deliberate attempt to obliterate it by means of a bomb during the Mexican government's persecution of the Church in the 1920s. Maguey-fiber is the most unsuitable material imaginable for painting, and there is no evidence of brush strokes or pigments of any kind. The image just *is*. It remains as bright and vibrant as ever, and exhibits several characteristics in common with a living human body, including a constant temperature equivalent to that of a living person, 98.6°F, no matter what the ambient temperature, pupils that seem to dilate and contract in reaction to light, and within which can be seen, under high magnification, what appears to be a snapshot of the instant Juan Diego revealed the image.

Science cannot explain it.

Of all the reported apparitions of the Blessed Virgin Mary through history, this one is unique, Taylor concluded. It is a continuing apparition; Our Lady remains present for each of us to see with our own eyes.

Arriving at the Plaza of the Americas, a large complex centered around the Guadalupe Event, we first availed ourselves of restrooms in the adjacent gift shop, where Roberto also showed us an example of the rough maguey-fiber cloth which comprised the *tilma*. As we entered the plaza, a photographer appeared out of nowhere for a pilgrimage group picture (we received our copies in the evening), then we walked to the New Basilica ... which is one of the ugliest churches I have ever seen.

The New Basilica was constructed in the 1970s, in the immediate post-Vatican II heyday of ecclesio-architectural devastation that ruined so many venerable churches. At least here that did not happen. They just built a new church that looks like a flying saucer has just landed, surmounted by an off-center circus tent of the same turquoise blue as Our Lady's mantle. The overall effect stands in absolute, diametrical contrast to the exquisitely beautiful churches that we were graced to see otherwise during this pilgrimage, including the immediately adjacent Old Basilica which we would visit a couple of days later. Nevertheless, the New Basilica houses the *tilma* - up high, behind the main altar, visible from the main body of the church, visible from a dozen or more chapels arranged in a mezzanine around the upper periphery, whose altars each (when correctly oriented with priest and people toward liturgical east together) face the *tilma*. Masses are said there continuously throughout the day, every hour on the hour. We walked around the outer periphery of the church, then made our way from the side, behind and below the wall behind the main altar, where a bank of parallel conveyer-belt people-movers running in opposite directions allow pilgrims to view the *tilma* from close proximity.

We were there - gazing up from a dozen feet or so at the miraculous image of Our Lady, one we had seen reproduced myriads of times even before coming here to Mexico where it is omnipresent. Each one of our group did several laps, back and forth, taking in the view of the image.

As we did so, Fr. Juan Diego was vesting himself. When he emerged from the nearby sacristy, we followed him and a sacristan up a winding flight of stairs (lined with windows of a design that reminded me so much of the 1970s that it hurt) to the mezzanine level and around to our assigned Chapel Eight, where Fr. Juan Diego said Mass facing the *tilma* along with us, all facing correctly *ad orientem*, toward liturgical east, toward the *tilma* and the image of Our Lady.[39] Because for his order, and indeed in Mexico and Latin America in general, 05 February is a the Feast of St. Philip de Jesus, a native Mexican martyred as a missionary in Japan in the seventeenth century as among the "companions" commemorated in the wider Church on 06 February as "St. Paul Miki and Companions," Fr. Juan Diego's homily was on martyrdom *"in odium fidei* – in hatred of the Faith" as suffered by the Japanese martyrs versus martyrdom *"in odium veritatis* – in hatred of the truth" as was that of St. John the Baptist, the subject of the Gospel reading. Again, Fr. Peter assisted, and Taylor Marshall read; notably, his nine-year-old son Jude, served at the altar for his very first time. After Mass, a brief period of further picture-taking included a few group shots around the altar.

Then it was hurry-hurry-hurry, very reminiscent of Rome in 2014 – such is the life of a pilgrim! So much to see and do in a limited amount of time. We exited the basilica, then worked our way around between the base of Tepeyac Hill and the back of the Old Basilica, into the little Templo del Pocito where once flowed a spring, then a well which is now dry, on around to the site of Juan Diego's latter-day home once the first chapel requested by the Virgin had been built, within two weeks of her appearance in December 1531. The chapel that exists

---

[39] I lay such emphasis on this because I consider one of the worst misapplications of "the spirit of Vatican II" to be the reversal of the priest's orientation away from "toward the east" or *ad orientem* to "toward the people" or *versus populum*. The priest is properly carrying out the Holy Sacrifice of the Mass on our behalf; we are participating in that sacrifice together with him; we should face with him the direction from which Our Lord will return (Matt. 24: 27). The priest is not putting on a show for us as mere spectators, which is the dynamic established by *versus populum*. It truly amazes me how thoroughly so much done in the name of Vatican II contradicts its stated goals when you think about it. Taylor and both our priests were of one mind on this, and it was generally no problem. Sometimes it could be otherwise, however – as it nearly was during our second Mass in the New Basilica, on Monday: The native sacristan setting up the altar insisted on doing so *versus populum*, despite Taylor's insistence otherwise. As soon as the sacristan left, however, Taylor turned it around as it should be and in accordance with our priests' preferences.

there now, the Antigua Parroquia de Indios, was unfortunately closed, I believe, preparing for Pope Francis' impending visit (within days of our departure). Since the museum behind the Old Basilica would not be open on Monday when we returned to Guadalupe for a more extended visit, we opted to put off lunch and go through it for a rushed half-hour visit. No pictures were allowed, and frankly, it is all a blur to me now except for the constant direction of docents "this way" up – up – up flight after flight of stairs.

It was then that I first noticed the altitude bothering me. I had not perceived it until those interminable stairs, but the fact is that Mexico City sits at about 7300-ft. above sea level, and the air is considerably thinner than at the 100-ft. elevation to which I am accustomed in Natchitoches. It is not something you usually notice, but with a bit of exertion, it can hit you. A little research found the reason – each breath takes in only about 75% of the oxygen as compared to sea-level. Luckily, only on that first full day did it bother me significantly, but for that day, it did so increasingly, especially given our next excursion.

Assembling back by the statue of John Paul II between the two basilicas, we went back to our bus and headed out toward San Juan Teotihuacan, about an hour and a half northeast of the city – far enough to get beyond the urban sprawl. Along the way, Roberto expounded on the differences between the pre-Aztec people who built the pyramids we would see there, about two thousand years ago, and the Aztecs themselves. He insisted they worshipped "good gods" who did not demand human sacrifice. To be honest, I believe he was drawing too stark a contrast. Admittedly, religious ideas and practices can change over time, and there could well have been a period at some time in their history when what Roberto said might have been true; nevertheless, there is plenty of evidence for human sacrifice at Teotihuacan during its height, between ca. AD 400 and 600. The people of Teotihuacan were, however, likely nowhere near as bloodthirsty as their successors, the Aztecs, would be ca. 1500.

Before we went to the pyramids themselves, we had lunch and a show, another excellent buffet with a mariachi band as well as a man and woman dressed up in neo-Aztec garb greeting, playing instruments (drums), and dancing. It was an interesting experience.

Then it was off to the site of the pyramids. In consideration of the sun, Roberto had passed out a "surprise" gift from 206 Tours: sombreros for the ladies, straw cowboy hats for the men. I hardly ever wore mine; just that one excursion, I believe. It just is not me. I had brought my own Pendleton, anyway.

Although it had been my declared intention from the beginning to make the climb up the Pyramid of the Sun, as we approached it closer, I knew that that was not going to happen. Neither pictures nor merely reciting its dimensions (216 feet tall; 750 feet square, more or less, at the base) convey its magnitude. It was just too high – by which I mean both the absolute altitude above sea level of the plain upon which Teotihuacan is located as well as the relative height of the pyramid above ground-level. It was, furthermore, too steep, with steps too large, and preceded by an even more precipitous drop-off that, as I told Anne, "I don't even want to climb down *this*, much less up *that*!"

I am too old, too fat, and a heart patient to boot; I was already experiencing shortness of breath that day from mild altitude sickness. That latter got better by a couple of days into the trip, but I don't think the other factors, both personal and inherent in the climb, would have let me do it – nor do I think Anne would have allowed it. Many others of our group did make the climb, including Joy Marshall with baby Margaret strapped to her chest. How many other people will ever be able to say they were atop the Pyramid of the Sun when they were four months old? Fr. Juan Diego heard several Confessions atop that summit, and later remarked that at one pronouncement of the words of absolution with the Sign of the Cross a "goth"-looking girl gave him a look of sheer hatred that reminded him that there are indeed those who hate God, His Church, and His ministers.

Anne and I opted instead to walk the length of the Avenue of the Dead to the slightly smaller Pyramid of the Moon. A fellow pilgrim accompanied us part of the way, an Australian named Neil who had come the furthest to join this pilgrimage. He was brought to join this pilgrimage specifically by devotion to St. Michael and a determination to visit every shrine to that warrior archangel, one of which we would visit a couple of days hence.

I did try to scale the Pyramid of the Moon, at least up to the lower level. I made it about halfway before deciding that I did not need to do even that. That conviction was reinforced only moments later when I witnessed this young buck bounding up the steps slip, and had he been going down there could have resulted a tragedy. As it was, he just went down on all fours, regained his balance, and continued his ascent. I, on the other hand, gingerly made my way back down to *terra firma*. Anne and I both climbed atop a platform at the center of the plaza facing the Pyramid of the Moon, where I overheard a conversation about a cool phenomenon that I was able to duplicate. If you stand at the very center of that platform and give a loud, solid CLAP, echoes will resound off the surrounding pyramid and smaller temples. How many from our group did that, huh?

We made our way back to the bus through a gauntlet of vendors hawking cheap souvenirs. An unexpectedly short trip took us to a souvenir shop where a lady demonstrated the various products that can be derived from the agave cactus that the Mexicans call "maguey." Besides the rough cloth from which the *tilma* was made and even a ready-made needle-and-thread from the spines which connect directly to lengths of the fiber, those products include a mildly alcoholic drink called *pulque* as well as a more potent form of tequila (yes, there were samples). I am sure there were more – it seems like Roberto mentioned shampoo, but anything beyond that escapes me. We did some souvenir shopping there, and I experienced the first frustration I would get used to over the next few days. I always try to get a necktie from places I visit, but in Mexico; time and again, I found that what I tried to describe as a necktie the Mexican vendors took to mean what we would call a bolo – a corded "necktie" consisting of a cord with decorated metal end-pieces bound by an ornamental clasp, sometimes simple, sometimes quite elaborate. I never found an actual necktie in Mexico.

Returning to our bus, we set out back to the hotel. Along the way, we prayed Evening Prayer and a Rosary.

Anne and I enjoyed supper with Fr. Juan Diego and a lady named Pat. We had decided to try to vary our table partners as much as possible. While the arrangements at the Galeria Plaza – typically four to a table – allowed for more intimate conversation over dinner, they also posed the danger of falling into the habit of always dining with the same people. We had found Gemma and Arsenio amiable partners for both dinner the previous night and breakfast, but we wanted to get to know others as well. The group was too large for us to make our way through the entire list in the few days we had, especially as the inevitable happened, and some small groups quickly coalesced, always sat together, and verged on becoming cliques, but we did share meals with a number of our fellow pilgrims, which paid off. We met many interesting fellow Catholics in those few days. Each had unique stories and reasons for being there. Not as many were members of the NSTI, or even listeners to Taylor's show, as I expected. Some had availed themselves of this particular pilgrimage because it was happening at the right time. One couple was a last-minute addition because the pilgrimage they were signed with canceled at virtually the last minute due to the congestion predicted for the Pope's upcoming visit. (I wish I knew what broker that was because I would not use them.) One pilgrim I mentioned already, Neil from Australia, was there not specifically for Our Lady of Guadalupe but rather from devotion to St. Michael the Archangel and an intention to visit every shrine to St. Michael *everywhere*. He did not lack in devotion to Our Lady, though. He proved quite knowledgeable about the various mysterious qualities of the *tilma*. As we expected, all the pilgrims proved to be genuinely nice. Sure, some irritated us a bit at first, but we grew fond of them; others grew more irritating due to little personality quirks or mannerisms that became more apparent over time; overall, however, we quickly formed a group bond that made it difficult to leave them all in the end. As I would tell Anne on the way home, we knew none of them before last Thursday, but by Tuesday evening, I was missing them all.

After supper, Anne and I replenished our supply of bottled water across the street, then retired to our room and rested. Every night I downloaded the day's pictures from my phone to my computer and thence to an external hard drive and made notes about the day's activities. That latter was a good thing, because once again, as in Italy, we did so much each day that everything very quickly started blurring together. I tried something new, in fact, with remarkable success. I used an audio recorder app on my phone to make summary notes at the end of each day. Those proved to be extremely helpful in eventually composing my blog entries, even if the daily exhaustion that kept me from making written notes also made those audio notes rather frustrating to listen to given numerous pauses, "ums" and "ers," even occasional incoherent mumblings.

Saturday 06 February 2016 – Mexico Day Three: *Mexico City*

We were able to sleep in about a half-hour later, getting to breakfast about 07:00 then to the bus for an 08:00 departure. We went directly to the Parroquia Verbo Encardado y Sagrada Familia, having just enough time along the way for Morning Prayer. This Church of the Holy Family contains the shrine and relics of Padre Miguel Augustin Pro, a priest-martyr of the Mexican government's brutal persecution of the Church in the 1920s, which gave birth to the *Cristeros* rebellion about which I will say more later. In secret, during the darkest days of the repression, when the government went so far as outlawing the Church and any religious expression whatsoever, the young Jesuit priest went around, often in disguise, celebrating Holy Mass and dispensing the Sacraments, until he was eventually captured and executed on trumped-up charges without even the benefit of a trial. His execution was the first martyrdom ever captured on film, giving us the iconic shot of Padre Pro standing cruciform, a crucifix in one hand and a Rosary in the other, facing the firing squad. He was beatified in 1988, and so is properly "Blessed Miguel Pro," although common parlance tends to retain the simpler "Padre Pro." I am confident he will be canonized one day. Incidentally, the effect of the government's attempted use of his public execution as propaganda was precisely the opposite of what they wanted. Intended to dishearten the opposition, the famous picture instead helped fan a smoldering resistance into full-scale war.

Fr. Juan Diego celebrated Mass in yet another strikingly beautiful church. We all venerated the relics of Padre Pro, then stepped out of the church and into the adjacent museum containing many of his personal items, relics of his life, priesthood, period in hiding, and eventual martyrdom.

Leaving Sagrada Familia, we traveled to the Shrine of Our Lady of Covadonga, memorializing one of the few Christian victories against the Moors in the early eighth century when the explosive spread of Islam out of Arabia was still going strong. Muslims from North Africa swept across Spain after 711 and reduced the Christian Spaniards to only a small corner in the northwest, the majority in the rest of the peninsula suffering dhimmitude for hundreds of years. As the story goes, a Spanish nobleman named Pelayo rallied the defeated Christians to make a stand in 722 at a place of many caves called Covadonga. Pelayo prayed to the Virgin Mary for victory, and subsequently credited the Christians' success and very survival to her intercession. Pelayo became king of the remaining free Christians in Spain, and Our Lady of Covadonga became a patron of the hundreds-of-years-long war to drive the Muslims back out of Spain, the Reconquista, which concluded only shortly before the Conquest of Mexico began. Many of the conquistadors naturally had a great devotion to Our Lady of Covadonga.

From there, we had a fair distance within the city to drive, which Taylor filled with a talk on the connections of the Mexican Our Lady of Guadalupe with St. Luke the Evangelist and the Spanish Lady of Guadalupe – which I blended into my summary given previously. We ended up at the main square of Mexico City, properly the Plaza de la Constitución but commonly called the Zocalo, where we first took lunch in VIP's, a restaurant on a side street half a block or so from the southwestern corner of the Zocalo. Anne and I ended up at a table with Joy Marshall and baby Maggie, as well as our guides Roberto and Paolo, our first chance to visit with any of them. After lunch, we walked back to the Zocalo, which is surrounded by high-end hotels, offices, the National Palace, and the Metropolitan Cathedral at the northern end. There was a great deal of preparation underway for the Pope's visit the next week – and one lone protester there opposing the Pope's visit. He was a bit pathetic, basically being ignored.

Although it was on our itinerary, we saw the National Palace only from the outside, from the other side of the Zocalo, as we walked directly to the Metropolitan Cathedral. The Zocalo proper, or at least this area of Mexico City, is on the very site of the old Aztec city of Tenochtitlan; the Metropolitan Cathedral of the Assumption of the Most Blessed Virgin Mary into Heaven rests on the site of the principal pyramid-temple to the blood-thirsty war-god Huitzilopochtli. Through thick glass plates embedded in the sidewalk before it, you can see Aztec brickwork from that era.

The Metropolitan Cathedral is one of the most magnificent churches I have ever beheld, a mixture of architectural styles and design aesthetics from Renaissance to Baroque to Neoclassical, reflecting more than two hundred years of construction from the sixteenth to the nineteenth centuries. It is breathtaking. Entry presents you with a smaller church literally within the larger church, with multiple side-chapels all around; a colossal organ backs the smaller chapel which lies in the foreground immediately upon entry; past the organ, in the distance at the end of the nave, can be seen the magnificent high altar of the cathedral.

By the way, when I say breathtaking, I mean it. I was wearing my hat when I stepped through the door into the church and was absolutely gob-smacked. I stood there, in slack-jawed amazement, overwhelmed by beauty – until an attendant sternly got my attention to remove my hat as is customary for men upon entering a church. It was quite embarrassing – but that I neglected to do so is, to my mind, a telling sign of how out of myself I was suddenly taken by the sight.

We spent a great deal of time wandering around inside the cathedral. It was so much to take in. The cathedral overall is dedicated to Our Lady's Assumption into Heaven, but inside there are multiple chapels dedicated to Our Lady under a number of titles, including some I had never heard of and have never encountered since: Nuestra Señora de la Soledad; Nuestra Señora de los Dolores; Nuestra Señora de Zapopan, Nuestra Señora La Antigua; Nuestra Señora de la Immaculada Concepción; Nuestra Señora las Angustias de Granada – and, of course, Nuestra Señora de Guadalupe. Then there were a few chapels dedicated to Our Lord: Señor del Buen Despacho, El Divino

Salvador; Santo Cristo; and to other saints: Los Santos Cosme y Damian; San Jose; San Felipe de Jésus (whose feast was, recall, the day before); San Pedro; and I probably missed some. There were that many. Before the high altar, we viewed the tomb of Bishop Zumárraga, who requested and received the sign from Our Lady of Guadalupe. And there was so much more. We tried to give proper reverence to all these altars and a myriad of relics – but just could not. There were too many. This is definitely on my list of things that I would like to do again – remembering to remove my hat, of course.

There was one final sight in the cathedral, having nothing to do with religion per se, that I found impressive. What is now Mexico City was once a large lake. When the Spaniards arrived, the Aztec capital of Tenochtitlan was on an island in the middle of that lake. The lake is gone now, drained long ago. But the soft clay of the lakebed makes a feeble foundation for a modern city. Central Mexico is, moreover, prone to earthquakes, a fact that I have known all my life just from news reports. I remember well horrific images from the 1985 Mexico City Earthquake that killed over five thousand people. We would see one reason for frequent seismic activity the next day, although the main cause is the intersection of three tectonic plates just off the southwestern coast of Mexico. We saw one of the effects right there, in the center of the cathedral, where a massive pendulum hangs with its point bare millimeters from the floor. Beneath it, inscribed in stone, are markings showing where the pendulum has pointed over centuries, indicating a continuous shifting of the center of gravity resulting from the succession of tremors, sometimes severe earthquakes, the church has endured over those centuries. One of our pilgrims, Tom from California, an engineer, commented over lunch a couple of days later that the clay beneath Mexico City can jiggle like a bowlful of jelly in a particularly severe quake – and launched off into a discourse on the efforts the Mexican government has made to stabilize its significant historical and cultural landmarks, such as the Metropolitan Cathedral and the Old Basilica at Guadalupe. It was amazing and unsettling.

As we exited the cathedral, we beheld a larger-than-life statue of Pope St. John Paul II made entirely of melted-down keys. Within it is an image of Our Lady of Guadalupe. There was a bit of an uproar as one member of our group was found missing. I am not sure exactly what the issue was, whether she had wandered off alone or her Whisper was off and she did not hear the guides calling her as she continued exploring the nooks and crannies of the great cathedral, but she turned up presently. We proceeded to walk several blocks through the streets of downtown Mexico City to the Plaza and Church of Santo Domingo (St. Dominic). This church was similarly impressive on a smaller scale than the cathedral. It was to St. Dominic that Our Lady revealed the fifteen traditional mysteries of the Rosary. We were told that this church is noted for hosting the very first Rosary Confraternity in the world (although there are competing claims to that honor) and that the Rosary has been prayed every day since the sixteenth century at 18:00 in its Shrine of Our Lady of the Rosary.

We walked back to the Cathedral, where we had to wait quite a while for the bus to meet us. Traffic was very dense. On the way back to the hotel, we prayed Evening Prayer and the Rosary. As we neared the hotel, Roberto pointed out a small crowd of people at the Angel Monument a few blocks over from where we passed. Although we passed at a distance, several young ladies' colorful dresses stood out even in the lowering dusk. The monument provides a popular backdrop for *Quinceañera* photographs as Mexican girls celebrate their coming of age at fifteen. Having a while between arriving at the hotel and supper at 19:00, Anne and I went walking. We tried to get to the Angel Monument, but it is the center of a traffic circle with multiple lanes and no immediately apparent place to cross, at least from the direction we approached. We therefore walked back around some other local streets, popping into various stores, including a liquor establishment where we purchased a couple of gifts, a pharmacy where we bought a couple of toiletry items we needed, and so forth. Incidentally, at some point on the pilgrimage, the subject of "our" street's name came up - Calle Hamburgo. The explanation given was that such names evocative of various locations across Europe reflect the character of this part of Mexico City as an old diplomatic district. The street is thus named for Hamburg, Germany.

After supper - I do not remember with whom we sat - and a half an hour or so spent transferring the day's pictures to my laptop and external hard drive, Anne and I went all the way up to the top of the hotel, the "penthouse" level, where there was an open-air pool, exercise rooms, conference rooms, allegedly a bar, and so forth. We found it deserted although we had heard of members of our group congregating there in the evening for drinks. We did not even find the alleged bar. We did find quite an impressive view out across the city, but it was windy and cold. Within just a few minutes, we went back down to the bar. No one from our group was there, either, so we enjoyed drinks on our own - another margarita for me (unfortunately not blue), a mojito for Anne. Halfway through my margarita, I realized that both of our drinks were "on the rocks." We had been prudently avoiding water even in the hotel, although we had gotten conflicting advice on that point. I thought back to Thursday night; had the blue margarita had ice in it? I could not remember – nor did I remember it *not* having ice. There had been no ill effects then. Perhaps the Galeria Plaza's ice was indeed from filtered water, as we had been told. Praying for the best, I finished the present margarita, and then we returned to our room to prepare for a very early morning on Sunday, to begin a very long day that we were warned would not have us back to the hotel before 20:00. Given that Sunday 07 February was the date of Superbowl 50, I braced myself for howls of protest. There were none.

This a pilgrimage, I thought.

Sunday 07 February 2016 – Mexico Day Four: *Tlaxcala and Puebla*

We were up for an early breakfast and departure on the bus by 07:30, headed out of Mexico City entirely toward San Miguel del Milagro, about two hours to the east in the state of Tlaxcala. We could feel our ears popping as we left the huge bowl amid the mountains in which is Mexico City – I think Roberto might have said at one point that we topped out at about 10,000 feet above sea level. And that was going through a pass between Monte Tlaloc to the north and two mountains to our south that had all our attention.

It was a beautiful, albeit hazy, day, perfect for viewing Popocatepetl ("The Smoking Mountain") and Iztaccíhuatl ("The White Woman," also called La Mujer Dormida, "The Sleeping Woman," because from a certain aspect that mountain looks like a sleeping woman draped in a white blanket). Both mountains, respectively the second and third highest in Mexico, are volcanoes; Iztaccíhuatl is dormant, but Popocatepetl is quite active and had become more so in recent days. As we slowly rounded the mountains to the north, Popocatepetl greeted us by belching out several clouds of steam.

We stopped partway along the journey for a pit stop and extended view of the vista – and photos – then continued toward San Miguel. Along the way, we saw groups of pilgrims on foot and on bicycles, heading the direction from which we came. They were making their way to Mexico City and the Shrine of Our Lady of Guadalupe, to be there for the impending Papal visit. Banners, signs, crosses, and crucifixes proclaimed their intention. One group followed a pickup truck driving slowly along the shoulder of the road, its bed having been made into a shrine with the image of Our Lady of Guadalupe surrounded by flowers. Lots of flowers.

Also, during that drive, Roberto told us the history of Mexico and the Church during the nineteenth and twentieth centuries. Again, although I did not record it, I later reconstructed it to go something like this:

> After generally prospering during the sixteenth and seventeenth centuries, when Spain was under the rule of the Spanish branch of the Central European Habsburgs, New Spain – the colonies in the Americas – found things quite different once the French Bourbons gained control of the mother country as a result of the 1700 War of the Spanish Succession. Spain's New World possessions were treated more thoroughly as an exploited colony than ever before, and discontent rose. Increasingly disgruntled, many Mexicans saw the American Revolution of 1776 as a model and its success as an inspiration. Tensions only rose in 1808 when the French Emperor Napoleon imposed his brother Joseph Bonaparte as king of Spain.
>
> Outright rebellions broke out in Mexico two years later, the first led by a priest, Miguel Hidalgo, who was captured and executed in short order. But the rebellions could not be suppressed so easily. In 1821, a Spanish general, Augustin de Iturbide, switched allegiances and declared Mexico independent on 24 February 1821. A constitutional monarchy was established, with Iturbide being declared Emperor on 18 May 1822. He quickly found the factions coalescing during this period to be irreconcilable and unworkable and was forced to abdicate within less than a year. By that time, however, two camps of rebels had coalesced: the conservatives, who were centralists, monarchists, and clericalists, wanting a centralized government ruled by a king with Catholicism being the sole religion; and the liberals, who were federalists, republicans, and anticlerical, demanding a decentralized, representative form of government with the Church being disestablished.
>
> The downfall of Iturbide was followed by chaos that invited a Spanish attempt at recapturing its wayward colony – but resulted in the rise of General Antonio Lopez de Santa Anna, whose successful repulsing of an invading Spanish army (1829) united the factions for a time and won him the

1833 presidency of the United Mexican States. Santa Anna's new constitutional government mostly balanced the demands of the conservatives and liberals – but his humiliating defeat that lost Texas (1836), then an unsuccessful war against the United States of America (1846-1848) which lost Mexico much of its northern territory in what is now the American southwest by the 1848 Treaty of Guadalupe-Hidalgo, ultimately cost him his office (1855). Liberals then forced through constitutional changes that cost the Catholic Church its privileged position and instituted their dream of a federal republic, but the resurgent conservatives would not submit.

By 1861 the liberals had won the civil war that resulted, at which point Mexico repudiated its mounting debt to England, France, and Spain. The three creditors briefly occupied Vera Cruz to force payment, which was rescheduled. England and Spain withdrew – but the French Emperor Napoleon III rejected the agreement and instead attempted to force a puppet ruler on Mexico in the person of Archduke Maximilian of Austria. He failed in the short term – the French loss of the Battle of Puebla on 05 May 1862 gave the Cinco de Mayo – but the French rallied and by 1864 had succeeded in forcing the hapless Maximilian von Habsburg on Mexico. The Mexicans took the conflict underground, continuing it as a guerrilla war. When the concurrent US Civil War had ended, and the victorious US government demanded that France withdraw from Mexico, Maximilian found himself with no support – he was defeated, captured, and executed in 1867.

Turmoil continued. A brief return to the republic under President Benito Juarez ended in a coup establishing the Porfirio Diaz dictatorship in 1876. Diaz forced economic growth, but there was a widening gulf between the mass of the poor and a small class of Diaz' allies that climaxed in a sham presidential election, which Diaz blatantly stole in 1910. His challenger, Francisco Madera, fled to Texas and called for rebellion, which was answered by Pascual Orozco, Pancho Villa, and Emiliano Zapata; Madera returned and forced a fair election in 1811, which Madero won – but then he was killed in another military coup led by General Victoriano Huerta, 1913. Another series of rebellions by Pancho Villa and others, who fought amongst themselves as much as against the *Federales* – plus US involvement when fighting spilled over into

American territory – led to general chaos until 1919, by which time Venustiano Carrera had drawn up a new liberal constitution for Mexico, which included total separation of Church and state. The Church hierarchy in Mexico had generally supported the anti-democratic regimes of Diaz and Huerta; it now found itself disestablished and banned from public life entirely. In short order, the ban turned into outright persecution (including, e.g., the martyrdom of Padre Pro), provoking the mass uprising known as the Cristeros War of 1927. The rebels took a banner of Our Lady of Guadalupe as their standard and "¡Viva Cristo Rey! – Long live Christ the King!" as their battle cry. By the 1930s a measure of accommodation had been reached with a new government instituted by the Revolutionary Party that would rule Mexico for the rest of the twentieth century, generally well although world economic unrest in the 1970s struck Mexico harder than other countries. The Church remained disestablished and allowed no public expression but was generally tolerated otherwise; in the 1980s, most restrictions were lifted, and a state of relative normalcy in Church-state relations has prevailed ever since.

Then, Pablo told us the legend of the mountains we were passing:

When the young warrior Popocatepetl and the beautiful princess Iztaccíhuatl fell in love, her father, the emperor, was outraged. He imposed a seemingly impossible task on the suitor – to defeat and bring back the head of the greatest warrior of an enemy tribe. In time, a messenger arrived, bearing news that Popocatepetl had been slain in the attempt. Iztaccíhuatl was grief-stricken– she fell ill and died of a broken heart. Then Popocatepetl returned triumphant, bearing the enemy's head. He had succeeded in the task despite betrayal by a rival who, seeking the hand of the princess, had sent the false news of Popocatepetl's defeat. The traitor was seized and killed, but Popocatepetl was disconsolate. He took the body of his beloved princess into the mountains, lay her out as if sleeping, and took up vigil beside her, awaiting his own death. The gods, touched by his devotion, transformed them both into mountains – the snow-covered "White" or "Sleeping Woman" and the volcanic "Smoking Mountain" that periodically spews forth fire and smoke as a sign that Popocatepetl keeps his vigil still....

As we approached San Miguel del Milagro, Roberto took back up with the eponymous story of the apparition and great miracle worked by St. Michael the Archangel in 1631 - one hundred years after Our Lady of Guadalupe.

> Unlike a century earlier when Juan Diego had received a visitation and instructions from a young maiden which he promptly followed, when Diego Lazaro encountered a heavenly warrior commanding him to find a healing well in far-off Tlaxcala the young Indian peasant was incredulous as well as doubtful that anyone would believe him. He thus kept silent and fell deathly ill with a fever. His relatives took up deathwatch beside him and were there when he seemingly breathed his last. At that moment, a brilliant light appeared, frightening them into flight. When the light subsided and the relatives returned, they found Diego Lazaro apparently dead. Then he opened his eyes, sat up, and began to speak, telling them of a second visitation, in which the warrior - the archangel St. Michael - raised him up and took him to the place he had only described before, showing him the healing well, and promising him true death if he did not fulfill his mission. Healed, Diego Lazaro arose and led his relatives to the governor of Tlaxcala, some days' journey away, where he found his original fear realized: The governor berated him for purporting that God's archangel would appear to a worthless peasant and drove him away with promises of awful punishment should he continue putting forth such nonsense. Diego Lazaro and his relatives secretly made their way to the site revealed by the vision, where they did find the well. Recalling the governor's threats, however, Diego Lazaro exacted a promise of secrecy from his relatives, at which point St. Michael appeared again, gave him a beating, and commanded him to take some of the well water to the bishop. The bishop tested the water by distributing it to the ill and infirm, all of whom were healed. Word spread quickly, and so the site of the well became a destination for pilgrims seeking miraculous healing.

Many such miracles have been attested over the years since in the place now known as "St. Michael of the Miracle." We spent a couple of hours there, passing through an open-air market, witnessing the colorful enthusiasm of Mexican piety, including a custom, that first Sunday after the Feast of the Presentation (02 February), in which they brought dolls of the Infant Jesus to the Church of St. Michael to be blessed. Sunday Mass was in progress as we passed the main church. The congregation was standing room only, spilling out the doors; there was no getting in there, but Fr. Peter said Mass for us in a chapel at the adjacent Shrine of San Miguel del Milagro. We were able to have bottles filled with healing waters from the well. A tiny bit of water from the well. The well, just outside the main church, is now almost dry, so the brothers who staff the shrine carefully allocate its water to pilgrims, distributing holy water "enriched" with a dash of water from the holy well.

Afterward, we wandered around the market for an hour or so. I bought pastry from some nuns selling through a window onto the square directly out of their convent; Anne picked up several small items of pottery, one of the wares for which this area is known. Back on the bus, as we drove about a half an hour or so to Puebla, Taylor talked about the role of Our Lady as Mediatrix of All Graces and Co-Redemptrix, two doctrines that especially raise the ire of Protestants who do not understand the central role Our Lady played in the Plan of Salvation and consider that recognizing her participation somehow denigrates Christ's unique position as Redeemer. It does not.[40]

We arrived in Puebla at lunchtime. There, at the Hotel Colonial Restaurant in the city that is the reputed home of the dish, we enjoyed a wonderful meal of the Mexican chocolate-based gravy known as *mole* ("MO-lay") on chicken wrapped in corn tortillas like fajitas. It was wonderful! After that, we walked a fair distance through a more extensive

---

[40] Given its timing, which came during my writing and editing this manuscript, I feel compelled to offer at least some comment on Pope Francis' 12 December 2019 comments on the prospect of formally declaring Our Lady the title "Co-Redemptrix" (widely reported, e.g. Inéz San Martin, "Pope calls idea of declaring Mary co-redemptrix 'foolishness'," *Crux* [13 December 2019] [https://cruxnow.com/vatican/2019/12/pope-calls-idea-of-declaring-mary-co-redemptrix-foolishness/]). As with many other of this Pope's declarations, I consider characterizing that prospect as "foolishness" to be problematic given how entrenched the idea of Our Lady's cooperative role in our redemption is in the Church's authentic magisterium. Dr. Mark Miravalle, a vocal advocate of such a declaration, charitably points out that the Pope does not so much characterize the title itself as "foolishness" as the idea of defining new dogmas in general ("Clarifications on Pope Francis' Guadalupe Homily Concerning 'Co-redemptrix'," *Mother of All Peoples – The Marian Library* [13 December 2019] [https://www.motherofallpeoples.com/blog/clarifications-on-pope-francis-guadalupe-homily-concerning-co-redemptrix]). That is not the prevailing characterization, however.

market toward our next church. But, on the way, Anne and I had a little adventure.

The day before, at lunch, Anne had mentioned to Pablo her wish to be able to bring our son Tristan back some kind of soccer memorabilia – a scarf or a jersey. Pablo at once replied that he knew just the place, in Puebla. Anne reminded him now, and we three broke off from the group for a few minutes to go into a sports shop where she found what she wanted. I was having flashbacks of when she and I had briefly broken ranks in Italy for exactly the same reason – only that time we did not have an accomplice! With Pablo's help, Anne completed the transaction in mere minutes – which did not keep our absence from being noticed. It was somewhat amusing as we dashed to catch up to the group and began hearing on our Whispers as they realized someone was not present, including Pablo! – "Where's Pablo?" We were, of course, unable to respond and let them know we were returning; Whispers only go one-way.

In any case, we all made it to the Templo de Santo Domingo in Puebla and went inside. Among the many notable sights in that church was what is definitely in the running for the single most impressive thing I saw on this trip (not counting the image of Our Lady, which is in a class all its own) – a side chapel, really a full transept, dedicated to Our Lady of the Rosary. The seventeenth-century *Capilla del Rosario* was stunning in its Baroque beauty, with huge oil paintings of the Mysteries of the Rosary lining the walls. As usual, the central nave of the church was flanked by numerous other side chapels dedicated to various saints, including one dedicated to St. Thomas Aquinas, the Dominican patron saint of Taylor Marshall's online enterprise which sponsored this pilgrimage. I managed to get a picture of Taylor venerating the shrine of the saint being girded by angels.

Assembling in the plaza fronting of the church, we walked a short distance back to where the bus would pick us up and were treated to a few minutes listening to a street band and watching people dancing. Among the latter were Pablo and one of the ladies from Houston, Molly! I heard someone say it was "Mexican Mardi Gras" (which was just two days hence), but I am not sure if that was serious or just a quip.

Back on the bus, we made a quick transfer to another area of Puebla, to the Templo de San Francisco de Asis, which holds the incorrupt body of St. Sebastian of Aparicio, an early Spanish colonist in Mexico who lived a full life as the first Mexican "cowboy," domesticating wild cattle, harnessing them to wheeled carts (the native Americans had no knowledge of either) and building a smooth highway to facilitate movement and trade across Mexico, all by the time he was seventy – at which time he gave up his fortune and became a friar, and spent most of the next thirty years as a beggar, finally dying at age 98.

Finally, on the long ride back to Mexico City and the Galeria Plaza, after Evening Prayer, we were treated to a movie – *For Greater Glory*, starring Andy Garcia, the story of the 1920s *Cristiada* in Mexico. Anne and I had seen this 2012 film only a couple of weeks earlier in preparation for this trip since I knew that conflict provided the context for Padre Pro's martyrdom, but we appreciated seeing it again. Briefly, set mainly in the west of Mexico, the movie tells the true story of an atheist retired general, Enrique Gorostieta, who is hired by the *Cristeros*, faithful Catholics taking up arms in resistance to the persecution initiated by President Plutarco Calles, to bring military discipline and leadership to their cause. Through the conflict, as well as the witness of a young boy who runs away from home to join the war and then is captured and killed, the general finds his faith just before he too falls in an ambush by the *Federales*. But that night, we ended on a cliff-hanger – when we arrived at the hotel, we had just witnessed the martyrdom of the boy, Jose Sanchez, who refused to forsake his God, even in the face of horrific tortures. We would, of course, finish out the movie, about another twenty minutes, the next evening. But from that moment on, our group gained another rallying cry. To Taylor's "*Ave Maria!*" (and "*¡Bueno Bueno Bueno!*" which began as Roberto's mike check), which we had from the beginning, now was added the *Cristeros*' "*¡Viva Cristo Rey! – Long Live Christ the King!*"

Later that same year, 2016, Pope Francis canonized St. Jose Sanchez del Rio. At the time we were in Mexico, the recent authentication by the Congregation for the Causes of Saints of the third miracle required for canonization had resulted in speculation that the Pope would use his upcoming visit to Mexico as an opportunity to canonize him, but he did not. The ceremony took place on 16 October.

Roberto had pegged our return time almost exactly. We pulled back up to the hotel just after 20:00. A more limited, but still excellent spread, was available to us in the dining room. Many people did not seem to avail themselves of it, or did so only quickly, to get to their rooms or the bar to watch what remained of the Superbowl.

Yes, this was a pilgrimage. But that was the Superbowl.

Not being huge football fans, however, Anne and I joined a smaller group for a quieter dinner before we went up to our room, where I backed up my photos as usual, and we wound down to get a good night's sleep for our last full day in Mexico.

Monday 08 February 2016 – Mexico Day Five: Guadalupe and Coyoacán
 We were up for breakfast at 07:00, to leave on the bus at 08:30, headed for our second visit to the Shrine at Guadalupe. On previous mornings Anne had spied a lovely white lacey scarf with the image of Our Lady of Guadalupe, Juan Diego, and Pope St. John Paul II on it among the wares offered by one of the street vendors swarming around the bus as we were boarding. They were always the same ones, and to my surprise, Pablo said these vendors were legit, but on Sunday morning, the particular vendor did not happen to have the one Anne had seen. He promised he would have it *"mañana"* – and so he did. She bought it, and I ended up purchasing a large banner of the image of Our Lady of Guadalupe from him as well, mainly in appreciation that he had followed through.

Along the way to the Shrine, after Morning Prayer, Taylor presented the group with options. A number of us, myself included, had expressed concern that we would not have sufficient time to take it all in on this second, visit to the shrine of Guadalupe, including time to sit and pray and present the intentions that we had brought with us to Our Lady, given the afternoon was to be spent at several other churches. So, he put it to a vote – after, at my suggestion, having Roberto and Pablo tell us a little about the three other churches we were scheduled to visit. Of the choices – 1) to ditch the three other churches entirely and stay at Guadalupe all day, or 2) to stay longer at Guadalupe, take a late lunch, and go to one of the churches, described by Father Juan Diego as "worth seeing," or 3) to keep the original schedule. The consensus was for option two (I voted for option one but was outvoted). It was, however, a happy compromise.

Also on the way to the Shrine, Roberto passed out lyrics for Guadalupan pilgrim songs, most notably *La Guadalupana*:

> *Desde el cielo una hermosa mañana,*
> *Desde el cielo una hermosa mañana,*
> *La Guadalupana, La Guadalupana,*
> *La Guadalupana bajó al Tepeyac....*[41]

---

[41] *The Virgin of Guadalupe*

> Down from heaven on a beautiful morning,
> Down from heaven on a beautiful morning,
> The Virgin of Guadalupe, The Virgin of Guadalupe,
> The Virgin of Guadalupe came to Tepeyac....

We could have used more than a single run-through of its *nine verses* on the bus before we got to the Shrine, but that is all we got. When we arrived at the Shrine, we went into the same gift shop for a bathroom break before we proceeded into the Plaza of the Americas and directly into the New Basilica, belting out *La Guadalupana*. Our hearts were in it, but frankly, the quality of our sung Spanish was not there. No matter.

A great deal of preparation for the Pope's impending visit was visible, both in the plaza and inside the basilica, where the number of people was easily as large as it had been on Friday. Mass was once more underway at the main altar, with a constant stream of Mexican pilgrims processing in with banners and other religious iconography. In fact, although we had planned on celebrating Mass in one of the upper chapels at 10:00, we could not. All were in use, and so we had to delay our Mass until 11:00. Having a free hour, we walked across into the Old Basilica, which is now mainly devoted to Eucharistic Adoration.

The official reason for the building of the New Basilica in the 1970s was that the Old Basilica, as magnificent as it is – and in my opinion it has a far more suitable ambiance for the miraculous portrait of the Mother of God than the dated 1970s-chic décor of the New Basilica – it was far too small for the vast number of pilgrims that now make their way to Guadalupe each year. That was an important consideration, yes, but not the decisive one. Built at the base of Tepeyac Hill, the Old Basilica sits atop even more sandy soil than the Metropolitan Cathedral downtown and lists to an even more noticeable degree. Looking closely at it from certain angles, the façade at once brought to mind the Leaning Tower of Pisa, although the cant is obviously not to the same degree. It is especially noticeable inside, where you feel as if you are walking on a slanted floor, generally uphill from the doors to the high altar at the front of the church. The foundation had shifted so much by the mid-twentieth century that the building was unsafe, and it was indeed closed for many years. Once again, however, the wonders of modern engineering have stabilized it and allowed it to be opened to the public. (The Old Basilica is what inspired Tom's discourse later at lunch.)

It was quite an experience standing inside the Old Basilica. Besides the dark carved-wood beauty, I felt a little off-balance all the while.

Roberto took us to the front of the Old Basilica, to a life-size replica of the *tilma* now occupying the spot where the original resided for many, many years. He used it to explain a lot of the iconography of the image which the Aztecs could read like a book. The colors of her dress and mantle, the pattern of stars on the latter, the flower-like designs on the former, the band around her waist above her pregnant abdomen, and so forth – all have meaning and told the Indians that the Mother of the Spaniards' God was their mother as well, and wanted her two peoples to be one.[42]

There was a smaller gift shop in the Old Basilica, just outside the Adoration Chapel, but I think most of us spent more time in the chapel than in the shop.

We reassembled in the front of the New Basilica and were finally able to make our way to one of the upper chapels, where Fr. Peter celebrated our last Mass of the pilgrimage to Mexico City. Afterward, we scattered, as usual, each to do our own thing – or, rather, each of us to do pretty much the same things just not necessarily in the same order. In my and Anne's case, it was first to make our way up Tepeyac Hill to the church on the spot where Juan Diego found the miraculous roses, back down and around to the gift shop where we made the bulk of our purchases of sacramentals and memorabilia for this trip, and then again to the New Basilica for our time with Our Lady.

As far as the gift shop goes … Well, it was an indescribable experience. Words cannot convey the confusing chaos of the way shopping and transactions were conducted. The process, as it were, was rendered almost unnavigable by the language barrier. It seems that there were little areas of "jurisdiction" for the various salespeople. When I found a T-shirt right inside the front door, a young lady started right away writing me up a ticket; when I indicated I would like her also to help me with an item not seven to ten feet away, she made it clear that she could not help me with that and another clerk had to take up – generating a separate ticket. Nor could we take our merchandise with us as we shopped around the store. No, we got a ticket representing each purchase, which the clerk holding jurisdiction took away. So, we ended up assembling a stack of handwritten tickets and nothing to show for it. *A large stack of handwritten tickets*, because, as I said, we did most of our souvenir and sacramentals purchasing there. *And nothing to show for it*. Then we were to present the tickets to a central cashier and pay … at which point I was really feeling stressed by the total chaos, experiencing sensory overload, and commented to Anne that we were

---

[42] A good point-by-point illustrated summary of the iconography, among much else, may be seen at the page, "Guadalupe, Mexico (1531)," Michael O'Neill, *The Miracle Hunter* [http://www.miraclehunter.com/marian_apparitions/approved_apparitions/guadalupe/index.html], accessed 08 August 2019.

paying all at once for such an accumulation of merchandise that I was not sure we would even remember what all we had bought – *or how to go about finding it*! Luckily, one of the young clerks had perceived how clueless I was and managed to communicate to me that I should pay then bring the stack of tickets back to her. I did that. And, sure enough, she took them and scurried around from here to there and back again, and suddenly, we had all our purchases in hand and were ready to go. She was a lifesaver! – or at least a sanity-saver for me!

Leaving the gift shop, Anne and I returned to the New Basilica. I spied Fr. Juan Diego by one of the large columns inside, hearing the Confession of one of our group. That was something I had been meaning to avail myself of during this pilgrimage but had never found the right time. The only time I knew that he was planning to hear Confessions was when he announced that he would do so atop the Pyramid of the Sun. Now was my chance. I went over and got in line, and a few minutes later, I Confessed and received Absolution. Anne had meanwhile found a pew– this was in one of the rare lulls in the liturgical activity that is almost constant in the basilica. When I joined Anne, she went and Confessed. Meanwhile, I prayed the prayers to receive the Holy Door Indulgence that was available for Pope Francis' Jubilee Year of Mercy. The main door of this basilica was, like in all basilicas including our own in Natchitoches, designated as a Holy Door through which pilgrims could pass and, under the usual conditions, receive a plenary indulgence.[43] I also prayed for all the intentions that had made it into my little "pilgrimage notebook," adding some others that came to mind. It was there that the presence of Our Lady in that place really did hit me, perhaps not as intensely as others have reported in the presence of the *tilma*, but as a concrete reality.

We remained there in prayer for about a half an hour, bringing us up to the 14:00 time appointed for the group to gather again by the big statue of Pope John Paul II between the two basilicas. We did so. As usual, it took about twenty minutes for stragglers to make their way there, then we walked to where the bus awaited us, and we set out again through Mexico City.

---

[43] The "usual conditions" are Sacramental Confession within a few days either way of performing the indulgenced exercise, receiving the Eucharist on the day of performing the indulgenced exercise, having no attachment to sin, and praying for the intentions of the Holy Father. Sometimes the prayers for the intentions of the Holy Father are specified, sometimes not. In the case of the Extraordinary Jubilee Year of Mercy extending from 08 December 2015, the Solemnity of the Immaculate Conception, to 20 November 2016, the Solemnity of Christ the King, the suggestion was one Our Father and a Hail Mary.

I do not believe it was far or long before we stopped for lunch at a cafeteria attached to a department store called Sanborn's.[44] Once again the food was excellent, and we had a bit of time afterward to wander around in the store. It was clear that, for all the abject poverty that may be witnessed in various parts of Mexico City as well as in the countryside, and the drug-trafficking violence that is notorious in certain regions (mainly the borders, both north and south, as I understand it) this "third-world" country does have access to all of the amenities of a "first-world" state, at least in the cities and most of the places we visited. The Galeria Plaza Reforma was definitely first-class. One thing that I did find surprising, however – and perhaps this is the difference between "first-" and "second-world" countries and the standards of education – was that, in contrast to my experience in Europe and despite the relative proximity of Mexico to the United States, it seemed that relatively fewer people with whom we interacted here had any facility with English. But what can I say? So few people in the US have any language skills whatsoever beyond English, and, as I apologized to one clerk along the way, when I caught myself attempting my pitifully limited Spanish even after she had demonstrated that she was perfectly able to communicate in English, "I'm sorry – your English is much better than my Spanish!"

Then we set out for our last excursion, about an hour and a half drive south to the suburb of Coyoacán. Along the way, we watched the last half-hour or so of *For Greater Glory*, then Fr. Juan Diego related his vocation story, revealing how an Irish Canadian ended up as a friar with the name "Juan Diego," in prison ministry in Nicaragua. It was a fascinating story, especially his description of his relationship with the inmates to whom he ministers.

In Coyoacán, we visited the Franciscan church of San Juan Bautista (St. John the Baptist), the last of the many stunningly beautiful Catholic churches we toured. Obviously, the architectural disaster of the Post-Vatican II era struck Mexico just as it did the US – the New Basilica at Guadalupe is a case in point, I would say – but in the admittedly statistically limited (and doubtless skewed) sample set we experienced, the post-Conciliar design ethos was otherwise mostly absent. *Thanks be to God!* Each church did have its distinct flavor, of course. Along the way, visiting mainly Dominican and Franciscan churches, the differing "architectural sensibilities" of the respective

---

[44] Sanborn's are ubiquitous in Mexico City, making which one we visited impossible to ascertain.

orders was pointed out, and when it came to my attention, I noted how much the simpler Franciscan churches resembled my Minor Basilica of the Immaculate Conception at home in Natchitoches. That makes sense historically. There was a heavy Franciscan presence in early Natchitoches, as I understand, and in fact until the 1850s the original name of the church which eventually became our basilica was indeed "St. Francis"; there is indeed a statue of St. Francis on the grounds behind the sacristy.

Here, in San Juan Bautista Church, there were a couple of features notably unique among the churches we visited. First, whereas I previously commented on the many effigies of the crucified Jesus, just down from the cross, lying shrouded in a glass coffin, here there was to my surprise a similar life-size depiction of the Blessed Mother lying in the sleep of (perhaps) death – her "Dormition"[45] – wrapped in the blue mantle studded with golden stars that she wears in the image on the *tilma*.

Also, nearby.... If there were depictions of the *Spanish* Our Lady of Guadalupe in any other church we visited, I did not notice them. (There was so much to see – sensory overload was constant!) But here there was one. There were also huge paintings depicting the conversion of the native Mexican peoples. San Juan Bautista occupies land donated by Hernan Cortes, near what became the conquistador's *hacienda*. There was also an Adoration Chapel off the left transept where the Blessed Sacrament was exposed. We stopped, and we worshipped.

Once again, breathtaking.

Outside the church, just across a small plaza, Anne's new buddy Pablo made sure we experienced two of the three culinary delights he said people come to Coyoacán to experience – the coffee, the ice cream, and churros. Churros are fluted, ridged, deep-fried dough that is well-dusted in sugar while hot – crispy on the outside, warm and soft on the inside – and in this case filled with ice cream! Wonderful!

---

[45] Although the bodily Assumption of Mary into heaven at the end of her earthly life is a dogma of the Church, whether she was Assumed into heaven before or after experiencing death has never been formally defined. If the former, she would enjoy the company of Enoch and Elijah as the only humans never to have experienced death, as would have been most fitting for her since she was preserved completely free from Original Sin by her Immaculate Conception; it would thus be theologically fitting. On the other hand, the preponderance of tradition holds that, in order to unite herself more perfectly with the salvific Passion of her Son, she chose willingly to experience death in this world before being rejoined with Him in heaven. In any case, "Dormition" means "Falling Asleep," even if euphemistically referring to bodily death.

Finally, back on the bus, we headed back to the hotel for a half-hour chance to freshen up before heading back out for our last meal together as a group in Mexico City. The stop back by the hotel would also allow us to pick up one pilgrim who was not with us for the day to join up with us for the farewell dinner. This 88-year-old gentleman could not walk well. He had come with us on Friday and Sunday, spending much of his time in a wheelchair which Pablo generally pushed (as well as, at least at one point, little Jude Marshall), and his wife said that with the first visit to Guadalupe he had already accomplished his goal for this trip. As my understanding is that most pilgrimage brokers do not make allowances for such situations, this was a gracious concession whether on the part of Taylor or 206 Tours, which I do not know.

The trip back from Coyoacán afforded time for Fr. Peter to follow Fr. Juan Diego in sharing his vocation story, telling how a "book-priest," a priest who trained mainly in canon law and did not end up in the "pastoral track," nevertheless ended up as the Rector of the cathedral in Shreveport. Then Roberto read off the flight, departure time, and gate information for the various small groups and individuals who, it turned out, would be leaving the hotel the next day as we arrived on Thursday – scattered across pretty much half the day. The earliest group had to be up and ready to roll out by 06:00; Anne and I, however, were in the latest group, not departing the hotel until noon.

After the brief stop at the Galeria Plaza, and a short bus ride further, our final meal together was at a fine "French-Mexican" restaurant called "Mexsi Bocu," a pun on "*Merci Beaucoup*," opened a few years previous (as I understand it) by a French chef who married a Mexican and decided to create a unique cuisine combining their respective heritages. Anne and I ended up sitting at a table with one of our group whose husband decided he was too tired for this last excursion – and it was indeed quite late, after a full day; we were verging on 21:00 before we were placing our orders and pushing 23:00 before we loaded up for the return to the hotel. Roberto, Pablo, and even Mario, the driver, joined us at our table, and although Mario evidently had little or no English, it was a welcome opportunity for us to get to know Roberto and Pablo even better. As I said, we became quite fond of both by the end of our few days with them, and in addition to their considerable skills as guides (and Pablo's going the extra mile to help out Anne the day before) this meal cemented that affection. They kept up a lively conversation about their personal histories as well as the joys and travails of a tour guide. I discovered, to my surprise, that they had never worked together; in my judgment, they make an effective team, complementing each other perfectly. During the meal, I passed around my little brown pilgrimage notebook, and everyone present wrote their name and email address into it, from which I later compiled a master list on Google Docs and shared it with all.

Finally, no earlier than 23:00, we were back at the hotel. Anne and I had previously sought out a rumored small group of pilgrims who would end the day up on the roof of the hotel and decided to give it another shot. This time we found them there, and, although it was too cold to sit out by the pool, we found a table and chairs just inside where a small group of us, including Fr. Juan Diego and Taylor - who brought up half a bottle of fine Oban Scotch that we all enjoyed - visited, shared stories about how we had come to be there; reminisced about various things that had really struck, impressed, or moved us; and generally just did not want to let go of the bonds that had been forged in a few short days.[46] But eventually - sometime after midnight - we had to surrender and head to our rooms.

Tuesday 09 February 2016 –Mexico Day Six: *Departure*

As Anne's and my flight would not be departing until 15:00, and Roberto told us our shuttle to the airport would not leave the hotel until noon, we slept in, sort of. We were up about 07:00 and went down for our last breakfast in the Galeria Plaza. Then we returned to our room and set about the arduous task of packing to go home. It is always challenging, trying to put more into our suitcases than we arrived with, because of the various souvenirs and other items we purchased, which included a small statue of Our Lady of Guadalupe that Anne was concerned would not survive the tender mercies of baggage handlers and thus included in her carry-on. But we always manage it - one trick is to bring at least some items, including in my case some shoes which were very comfortable but ready to be retired, that can be left behind to free up space. I had packed a nicer pair of shoes that I wore Sunday, so it was indeed a net saving on packing volume. Once we had accomplished that task, by about 09:30, we

---

[46] Kind of like me in writing this account of the last full day of our pilgrimage. My subsequent trip-journaling, which gave birth to the "travels blog" and ultimately to this book is always an enjoyable experience allowing me to relive the experience all over again as I scour my notes, my memory, my pictures, as well as the Internet regarding the things we saw and did, and I always find myself not wanted to bring it to a close.

decided to go ahead and check out early and take some time wandering around the nearby streets. Anne still had a few souvenirs and sacramentals that she wanted to obtain, including some more medals and rosaries.

As it happened, a couple of people from our group – Neil from Australia and Steph from South Carolina – were interested in venturing out. It also turned out that Roberto, who was going to oversee all our transfers from the hotel to the airport at noon, was "stuck" at the hotel with nothing to do for the next couple of hours. So out we all went, and Roberto proved invaluable this last time as well, taking us right to a big indoor market just a few streets away, that reminded me somewhat of the *Mercado* in San Antonio. We spent some time in there, and at the end, while we were waiting for Steph to rejoin us, Anne took Roberto a couple of stores down and bought him a big cup of coffee as a token of thanks.

We made our way back to the hotel, waited around for maybe half an hour as various others in our airport-transfer group assembled in the lobby, then we were back in the shuttle vans and headed to the airport. The trip did not seem to take nearly as long, perhaps because, strangers having become friends through shared religious experience, animated conversation quickly passed the time. Or maybe it was that the van was not so uncomfortably hot as it was Thursday! In any case, we were at the airport before we knew it.

And final farewells were said. As Anne commented, it was quite different than on our way back from Rome, when most of the pilgrimage group were all returning to the same place. This time, we knew we probably would never again lay eyes on most of these new-found friends, even if the wonders of modern technology (email, social media) make it possible to keep some form of contact. I do not know of any tears being shed, but it was hard parting from them.

Not much need be said of the rest of the day. The flights went as smoothly as those did on Thursday. The only glitch came in the Dallas airport when Tom, the engineer, discovered his wallet missing in the chaos of passing through security. The immediate suspicion was foul play, and Anne and I felt terrible leaving him as we had to head off to catch our flight to Shreveport. Thankfully, a subsequent email the next day revealed that the wallet had been found, contents intact. The Velcro that holds it shut had somehow caught on the conveyor through the X-ray machine, and it had not come out the other side. I am not sure how or when exactly the mystery was solved, but it was, and all's well that ends well.[47]

Finally, near midnight, after our flight to Shreveport and an hour-plus drive, Anne and I pulled back up at home in Natchitoches, to the varyingly enthusiastic welcomes of three cats.

Ave Maria! ¡Viva Cristo Rey! ¡Bueno Bueno Bueno!

Addendum 1: Counting the Cost

As best I can figure based on the package from 206 Tours, the cash we took with us and exchanged into pesos (and spent virtually to the last centimo), plus my credit card record, this trip came in at $6,365.00. Not quite as much less for six days (as it was billed) in Mexico City than ten days in Italy ($9,155.00) as I would have expected, but in the same ballpark. It must be considered that a sizable portion of both of those totals was what might be termed "discretionary," i.e., not part of the package, money we did not *need* to spend. Discounting that, 206 Tours' $5,364.00 for six days in Mexico City comes to $894 per day and is significantly more than Magnificat's $7,204.94 for ten days in Italy, $720.49 per day. Also, those totals are for myself *and* my wife. So, the ballpark per person price, respectively, was about $360 per day for Italy with Magnificat vs. about $450 per day for Mexico City with 206 Tours.

Addendum 2: Reflecting on the Pilgrimage to Mexico

About a week or so after our return, I received an email from Taylor asking if I would be willing to be interviewed for an episode of his podcast, *The Taylor Marshall Catholic Show*. Of course, I said yes, and a few days later, we spent a pleasant twenty minutes chatting about the pilgrimage via Skype. Within a few days, our conversation appeared as Episode 105, "Our Pilgrim Interviews on Our Lady of Guadalupe."[48] I was the last third of the hour-long show, preceded by Fr. Juan Diego and Chantal Dickson from Shreveport. Both have fascinating insights.

---

[47] Did I say Tom's wallet was the only glitch? There were also – possibly – effects of the margarita with ice from a couple of nights before, finally catching up with me. It seems long, and maybe had nothing to do with it; Anne was unaffected. But let's just say that although I was not dreadfully sick during those flights (thanks be to God!), I made sure I always knew where the men's room was and never got far from it.... Don't. Drink. The water.

[48] Taylor Marshall, "105: Our Pilgrim Interviews on Our Lady of Guadalupe [Podcast]" *Taylor Marshall.com* [https://taylormarshall.com/2016/02/105-our-pilgrim-interviews-on-our-lady-of-guadalupe-podcast.html], accessed 09 August 2019.

Listening to the podcast three and a half years after the event is an interesting experience. Here is an abstract of some comments I made, including points that never made it into my blog or the narrative above, set up as a short question-and-answer session from Taylor to me:

Why did you want to visit Our Lady on a pilgrimage to Guadalupe?
Actually, I had never really given it any thought. I had been on one pilgrimage, to Italy in 2014, and found it very moving, but really did not anticipate going on another. In fact, another pilgrimage with many of the same people is coming up (to Fatima and Lourdes [October 2016]), but I am unable to go because of both cost and timing. I never *ever* expected to want to go to Mexico, though. *Then*, listening to your podcast last October, you announced this pilgrimage – the timing was right – and the cost was lower. It did not take long for my wife and me to say, *Let's go!*

What was it like to see the tilma for the first time?
I'm going to lead with something I bet you do not expect: The first time I found a bit underwhelming – and overwhelming at the same time. Friday's visit to the Shrine was too rushed. We went into the basilica and discovered the total chaos of multiple continuous Masses being said all over the church; other pilgrims milled about seemingly aimlessly, making devotions, leaving offerings, praying, I was stunned. We went on the People Mover, heard Mass, were out for a short tour of the overall area – and away. And I was like – "?!"; I heard others say the same thing – "?!"; *That was it? We've done it?* It took some time for me to process it, to really develop some perspective. For instance, the "chaos" ... as I said later in answer to one of your general questions on the bus, I came to see it as a sign of the authenticity of the Mexican people's religion. I tend to prefer order and get really uncomfortable in the midst of such chaotic crowds, but even I could see these people were here for one and one reason only – out of love for Our Lady. It took a while for that perception to develop, but once it did, I was able to get the payoff on the second visit, which was entirely different. On Monday, we got the "real" pilgrim experience, walking into the basilica singing "*La Guadalupana*" (however badly), down to the People Mover ... Later, after Mass, we had the chance to do our own thing ... My wife and I took the chance to spend some time before the *tilma* – not as close as from the People Movers, but we were able to find a pew (we were lucky enough to catch a lull between Masses), make our

Confessions to Fr. Juan Diego, then just sit, pray, present the petitions we'd brought to Our Lady, and listen. And that's when her presence became *real* to me. You said at one point in your lectures on the bus that the Apparition at Guadalupe is unique, given the totally unexplainable qualities of the *tilma* (the images in the eyes, the constant body temperature – I've even heard that it has the heartbeat of an unborn child in it) – *It is a continuing apparition. Our Lady, I believe, continues to be present there, in a unique, mysterious, and wonderful way.*[49]

What were some highlights of the pilgrimage other than Our Lady?
Besides the *tilma*, the single most awesome thing I saw was that chapel of the Rosary in the Church of Santo Domingo in Puebla (I think). Absolutely beautiful. All the intricate carving and gold leaf, the great oil paintings of the Mysteries of the Rosary. Words cannot describe it. That is possibly the most beautiful church I've ever been into. The only thing remotely comparable to it on this trip was the Metropolitan Cathedral in Mexico City. Here's a funny story: We stepped through the doors, and I was so stunned by its size and the spectacle of that chapel in the foreground, the massive organ, and in the distance the main nave of the church and the high altar, that I completely forgot to take off my hat. I was just getting my bearings, getting ready to take some pictures, when a docent came up and rebuked me. Boy was I embarrassed!

What spiritual truth or lesson did you bring home with you?
1) The absolute, wondrous beauty of our Catholic Faith.

2) How ours is a historical religion. In my history classes, one of the things I stress as a strength of Christianity in its beginning is that, as much as it was like the host of other mystery religions that flourished in the period of the Early Roman Empire, it had one thing that set it apart. Jesus existed – all kinds of sources outside the Bible attest to it – Josephus, Tacitus, and so forth – Christianity was not like the cult of Isis or Mithras. People could point to a specific time and place and say, "*There, in Jerusalem, ca. AD 30, GOD WALKED THE EARTH AS A MAN.*" Well, similarly, I'd read about Juan Diego and Our Lady of Guadalupe, and a lot of the other saints and shrines we saw. But being able to go there, to be able to be within a dozen feet or so of that *tilma*

---

[49] Several years later, pondering this, I am reminded of the quotation from the tomb of St. Martin of Tours presented in the Introduction, and would paraphrase it to say that "[she] is fully here, present and made plain in miracles of every kind" (see p. 23). Many miracles of healing have been attributed to Our Lady of Guadalupe.

and see the image of Our Lady – to be able to walk on Tepeyac Hill, and see placards saying *"Here, on such and such a date, Juan Diego saw Our Lady."* We did that over and over again – we were in the presence of the incorrupt body of Blessed Sebastian of Aparicio, the relics of Padre Pro – and many other examples.

3) Finally, whatever problems Mexico might have as a country – and frankly we didn't witness anything like that, nothing to make us feel in the least unsafe through the whole of our days in Mexico – it's my opinion that, given the overt, manifest love the people display for Our Lady of Guadalupe, whose image is literally everywhere – even in a garage across the street from our hotel, on the wall, with flashing Christmassy lights all around it – visible from our dining room – Mexico has not lost its soul like I'm afraid, given recent developments in our own "more sophisticated" society, we have as a country.

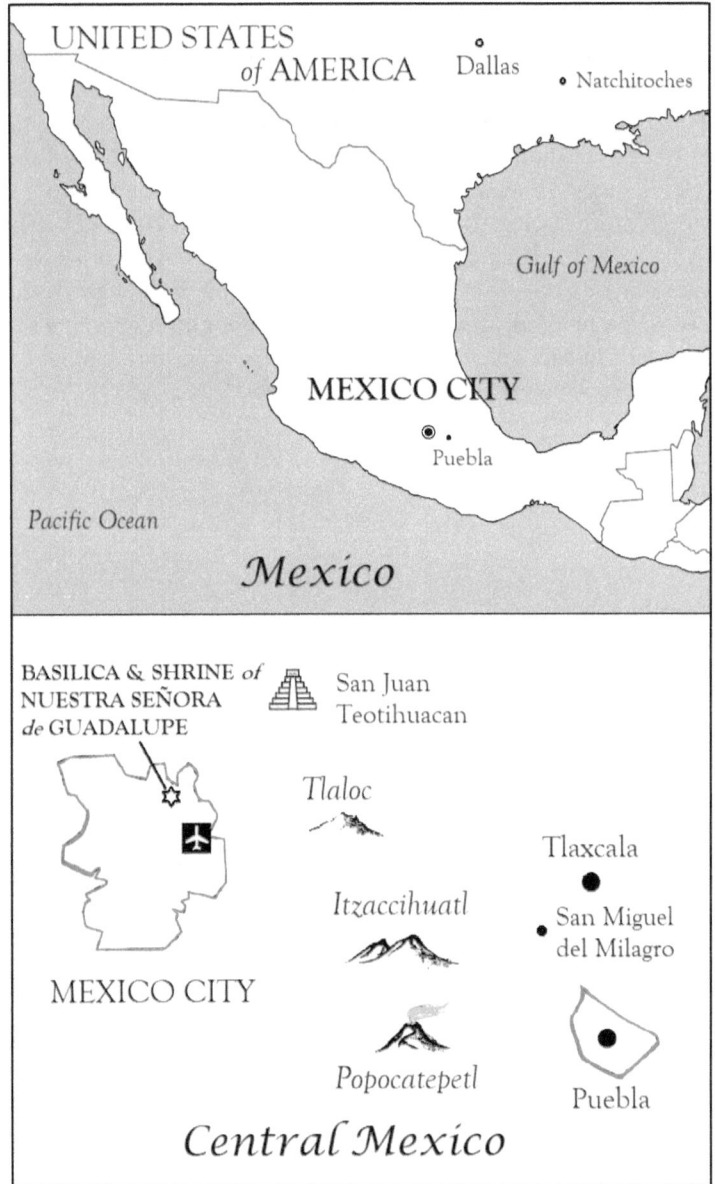

Figure 13: Map of Mexico

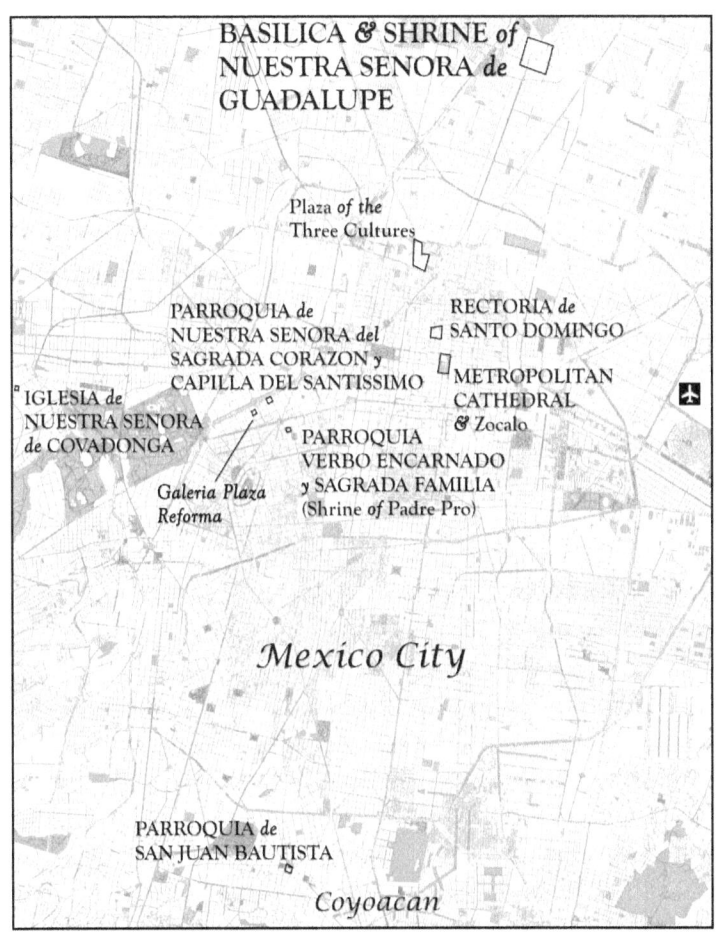

Figure 14: Map of Mexico City

Figure 15: The *Tilma* bearing the image of Our Lady of Guadalupe, in the New Basilica, Mexico City, as seen from the people-mover immediately below. Photo by the author.

Figure 16: The Spanish *Virgen de Guadalupe*. Image from Wikimedia Commons, there stated to be in the Public Domain. Uploaded to Wikimedia Commons 27 November 2005. Attributed to Bernard Higonnet. Accessed 08 January 2020. [https://commons.wikimedia.org/wiki/File:Virgenguadalupe.jpg#/media/File:Virgenguadalupe.jpg] (No higher quality image in the Public Domain was currently available.)

Kent G. Hare

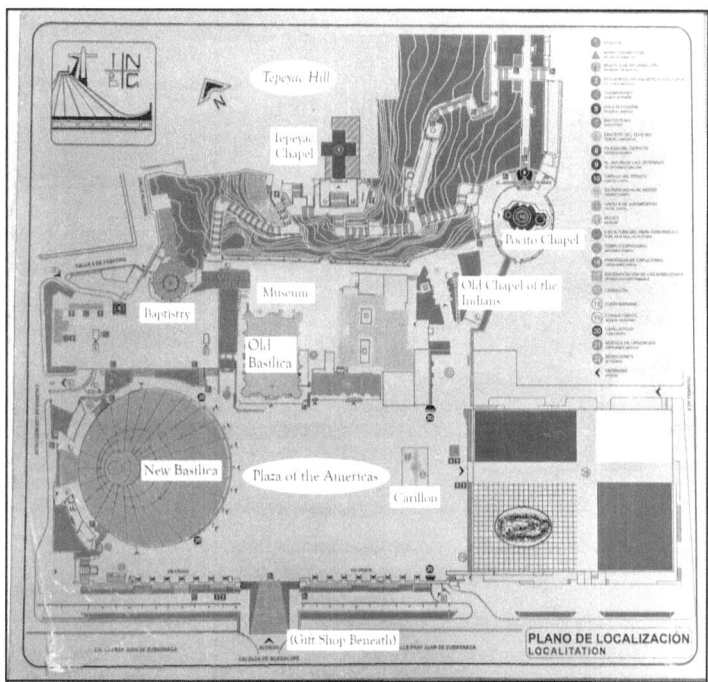

Figure 17: Layout of the Shrine of Our Lady of Guadalupe, Mexico City.
Photo of a plaque on site by the author; Labels added.

Figure 18: The Old Basilica of Our Lady of Guadalupe, Mexico City. Interior.
Photo by the author.

Figure 19: Kent and Anne; Taylor, Jude, Joy and Maggie. The New Basilica of Our Lady of Guadalupe. Photo taken by a fellow pilgrim.

Figure 20: Our Mexican guides: (L) Roberto; (R) Anne and Pablo. Photos by author.

Figure 21: Father Juan Diego, our Spiritual Director. Photo by author.

Figure 22: Templo de Santo Domingo, Puebla – Capilla del Rosario.
Photo courtesy of Anne G. Hare.

Figure 23: Radio Maria Pilgrimage to the Holy Land, August 2018.
Photo courtesy of Ingrid Cannella-Newell.

Figure 24: Brother Miguel, Father Emilio, and the author.
Photo courtesy of Ingrid Cannella-Newell.

CHAPTER THREE

IT WAS HERE! IN THIS PLACE!
Pilgrimage to the Holy Land

Of all possible Christian pilgrimage destinations, the Holy Land is and has always been the most popular, the one, it is said, every Christian should visit at least once in their lifetime – to "Walk in the Footsteps of Jesus," as countless advertisements have urged, including the one that caught me.

It is an ambition I have not had all my life. Only after the 2014 pilgrimage to Italy did I consider it even a remote possibility. Before that, I had little interest, for much the same reasons that made it even then seem unlikely. The ever-present turmoil in the Middle East was a primary concern, of course. Who would not think twice before willingly setting foot into that mess? – as it seemed from eight thousand miles away, watching near-daily reports of terroristic violence.

Nevertheless, as I related briefly in the Introduction, while on the pilgrimage to Mexico City in February 2016, the subject came up. The seed was sown over one of the meals that Anne and I shared with Kate and Molly, the ladies from Houston, when conversation about respective pilgrimage experiences turned to their earlier pilgrimage to the Holy Land sometime before. They strongly encouraged us to put aside our hesitation and go. Then, the last evening, conversation with Taylor revealed that he wanted to *lead* a pilgrimage to the Holy Land – "Maybe next year." After talking to Kate and Molly, I had investigated the cost of such a trip and seen that they tend to run at least $4000 per person, base price. While letting Taylor know I would love to accompany him, I also expressed doubt that I would be able to swing it financially – to which he replied, "Pray a novena!"

Anne and I talked about it from time to time after that, but she remained adamant in her lack of desire to travel to the Middle East. She did not want to keep me from going, but it was clear that she had no interest in going with me or spending that kind of money to do so. It is also unfortunate that her job does not afford her the flexibility that mine does as an academic. It is not like I sit around doing nothing all summer, but outside of the spring and fall terms, my schedule is whatever I want it to be even when teaching Internet courses as I do every summer.

As it happened, "next year," 2017 came and went, and in early 2018 an exchange of text messages on the subject left me feeling that a pilgrimage to the Holy Land with Taylor was a year or more away, at least. I told myself that I therefore had more time to save up; I remained interested in going, especially since it looked like my brother and his wife were going to make it there before me! But I did not think much more about it, except....

While driving around town, if I am not listening to Taylor's podcasts, I will often tune in Radio Maria, a Catholic network headquartered in Alexandria, Louisiana (for the US), with a station right here in Natchitoches. As I listened intermittently that spring of 2018, I started half-hearing a short ad for a pilgrimage to the Holy Land sponsored by Radio Maria. Again, I did not think anything of it. The finances just were not right, and I was set on waiting and traveling with Taylor.

Then came Good Friday (30 March) 2018. As is our custom, Anne and I joined in the annual Walking Way of the Cross around downtown Natchitoches, beginning and ending at the Minor Basilica. As we were retiring afterward from the church itself into the parish hall next-door for what one of our former priests dubbed "a light, penitential lunch" of cheese, tuna, and PBJ finger-sandwiches, Anne stopped me by the door and pointed out a poster hanging in the window – announcing:

> **9 Days: Pilgrimage to the Holy Land**
> "Walking in the Footsteps of Jesus"
> Spiritual Director: Fr. Emilio Garreaud
> National Director of Radio Maria
> **July 30 – August 7, 2018**
> **$2,990 PER PERSON**
> Round Air Trip from Houston, Miami, and New York

"Wow," I said (really). "That's a good price." I snapped a quick picture with my phone and went on in.

Once the intense schedule of the Easter Triduum was behind us, my thoughts turned back to that announcement, and I started giving it some thought. I will not bore you with the details, but more research confirmed my "Wow" – that *was* a good price! I checked out the listed broker, Nativity Pilgrimage, of which I had never heard. As far as I could tell from a quick Internet search, they seemed legitimate; I called one of the contact numbers on the poster and found out from one of the volunteers at Radio Maria that Fr. Emilio had experience with this company and had been pleased with it. The lady with whom I spoke sent me a brochure with a bit more specific information about this particular trip, which I received a couple of days later.

And, yes, I prayed a novena – nine days of Rosaries – specifically asking to be guided in deciding whether to take this opportunity. I knew it would be just me. Anne remained uninterested in going, having designated all her available time off for a week in late May when our son would be graduating from University, and her sisters (and her sister-in-law) would be coming into town to attend. Both of my wife's parents are deceased, and their children are scattered across much of the country – it would be so easy to drift apart, but they make earnest efforts to come together periodically. She encouraged me to go if I wanted. Two things then happened that I took as being signs in answer to my prayers. First, on the second day of the novena (I believe), my tax preparer called bearing particularly good news. Although circumstances peculiar to tax-year 2017 had left me fearing we might end up owing a substantial amount rather than get a tax refund, it turns out we did indeed get a refund. The amount was just enough to cover this pilgrimage. Anne was okay with me using the money for this purpose. Second, on the last day of the novena, having had no further revelation and still being a bit hesitant, I asked for another sign. In this case, on that last day, I did so after morning Mass in the basilica when I prayed the Rosary in front of the side-altar dedicated to the Blessed Virgin Mary. Finishing up the Rosary, I went out to my car, got in, and when the radio came on, the first words I heard were, "Our celebrant is going to be Fr. Emilio Garreaud, the National Director of Radio Maria USA." The leader of the pilgrimage was just beginning to say Mass.

I took that as the sign for which I had asked.

As an aside, it also bears mentioning that on the same day I called Radio Maria I had found an announcement online from Catholic evangelist Steve Ray, who was just starting a nine-day pilgrimage in the Holy Land, that he would be video-blogging daily.[50] I was, therefore, able to follow pretty much the announced itinerary for the Radio Maria pilgrimage over nine days, even as I was praying over nine days for guidance whether to go on it!

---

[50]"Holy Land with Fr. Scott Courtney April 2018 (SOLD OUT) 04 April 2018 to 13 April 2018," *Footprints of God Pilgrimages* [https://www.footprintsofgodpilgrimages.com/pilgrimage/holy-land-with-fr-scott-courtney-april-2017/]. (Note that the "2017" tag in the URL is correct, and takes you to the right place, the April *2018* pilgrimage.) I discuss this wonderful resource in more depth in Chapter Six.

Later that day, I called Nativity Pilgrimage and got the ball rolling – letting them know to expect my registration in the mail within a few days. I had other things I needed to do in preparation, as well. For one thing, my passport had expired late in 2017, so I jumped on getting it renewed. The posted turnaround time was eight weeks, so I knew I could not waste time. At that point, mid-April 2018, we were about fourteen weeks out. Well, it turned out that my new passport arrived much quicker than eight weeks – more like about four weeks.

I also tried to drum up a traveling companion, unfortunately to no avail. Going without Anne continued to bother me, both because we had never been apart for so long or so far and because I am a heart patient whose one brush with death via cardiac event had occurred at the end of an international flight. That had been eight years before, in 2010, landing back in Houston after two weeks in the UK, and resulted in the implantation of two stents. So far – despite my doing less than I really should to keep myself in shape (and despite yearly asschewings by my cardiologist mainly about my weight) – there had been no recurrence. But especially every time I fly, that weighs heavily on my mind. What if something similar, or worse, happened halfway around the world from Anne? If the situation were reversed, I know I would want to be right there.

But with her support and encouragement, I refused to let that fear dictate my actions.

And so, I was signed up and going off "by myself." Then....

In early June, the whole trip threatened to implode. By then I was wondering why no more information had been coming regarding itinerary, flights, and so forth. Then an email did come, bearing news that we were one pilgrim short from the required ten to make the trip. Nativity Pilgrimage had pushed the dates out by two weeks in an attempt to make the number. The revised dates – 13 to 21 August – impinged into the beginning of the fall semester 2018 at NSU, so that I would effectively miss the first week of classes. I gave the matter some thought and proposed a way for my classes to be covered, and my department head readily cleared me to go. At the same time, I took the initiative in recruiting a tenth pilgrim. A few weeks previously, when we were all together during my son's graduation, I told my wife's sister-in-law, Kristal, about the trip. Her response was a wistful, "I'd like to do that." So, I reached out to her. My wife and I agreed that Kris being Baptist and this being a Catholic pilgrimage would not be a problem – and it was not. She jumped at the chance, signed on, and fit right in. I know that her being along for the trip was a great comfort to my wife, for reasons that will become clear shortly.

Nativity Pilgrimage evidently jumped right on finalizing the logistics as soon as the requisite number of pilgrims were confirmed, because in short order I received an email with much more specific information: flights and times, an itinerary, lodging, and even the names of all the pilgrims, totaling twelve including Fr. Emilio and a "religious brother" of his order. Twelve? I never quite understood how that brother fit into the numbering, but he may have been supernumerary, benefiting from a frequent practice whereby a travel group includes a "free" traveler for every x who are paying. I do know that some months later, being on Nativity Pilgrimage's email list, I received notification of a promotion whereby for every five paid pilgrims a sixth would be included free. In that latter case, a minimum total of twenty paid travelers was necessary. From the very beginning, when I was inquiring about the pilgrimage to the Holy Land that I was considering joining, I was told that Nativity Pilgrimage was giving Radio Maria and Fr. Emilio a "special deal" because Jakoub Khaled, the owner of Nativity Pilgrimage, likes Radio Maria and Fr. Emilio in particular. It may be that over and above a comparable deal to what was later announced – one free for five paying, minimum twenty paying – the special deal behind our pilgrimage was essentially one free for five paying, minimum *ten*, with Fr. Emilio and his fellow religious being the two free. We were not, of course, privy to such information, so that is no more than speculation.

All in all, the itinerary closely matched the sample for a nine-day pilgrimage available on Nativity's web site. Examination of the hotels' web pages also was reassuring. Both were visually quite nice; I was particularly impressed by the fact that we would be staying in the Ron Beach Hotel in Tiberias – that is the very hotel frequented by Steve Ray for his pilgrimage groups. Given the excellent price on this pilgrimage, I had wondered what our accommodations would be like.

The itinerary also confirmed that, given the departure from Houston very late in the evening of "Day 1" and the even later arrival in Tel Aviv on "Day 2," plus a *very long* Tuesday 20 August as a result of flying westward on our return flight, it was apparent a full three days of this "Nine-Day Pilgrimage" were going to be taken up with travel. Only six days would be on the ground. But we would pack a lot into those days.

With much more "hard" information in hand, my excitement mounted and I doubled down on my "prep" work, mainly reading about the history of the Holy Land and Israel in general as well as doing specific research on the various things I knew we would be seeing, composing material to "drag and drop" into my travel blog when the time came. As far as the former goes, regarding the Holy Land both my religious background and my historical training give me solid grounding in Biblical History. I even teach an advanced-level course on the subject. After the Biblical period, however, ending about AD 70 with the destruction of the Temple, my knowledge got very sketchy beyond the region's peripheral significance in Roman and European history, mainly through the era of the Crusades (1095 1291), whereupon the region became a great historical black hole about which I knew virtually nothing. Even though I have lived through most of the history of the modern state of Israel, I had only a reasonably aware layman's knowledge of recent history, either. Yes, I read James Michener's *The Source* thirty-odd years ago, but I remembered almost nothing specific other than a haunting image of an Israeli chasing fleeing Arab Palestinians, begging them not to go – "We *need* you!"[51]

Deciding to rectify that lacuna in my knowledge, I read several good books and watched a couple of interesting movies – and kept a better record while doing so than I did for either previous pilgrimage.

Almost immediately, my scouting around on the Internet and mainly in Amazon turned up an interesting movie: *Cast a Giant Shadow* (1966), starring Kirk Douglas leading a cast that included John Wayne, Yul Brynner, and Angie Dickenson. Douglas played American Col. David "Mickey" Marcus, recruited by the fledgling Israeli state just after the United Nations voted for the partition of Palestine in November 1947, first as an adviser then ultimately as the first commanding general, overseeing the monumental task of building an alternate route through the mountains from Tel Aviv to the starving, besieged city of Jerusalem when the Arabs had blocked all other access. The movie ends tragically, just after that triumph in June 1948, with Marcus being killed by one of his own Israeli sentries late one night when, unrecognized in the darkness, he is unable to reply to a challenge with the proper password – in Hebrew.

Ending with the death of Mickey Marcus, however, left a huge part of the story of the 1948 War of Independence untold. As far as I am

---

[51] The scene is at approx. 91% through the Kindle edition, loc. 17637. I misremembered the details, of course. He Israeli was driving slowly along a column of Arab refugees, pleading in Yiddish, to no avail. His fellow Israelis considered him mad.

concerned, the best entrée into the events giving birth to the modern nation of Israel is to be found in the pages of *O Jerusalem!* by Larry Collins and Dominique LaPierre. Their book provides a wonderful, majestic account. It is solidly researched history written in an engaging, almost novelistic style that balances a myriad cast of characters from both sides of the conflict, Israeli and Palestinian, both in the attention they get and in the sympathy with which the authors treat them. By the time I finished it – it is a long book – I felt like I had practically lived through the events! The book is quite old at this point – it came out around 1970 – but it still would be my recommended starting point for anyone interested in the events of 1948. The more recent (2005) movie of the same name (at least outside the US; in the US it went by the title, *Beyond Friendship*) is, on the other hand, a disappointment. It clocks in at considerably less than two hours long (a mere 101 minutes) while attempting to tell a story that took over seven hundred pages in written form; the attempt to create new main characters to focus the narrative fails because they never get a chance to be developed into people worth the audience's concern.

I moved directly into *Return to Zion: The History of Modern Israel* by Eric Gartman, which is a more comprehensive account from the beginning of the Zionist movement in the late nineteenth century through just a few years ago, with reasonably heavy emphasis on the wars that Israel has endured and the seemingly irreconcilable conflict with the Palestinians. After *O Jerusalem*, *Return to Zion* made for pretty dry reading, but it went quickly, and I did feel like I now had a good handle on the overall history of the modern state up to just a few years ago.

Wanting something with a longer perspective, especially bridging the gap that I felt between the late thirteenth century and the twentieth century, I turned to *Jerusalem: The Biography*, by Simon Sebag Montefiore. Beginning with a detailed and compelling narrative of the siege and fall of Jerusalem and the destruction of Herod's Temple in AD 70, Montefiore then turns back to the city's earliest beginnings and proceeds to retell much of the story of the Bible quite solidly, albeit with a surprisingly secular slant, before continuing on into the post-Biblical history of the city with which I was much less familiar and which I found increasingly engaging. I picked up a lot of nuggets of information that I had never known before, such as that the Armenian Cathedral of St. James is dedicated to *both* of the Apostles by that name, both the Greater (son of Zebedee and brother of John) *and* the Lesser ("brother" of Christ)! That is just one example. As the book gets into the last couple of hundred years, characters become more fleshed out, most notably when telling the story of Montefiore's twice-great-uncle Moses Montefiore, an international financier and philanthropist involved with the Rothschilds in rendering great aid to Jews among whom the stirrings of what would become the Zionist movement were just being born. It is a fascinating book I am sure I will read again, especially if, as I hope, I return to the city.

Soon after I committed to the pilgrimage, I ordered the travel guide for *Jerusalem, Israel, Petra, and Sinai* from the excellent DK Eyewitness Travel series. Fully illustrated in color, with tons of cut-away schematic diagrams of significant sites as well as a pull-out city map and tons of information, I love these books - I have picked one up for every trip I have made in the past ten years and have never regretted it. They do tend to be a little pricey, which is why I usually drop back a couple of years to the previous edition. My one caveat would be DK's non-religious perspective.

Another guidebook that drew my attention was *The Holy Land for Christian Travelers: An Illustrated Guide to Israel*, by John A. Beck. Similar to, but not nearly to the degree of the DK guide, there are a lot of illustrations, maps, and diagrams - although rather than the terse descriptions offered by DK, the text is more of a narrative, with a heavy emphasis on pulling in scriptural references. It is from a general Christian perspective.

On the other hand, Rev. Charles Samson's similar *Come and See: A Catholic Guide to the Holy Land* is explicitly Catholic. It is a bit smaller in format than I anticipated - including the print - very dense but in concept very much like Beck's work except meticulously referenced and with considerable theological and spiritual discussion - "Issues Raised (what aspects of our faith are relevant to what we experience [at each location]; [and] Points of Reflection (in other words, how this spot might speak to you in your spiritual life, with special sections to aid seminarians in their formation to the priesthood)" (p. xix). It seems to have more illustrations, etc., than Beck, but they seem smaller and "muddier" - and it has very small type in order to fit it all in a mass-market paperback size book; nevertheless I found it a useful aid in prepping and expect it to be a valuable companion reference for years to come.

There was one final area of research I undertook as well, not so much for its relevance to the Holy Land as because of the circumstances in which Radio Maria was created and which remain central to its proclaimed mission: to spread the news of alleged apparitions of

Our Lady at Medjugorje that have been occurring on more or less a daily basis for nearly four decades. Contrary to my expectation, although it was mentioned from time to time while we were in Israel, Medjugorje did not turn out to be a major topic of conversation, and since I consider the Medjugorje phenomenon in more detail elsewhere in this book, I will leave discussion for that time.

About three weeks before our new departure date of 13 August, on 25 July, eight of our pilgrims met at the Radio Maria station and national headquarters in Alexandria, Louisiana, where Fr. Emilio said Mass and then presided over a meeting to discuss the pilgrimage, logistics, safety, what Fr. Emilio's experience has been with Nativity Pilgrimage and Turkish Airlines, and so forth, over a satisfying meal of homemade lasagna. That was the first time I met most of my fellow pilgrims: Fr. Emilio, of course; Kathie and Robert Duggan from Pineville, just north of Alexandria (and with whom I had previously talked over the phone); and Ann Bonnette, Ingrid Cannella-Newell, Donna Young, and Jennifer Stevens, all from Alexandria itself. Missing were Maria Biancavilla and Angela Spinelli from New York; Mary Bourgeois from Lafayette, Louisiana; Kris from Topeka, Kansas; and "Br. Miguel," the religious brother from Costa Rica.

But if you added up the names I just mentioned, you may have noticed that they total ... thirteen. I believe it was at this meeting that we discovered that there had been some kind of miscommunication regarding one of the pilgrims so that we were never actually down one from the required ten at all. Nor had there really been any need to push the dates out as was done. The way it turned out, however, ended up being for the best. For one thing, Kris got the opportunity to come along. For another, had we kept the original dates, I would have been either in the Holy Land or over the north Atlantic when I suffered a medical crisis.

Without going into needless detail, on the morning of Tuesday 07 August I presented at the Natchitoches Regional Medical Center emergency room with chest pain that had begun the previous day and occasional momentary lightheadedness that had begun earlier in the summer and increased in frequency to the point that I had consulted with my primary care physician a week or so prior. Given the number of medications I am on, every one of them listing "dizziness" and "lightheadedness" as side effects, we planned on doing a full medicines evaluation upon my return. Then the chest pain started – feeling *nothing* like when I had a heart attack eight years previously, by the way. There in the ER, everything looked just fine. Tests quickly determined that I did not have another heart attack. Then, while I was still connected to the monitor, awaiting discharge, I felt a wave of lightheadedness at the same time that the heart monitor started beeping frantically. My heart went into intermittent bradycardia – to the degree that at times there were several seconds between beats. This had been happening for months, explaining the dizziness, as my brain momentarily lacked oxygen, and ultimately the chest pain, as my heart muscle protested the diminished blood flow.

Things started happening very quickly at that point. By the end of the day, I had received a pacemaker.

I thought my pilgrimage was off, of course – but my cardiologist, Dr. Chris Ingram, whose office is in the hospital, was in the ER within minutes of the event and did not agree. He expedited the procedure to be performed immediately by his surgical partner, Dr. Dennis Britten, rearranged his own schedule to be able to check me out first thing on the morning of the following Monday 13 August – the day I was to depart – and cleared me to fly. I would spend the entire pilgrimage with my arm in a sling to keep the pacemaker leads from pulling loose from my heart before they had a chance to scar into place, but I would go.

Monday 13 August – Holy Land 2018 Day One: *Embarkation*

And so, within an hour of being cleared by Dr. Ingram at 08:00, following 06:30 Mass at the Minor Basilica and a Blessing for Travelers given by Fr. Luke LaFleur, Anne was driving me to Pineville, just north of Alexandria. There I joined and rode to Houston with Kathie and Robert, to join Fr. Emilio, Kris (who had spent the night before with Anne's sister in Houston), Mary, Donna, Ingrid, Jennifer, and Ann at the George Bush International Airport for a 19:05 flight (which actually left about 19:30). Flying Turkish Airlines, we would connect through Istanbul and ultimately land in Tel Aviv.

Tuesday 14 August 2018 – Holy Land Day Two: *Arrival in Israel*

I managed to briefly nap a couple of times during the thirteen-plus hour flight, maybe an hour or two each, but I never sleep well on a plane. We landed in Istanbul, Ataturk Airport, at about 09:00

CDT, almost on schedule despite our late departure. My phone's international plan kicked in almost at once after coming off "Airplane Mode," and I let Anne know we were on the ground via text message. Its time also shifted to the local time of about 17:00 TRT (the same time zone as Israel, just with a different abbreviation, so that I will report that from now on). Flying eastward as the sun progressed westward meant that we had a very short "night." By my calculations, we had crossed the dawn terminator in the mid-north Atlantic at about 50-55 degrees north latitude at a bit before 03:00 CDT. There was no Internet, however, which was frustrating.

Ataturk Airport itself was, as I overheard an irate woman describe it in a British accent, "crowded worse than a Mumbai train station." It was also sweltering. The men's bathroom was indescribably filthy. And we had a layover of almost three hours.[52] Our schedule had us departing Istanbul at 19:45 for a two-hour flight to Tel Aviv. We did not leave for an hour after that, for reasons I do not know. But we were finally off for the second and last leg of our trip.

> Now the LORD said to Abram, "Go from your country and your kindred and your father's house to the land that I will show you. And I will make of you a great nation, and I will bless you, and make your name great, so that you will be a blessing. I will bless those who bless you, and him who curses you I will curse; and by you all the families of the earth shall bless themselves." ... and they set forth to go to the land of Canaan. When they had come to the land of Canaan, ... the LORD appeared to Abram, and said, "To your descendants I will give this land." So he built there an altar to the LORD, who had appeared to him. (Gen. 12: 1-3, 5b, 7)

So did the Father of the three Faiths calling this land "holy" first come to it. As pilgrims, we too were answering the call of God, although our journey had not been so far (in time, whatever the distance), nor would our presence here last so long (at least physically, although I dare say its effects will last a lifetime, and a part of my spirit will always be there).

---

[52] Only later would I learn that commercial passenger traffic through Ataturk Airport would soon be shifted to a newly built Istanbul Airport, Ataturk being reserved to cargo and government flights. That undoubtedly explains – without excusing – the general sense of neglect.

We arrived outside Tel Aviv at Ben-Gurion International Airport, Terminal 3, at 22:30 Israel time. A kind young man in the passports line helped several of us get on the airport Wi-Fi, and immediately Internet and data kicked in.

This airport takes its name from David Ben-Gurion (1886-1973), the wild-haired first prime minister of Israel. An ardent Zionist, Ben-Gurion personally proclaimed the new State of Israel in May 1948 even as the British withdrew from the Palestinian Mandate which they had hitherto overseen, and the armies of the surrounding Arab powers invaded. He united the various Jewish militias into the new Israeli Defense Force and oversaw their successful defense of the fledgling nation. He earned the right to be called "Israel's Founding Father."

We met up with the last members of our party, Br. Miguel Alfaro, S.C.V., from Costa Rica as well as Maria Biancavilla and Angela Spinelli from New York. Maria was the Secretary of the Board of Directors of Radio Maria USA. We were all together now, and over the next week or so we would form a bond I believe will endure even if some of us never cross paths again. I wrote the following in my blog a day or so later when I finally got a chance to post something:

> As an aside, I must say that these are all incredibly nice people. Not that I doubted they would be, but I am really touched by how solicitous they are of my semi-handicapped state at this point, unable to use my left arm for much of anything for fear of 'unplugging' myself.... I could not ask for better companions!

As late as it was, we still had miles to go ... well, maybe not "before we slept." About midnight, we boarded our bus and headed north to Tiberias on the western coast of the Sea of Galilee, a little less than two hours away. Part of the way, Padre gave us an overview of the history, peoples, and cultures of Israel and Palestine, which he considers two separate countries. Tiberias itself began as a Roman city built by Herod Antipas (son of Herod the Great) and named in honor of the Emperor Tiberius. But it was not too long before the bus settled down to quiet and I am sure others, like me, dozed a bit despite the excitement of being in the Holy Land – even at night when we really could not see much.

We arrived at the Ron Beach Hotel about 01:45, I think. From watching Steve Ray's video blogs, I immediately experienced a somewhat disorienting sense of familiarity – even *déja vù* – when we pulled up and entered the lobby!

By the time I hit the sack, having unpacked what I needed, set up for the "next" day, showered, and eaten a very light snack left by the hotel since we were arriving so late, it was after 03:00. With eight hours' time difference from home, the time there was about 19:00 CDT, *still Tuesday evening* but making it now about 38 hours since I got up to head to Mass on Monday morning. It was nevertheless going to be a short sleep. We had arranged to meet for breakfast at 08:00, to head out for our first day's adventures at 09:00.

But I was in the Holy Land, the Land of the Patriarchs, Prophets, and Kings, the Land of Jesus. Even at night the view out across the Sea of Galilee from my balcony was impressive.

Wednesday 15 August 2018 – Holy Land Day Three: *Around the Sea of Galilee*

Our first full day in the Holy Land was the Solemnity of the Assumption, a Holy Day of Obligation commemorating the Assumption of Our Lady into heaven at the end of her earthly life. Preserved free from Original and Actual Sin by the prevenient graces of her Son, it was only right that her body should not know corruption any more than that of her Son. Such has the Church believed since time immemorial although it was only declared a dogma of the Catholic Church in 1950. We would be going to the Church of the Dormition on Mt. Zion later during this pilgrimage – one of the reputed sites from which Our Lady was taken up bodily into heaven – and had our schedule not changed for reasons unknown to me, it would have been very fitting for our Mass on this holy day to take place at the site of another great event associated with Mary – Cana, where Jesus worked his first miracle at her urging. But Cana would have to wait for Thursday. Instead, Mass was at a site central to her son's mission in Galilee, where he proclaimed a truth central to his very identity.

A phone call woke me up at 07:30, but a more extended time getting ready due to my impaired left arm made me a little late to breakfast. It was a magnificent buffet spread, however! As we ate, Padre informed us of the departure from our published schedule that I just mentioned. In this case, we flip-flopped the first two days, for the present remaining in the environs of the Sea of Galilee. It turned out to be the least of changes our itinerary would undergo.

I took the opportunity just before we were to assemble at the main door of the hotel to duck into the gift shop just off the lobby and pick up a simple wooden cord Rosary. I had discovered the one I meant to bring with me missing during the previous day, in the midst of our travels. As it would turn out, I had mislaid it before ever leaving home.

We boarded our George Garabedian Co., Ltd., tour bus a bit after 09:00, to be greeted by our guide, Anton "Tony" Azraq, and our driver, Wael. I do not believe I ever got Wael's last name, and we did not learn much about him other than that he was a fantastic, attentive driver who kept a large cooler in the front of the bus well stocked with cold water, which we were encouraged to drink in large quantities given the oppressive heat. We would, on the other hand, get to know Tony quite well over the next six days. Both he and Wael are Israeli Christians; Tony told us that Nativity Pilgrimage only works with Christian, specifically Catholic, guides and drivers. Tony is Melkite Greek Catholic, one of the Eastern Rite Catholic Churches in union with Rome as opposed to Eastern Orthodox who are not. He was born in Jerusalem and has deep ancestral roots in the Christian Quarter. Duties as a reservist in the Israeli Defense Force had not ended until too late for him to join us the previous night. I was particularly excited to find that he is a Biblical archaeologist, so that he and I could "talk shop." It quickly became obvious that he knows his stuff both historically and religiously. His professional knowledge and experience working on at least one of the sites we would be seeing added immeasurably to our pilgrimage experience. We all liked him at once with an affection that only grew over the next few days.

Our day began with a short bus trip around the northwestern shore of the Sea of Galilee to Capernaum. In the daylight, the rugged nature of the landscape was even more impressive than what I could see from the bus the night before.

Capernaum - "CAPHARNAUM THE TOWN OF JESUS," as the sign declares - was Jesus' home and base of operations for most of his period of ministry as described in the Gospels. It was also the home of half of the disciples, including the fishermen among the group - Peter and Andrew, James and John - as well as of Matthew the tax collector. Not inhabited for over a thousand years, the site is now an important archaeological site which includes a synagogue that has been dated mostly to the AD fourth century (the white part) atop a first-century foundation (the black part), as well as a church built over the ruins of what is said to have been St. Peter's house, where Jesus healed Peter's mother-in-law and many others:

> And when Jesus entered Peter's house, he saw his mother-in-law lying sick with a fever; he touched her hand, and the fever left her, and she rose and served him.
>
> That evening they brought to him many who were possessed with demons; and he cast out the spirits with a word, and healed all who were sick. This was to fulfil what was spoken by the prophet Isaiah, "He took our infirmities and bore our diseases." (Matt. 8: 14-17)

As a "church" it is dreadfully modern in its construction – in the round, open and airy. One might excuse its appearance because, in truth, its primary function is not as a church at all, but instead as a showcase for the archaeology. In the center, below a glass floor surrounded by rails visitors can see the excavated first-century remains of Peter's house, overlain by the remains of an octagonal fifth-century Byzantine church. Those same remains are also visible from the side, beneath the church, which is built specifically to leave the excavation undisturbed and protected from the elements.

One *might* excuse it for those sound reasons ... but did it *have* to look like the *Millennium Falcon* had just landed?

Padre said our first Mass in the Holy Land. His homily emphasized how *it was here, in this place* – at Capernaum, in the Galilee, in Israel in general – that the Son of God came into history and changed everything. *It was here, in this place* would figure in Padre's every homily and much of Tony's exposition throughout the coming week.

Immediately upon the Mass beginning, however, I noticed something odd. It was, as I mentioned above, the Solemnity of the Assumption, a primary feast day – and yet that is not the Mass that Fr. Emilio said. That was how I discovered that Pilgrimage Masses in the Holy Land generally do not follow the standard Catholic liturgical calendar. Instead, the Masses at the major pilgrimage sites are "of the place," wherever that place is, whatever day it is, following the Missal of the Franciscan Custody of the Holy Land. Tony would mention this Franciscan apostolate often during our pilgrimage. It has charge of most of the holy sites under the authority of the Catholic Church – and has held that charge since at least 1342. The Franciscan presence in the Holy Land began over a century earlier, with St. Francis' attempt to convert the Sultan of Egypt, as told in Chapter One. Francis failed in that effort, of course, but did so captivate the Sultan that he decreed that Francis' "little brothers" should not be molested. It was an indulgence that could not last, as such, beyond the death of that Sultan in

1238, but it set a precedent for Franciscan Catholic primacy in the Holy Land that would be renewed over a century later. In 1342, a half-century after the age of Crusades effectively ended with the fall of Acre (1291), Pope Clement VI secured an agreement with the Sultan of Egypt that the Franciscans would hold several holy places (including the Holy Sepulcher and the Cenacle, the Upper Room of the Last Supper) in custody for the Papacy, establishing the "Custody of the Holy Land." Over time the Franciscans slowly added to their holdings by maintaining a skillful *détente* with the various Muslim powers that came and went. Were it not for the Franciscan Custody, western Christians would doubtless have lost access to most or all of these sites. It has not been without cost, however. At times, under weaker or even hostile authorities the Franciscans have suffered grievous persecutions, and not always from Muslims – sometimes from various Orthodox sects, fellow Christians, as well. Their faith and determination to protect and preserve the holy sites has endured, nonetheless, and to that end, they have overseen archaeological digs, built and maintained churches and hostels, and welcomed pilgrims.

We quickly came to recognize the sites under the custody of the Franciscans by the presence of the Jerusalem cross, the distinctive "five-fold cross" or "cross and crosslets," a large "cross potent" (with four arms of equal length, each ending in a bar) with a smaller "Greek cross" (four arms of equal length *not* ended in a bar) in each quadrant. For almost a thousand years this emblem has been identified with the Holy Land. Said to symbolize variously the Five Wounds of Christ and the City of Jerusalem with the Four Gospels transmitting the Good News to the ends of the earth, it appeared on the coat-of-arms of the later Crusader Kings of Jerusalem in the thirteenth century. Today, the Jerusalem cross *gules* on a field *argent* (red on white) appears all over the Holy Land as the symbol of the Franciscan Custody. It marked most of the sites we visited during our time in the Holy Land, and our Pilgrimage Masses were consequently celebrated according to the Custody Missal. For the church above the house of St. Peter, that meant prayers and readings that were effectively those of 22 February, the Feast of the Chair of St. Peter, including Christ's entrusting the Prince of the Apostles with the Keys to the Kingdom of Heaven in Matthew 16: 19.[53]

---

[53] I will note the theme of each Mass of our pilgrimage and its Franciscan Custody readings. Here, of course, the theme was St. Peter the Apostle and his authority. The readings were 1 Peter 5: 1-4, Psalm 89, and Matthew 16: 13-19.

Afterward, we received our first exposure to Tony's insightful narrations as he described the archaeology of the site, including the adjacent ruins of the Jewish Synagogue – the one where Jesus preached.

> **And they went into Capernaum; and immediately on the sabbath he entered the synagogue and taught. And they were astonished at his teaching, for he taught them as one who had authority, and not as the scribes.** (Mark 1: 21-22)

According to John's Gospel – in the long Bread of Life Discourse in chapter 6 – this was where Jesus scandalized the people and many of his own followers by declaring:

> "Truly, truly, I say to you, unless you eat the flesh of the Son of man and drink his blood, you have no life in you; he who eats my flesh and drinks my blood has eternal life, and I will raise him up at the last day. For my flesh is food indeed, and my blood is drink indeed. He who eats my flesh and drinks my blood abides in me, and I in him. As the living Father sent me, and I live because of the Father, so he who eats me will live because of me. This is the bread which came down from heaven, not such as the fathers ate and died; he who eats this bread will live for ever." This he said in the synagogue, as he taught at Capernaum. (John 6: 53b-59).

Here! In this Place!

Tony also explained the social and political context of first-century Capernaum – near the border between Tiberias to the south, under the Tetrarchy of Herod Antipas, and Caesarea Philippi to the north, under the Tetrarchy of Antipas' brother Herod Philip. As such, it was a center for the collection of taxes and tariffs – and it was of course at Capernaum that the gospels introduce Levi, also known as Matthew, the tax-collector.

> [Jesus] came to his own city. ... [where] he saw a man called Matthew sitting at the tax office; and he said to him, "Follow me." And he rose and followed him. (Matthew 9: 1b, 9b)

Departing Capernaum, we drove only a short distance – none of our drives were long that day – to Tabgha, the putative site of the

Miracle of the Multiplication of the Loaves and the Fishes. The name comes from the Greek *Heptapegon*, "Seven Springs."

> Now when Jesus heard this, he withdrew from there in a boat to a deserted place by himself. But when the crowds heard it, they followed him on foot from the towns. When he went ashore, he saw a great crowd; and he had compassion for them and cured their sick. When it was evening, the disciples came to him and said, "This is a deserted place, and the hour is now late; send the crowds away so that they may go into the villages and buy food for themselves." Jesus said to them, "They need not go away; you give them something to eat." They replied, "We have nothing here but five loaves and two fish." And he said, "Bring them here to me." Then he ordered the crowds to sit down on the grass. Taking the five loaves and the two fish, he looked up to heaven, and blessed and broke the loaves, and gave them to the disciples, and the disciples gave them to the crowds. And all ate and were filled; and they took up what was left over of the broken pieces, twelve baskets full. And those who ate were about five thousand men, besides women and children. (Matt. 14: 13-21)

The site has been venerated as such since at least the fourth century when the Spanish pilgrim Egeria described it clearly:

> By the sea is a grassy field with plenty of hay and many palm trees. By them are seven springs, each flowing strongly. And this is the field where the Lord fed the people with the five loaves and two fish. In fact the stone on which Lord placed the bread has now been made into an altar.[54]

Nevertheless, the Bible itself read against the local geography makes this identification unlikely at best. In the first line of the passage from Matthew quoted above, Jesus reacts to news of the death of his cousin and herald John the Baptist (told in Matt. 14: 1-12) by seeking solitude, "with[drawing] from there in a boat to a deserted place by himself" (14: 13). From exactly where he is withdrawing is uncertain, given that the passage immediately preceding the digression about John the Baptist is that commonly entitled, "The Rejection of Jesus at

---

[54] "Egeria, describing the church at Tabgha," quoted in Lawrence R. Farley, *Following Egeria: A Visit to the Holy Land through Time and Space* (Chesterton, Indiana: Ancient Faith Publishing, 2014), chapter 7: "Galilee," Tabgha (Kindle edition at 66%)

Nazareth" (Matt. 13: 54-58).[55] Nazareth is miles away from any body of water. No one withdraws from Nazareth to *anywhere* in a boat. After being rejected by his hometown, Jesus evidently returned to the shore of the Sea of Galilee. The most natural assumption is that the disciples of John found him in Capernaum, his base during the Galilean ministry. That assumption only creates a bigger mystery, however. As we had just experienced, Tabgha is only about two miles from Capernaum, right along the shore. Hardly a place where Jesus would have sought refuge – by boat no less. The Gospels of Luke and John suggest an alternate location for the Multiplication, at Bethsaida, a bit further away, around the arch of the northern end of the Sea of Galilee, past the inlet of the Jordan River, more likely to have been accessed by boat. The whole conundrum is complicated, however, by the presence of a *second* miracle of Multiplication, the similar Feeding of the Four Thousand as related by Matthew and Mark, with *seven* loaves of bread and a small but unspecified number of fish. The Feeding of the *Five* Thousand identified by tradition with Tabgha was the *five* loaves and *two* fishes. Frankly, no explanation I have ever encountered, including that presented by a sign at Tabgha which acknowledges the mystery, really untangles the mess convincingly.

What is the significance of this? For me it is this: I am confident that the traditional identification of most of the holy sites is correct. Memories from generation to generation can be quite long, especially regarding astounding events such as surrounded Jesus in his earthly life. Archaeology has, moreover, confirmed the vast majority beyond any reasonable doubt. Some, nevertheless, may be and probably even are incorrect. Does that make visiting them superfluous? Not at all. Taking Tabgha as an example, recall that it has been revered as a holy site for at least 1700 years! Such longevity of cult can, itself, impart a sacrality worth experiencing. For so very long, our forefathers in the Faith have looked to Tabgha as the place to tangibly meditate on one of Jesus' greatest miracles – and I am perfectly happy to continue that tradition.

One way I did so was that in that church I lit my first candle on behalf of my friend Angel Kitishian, who grew up in the Armenian Quarter of Old City Jerusalem. She asked me to light a candle for her intentions in every church we visited. Sometimes in the overwhelming excitement and rush, I forgot (as I had at Capernaum), but in most cases, I did so.

---

[55] E.g., the New American Bible.

The Church of the Multiplication of the Loaves and the Fishes is another excellent example of our - or at least my - false expectation that the churches we would see in the Holy Land would be uniformly ancient, monumental, and majestic. The Church of the Holy Sepulcher in Jerusalem and the Church of the Nativity in Bethlehem are certainly all those things. Most are not. Most churches that we visited turned out not even to be that old. They are relatively modern, although they have ancient elements, as did the church at Tabgha, which specifically incorporates restored mosaics from the fifth-century church, including one laid directly in front of the rock which Egeria may have seen in an even earlier church. Overall, however, the churches of the Holy Land are, I am sad to say, relatively bland as far as decor goes. They are nothing like the spectacular churches of Italy or even more so Mexico, which *are* monumental and majestic even if not truly "ancient" in the case of Mexico.

I think there may be a reason for both "oddities," the lack of antiquity and the "blandness." As to the first, most of the churches are of recent construction because of the historical violence of that part of the world. We repeatedly heard from Tony how, during the invasion of 614, the Persians destroyed most of the earliest churches from the Byzantine era (taking that to be from the legalization of Christianity in 313). Although Emperor Heraclius famously expelled the Persians in 629, rebuilding had barely begun before the Muslims overran the Holy Land (636-638). During the Crusader Period (for simplicity's sake, roughly the 1100s) there was a flurry of church and monastery building, but before and after that period the status of Christian buildings remained precarious and dependent on the whim of the current Muslim ruler. Even the so-called "chivalrous Muslim" Saladin, the conqueror of Jerusalem in 1187, wiped out most of the churches of his day or converted them to mosques. The Franciscans had some success in mitigating the damage, especially once the Custody was formally established in 1342, but again it very much depended on the whim of the current Muslim ruler. Only during the last couple of centuries of the Ottoman Turkish period (1516-1917), could Christians build with any degree of security whatsoever. That was mainly because the Ottoman Empire's dubious status as "The Sick Man of Europe" (it nominally ruled much of the Balkans and was thus considered a European power, although one in a long, slow but accelerating decline from the mid-eighteenth century at the latest) put it at a disadvantage in dealing with other Christian European powers positioning themselves as protectors of the various groups of Christians in the Holy Land.

Some of the present churches date to that period, but the real game-changer came when the British captured Jerusalem in December 1917 and the subsequent Treaty of Versailles and nascent League of Nations confirmed their control of the area in the "British Mandate for Palestine." Of the 23 churches we visited in the Holy Land, the present buildings of eleven date from that later period, after 1917. Seven were built between 1750 and 1917, and only five date from before 1750. Since 1948, the Israelis have given full support to new Christian church construction – if only for the tourist revenues they generate.

As to the disappointing visual aspect of many of the churches, I imagine that, while almost every church we entered was Catholic, because pilgrims and Christian tourists from every faith tradition imaginable come to Israel and worship at them, the relative blandness is considered "ecumenical." Moreover, even those built before the 1960s have been renovated post-Vatican II, with predictable results. The few truly ancient churches we saw are, of course, exceptions to either of those rules, especially since they are governed under a different set of rules entirely – those of the "Status Quo" which I will explain in its time.

All that being said, even the plainest modern church in the Holy Land does, nonetheless, possess a unique aura stemming from the mystery it commemorates, if not from exactly *how* it does so. The power of place transcends any time-bound particulars of decoration. As I will elaborate presently, many of the early to mid-twentieth-century churches were designed by a single visionary architect intent on expressing the essence of the place and its mystery, its significance. Finally, preservation of elements from the most ancient buildings on the site is common. In the Church of the Multiplication, there is, beneath the altar straddling a large, flat rock (a post-Vatican II free-standing altar, naturally), a restored mosaic possibly dating from the fourth century, which has become iconic – that of two fish flanking a basket of bread like a set of parentheses. Oddly, the basket has only four loaves ... "oddly," until the symbolism is explained: Jesus Himself is "the fifth loaf." The symbolism is particularly effective during the celebration of Holy Mass on that altar – at which point the "fifth loaf" becomes tangibly present in the Consecrated Host.

We then drove a short distance to the Church of Peter's Primacy, right on the shore of the Sea.[56] The story is told basically as the last chapter of John's Gospel:

> After this Jesus revealed himself again to the disciples by the Sea of Tiberias; and he revealed himself in this way. Simon Peter, Thomas called the Twin, Nathanael of Cana in Galilee, the sons of Zebedee, and two others of his disciples were together. Simon Peter said to them, "I am going fishing." They said to him, "We will go with you." They went out and got into the boat; but that night they caught nothing.
>
> Just as day was breaking, Jesus stood on the beach; yet the disciples did not know that it was Jesus. Jesus said to them, "Children, have you any fish?" They answered him, "No." He said to them, "Cast the net on the right side of the boat, and you will find some." So they cast it, and now they were not able to haul it in, for the quantity of fish. That disciple whom Jesus loved said to Peter, "It is the Lord!" When Simon Peter heard that it was the Lord, he put on his clothes, for he was stripped for work, and sprang into the sea. But the other disciples came in the boat, dragging the net full of fish, for they were not far from the land, but about a hundred yards off.
>
> When they got out on land, they saw a charcoal fire there, with fish lying on it, and bread. Jesus said to them, "Bring some of the fish that you have just caught." So Simon Peter went aboard and hauled the net ashore, full of large fish, a hundred and fifty-three of them; and although there were so many, the net was not torn. Jesus said to them, "Come and have breakfast." Now none of the disciples dared ask him, "Who are you?" They knew it was the Lord. Jesus came and took the bread and gave it to them, and so with the fish. This was now the third time that Jesus was revealed to the disciples after he was raised from the dead.

---

[56] And when I say "we ... drove a short distance," I mean *a short distance!* – literally on the bus, around a corner, off the bus, and Bob's your uncle. Less than a minute, but even so I did not realize how close the two sites are until I traced our steps on Google Maps after I returned home. In fact, they are both technically considered to be at Tabgha, although it seems that the most common parlance seems to have that name, when used without qualification, connote the putative site of the Multiplication of Loaves while the Church of St. Peter's Primacy is accorded its specific name.

When they had finished breakfast, Jesus said to Simon Peter, "Simon, son of John, do you love me more than these?" He said to him, "Yes, Lord; you know that I love you." He said to him, "Feed my lambs." A second time he said to him, "Simon, son of John, do you love me?" He said to him, "Yes, Lord; you know that I love you." He said to him, "Tend my sheep." He said to him the third time, "Simon, son of John, do you love me?" Peter was grieved because he said to him the third time, "Do you love me?" And he said to him, "Lord, you know everything; you know that I love you." Jesus said to him, "Feed my sheep. Truly, truly, I say to you, when you were young, you girded yourself and walked where you would; but when you are old, you will stretch out your hands, and another will gird you and carry you where you do not wish to go." (This he said to show by what death he was to glorify God.) And after this he said to him, "Follow me."

Peter turned and saw following them the disciple whom Jesus loved, who had lain close to his breast at the supper and had said, "Lord, who is it that is going to betray you?" When Peter saw him, he said to Jesus, "Lord, what about this man?" Jesus said to him, "If it is my will that he remain until I come, what is that to you? Follow me!" The saying spread abroad among the brethren that this disciple was not to die; yet Jesus did not say to him that he was not to die, but, "If it is my will that he remain until I come, what is that to you?"

This is the disciple who is bearing witness to these things, and who has written these things; and we know that his testimony is true.

But there are also many other things which Jesus did; were every one of them to be written, I suppose that the world itself could not contain the books that would be written. (John 21: 1-25)

The large rock upon which was the "charcoal fire" over which Jesus grilled some fish and baked some bread is called the *Mensa Christi*, the "Table of Christ." There, by his threefold affirmation of love for Christ, Peter atoned for his earlier threefold betrayal during the Passion (by a *charcoal fire*). There, Jesus commissioned specifically him,

Peter, to feed and tend his sheep – but also foretold Peter's ultimate end in martyrdom.

As might be expected, given the story, there was easy access to the shore via a beach; several went down to the water, but I did not. I took the chance to chat a bit with Brother Miguel and satisfy my curiosity about his religious status. He had been introduced to us as a "consecrated layman" of the same order that Padre Emilio belongs to, the *Sodalitium Christianae Vitae* (Sodality of the Christian Life), a society of apostolic life founded by a layman in Peru in the 1970s. Specifically, I had wondered if his status was anything like a Benedictine Oblate such as I am. It is not. As I understand it, Brother Miguel's status is more akin to a monk or a friar, although his promises of poverty, chastity, and obedience are not considered religious vows. Members of the society live together in communities dedicated to the work of evangelization, especially to the marginalized, the youth, and the culture in general.

Lunch was at the nearby Tanureen Galilee Restaurant, where I had the full St. Peter's Fish, with the head left on it. I got it that way, I readily admitted, mainly for "bragging rights." Of course, the fish is really tilapia – but I had St. Peter's Fish full-on, on the Sea of Galilee!

I did not do it justice in the eating (especially the head, *especially* the eyes!). I just picked at it around the many bones.

Brother Miguel, on the other hand, *demolished* that thing.

It bears mentioning that the proprietors at Tanureen are Lebanese Christians. Throughout our pilgrimage, Tony steered us, whenever possible, to Christian establishments, for reasons that would become clear. Also, although our breakfasts and dinners were included in the pilgrimage package overall, our lunches were not. We were technically "on our own." Nevertheless, quite wisely, rather than letting us scatter, Tony always kept us together and handled everything, including collecting our money (typically ten to twenty dollars) and paying out. So, we all ate together, which is, I repeat, best. I cannot imagine the difficulty of trying to gather us back in after lunch to head out on our next jaunt were we *not* already together! Tony consistently chose our lunches well. *Everything* was quite good.

After lunch, it was time for the boat ride on the Sea of Galilee, departing from the Kibbutz Ginosar. A *kibbutz* is a Jewish commune. Kibbutzim originated as farming collectives during the early *Aliyah* (Return) movement that gave birth to the modern state of Israel. Most Jews stepped off the boats which brought them with nothing whatsoever to their name. They faced a landscape of largely wasteland. The current residents of the land, however sparsely it was settled, were increasingly hostile to the newcomers. None stood a chance on their own; cooperation was essential for any of them to survive. Initially agricultural, kibbutzim made the desert bloom, but have also diversified into many different activities as the Israeli economy has boomed. This particular kibbutz now derives the bulk of its income from tourism.

Kibbutz Ginosar is the location of the Yigal Allon Museum displaying the famous "Jesus Boat," a first-century fishing boat discovered during a drought in 1986, almost miraculously preserved intact. It also serves as the base for the popular excursion boats (of which there are at least two) which are close replicas of the Jesus Boat, albeit a bit larger. Ours was auspiciously named "*Noah*." As we motored out (which is another big difference between *Noah* and its prototype), once they had run up the American flag and played the *Star-Spangled Banner*, Tony gave an excellent talk about the Jordan River and the Sea of Galilee as an image of the Life of Christ, as well as describing the terrain we could see surrounding the Sea and the region of Galilee in general. Near the end of our cruise, which lasted about an hour, the boat captain invited everyone to learn to dance the *Hava Nagila, the* traditional Israeli celebration dance. I begged off since I cannot extend my left arm. I instead videoed it, to become one of the few items I posted to the Internet during the pilgrimage itself.

The Kibbutz Ginosar preserves the name of an important Bronze and Iron Age city located nearby, Kinneret, which also gave the Sea one of its several names through history. What we today generally call the "Sea of Galilee" has also been known variously as the "Sea of Tiberias," "Lake Tiberias," "Sea of Kinneret," "Lake of Gennesaret" – or "Sea of Ginosar."[57] Something I did not know but should have put two and two together to realize is that, although the Dead Sea to the south is famously the lowest lake in the world, at approximately 1300 feet below sea level, the Sea of Galilee is the *second*-lowest lake in the world at about 700 feet below sea level. Both are part of the northern extension of the geological fault line in the earth's surface known in East Africa as the Great Rift Valley. One effect of the lower altitude is a slightly higher atmospheric pressure, which made the heat (about 100°F) and humidity in that great bowl surrounded by mountains even

---

[57] Those names are all derived from Hebrew, Greek, or Latin. Another name, Turkish and used during the Ottoman period, is "Sea of Minya." Wikipedia, s.v. "Sea of Galilee," accessed 04 October 2019.

more oppressive than similar temperatures and humidity back home in Louisiana.

Returning to the dock, we did not go into the exhibit of the actual Jesus Boat but instead mounted back up for the ride to the Mount of the Beatitudes, during which we had time to pray the Divine Mercy Chaplet.

Of course, the Beatitudes are just the opening of the long Sermon on the Mount (Matthew chapters 5 through 7), but they are the most familiar part to almost everyone. They are perhaps the best exposition of Jesus' preaching of the Kingdom of Heaven and the blessings that are ours as part of the New Covenant:

> Seeing the crowds, he went up on the mountain, and when he sat down his disciples came to him. And he opened his mouth and taught them, saying:
>
> "Blessed are the poor in spirit, for theirs is the kingdom of heaven.
>
> "Blessed are those who mourn, for they shall be comforted.
>
> "Blessed are the meek, for they shall inherit the earth.
>
> "Blessed are those who hunger and thirst for righteousness, for they shall be satisfied.
>
> "Blessed are the merciful, for they shall obtain mercy.
>
> "Blessed are the pure in heart, for they shall see God.
>
> "Blessed are the peacemakers, for they shall be called sons of God.
>
> "Blessed are those who are persecuted for righteousness' sake, for theirs is the kingdom of heaven.
>
> "Blessed are you when men revile you and persecute you and utter all kinds of evil against you falsely on my account. Rejoice and be glad, for your reward is great in heaven, for so men persecuted the prophets who were before you.' ...
>
> And when Jesus finished these sayings, the crowds were astonished at his teaching, for he taught them as one who had authority, and not as their scribes. (Matt. 5: 1-11 ... 7: 28-29).

Along the path leading from the car park are stones inscribed with the Beatitudes, which a series of eight mosaics also depict iconographically inside the church, around the altar. Padre led a few of us inside the church in praying the Beatitudes. There was also, open on display, a manuscript of the Beatitudes in Gregorian chant. I so wanted to stand there and take the time to learn and intone them properly! – in Latin! – but there was too much else to see.

The Church of the Beatitudes was the first of several churches Tony pointed out to us as having been built by Antonio Barluzzi, an Italian known as the "Architect of the Holy Land." Between 1912 and his death in 1960, Barluzzi assisted or oversaw the building or restorations of at least 23 holy sites, mostly churches, in Israel and Jordan. By my count, we saw, if only in passing in a few cases, eleven of them. While some of them were not entirely to my taste as far as church architecture goes, they were all quite striking, incorporating a variety of styles usually calculated to evoke something specific to the individual church and its historical significance. In this case, an octagonal plan represented the eight Beatitudes. One interesting fact that Tony related is that this church, built in the late 1930s, was financed by *Il Duce*, Benito Mussolini, the Fascist leader of Italy.

On the way back toward Tiberias, we made an unplanned excursion to a newly excavated and just being developed site at what is the *actual* town of Magdala, which is near, but not identical to, a place long misidentified as the town of Jesus' most famous female disciple (after the Blessed Mother, of course).

The nature of the town, as revealed by the excavations, seems to finally explain precisely what Mary Magdalene's unspecified "sin" was, if not adultery, which scholars have long rejected. Built in close proximity to a cliff, just across the highway today, in which are hewn tombs, and thereby rendered unclean to observant Jews, it seems that Magdala was a town settled specifically by the unclean, which included sinners and lepers,[58] whose descendants such as Mary would then bear the stigma of being identified with such a place. Perhaps ironically, therefore, the excavations at Magdala have uncovered the first intact Torah lectern in the ruins of the town's synagogue.

Just adjacent, we went into a new development, *Duc in Altum* (Cast into the Deep), a retreat complex including the "Chapel of the Boat." The altar is inside a boat before a great picture window overlooking the sea. While there we met a young lady from the States, Colorado to be specific, who is volunteering at this new chapel dedicated to the women of the Bible, as evidenced by the columns bearing the names

---

[58] It must be remembered that "leprosy" in the Bible was not necessarily Hansen's Disease. Just about any persistent skin condition could be considered leprosy and incur the social stigma of being outcast.

of many of them, beneath an image of Our Lady of Guadalupe arching above in the dome of the vestibule.

From there, we traveled back to the Ron Beach Hotel. Along the way, Tony pointed out shrubbery along the road, which he identified as the very same "thorns" woven into the "Crown of Thorns," which the Roman soldiers mockingly imposed onto Our Savior's Sacred Head during his Passion. Unlike the huge knitting-needle like thorns we usually envision, these were much smaller but ended in something akin to fishhooks that would dig into the flesh when pushed down on his head in the form, not of a ring-like "crown," but more of a full-head "*cap*" as scholars now believe.

Back at the hotel, we had about an hour or so to rest and refresh before dinner. Some went to the pool; others went down to the beach itself. I got my computer online and started finalizing the previous blog posts.

Supper was at 19:30, and was, like all our meals there at the Ron Beach, a substantial buffet on several tables - salads, main courses, desserts of many different varieties, always with ample pita and hummus. I got a little from each spread, and it was all good.

When we were driving back to the hotel earlier, Tony had offered anyone who wanted to accompany him a trip walking up the street to the Scots Hotel, which has in its old wine cellar a fine wine-tasting bar. Kristal and I and several others took him up on the offer, meeting him out by the pool and setting forth up the street. There was a minor mishap along the way - "minor" in the bigger scheme of things, although we could not know it then when it seemed devastating. The sun had set, and the light was rapidly failing; I was walking along chatting animatedly with Ann, one of the ladies from Alexandria, when she missed her footing and took a fall, twisting her ankle severely in the process. Her ankle started swelling immediately, and although the consensus was that it had not broken, she was in very great pain. Angela sprinted like The Flash back up toward the hotel to arrange for a wheelchair and ice to put on the ankle. Meanwhile, we flagged down a cab, and Tony proceeded to pick the injured lady up under one arm and put her in the cab - as if she were a child; it was a sight to behold - and Tony skyrocketed in our estimation. It may have been at that point that I learned that he is a combat medic as well as a pilgrimage guide and Biblical archaeologist.[59]

One may wonder why I include this story. These things happen. It was part of the experience of that pilgrimage for us all. I know a lot of prayers went up for Ann that this misfortune would not derail her pilgrimage.

Having ridden back to the Ron Beach Hotel with Ann and gotten her situated, Tony rejoined us in short order and we proceeded up the street to the Scots Hotel and into its wine cellar where a gentleman named Omri gave us a lesson in wine-tasting in general and in particular the history of enology in Israel, with six samples (three white and three red) all of which were good. One of the whites, if I recall, was from a strain of grape just recently recreated through DNA analysis of seeds found in ancient tombs dating from the time of Jesus.[60] My preference in wines being red, one of those struck my fancy, however, and I ended up buying a bottle to take home. It was an interesting experience.

Our return walk to the hotel was without further mishap, thankfully. We arrived back after 22:00, and I ended up working on the blog until midnight – far too long! I was determined to maintain the blog

---

[59] I later found the following interesting articles including comments and information about Tony Azraq. All are from 2015 and are related to an Archdiocesan Pilgrimage from Indianapolis for which Tony served as guide:

Nancy Hoefer, "A land of calm and chaos: 'There's a militarized wall around Bethlehem?' and other Holy Land pilgrimage observations," *Archdiocese of Indianapolis: The Criterion Online Edition* (13 March 2015) [http://www.archindy.org/criterion/local/2015/03-13/holyland.html]

Nancy Hoefer, "Life for Catholics in Holy Land involves persecution and economic hardship," *Archdiocese of Indianapolis: The Criterion Online Edition* (20 March 2015) [http://www.archindy.org/criterion/local/2015/03-20/holyland.html]

Nancy Hoefer, "A land of calm, chaos and other Holy Land observations," *Diocese of Oakland: The Catholic Voice Online Edition*, vol. 53, no. 7 (06 April 2015) [https://www.catholicvoiceoakland.org/2015/04-06/inthisissue15.html]

Nancy Hoefer, "Tour guide gives cultural, historical and archaeological insight," *Diocese of Oakland: The Catholic Voice Online Edition* (18 May 2015) [http://www.catholicvoiceoakland.org/2015/05-18/inthisissue11.htm]

Also interesting considering some of the things Tony would tell us over the course of our time together is Nancy Hoefer, "How Catholics in central and southern Indiana can help keep a Christian presence in the Holy Land," *Archdiocese of Indianapolis: The Criterion Online Edition* (13 March 2015) [http://www.archindy.org/criterion/local/2015/03-13/holyland-sidebar.html]

[60] Richard Gray, "Could we soon drink the same wine as Jesus? DNA from ancient seeds is being used to resurrect 2,000-year-old drinks," *Daily Mail.com* (01 December 2015; updated 04 December 2015) [http://www.dailymail.co.uk/sciencetech/article-3341187/Could-soon-drink-wine-Jesus-DNA-ancient-seeds-used-resurrect-2-000-year-old-drinks.html]

better than in the past. But I approached it somewhat differently this time. I focused more on getting just the bare sequence of events recorded, as well as downloading, backing up, and posting a few of the many (usually dozens, sometimes a couple hundred) pictures I had taken through the day. As much as anything, I was creating a placeholder to which I would add details once I was home. I easily could have spent the entire night, each night, recording such detail. Nevertheless, however valuable a thorough and illustrated narrative might be in the future, a pilgrimage is about the here and now drawing from the there and then pointing toward the eternal. So, each night, I pulled myself away so as not to be too fatigued the next day. I believe that first night was actually the latest I stayed up.

Thursday 16 August 2018 – Holy Land Day Four: *The Galilee*

A specific, definitive reason "Galilee" is as often as not called "The Galilee" I have not been able to discern. The only clue lies in the etymology of the name, which seems to come from a Hebrew root meaning "district" or "circle,"[61] that is, that it originated as "The District." The first occurrence of the name could indeed be translated so: Isaiah 9: 1, which many Bibles render "Galilee of the nations" (e.g., RSV) is translated "the district of the nations" by the J[ewish] P[ublication] S[ociety] in *Tanakh 1917*.[62] Whatever the origin, the usage seems as ubiquitous and yet as unexplained as a similar usage here in Louisiana of "The Avoyelles" to refer to Avoyelles Parish southeast of Alexandria.

My alarm went off at 06:45, and I got up within (a few) minutes, dressed, and was down to breakfast (only a few minutes after) 07:30. It was pretty much the same amazing spread.

Ann was already there, her ankle visibly swollen even through the bandage wrapping, and giving her pain. But the hotel kindly allowed the use of the wheelchair, and fellow travelers took turns pushing her around. Unfortunately, for all my lingering sense of guilt that I was talking with her and thus distracting her when she fell, with one arm out of commission, I was not able to help.

---

[61] Multiple sources, including the Wikipedia article s.v. "Galilee," and Felix Just, S.J., "Biblical Geography: The Galilee," *Catholic Resources.org* [http://catholic-resources.org/Bible/Geography-Galilee.html], both accessed 12 August 2019.

[62] *Bible Hub* s.v. Isaiah 9: 1 [https://biblehub.com/isaiah/9-1.htm], accessed 12 August 2019.

I wrote earlier that many prayers were being offered up on her behalf. She was able to hobble whenever the wheelchair was not usable, even that first day, and if I am not mistaken, she was pretty much ambulatory by the day after.

We were on the bus by 09:00, headed to Cana, saying a Rosary. Ever since St. John Paul II introduced them in 2000, the five Luminous Mysteries have been suggested for Thursdays: The Baptism of Jesus; The Wedding at Cana; Preaching the Kingdom; The Transfiguration; and The Eucharist. Two of them were perfectly suited for this particular Thursday.

Along the way, we passed by the "Valley of the Pomegranates" - *Rimmonim* - and as we neared and entered Cana, Tony told us a sad fact. What was, a mere generation ago, a town of almost 100% Christian is now overwhelmingly Muslim, about 80%. Later he would explain why, and why that fact is not just sad but sobering.

Cana is, of course, most commonly associated with the site of Christ's first known miracle, the beginning of his public ministry. John tells the story:

> On the third day [after his arrival in Galilee and calling of Philip and Nathanael] there was a marriage at Cana in Galilee, and the mother of Jesus was there; Jesus also was invited to the marriage, with his disciples. When the wine failed, the mother of Jesus said to him, "They have no wine." And Jesus said to her, "O woman, what have you to do with me? My hour has not yet come." His mother said to the servants, "Do whatever he tells you." Now six stone jars were standing there, for the Jewish rites of purification, each holding twenty or thirty gallons. Jesus said to them, "Fill the jars with water." And they filled them up to the brim. He said to them, "Now draw some out, and take it to the steward of the feast." So they took it. When the steward of the feast tasted the water now become wine, and did not know where it came from (though the servants who had drawn the water knew), the steward of the feast called the bridegroom and said to him, "Every man serves the good wine first; and when men have drunk freely, then the poor wine; but you have kept the good wine until now." This, the first of his signs, Jesus did at Cana in Galilee, and manifested his glory; and his disciples believed in him." (John 2: 1-11)

Without getting into the full exegesis of this passage, note that the first emphasis is on the presence of Mary, his mother, *then* Jesus and his disciples, and that she instigates him to the performance of this first known "sign," which "manifested his glory" such that "his disciples believed in him." Her command to the servants, "Do whatever he tells you," are Mary's last recorded words in scripture. Moreover, forget any idea that Jesus' addressing his mother as "woman" was a sign of disrespect; it was, on the contrary, a term of profound respect in the contemporary Middle East. Finally, the Church holds this event to effect Jesus' sanctification of the covenant of marriage,[63] sacramentalizing it by transforming into wine the very element of water which he had previously sanctified at his Baptism, the element by which we are likewise sacramentally reborn.

We parked and walked to the Wedding Chapel at Cana. "The Cana Catholic WEDDING CHURCH" – so proclaims the sign, in three languages: English, Arabic, and Hebrew – is a brilliant white church that would not be out of place in Italy, I think. It is, of course, under the Franciscan Custody of the Holy Land.

Although we passed through the main body of the church, we did not linger there, heading directly into the small chapel set aside for what was the highlight of that stop. There, in the Cana Catholic Wedding Church, our only married pilgrim-couple, Robert and Kathie with whom I rode from Pineville to Houston, renewed their vows of holy matrimony within a week of the 54th anniversary of their wedding. In a short homily, Padre Emilio expanded on Tony's commentary regarding the meaning of the Aramaic word, *ishshah*, "woman," and tied Jesus' usage here to the beginning and ending of the Bible, from Eve, the first woman in Genesis, to the Great Sign in Revelation, the Woman Clothed with the Sun.

Then Tony took us down to the archaeological area beneath the church, after which he let us loose to take pictures. I think he said that a large stone jar-like object usually described as being one of those described in the scripture quoted above was not that, but rather an olive press; the stone water jugs were quite a bit smaller, what is called a "gallon" in this case being more the volume of a liter or quart.

For whatever reason, some among our group dawdled when he called us via Whisper back to the bus, and we started for Nazareth late ... and consequently almost missed having Mass there. Some speculate, although I do not know for sure, that we may have been relegated to a

---

[63] *Catechism of the Catholic Church*, §1613.

smaller, nondescript chapel rather than the main basilica because we arrived almost fifteen minutes late. Tony mildly, but firmly and deservedly, rebuked the group later when he had a chance. It was not a mistake we made twice!

As we entered the town where Our Lord "grew and became strong, filled with wisdom," "increas[ing] in wisdom and in stature, and in favor with God and man" (Luke 2: 40, 52), in the loving home of his mother Mary and his earthly father Joseph, from whom he learned his trade of construction[64] through many unrecorded years, Tony described Nazareth then and now. Then it was a quiet village of a few hundred at most, perhaps founded as a refuge for descendants of David after the return from the Babylonian Captivity; now it is a city of over 100,000, only about one-fifth Christian. Again, the overall trend is an increasing Islamic population, nearing fifty percent. There has been friction in the almost exclusively Christian and Muslim lower or "Arab" town, including clashes, protests, and counter-protests surrounding preparations for Pope John Paul II's visit there in 2000, Muslim plans to build a large mosque overshadowing the basilica, and an Israeli government moratorium on any construction at the site at all – satisfying no one.

In any case, we entered Nazareth, parked, and hastily walked to where we did hear Mass *at* the Basilica of the Annunciation, albeit in a chapel which we reached via a spiral staircase that seemed to go up forever. We were nonetheless still within mere yards of where God entered history via a virgin's womb. Padre Emilio's homily focused on that as the obvious theme – "*here*" is where the Incarnation happened; "*in this place*" is where Mary said "Yes," "*Fiat.*" As the First Creation began with *fiat*, so did the New Creation.[65]

At that Mass, in the Basilica of the Annunciation, Padre let me lead the chanting of the *Magnificat*, and I believe that I also began chanting the Responsorial Psalm at that time. By the end of the pilgrimage, I had even managed to introduce chanting the *Kyrie* in Greek, and the *Sanctus* and *Agnus Dei* in Latin. Give me an inch when it comes to Latin in the liturgy, and I will happily take a mile! It was not totally

---

[64] "Carpenter," although the most common, is not the *best*, translation of the Greek *tekton*. "Carpenter" implies merely working with wood – which Joseph would have done – be he would have also worked with stone. "Builder" works; perhaps even better would be "Contractor."

[65] The Mass of the Basilica of the Annunciation was, per the Franciscan Custody Missal, that of the Feast of the Annunciation, 25 March. The readings were Isaiah 7: 10-14; 8: 10; Psalm 40; and Luke 1: 26-38.

HOLY RAMBLINGS

out of the blue, of course. After the first Mass, at Capernaum, had been without any singing, I had offered.

The Basilica of the Annunciation occupies the site of the home in which young Mary lived with her parents. Like many houses in the area in the ancient world, the house backed up to a hill, extending back into a cave, either natural or hollowed out. The parts of the house backed up into such a grotto enjoy somewhat ameliorated temperatures compared to the extremes – generally hot, as it was on the day we were there – out in the open.

> **In the sixth month the angel Gabriel was sent from God to a city of Galilee named Nazareth, to a virgin betrothed to a man whose name was Joseph, of the house of David; and the virgin's name was Mary. And he came to her and said, "Hail, full of grace, the Lord is with you!" But she was greatly troubled at the saying, and considered in her mind what sort of greeting this might be. And the angel said to her, "Do not be afraid, Mary, for you have found favor with God. And behold, you will conceive in your womb and bear a son, and you shall call his name Jesus. He will be great, and will be called the Son of the Most High; and the Lord God will give to him the throne of his father David, and he will reign over the house of Jacob for ever; and of his kingdom there will be no end." And Mary said to the angel, "How shall this be, since I have no husband?" And the angel said to her, "The Holy Spirit will come upon you, and the power of the Most High will overshadow you; therefore the child to be born will be called holy, the Son of God. And behold, your kinswoman Elizabeth in her old age has also conceived a son; and this is the sixth month with her who was called barren. For with God nothing will be impossible." And Mary said, "Behold, I am the handmaid of the Lord; let it be to me according to your word." And the angel departed from her.** (Luke 1: 26-39)

The basilica itself is what I might term "mod-exotic" – a conical tower above a brilliant white facade built in the 1960s. It is built, like most churches in the Holy Land are, on a site previously occupied by a series of earlier churches going back to the fourth century. The "conical tower" is said to be in the shape of an inverted lily, representing Mary's purity, but I would never have guessed that. Etched into the concave front of the main body of the church are images of Mary and the Angel, below which are the four Evangelists, with the words, in Latin, "*Verbum Caro factum est et habitavit in nobis* – The Word became Flesh and dwelt among us."

Inside the basilica, in the grotto where the Angel appeared to Mary, the altar bears a similar inscription – with a crucial addition: "VERBUM CARO HĪC FACTUM EST – THE WORD BECAME FLESH HERE." I think the dot above the *I* in *HIC* represents a macron, which I do not believe I have ever seen in an inscription. In Latin, vowel length matters, both in pronunciation and in distinguishing two different words, and is indicated with a macron: *hic* with a short *i* means "this one"; *hīc* with a long *i* means "here." But the orthographic convention of adding the macron is modern, a convenience for students. I, therefore, read it as lending emphasis – *"here!"* – to the word that is added – "The Word became flesh *here!*" *It was here, in this place!*

Again, the fairly recent construction of the church stripped away a little of the sense of antiquity even though intellectually, I knew I was standing on two thousand years of history going to the very beginning of our Faith. And it was overall quite magnificent, especially on the inside.

The magnificence was the perfect setting for something we barely finished Mass in time to witness – the Franciscan friars' Noon Procession before the grotto, beginning with the *Angelus* sung in Latin:

> *Angelus Domini nuntiavit Mariae. – Et concepit de Spiritu Sancto.*
> *Ave Maria....*
> *Ecce ancilla Domini, – Fiat mihi secundum verbum tuum.*
> *Ave Maria....*
> *Et Verbum caro factum est, – Et habitavit in nobis.*
> *Ave Maria....*

I said to Ingrid immediately afterward, "*Tell* me Latin is not better!" It was beautiful.

Taking us outside to a portico surrounding the plaza before the basilica, Tony explained the archaeology and history of the basilica with his usual skill and insight. One part I found particularly memorable: Why was Mary so "greatly troubled" by the appearance of the angel? The encounter is believed to have taken place in the grotto at the rear of the house, one of the uses of which was to isolate women during times when they became ritually impure, once a month. Suddenly, the angel appeared, not what we imagine as having wings and a halo, but rather in the form of a man, a *strange* man, in a culture where women, certainly young women, did not associate with men who were not related to them. What young woman, alone, suddenly confronted with a strange man where he should not have been – *in the most private part of her home* – would *not* be afraid?

He then again turned us loose to explore the site. I mainly concentrated on revisiting the grotto, *the* place where the Incarnation happened. I then returned to a bench in the shade of the portico by the entrance to the plaza and, along with a couple of others from our group, found cheap entertainment watching an elderly docent regulating entry into the basilica. He took his job quite seriously, especially regarding women with uncovered shoulders or knees. We watched him turn several away, and others would have been had they not been able to pull out scarves they could drape strategically to accomplish the job to his satisfaction. All the guidebooks say to dress with decorum when attending these holy sites, and it pays to heed them. Not all were policed so strictly as here, however!

I was, in any case, feeling a bit worn down at the time. Recall, I was only a little more than a week out from my pacemaker implantation. And although I knew of another holy site of interest nearby, I was dissuaded from seeking it out by Fr. Emilio's characterization when I asked where exactly I might find the Church of St. Joseph the Carpenter: "Many steps, many steps!" It is a decision I regret.

Part of the same complex with the Basilica of the Annunciation, connected to it by the Franciscan convent, St. Joseph's church stands over another grotto containing the ruins of what is said to be St. Joseph's house and workshop, likely where the angel appeared to Joseph:

> **When his mother Mary had been betrothed to Joseph, before they came together she was found to be with child of the Holy Spirit; and her husband Joseph, being a just man and unwilling to put her to shame, resolved to send her away quietly. But as he considered this, behold, an angel of the Lord appeared to him in a dream, saying, "Joseph, son of David, do not fear to take Mary your wife, for that which is conceived in her is of the Holy Spirit; she will bear a son, and you shall call his name Jesus, for he will save his people from their sins." All this took place to fulfil what the Lord had spoken by the prophet: "Behold, a virgin shall conceive and bear a son, and his name shall be called Emmanuel" (which means, God with us). When Joseph woke from sleep, he did as the angel of the Lord commanded him; he took**

his wife, but knew her not until she had borne a son; and he called his name Jesus." (Matt. 1: 18b-25)

The Holy Family would probably have lived here once they returned from their extended journey to Jerusalem and thence into Egypt. Such is the ancient belief, in any case. A round plaque declares, "*HIC ERAT DOMUS ILLIS* – HERE WAS THEIR HOME."

I did not actually see this, however.

Nor did I see something else – *the upper, main level of the Basilica of the Annunciation!* Only in research after returning from the pilgrimage did I learn that, like the Basilica of St. Francis in Assisi, there is another whole church atop that which I saw. Looking up from the area before the grotto into the conical tower, little did I realize I was looking up through another level.

There was so much to see and so little time. I do treasure the time I had, the memories I have of being there, in that place. But I want to go back!

We ate lunch in a little café almost directly next door to the basilica – wonderful, thick, and loaded *gyros* sandwiches, dripping with *tahini* sauce. Perhaps it was, as my wife later suggested, merely the time and place, but in my memory, that was the best *gyros* sandwich that I have ever eaten!

Walking back to where Wael waited with our bus the same way we had rushed earlier, we passed back through the Old Market of Nazareth, containing plenty of open-air shops and scads of souvenirs. Tony had, however, cautioned us against shopping indiscriminately, for several reasons. One, he said, was that most of the religious items we would find here would be cheap "fakes," made in China, whereas he promised to take us to a shop in Bethlehem whose wares he guaranteed would be authentic, crafted by local Christians, purchasing which would indeed be the best support we could offer in a society becoming increasingly hostile to them. Along those same lines, secondly, he said most of these sellers here would indeed be Muslims, and buying from them would, in effect, be supporting them against the local Christians. Thirdly, the prices would be inflated. Finally, especially, he warned us against using credit cards except where he advised. He promised to tell us beforehand of legitimate, safe sellers – and did, throughout the trip – but he also cautioned us never to *ask* him about one in their presence, which would put him in a bad spot.

On the way back to the bus, Tony ducked into a sweets shop and came out with a good-sized box of Israeli *baklava*, which was enjoyed by all once we got back on the bus.

Tony is *The Man*.

Leaving Nazareth, we set forth toward Mount Tabor. Along the way, we saw the Jezreel Valley, which figures prominently in several episodes in the Old Testament, and Tony pointed out Nain, the home of the widow whose son Jesus raised from the dead.

> **Soon afterward he went to a city called Nain, and his disciples and a great crowd went with him. As he drew near to the gate of the city, behold, a man who had died was being carried out, the only son of his mother, and she was a widow; and a large crowd from the city was with her. And when the Lord saw her, he had compassion on her and said to her, "Do not weep." And he came and touched the bier, and the bearers stood still. And he said, "Young man, I say to you, arise." And the dead man sat up, and began to speak. And he gave him to his mother. Fear seized them all; and they glorified God, saying, "A great prophet has arisen among us!" and "God has visited his people!" And this report concerning him spread through the whole of Judea and all the surrounding country.** (Luke 7: 11-17)

But we did not go there. Tony says it is not safe. Nain is, he said, a case study of the "Soft Jihad" by which Islamists are spreading their ideology so insidiously. The town was completely Christian in 2004, when they allowed one family of Islamic "refugees" from Iraq to move in. These were almost immediately followed by relatives, relatives of relatives, and so forth, and as soon as their population reached critical mass, they took over and imposed *shariah* law, Christians fled, and the town is now entirely Muslim. The church which sponsored that original family is now closed, virtually a garbage dump behind the newly constructed mosque. Tony related the story as a warning. Europe, he said, is already far along the same road; The United States has pulled back, for now, explaining why – for President Donald Trump's policies regarding Islamic "refugees" alone – *he likes Trump* (something he had said already several times, but not with such force as this time).[66]

---

[66] I have been unable to verify Tony's characterization of the recent history of Nain. The Wikipedia article on Nain (s.v. "Nein," accessed 12 August 2019) is quite short, sketchy in its coverage, and silent on recent history, but provides demographic information across

A lot of Israelis like Trump, we discovered. A surreal collective doubletake occurred the first time we saw signs proclaiming, "Trump Make Israel Great," which we did on several occasions especially once we arrived in Jerusalem. I found out later that these were relics of a massive campaign just a few months previous welcoming Trump to Israel for the long-proclaimed but just as long-delayed (through multiple presidential administrations, over twenty-plus years) formal recognition of Jerusalem as Israel's capital by moving the US Embassy there from Tel Aviv. The Muslim Palestinians are not nearly so fond of Trump, however, and in fact within our group of pilgrims there were a variety of opinions expressed about the US President.

Debating contemporary politics is not the purpose of a pilgrimage, however. We turned our attention to the imposing sight of Mount Tabor, most famously the traditional site of the Transfiguration:

> And after six days Jesus took with him Peter and James and John his brother, and led them up a high mountain apart. And he was transfigured before them, and his face shone like the sun, and his garments became white as light. And behold, there appeared to them Moses and Elijah, talking with him. And Peter said to Jesus, 'Lord, it is well that we are here; if you wish, I will make three booths here, one for you and one for Moses and one for Elijah.' He was still speaking, when lo, a bright cloud overshadowed them, and a voice from the cloud said, 'This is my beloved Son, with whom I am well pleased; listen to him.' When the disciples heard this, they fell on their faces, and were filled with awe. But Jesus came and touched them, saying, 'Rise, and have no fear.' And when they lifted up their eyes, they saw no one but Jesus only." (Matt. 17: 1-8).

Standing apart from the mountain range running southeast from Carmel directly to its west, between Nazareth to the nearer west and the Sea of Galilee to the east, Mt. Tabor rises like a great dome above the eastern end of the Jezreel Valley. It is only one possibility for the location of the Transfiguration, but since the fourth century, the

---

time that would seem to tell a different story: 1596, "119 households, all Muslim"; 1922, "a population of 157, all Muslims"; 1931 "189, still all Muslims"; "270, all Muslims" – but nothing more recent. The website *Seetheholyland.net* has an entry for the town, however, which while silent on any recent Muslim takeover does have an entry for a Catholic church at Nain, with pictures, noting that it is administered by the Franciscan Custody of the Holy Land but is "seldom open. The key is held by the Franciscans on Mount Tabor." [https://www.seetheholyland.net/nain/], accessed 12 August 2019.

tradition has been firm. Its relative isolation does make it a suitable "high mountain apart"; perhaps that relative isolation, similar to that of far-off Mount Sinai, helped inspire, long before the time of Christ, its association with the one true God, El Shaddai, "God Most High." At the summit today, built on fourth- to sixth-century Byzantine and twelfth-century Crusader foundations, the Franciscan Roman Catholic Church of the Transfiguration (finished in 1924) affords spectacular views both without and within.

Without: The great church is more traditional in its lines than others we've seen, with elements of the old Romanesque basilica design aesthetic evident in twin towers flanking a large round arch above the entryway, itself surmounted by arched windows – all visible for the length of a long avenue lined with palm, olive, and other trees, flowering gardens, between the Franciscan monastery, ancient monastic ruins, and low stone walls as you approach the church itself.

Within: Beyond the nave dominated by dark wooden pews and hardwood flooring focused on an altar (around which a group of pilgrims was finishing Mass), four or five features draw the eye's attention. First, directly behind the altar, a lower sanctuary, barrel-vaulted with mosaics of sunny-gold and sky-blue culminating in an exquisitely intricate stained-glass window featuring peacocks flanking a golden chalice – I hesitate to count the barrel-vault mosaic and the stained-glass window as one or two foci. To either side, however, long-narrow side-chapels each with altars beneath arching mosaics of sunny-golden angels adoring the Blessed Sacrament against a sky-blue backdrop. But the dominant focus is up – to an upper sanctuary on a second level, another altar visible behind which, in the apse, shines a brilliantly-glowing sun-golden mosaic of the transfigured Christ (with a sky-blue backdrop), flanked by Moses and Elijah in the clouds, with more earthly-hued (that is, *not* sun-golden nor sky-blue) disciples Peter, James, and John looking on in amazement from beneath. Overall, the impression is – and I cannot help but repeat it yet again – brilliant sunny golden light from the sky-blue heavens penetrating down into our darker, duller, earthly realm.

And without, again: The summit of Mount Tabor affords a commanding view in all directions, especially toward the south-southwest and the broad, flat Jezreel Valley shading into the foothills wherein lies Megiddo, the site of crucial battles past and future.

Getting to the top and seeing those sights, however, entailed a rather harrowing trip in a smaller van up a very windy road with a ton of switchbacks. I cannot imagine being a pilgrim of old having to climb this mount on my own two feet (more likely all fours, feet and hands). The ancient pilgrims' path has almost five thousand steps cut into the bedrock of this mountain. And until 1954 and the opening of the road, access to the mount is said to have been by donkey along a similarly oft-precarious path – which makes me wonder at the building of the various churches through time, especially the most recent, Barluzzi's church, finished thirty years earlier.

On the drive back to Tiberias, we prayed the Chaplet of Divine Mercy. Once again, we had a bit of free time before dinner. I took my prayer book and headed down to the beach, where I found, I believe, every one of the ladies with our group benefiting from a "fish pedicure." Tiny fish would school up around exposed flesh, especially the feet, and nibble away at any dead skin. I understand that it feels quite weird. I would not know; despite their urging, I did not take off my shoes and socks and dip my feet. I did take some video but did not post it. Let's just say that, after a couple of minutes, the clip ends abruptly with an indignant, "*Are you filming this?!*" – to which I admitted, "Y*es*," and shut it down.

I retreated up a way to enjoy the beach as I prayed the abbreviated version of Vespers in the *St. Benedict's Prayer Book* which I had brought along instead of my regular breviary. I knew I would not have time to pray the full Lauds and Vespers on most days. There is so much to see, so much to do, so much to ponder. *St. Ben's Black Book*, as I call it, is considerably lighter and more portable, as well.

After dinner, I returned to my room to get my packing in order. We were to have our bags outside our doors at 08:00, have breakfast, and head out for the south the next day, bidding the Galilee *adieu*. I was also a bit worried, however. At some point earlier in the day, one of my companions had pointed out a discolored spot on my shirt right where my still-bandaged-but-healing incision was under my left collarbone. The bandage, it turned out, was thoroughly saturated with blood-tinged watery secretions – something they had not warned me might occur. I knew by then that one of our pilgrims, Mary from Lafayette, was a nurse, so I asked her to take a look at it. She did so and seemed somewhat concerned that it might be a little inflamed.

In this case, the time difference and the wonders of modern technology worked well for me. The time in Israel – at that point about 20:30 – is eight hours ahead of the time back home, which was therefore in the noon hour. My wife works at the local hospital which hosts my cardiologists' clinic as well. I took a couple of good photographs of the incision and sent them to her, called her to explain, and asked her if she could walk over to the clinic and show it to one of the nurses. A few minutes later, she called me back. The surgeon who implanted the pacemaker had been standing just inside the door when Anne was explaining the situation to the nurse. He looked at the pictures and told her to let me know there was nothing to worry about, that it was looking about like he would expect at eight or nine days out from surgery. I was greatly reassured, and even though the wound slowly wept for most of the rest of our time in the Holy Land, I mostly managed to put it out of my mind.

Friday 17 August 2018 – Holy Land Day Five: *From Galilee to Bethlehem via Mount Carmel*

Our third day "on the ground" in the Holy Land deviated even further from what we had received as an itinerary. The first two days had swapped; this third would have had us either having driven to Bethlehem the night before or doing so first thing in the morning (I was never entirely sure which), followed by a full day's activities there. We did drive to Bethlehem, but we took all day to do it. And there was no activity in Bethlehem once we arrived except for happy hour in the bar and dinner in the restaurant. I asked Padre at that point how we were going to squeeze the announced four days' remaining activities into our three days remaining. He seemed not to see a problem.[67]

I did, but I had no say in the matter, and found that to be a source of grace. Not immediately, of course, and not until much later would I be able to begin to articulate why.

In March 2019, months after my pilgrimage to the Holy Land, Fr. Ryan Humphries, leader of the pilgrimage to Italy in 2014, returned briefly to Natchitoches and gave a presentation about his extended pilgrimage to various shrines in Europe the previous autumn, of 2018, including an attempt to walk the Camino de Santiago in which, as he said, "Nothing went right. Not a *single thing* went right." Unlike some others I know would have been (i.e., the man in my mirror), he was not upset by the experience, however, instead drawing from it a profound spiritual lesson which he conveyed to us in a near two-hour account he called, "Perspective, Journey, Docility." Calling his wayward journey a metaphor for the spiritual life (which is, in fact, quite

---

[67] To see just how far our actual itinerary departed from the original plan, check out Appendix One: *Itineraries: Ideal and Reality*. Other than arrival and departure, only one thing actually occurred on the day it was planned.

in line with the predominant, spiritualized, usage of the word "pilgrimage" in the *Catechism of the Catholic Church*[68]) Fr. Humphries furthermore defined "docility" as, with a nod to the old *Baltimore Catechism*, "that virtue by which we listen to the Holy Spirit and are then happy to do what the Holy Spirit directs us in any given moment, not being obsessed with my plans – which were thorough, complete, and reasonable – but be open to whatever it is that the Lord wants, whether or not anything at all in three months of travel goes right." Another way to look at it is etymologically, noticing the etymological connection of "docility" with "doctor" and "doctrine," all of which come from the Latin verb *doceo, docere*, "to teach." Not for nothing does the Vulgate Latin of 1 Kings 3: 9, wherein Solomon prays to the Lord for wisdom, in most translations rendered as his asking for an "understanding heart," in fact say that he asks for "*cor docile* – a *teachable* heart." As Fr. Humphries did with the various mishaps that befell him and repeatedly derailed his "thorough, complete, and reasonable" plans, we should seek God's will in the various mishaps of our own life – our own journey – especially our own pilgrimage.

In all honesty, "mishaps" is not at all how I would characterize much on our pilgrimage – Ann's stumble and briefly sprained ankle would be the most serious, I think; a mislaid wallet later in the trip being another; my condition not being precisely a mishap, it nonetheless provided me with an opportunity for grace – as did Ann's ankle injury, showing us the power of healing prayer; the mislaid wallet providing a demonstration of generosity by those who found it as well as those who went out of their way to return it to its owner; and my impaired state – most frustratingly having my left arm in a sling for the duration of the pilgrimage – made me more dependent on others than I am used to, forcing a certain humility on me that I am not used to either.

But "mishaps" were not causing the deviations in our itinerary, at least to my knowledge. Truthfully, to this day, I do not know precisely what was behind them, which is itself a source of frustration to me. The reasons were never explained to us and may well have had something to do with the chronic state of unrest in the Middle East. I have read and been told that having an experienced native guide when in the Holy Land, one who keeps his ear to the ground, who has connections, who can perceive the sometimes quickly-changing situation and judge when, for instance, it might not be a good day to venture into

---

[68] See footnote 4 above.

the West Bank Palestinian Authority regardless of what the packaged itinerary might dictate - and who has the ability to change plans quickly - can be crucial. Tony was, I believe, eminently qualified in all those areas. I have no idea whether such was behind any of our changes, but I trust that those changes occurred for good reasons, whatever they were. Nevertheless, I like to *know* these things. I like plans to be made - "thorough, complete, and reasonable" plans, as were Fr. Humphries'. And I like things to go as planned. When they did not - radically so on this pilgrimage - I consciously had to put my trust in Tony and Fr. Emilio ... and in God. It was a lesson in docility, humbling myself and submitting myself to the assuredly benign will of others. Such is the nature of any packaged group tour, of course, but it is even more so in the nature of a pilgrimage. Perhaps, in the context of a pilgrimage, by its nature, it was easier to give everything up to God, accept that all would play out as He willed it, taking from the experience a lesson in docility. But I pray it is a lesson that will stick with me in other aspects of my life.

As an aside, before taking up with the account of that third full day in the Holy Land, allow me to comment on something we unfortunately missed. Without a doubt, our pilgrimage provided us with a lot, covering an incredible amount of spiritual and religious geography in a very short time. With two calendar days getting to Israel and one getting back home, our "Nine-Day Pilgrimage" really comprised only six days on the ground. And, doubtless because of time as well as money, two places were never on our itinerary that I really wish had been. One is in the north, and one is in the south. I will leave discussion of the one in the south for later.

In the north of Israel, I would have liked to have gone to Banias. As a Catholic group, passing up Banias was ironic, because *it was there, in that place* (to paraphrase Padre), near Caesarea Philippi (not to be confused with Herod's seaport town of Caesarea Maritima), in the shadow of a great pagan shrine to Pan below Mount Hermon, that Jesus asked his Apostles the most crucial question of all - "Who do *you* say that I am?" ...

> Now when Jesus came into the district of Caesarea Philippi, he asked his disciples, "Who do men say that the Son of man is?" And they said, "Some say John the Baptist, others say Elijah, and others Jeremiah or one of the prophets." He said to them, "But who do you say that I am?" Simon

Peter replied, "You are the Christ, the Son of the living God." And Jesus answered him, "Blessed are you, Simon Barjona! For flesh and blood has not revealed this to you, but my Father who is in heaven. And I tell you, you are Peter, and on this rock I will build my church, and the powers of death shall not prevail against it. I will give you the keys of the kingdom of heaven, and whatever you bind on earth shall be bound in heaven, and whatever you loose on earth shall be loosed in heaven." (Matt. 16: 13-19)

Minimizing the significance of this exchange, including the event of Jesus changing Simon's name to "Rock," based on some fancied distinction in meaning between Greek *petros* (Peter's name bestowed here) and *petra* (the form used a few words later) as respectively "little rock" and "big rock," does not work contextually either in Greek (the language of the Gospel we have received) or Aramaic (the probable language Jesus and his apostles would have been speaking) or in the specific setting.

In Greek, since *petra* is grammatically feminine, giving that name to a man necessitated changing the grammatical gender to masculine ending in *-os*. In Aramaic, like in English, moreover, there is no distinction anyway – *kepha* is *kepha*, "rock" is "rock." What Jesus did *not* say was, "You are a pebble, and on this boulder I will build my church...." It would have made no sense whatsoever. He said, "You are a rock, and on this rock I will build my church...."

Where this happened, the geographical context is crucial, as well. The locale is rich in associations that converge uniquely *there, in that place*. The name, "Banias" derives from an ancient pagan shrine which the Greeks identified with the god Pan. It is an incredibly picturesque site, a colossal rock escarpment at the southwestern end of Mount Hermon, the highest peak in the area, permanently snowcapped at over 9,000 feet elevation, long considered almost to touch heaven and therefore one of the most sacred of mountains. The name "Hermon" is related to the Semitic root *h.r.m*, meaning "consecrated." A more ominous connotation in legend has Mount Hermon as the place where Lucifer and his angels fell from heaven to earth. Out of a cavern underneath the rock (an entry to the underworld, a gate to hell), there flows one of the primary sources of the Jordan River. A *rock* from which flow the *waters* which give Israel *life*. With the Roman imperial associations of Caesarea Philippi, finally, consider the immense symbolism of Jesus essentially founding the life-giving Roman Catholic

Church on Peter in that specific location! "And the gates of hell shall not prevail against it" (Matt. 16: 18 KJV). It is a shame we did not go there!

But we could not do everything. And the fact is that, again thanks to Nativity Pilgrimage and Tony, we ended up doing so much more than *was* on our itinerary – starting with Friday.

I woke up at 06:30 and went out on my room's small balcony, where I prayed Lauds from *St. Benedict's Prayer Book*. Then I finished packing up and had my bags waiting outside the door for the bellhop at 08:00. Breakfast was every bit as good as on previous mornings, although, at this point, I was really missing bacon! I stopped in briefly to the little gift shop and picked up a mug showing the mosaic from the Church of the Multiplication of the Loaves, then we were off.

About an hour's drive across northern Israel brought us to within sight of the Mediterranean Sea at Haifa, located on the spur of the long ridge of Mount Carmel that sticks out into the Sea. Along the way, Tony related the story of the Prophet Elijah and the Prophets of Ba'al:

> When Ahab saw Elijah, Ahab said to him, "Is it you, you troubler of Israel?" And he answered, "I have not troubled Israel; but you have, and your father's house, because you have forsaken the commandments of the Lord and followed the Ba'als. Now therefore send and gather all Israel to me at Mount Carmel, and the four hundred and fifty prophets of Ba'al and the four hundred prophets of Asherah, who eat at Jezebel's table."
>
> So Ahab sent to all the people of Israel, and gathered the prophets together at Mount Carmel. And Elijah came near to all the people, and said, "How long will you go limping with two different opinions? If the Lord is God, follow him; but if Ba'al, then follow him." And the people did not answer him a word. Then Elijah said to the people, "I, even I only, am left a prophet of the Lord; but Ba'al's prophets are four hundred and fifty men. Let two bulls be given to us; and let them choose one bull for themselves, and cut it in pieces and lay it on the wood, but put no fire to it; and I will prepare the other bull and lay it on the wood, and put no fire to it. And you call on the name of your god and I

will call on the name of the Lord; and the God who answers by fire, he is God." And all the people answered, "It is well spoken." Then Elijah said to the prophets of Ba'al, "Choose for yourselves one bull and prepare it first, for you are many; and call on the name of your god, but put no fire to it." And they took the bull which was given them, and they prepared it, and called on the name of Ba'al from morning until noon, saying, "O Ba'al, answer us!" But there was no voice, and no one answered. And they limped about the altar which they had made. And at noon Elijah mocked them, saying, "Cry aloud, for he is a god; either he is musing, or he has gone aside –

– at this point in Tony's narrative, I interjected that the original Hebrew basically means, "he's gone to the bathroom"! –

– or he is on a journey, or perhaps he is asleep and must be awakened." And they cried aloud, and cut themselves after their custom with swords and lances, until the blood gushed out upon them. And as midday passed, they raved on until the time of the offering of the oblation, but there was no voice; no one answered, no one heeded.

Then Elijah said to all the people, "Come near to me"; and all the people came near to him. And he repaired the altar of the Lord that had been thrown down; Elijah took twelve stones, according to the number of the tribes of the sons of Jacob, to whom the word of the Lord came, saying, "Israel shall be your name"; and with the stones he built an altar in the name of the Lord. And he made a trench about the altar, as great as would contain two measures of seed. And he put the wood in order, and cut the bull in pieces and laid it on the wood. And he said, "Fill four jars with water, and pour it on the burnt offering, and on the wood." And he said, "Do it a second time"; and they did it a second time. And he said, "Do it a third time"; and they did it a third time. And the water ran round about the altar, and filled the trench also with water.

And at the time of the offering of the oblation, Elijah the prophet came near and said, "O Lord, God of Abraham, Isaac, and Israel, let it be known this day that thou art God in Israel, and that I am thy servant, and that I have done all these things at thy word. Answer me, O Lord, answer me, that this people may know that thou, O Lord, art God, and that thou hast turned their hearts back." Then the fire of the Lord fell, and consumed the burnt offering, and the wood, and the stones, and the dust, and licked up the water that was in the trench. And when all the people saw it, they fell on their faces; and they said, "The Lord, he is God; the Lord, he is God." And Elijah said to them, "Seize the prophets of Ba'al; let not one of them escape." And they seized them; and Elijah brought them down to the brook Kishon, and killed them there.

And Elijah said to Ahab, "Go up, eat and drink; for there is a sound of the rushing of rain. So Ahab went up to eat and to drink. And Elijah went up to the top of Carmel; and he bowed himself down upon the earth, and put his face between his knees. And he said to his servant, "Go up now, look toward the sea." And he went up and looked, and said, "There is nothing." And he said, "Go again seven times." And at the seventh time he said, "Behold, a little cloud like a man's hand is rising out of the sea." And he said, "Go up, say to Ahab, 'Prepare your chariot and go down, lest the rain stop you.'" And in a little while the heavens grew black with clouds and wind, and there was a great rain. And Ahab rode and went to Jezreel. And the hand of the Lord was on Elijah; and he girded up his loins and ran before Ahab to the entrance of Jezreel." (1 Kings 18: 17-46)

One interesting perspective offered by Tony was his likening the priests and prophets of Ba'al, who did, after all, sacrifice babies to their god, to today's terrorists. So brainwashed and desensitized to the slaughter they committed, they became addicted to it, and there was little if any hope that they could be "rehabilitated." Alive, they would be an ever-present threat. Elijah *had to* execute them. Tony's implication was clear.

He also described what we were about to see. Haifa, the principal port, industrial, and military center of northern Israel, is now a heavily secularized city with a substantial representation of five different faiths: Judaism, Christianity, Islam, Bahá'í, and Druze. Rather amusingly, when someone asked for confirmation that the two cylindrical towers that could be seen off in the distance to our north were a nuclear power plant, Tony deadpanned, "No, that's a chemical plant." Right.

The first thing we stopped and viewed, from afar, was the shrine and gardens of the Bahá'í World Center. To summarize very quickly, Bahá'í was founded in Iran in the nineteenth century nominally as an offshoot of Shi'a Islam but in reality, a syncretic hodge-podge of different religions. Its two founders were the Báb, a forerunner figure proclaiming the advent of a new messiah, and his disciple Bahá'u'lláh. Thirteen years after the Báb's martyrdom in 1852, executed by the Iranian authorities, Bahá'u'lláh proclaimed himself to be that new messiah, and spent his final quarter-century in a Turkish prison in Acre (just north of Haifa), where he died in 1892. Their followers eventually honored Bahá'u'lláh's wishes that he be buried on Mount Carmel. They purchased a large tract on the side of the ridge which they developed into the immense terraced gardens that can be seen today. Tony likened them to the Hanging Gardens of Babylon. They were spectacular, supplying a great photo-op for everyone in our party.

(There is another amusing tidbit: Bahá'í is by no means a large religion by numbers, only a few million adherents around the world, but each member is obligated to automatically deposit one dollar per day into the bank account of the religion. The religion is not large, but it is very, very rich! Also, each member is obligated to spend one month during his life there in Haifa, tending the tomb and the gardens, for free.)

It was only a short ride from the Bahá'í Gardens to the Stella Maris Monastery of Discalced Carmelite monks. Overlooking the Mediterranean Sea, named for one of the titles of Our Lady, "Star of the Sea," Stella Maris is the center of Carmelite spirituality throughout the world. Although for much of its history the order founded on Mount Carmel during the Crusades suffered intermittent exile from the mountain, in the nineteenth century they returned for good and rebuilt the current church right above the cave in which Elijah hid from Ahab's Queen Jezebel immediately subsequent to the prophet's execution of her priests of Ba'al as described by Tony only a short time before we arrived in Haifa.

Padre said Mass again in a side chapel, taking as his theme that Mary is our Mother in heaven, praying for us constantly.[69] We then had a few minutes taking pictures in the monastery's church, which is another gorgeously accoutered basilica. A magnificent dome contains colorful scenes from both the Old Testament and the New Testament,

---

[69] The Custody Missal Mass of the Place for Our Lady of Mount Carmel included the readings Galatians 4: 4-7, Psalm 15, and John 19: 25-37.

including Elijah in the chariot of fire. The main altar is raised above the grotto, into which we could enter and stand where Elijah had taken refuge. A famous statue of Our Lady of Mount Carmel can be seen there as well.

Outside the front of the church stands a sad monument to French soldiers slaughtered on the site in 1799. The way the story goes, when Napoleon Bonaparte's campaign against the Ottoman Empire that year floundered, he left his sick and injured soldiers in the care of the Carmelites as he retreated. The Turks overran the monastery, killed the helpless French, and drove out the monks. The truth is, however, far worse. Rather than have his casualties slow down his retreat or possibly be captured by the Turks, Napoleon himself ordered them killed. The Turks did overrun the monastery and expel the monks, who would not return for almost forty years, but they are not guilty of the atrocity of which they are accused. [70] When the Carmelites returned, almost forty years later, they built the present church and monastery, not surprisingly, as a fortress.

Several of us stepped across the street to an observation area looking out across the Mediterranean Sea to the left and Haifa Bay ahead to the right, toward the mountains of southern Lebanon in the distance, Acre (the last Christian stronghold in the Holy Land, whose fall marked the end of the Age of Crusading in 1291) a bit closer. We also checked out the souvenir shop. Although Padre and Tony had cautioned us again that we should buy our tourist items in Bethlehem, I went ahead and picked up specifically Carmelite items – a new scapular and a wooden Rosary with the Carmelite emblem on it.

Tony had planned for us to eat at the immediately adjacent Santa Maria Coffee and Snacks, where Wael had parked the bus, but it was too full. So, we loaded back up and rode maybe half an hour south before stopping at a small restaurant beside the road to Jaffa-Tel Aviv. Along the way, Tony gave us another very impassioned and frank assessment of the current state of Christians in Israel vs. those in the Palestinian territories, the latter of whom he insists are not "Palestinian" at all but rather "Aramaean." "Palestinian," he says, is a political neologism created to describe a comprehensive ethnic nationalistic identity that never truly existed for the multiethnic peoples inhabiting the land of Palestine before the establishment of the state of Israel. It was coined to further the aims of Muslim Arabs who refused and refuse to recognize the new state. The condition of Christians in the

---

[70] Simon Sebag Montefiore, *Jerusalem: The Biography* (New York: Knopf, 2011) p. 349.

Palestinian territories is grim; Islam is quickly worming its way into the remaining historically Christian territories, with Christians as quickly being squeezed out. It seems a demographic inevitability, the "Soft Jihad" described before with reference to Nain compounded by the fact that although under Israeli law a man can have only one wife, under Muslim *shari'a* law he may have up to "four." As far as the state is concerned, only one of those is legally his wife; the other three are not. They are consequently classified as "unwed mothers," entitling them to state support. Effectively, that gives the "husband" four incomes, and puts the state in the position of economically subsidizing the expansion of Islam. The same is happening in Western Europe and to a lesser degree in the United States. Tony again expressed his support for Trump and vigorously defended the recent "Nation-State" Law passed by the Israeli Knesset, affirming that Israel is a Jewish state. Predictably, that drove the Muslims into another periodic frenzy of riots and protests. The law does not disenfranchise other faiths, Tony insisted; it merely requires that the government be officially Jewish, and that the president and the prime minister be Jewish. It disenfranchises no one; it explicitly grants freedom of religion and worship for Israeli citizens although it gives a preferential option to Judaism. As an Israeli Christian, Tony expressed his strong preference to be governed by a tolerant Jewish government rather than to be persecuted as would be inevitable under an Islamic *shari'a* state.[71]

We pulled up at the restaurant, the name of which I, unfortunately, did not note, and considerable time trying to nail it down has been fruitless. I am almost certain it was run by a Druze family. The Druze are another minority religious sect with some pretty odd beliefs (for instance, the Messiah, when he comes, will be born of a man!), usually persecuted by Islam but historically allies of similarly persecuted Christians. A large courtyard centered around a fountain with many hanging plants. It was too hot to eat outside, however. Inside, our choices for lunch were chicken or felafel; it being Friday, I got the felafel, which was exceptional. I shared a table with Brother Miguel, who told me more of his background and life in Costa Rica, including how he got to know Fr. Emilio, who was instrumental in bringing him into the Sodality, their religious order.

---

[71] Recall that I said he joined us fresh off a term of service in the IDF. He specifically serves in the Reserve. He nevertheless puts the lie to the statement I have heard that only Jewish Israelis are allowed to serve in the IDF. Jewish Israelis are *required* to serve; most others are not required, but many, such as Tony, *choose* to serve as volunteers.

As we continued the drive southward, it was time for our daily Rosary. We said one, as well as a Divine Mercy Chaplet, almost if not every day we were in the Holy Land.

By the standards of this pilgrimage and the size of Israel, it was a relatively long drive to Jaffa, just north of (and technically part of) Tel Aviv. Tony described the highly secularized Tel Aviv as essentially the San Francisco of Israel – with all the decadence that implies. Little more than a hundred years old, founded on wasteland essentially as a beachhead for Zionism's fledgling *Aliyah* "Return" movement, it is the most populous and wealthiest city in Israel. It is the world center for diamond trading, which is the number one source of Israel's national income. Second is military manufacturing. Third is Jesus – i.e., the pilgrimage industry. Tel Aviv is also renowned for its beaches, where the immoral depravity comes out full swing. Tony said he would not take his children there.

Jaffa stands just to the north of, and is a stark contrast with, shiny new Tel Aviv. Ancient "Joppa" is the oldest harbor in the Mediterranean Middle East, dating from the fourth millennium BC. It figures in myth and legend as well as history. Biblically, it is the site of two critical events involving St. Peter: the raising of Tabitha and the vision which began the evangelization of the Gentiles.

The first story goes like this:

> Now there was at Joppa a disciple named Tabitha, which means Dorcas or Gazelle. She was full of good works and acts of charity. In those days she fell sick and died; and when they had washed her, they laid her in an upper room. Since Lydda was near Joppa, the disciples, hearing that Peter was there, sent two men to him entreating him, "Please come to us without delay." So Peter rose and went with them. And when he had come, they took him to the upper room. All the widows stood beside him weeping, and showing coats and garments which Dorcas made while she was with them. But Peter put them all outside and knelt down and prayed; then turning to the body he said, "Tabitha, rise." And she opened her eyes, and when she saw Peter she sat up. And he gave her his hand and lifted her up. Then calling the saints and widows he presented her alive (Acts 9: 36-41).

Which is immediately followed by the second story as the entirety of Acts 10:

At Caesarea [Maritima] there was a man named Cornelius, a centurion of what was known as the Italian Cohort, a devout man who feared God with all his household, gave alms liberally to the people, and prayed constantly to God. About the ninth hour of the day he saw clearly in a vision an angel of God coming in and saying to him, "Cornelius." And he stared at him in terror, and said, "What is it, Lord?" And he said to him, "Your prayers and your alms have ascended as a memorial before God. And now send men to Joppa, and bring one Simon who is called Peter; he is lodging with Simon, a tanner, whose house is by the seaside." When the angel who spoke to him had departed, he called two of his servants and a devout soldier from among those that waited on him, and having related everything to them, he sent them to Joppa.

The next day, as they were on their journey and coming near the city, Peter went up on the housetop to pray, about the sixth hour. And he became hungry and desired something to eat; but while they were preparing it, he fell into a trance and saw the heaven opened, and something descending, like a great sheet, let down by four corners upon the earth. In it were all kinds of animals and reptiles and birds of the air. And there came a voice to him, "Rise, Peter; kill and eat." But Peter said, "No, Lord; for I have never eaten anything that is common or unclean." And the voice came to him again a second time, "What God has cleansed, you must not call common." This happened three times, and the thing was taken up at once to heaven.

Now while Peter was inwardly perplexed as to what the vision which he had seen might mean, behold, the men that were sent by Cornelius, having made inquiry for Simon's house, stood before the gate and called out to ask whether Simon who was called Peter was lodging there. And while Peter was pondering the vision, the Spirit said to him, "Behold, three men are looking for you. Rise and go down, and accompany them without hesitation; for I have sent them." And Peter went down to the men and said, "I am the one you are looking for; what is the reason for your coming?" And they said, "Cornelius, a centurion, an upright and God-fearing man, who is well spoken of by the whole Jewish nation, was directed by a holy angel to send for you to come to his house, and to hear what you have to say." So he called them in to be his guests.

The next day he rose and went off with them, and some of the brethren from Joppa accompanied him. And on the following day they entered Caesarea. Cornelius was expecting them and had called together his kinsmen and close friends. When Peter entered, Cornelius met him and fell down at his feet and worshiped him. But Peter lifted him up, saying, "Stand up; I too am a man." And as he talked with him, he went in and found many persons gathered; and he said to them, "You yourselves know how unlawful it is for a Jew to associate with or to visit any one of another nation; but God has shown me that I should not call any man common or unclean. So when I was sent for, I came without objection. I ask then why you sent for me."

And Cornelius said, "Four days ago, about this hour, I was keeping the ninth hour of prayer in my house; and behold, a man stood before me in bright apparel, saying, 'Cornelius, your prayer has been heard and your alms have been remembered before God. Send therefore to Joppa and ask for Simon who is called Peter; he is lodging in the house of Simon, a tanner, by the seaside.' So I sent to you at once, and you have been kind enough to come. Now therefore we are all here present in the sight of God, to hear all that you have been commanded by the Lord."

And Peter opened his mouth and said: "Truly I perceive that God shows no partiality, but in every nation any one who fears him and does what is right is acceptable to him. You know the word which he sent to Israel, preaching good news of peace by Jesus Christ (he is Lord of all), the word which was proclaimed throughout all Judea, beginning from Galilee after the baptism which John preached: how God anointed Jesus of Nazareth with the Holy Spirit and with power; how he went about doing good and healing all that were oppressed by the devil, for God was with him. And we are witnesses to all that he did both in the country of the Jews and in Jerusalem. They put him to death by hanging him on a tree; but God raised him on the third day and made him manifest; not to all the people but to us who were chosen by God as witnesses, who ate and drank with him after he rose from the dead. And he commanded us to preach to the people, and to testify that he is the one ordained by God to be judge of the living and the dead. To him all the prophets bear witness that every one who believes in him receives forgiveness of sins through his name."

While Peter was still saying this, the Holy Spirit fell on all who heard the word. And the believers from among the circumcised who came with Peter were amazed, because the gift of the Holy Spirit had been poured out even on the Gentiles. For they heard them speaking in tongues and extolling God. Then Peter declared, "Can any one forbid water for baptizing these people who have received the Holy Spirit just as we have?" And he commanded them to be baptized in the name of Jesus Christ. Then they asked him to remain for some days. (Acts 10: 1-48)

We had, of course, bypassed Caesarea Maritima, but we were now in Jaffa, at the Church of St. Peter. It is one of two Catholic churches in Israel oriented toward the west, toward Rome, giving physical expression to the symbolism of the latter story, the shift in narrative focus in the book of Acts from evangelization of the Jews to its great missionary drive *toward Rome*. We entered the church and prayed our Divine Mercy Chaplet for the day. Then we took pictures both inside the church and looking down on the waterfront. In the distance, we could see the blue waters of the Mediterranean Sea lapping against a long, white-sand beach. Nearer where we were, the waterfront was rockier, an appropriate setting for a plaque briefly describing this ancient port as well as the myth of Andromeda, princess of Joppa, chained to those rocks as a sacrifice to a sea monster but rescued by Perseus. Yes, I saw *Clash of the Titans*.

Then we were off once more, on the last leg of this day's drive – *toward Jerusalem* – passing Tel Aviv, passing Ben-Gurion Airport, and passing at least one area where burned-out husks of transport vehicles form a memorial of a tragic incident in the lead-up to the outbreak of the 1948 War. I had asked Tony if we would see these as we started along the highway, remembering the evocative passage in Dominique' Lapierre's 2015 introduction to his and Larry Collins' 1972 opus, *O Jerusalem!* Recalling how his first sight of those "tortured carcasses" inspired several years of research and writing culminating in the book, Lapierre conveys his driver's outrage that the story is so little known that his passenger knew nothing of it. In the spring of 1948, shortly before the 14 May declaration of the state of Israel, armed Muslim

Arabs had already laid siege to the city of Jerusalem, trapping a hundred thousand Jews within. Food and water rapidly ran out. David Ben-Gurion commandeered trucks and utility vehicles – and newly arrived immigrants from Europe – into an attempted relief convoy that rapidly became a suicide mission. Miles short of the starving city, the Muslims overwhelmed the convoy, slaughtering the drivers, looting the supplies, and burning the trucks. "Fire, blood, and hatred ruled that night," Lapierre concluded his recollection. "Not one single ounce of food or a drop of water leaked through to Jerusalem."[72]

A few miles later, the effect of nearing the city from the west today is somewhat different from Lapierre's first sight of "the Queen of all cities rising majestically in all her splendor ..., as if spread on a lunar landscape."[73] The highway itself is more modern than the winding, two-lane road that Lapierre traveled in the 1960s. We ascended into Judean hills that, although arid, are in all likelihood greener than at any time in history, resulting from an aggressive program of forestation that, since 1948, has planted trees provided by millions of Jews from around the world, many in lieu of making *Aliyah* themselves. We also caught glimpses of modern "West" Jerusalem through our bus windows. That expanded and modernized city is, however, all we saw that first day. We never caught sight of "East Jerusalem" or the "Old City" as we skirted to the south and directly toward Bethlehem.

As we approached the City of David,[74] Tony got serious in cautioning us *not* to leave our hotel after dark. We would not be in Galilee, in Israel, anymore, he said, but for all intents and purposes in another country. Then, in the late afternoon sun, we saw the massive security wall with watchtowers and barbed-wire fencing running along its top. Scant miles south of Jerusalem, Bethlehem is part of the West Bank – under the Palestinian Authority – and its people are strictly forbidden to enter Israel without permission, which is seldom given.

---

[72] Dominique Lapierre, "Introduction" (2015) to Larry Collins and Dominique Lapierre, *O Jerusalem!* (New York: Simon & Schuster, 1972; ebook: Beverly Hills, California: Renaissance Literary & Talent, 2015), Kindle ed., locations 130-148.

[73] Ibid., loc. 148.

[74] So it is called in Luke 2: 4 and 11 ... and nowhere else in the Bible. The phrase, "City of David," is used a total of 51 times in the Bible, and every other time (all in the Old Testament) it clearly refers to Jerusalem, from its first appearance at 2 Samuel 5: 7 to its last, at 1 Maccabees 14: 36. Why, then, in the face of clearly overwhelming scriptural precedent, did the Evangelist pointedly apply the term to Bethlehem? Protestant Biblical scholar Larry Eubanks posits in an online article that Luke was making a political statement against the Jewish authorities who had crucified the Messiah, the Son of David, and continued to persecute the early Christians – "Bethlehem: City of David?" (02 December 2015 [larryeubanks.com/bethlehem-city-david/].

This sad state of affairs is a relatively recent development – a legacy of the 2000-2005 Second Intifada, when Muslim Palestinians started sending continuous waves of suicide bombers into Israel, many of them into Jerusalem through Bethlehem. The Israeli response was to initiate a great building project variously called the "West Bank Barrier" and far worse names, but most practically just "The Wall." The Israelis consider such a defensive measure imperative. The rest of the world largely considers it a gross violation of international law and the Palestinians' rights. The rest of the world, however, does not have to live with the threat of daily suicide attacks that went from an everyday occurrence to a rarity. The Wall has, however, had devastating consequences. Hardest hit by this stern measure have been the Christians of Bethlehem, regarded with suspicion as "Palestinians" by the Israelis, considered Israeli collaborators by the Muslims. Many Christians are leaving, making their way out through Jordan to the east, abandoning their ancestral home and that of their fathers for near two thousand years. It is a tragedy that the light of Christianity is slowly being snuffed out in the very town where the Light first came into the world.

We passed through the checkpoint without incident. Passage from Israel into the Palestinian Authority is easy; it is the getting out that is so difficult. We would pass through the Wall several more times over the next few days, but that first time made quite an impression. Then, as Tony had warned us, we were suddenly in essentially another country. Whether it really is or is not is immaterial. It certainly *feels* like another country. Immediately conspicuous was no Hebrew signage – just Arabic and English. There were clearly visible signs of a moribund economy – I have seen figures that the overall unemployment rate in Bethlehem is around 70 percent – and among the Christians, it is even worse. Graffiti – most of it political, much of it anti-American – covered the walls as well as *The* Wall.

For all that, I will say that we never felt unsafe – in our bus, during any of our outings, or in our hotel. We heeded Tony's advice. None of us ventured alone or even in a group further than line-of-sight of the hotel, and that only during daylight.

The troubled little town of Bethlehem….

> In those days a decree went out from Caesar Augustus that all the world should be enrolled. This was the first enrollment, when Quirinius was governor of Syria. And all went to be enrolled, each to his own city. And Joseph also went up from Galilee, from the city of Nazareth, to Judea,

HOLY RAMBLINGS

to the city of David, which is called Bethlehem, because he was of the house and lineage of David, to be enrolled with Mary, his betrothed, who was with child. (Luke 2: 1-5)

Greeted by a statue of the messenger archangel, entering through a revolving door, we passed immediately from an atmosphere of urban stagnation into the fine, clean, splendidly outfitted Saint Gabriel Hotel. Checking in, Kristal and I, as well as several others of our group, found our rooms on the first floor, which was really, as we Americans would count it, the fourth floor. The ground floor was the lobby; above that was the bar; above that was the restaurant, *then* "the first floor." Others of our group were on the two floors above our own, and there were several floors above that, but as far as we could tell, we were the only guests for the first few nights of our stay. We received cards making it happy hour for us in the bar all that first evening, and a group of us ended up there as soon as we freshened up. I enjoyed an excellent local beer, Taybeh, brewed in a historically Christian town in the West Bank,[75] then we went up to supper at 19:00. Since we were the only group present, there was no expansive buffet like at the Ron Beach Hotel. The food was instead served to two tables seating eight people each, in what we would call "family style." But it was all every bit as good, and the arrangement made for a somewhat more intimate ambiance.

After supper, I excused myself, went back up to the room, and worked on my blog until soon after 22:00, when I decided I needed to get to bed.

Saturday 18 August 2018 – Holy Land Day Six: *Bethlehem and Mount Zion*

I got up a little after 06:30 for 07:15 breakfast. Again, it was smaller in scale than at Ron Beach, but every bit as good.

At 08:15, we departed for Bethlehem Nativity Souvenirs, about which we had by then heard so much. As we rode through the streets of Bethlehem, Tony explained more about how this religious articles

---

[75] Given everything we learned, I wondered if it still were Christian. Wikipedia, s.v. "Taybeh," cites *Time* magazine from 2009 in noting it as the "last all-Christian community in the West Bank." Its population is, however, declining. At the time of this writing, morover, the Christians of Taybeh have recently (October-November 2019) been the victims of several well-publicized attacks by Israeli settlers in the West Bank – Shatha Hammad, "Israeli settlers target Christian Palestinians in West Bank town," *Middle East Eye* (29 November 2019) [https://www.middleeasteye.net/news/israeli-settlers-target-christian-palestinians-west-bank-town].

co-operative came to be. During the height of the Second Intifada, in April and May of 2002, Bethlehem suffered a five-week siege from the Israeli army (centered on the Church of the Nativity), and tourism dried up to a trickle. Many Christian sellers of religious articles went bankrupt. The construction of the Wall retarded the recovery, a situation compounded by the rapidly changing demographics. In 2009, the Knights of the Holy Sepulcher, the Papal Equestrian Order devoted to protecting the Holy Land and supporting our Christian brethren there, spearheaded the new venture in which Nativity Pilgrimage has participated from the beginning. Sixty-four Christian families of Bethlehem participate in the co-op, rather than competing against each other with religious articles shops individually too small to survive. It provides jobs to young Christian Bethlehemites for whom there is virtually no other opportunity in the increasingly Muslim-dominated town. According to Tony, it is the only religious articles store in Bethlehem run by Bethlehemite Christians dealing exclusively in items made in Bethlehem by Christian artists and craftsmen. Outside support of such ventures is essential to the survival of the Christian community in Bethlehem. We certainly did our part!

I do not know how much time or money we spent there. A large showroom displayed every kind of religious souvenir imaginable – jewelry, rosaries, icons, statues. By far, the most impressive were a large quantity of obviously high-quality, individually hand-carved articles made from olive wood, ranging from small rosaries to nativity sets that seemed the size of small houses!

I am reasonably sure that the people who appear at my home basilica just about every year are from this co-operative. I almost immediately spied a statue of St. Francis that, while not identical to, was so like one that my wife purchased during one of their visits several years ago that it had to be from the same pattern if not from the same artist.

Gathering us together at the rear of the showroom, one of the associates, Bashir, showed off various wares – all the above, including fascinating Jerusalem cross necklaces that expand into a representation of the walls of the Old City. He demonstrated the differences by which to discern authentic hand-carved items from similar but machine-tooled, mass-produced imitations. He emphasized the craft and prayer put into the objects sold through the co-op by the local artists, some of them in families who have passed on the art through generations. Then Tony explained the religious, cultural, and artistic significance of Orthodox icons also available there, mainly displayed in a side gallery that I never got around to entering. At the end, we each received a complimentary olive-wood Jerusalem cross pendant, which Fr. Emilio blessed at once.

We were then given plenty of time to browse. I did some of that, but first, I approached Tony and asked him if a ring like the one he wore might be available here; I was sure it would, but there was so much that I did not want to waste time looking. I had noticed Tony's ring, bearing the Jerusalem cross, almost immediately that first morning in Galilee, had pointed it out to Kristal, and declared, "I have *got* to get me one of those!" Of course, the answer to my question was yes; Tony brought me just a few steps over, got Bashir's attention, and the fun began. He showed me several such rings, but my heart sank when he quoted prices to me. I am not a natural haggler. I am not going to detail the process, which went back and forth for some time; let's just say that in the end, I did purchase a ring, yellow and white gold with a deep blue head encrusted with small diamonds forming the distinctive five-cross design identified with Jerusalem. It is the largest single purchase I have ever made short of my house, a vehicle, or home appliances – or international travel (!) – far more than I anticipated. I wear it proudly as my primary memento of the Holy Land, one which I touched to every subsequent holy spot or shrine we visited, rendering it a third-class relic[76]; as far as what I paid goes, I take consolation in knowing that the money went for an excellent cause.

Here is an interesting story: The evening before, when we arrived at the Saint Gabriel Hotel, one of the ladies among our number missed her wallet, which she had been carrying with her throughout the pilgrimage thus far. Donna had no specific memory of when she last had it in hand, other than that she had it at lunch when she paid for her meal. We knew where we had been from that point forward (one of the advantages of our trip being so structured), so, with Tony's help, inquiries were made backtracking along the way. At some point either later in the evening or early the next morning, the wallet was reported found, with all money and cards undisturbed, at the Church of St. Peter in Jaffa. Some kind soul had noticed it in a pew and turned it in to the Franciscans who oversee the church. But the problem then presented itself as to how to reunite it with its owner. As it turned out, hearing of the debacle as he showed her a necklace in Nativity Souvenirs, the manager dispatched one of his employees to drive the hour to and from Jaffa and bring the wallet to the Saint Gabriel, where it

---

[76] See the short discussion of relics in the Introduction.

was waiting when we returned in the evening. Although Nativity Souvenirs is in Bethlehem and "Palestinian" residents of Bethlehem are forbidden to cross into Israel, the co-op obviously has Israeli citizens in its employ who *can* pass freely through the Wall, as might be expected. Running the business would be virtually impossible otherwise.

I include this story as an example of how genuinely good the Christians of Bethlehem are, as well as the unknown individual who found the wallet in the church and turned it in with all its contents intact. And, of course, the power of prayer, because I know we were all praying that Donna would be reunited with her belongings. Yes, Nativity Souvenirs did obtain a sale by this good deed, but the drive to and from Jaffa as Donna continued her pilgrimage was a genuine act of kindness.

Just before we left the co-op, Tony handed off the job of guiding us in Bethlehem to a native Bethlehemite Christian named Sana – when I confirmed her name to jot it down in my notebook, she told me it means "light." She, too, gave a very impassioned description of the plight of Christians in Bethlehem – not in a self-pitying way but making clear her own family's defiant determination not to retreat and let the Muslims turn Christ's birthplace into another Nain. She described the nineteenth-century *Status Quo* agreement that has helped thus far. After centuries during which various groups had competed for control of the various holy sites which were all under the rule of the Ottoman Turks, resulting in frequent changes of hand usually accompanied by substantial bribery – not to mention no little violence as passions remained in constant turmoil driven in part by the uncertainty, between 1757 and 1853 the Turks issued several *firmans*, decrees, that no further transfers could be made, nor could changes to any of the sites be made without a consensus among the six Christian communities historically resident in the Holy Land – Roman Catholic, Greek Orthodox, Armenian Apostolic, Syriac Orthodox, Coptic, and Ethiopian. Although usually focused on the agreement between those six Christian groups (more usually, *disagreement* which has impeded even simple upkeep of the Church of the Holy Sepulcher in Jerusalem and the Basilica of the Nativity in Bethlehem), the Status Quo also governs certain sites of interest to Jews and Muslims. Considerable difference in interpretation keeps tensions high, and some argued that with the dissolution of the Ottoman Empire in World War I the Status Quo became null and void, but the British wisely chose to maintain it during their period of rule (the Mandate Period, 1922-1948), during which Archer Lord Cust established the summary that has more or less guided relations ever since, *The Status Quo in the Holy Places* (1929).

The United Nations affirmed the Cust Summary soon after the establishment of the State of Israel in 1948. Regarding Bethlehem, Sana said that part of the agreement mandated that the mayor must always be Roman Catholic, while the vice mayor must be Greek Orthodox. Harsh realities since the mid-2000s have nevertheless driven an insidious emigration dropping the percentage of Christians in Bethlehem to only twenty percent of the population of 39,000, who are extremely cautious about wearing their faith on their sleeves. The other eighty percent are Muslims, but she reiterated that there are many Christians in Bethlehem who are determined to remain. She certainly is.

Making it to Manger Square (the site of major celebrations televised around the world every Christmas Eve - even if muted in some years by the ever-present troubles), we arrived at the complex of the Basilica of the Nativity. When I say "complex," I mean "complex." Approaching it from Manger Square, passing through the smaller Nativity Square bounded on the left by a garden or park, on the right by an Armenian convent, straight ahead is a hodgepodge of ponderous, fortress-like architecture - the product of almost fifteen centuries of building, rebuilding, and haphazard additions by disparate religious groups. Besides the basilica proper and the Armenian convent, the complex includes, immediately to the left a Franciscan monastery, and to the right rear a Greek Orthodox monastery. The Basilica of the Nativity gave us our first exposure to the reality of the Status Quo. Custody is shared by those three major Middle Eastern Christian bodies - Roman Catholic (represented by the Franciscans), Greek Orthodox, and Armenian Apostolic. Sometimes characterized as "cooperative," that is far too positive a term! - it is really an uneasy, sometimes downright hostile, truce more than anything else. Nor are the "shares" equal. Under the Status Quo, the Greek Orthodox enjoy primary custody of the main church, with Catholics and Armenians having lesser rights.

The present church occupies the oldest site continuously venerated by Christian worshipers. Its history goes back even further than the fifteen hundred years I just indicated - that is just the present church! Two centuries earlier, in AD 327, Constantine the Great and his mother St. Helena commissioned the first structure on the site already long reverenced as the birthplace of Jesus. That church was destroyed, however - *not* by the Persians during the 614 invasion, by which time it had already been rebuilt; *not*, most likely, by the Samaritans rebelling against the Byzantines, although they have long been blamed, because the Samaritans were probably not active this far south. It was destroyed by the Byzantine Emperor himself, Justinian the Great, who wished to build something more conducive to the Divine Liturgy than Constantine's church, which was more suited to pilgrims visiting the holy site than to active worship. For instance, the previous building centered around a raised octagonal gallery surrounding a twelve-foot hole peering down into the grotto where Our Lord was born. The raised eastern end of the nave of Justinian's church now covers that area, shifting the focus to the iconostasis and the sanctuary beyond, where the Great Sacrifice of the Divine Liturgy occurs. Access to the grotto is through small doors opening to steps leading downward on either side.

The basilica as it stands today essentially dates from Justinian's time, although it has suffered fire, earthquake, siege, and other calamities through the centuries. One thing it did not suffer, surprisingly, was destruction by the Persians who leveled almost every other church in the Holy Land about a half-century after its construction ended. According to legend, the Zoroastrian Persians spared the basilica because the invaders saw mosaics depicting the Magi in the garb of their own priests.[77] Most recently, during the Second Intifada in 2002, about fifty armed Palestinians wanted by the IDF invaded and were not evicted for over a month. Reports of what happened during that time vary: The IDF claims that the Palestinians held the monks of the various faith groups hostage and even used them as human shields; statements from the monks themselves and their orders, e.g., the Franciscan Custody, insist otherwise, that the monks stayed willingly at their posts and ministered to the Palestinians, attempting to broker a peaceful solution. As I see it, the two stories are not necessarily contradictory, and it must be remembered that the Christian religious must live and work within the increasingly Palestinian society of Bethlehem, rendering it unlikely they would openly denounce the invaders.

Its great age also, inevitably, deteriorated the condition of the church, such that in the early 21st century, the roof regularly leaked, rendering the interior vulnerable to water damage. A major restoration project began in 2013 and was still underway while we were there – running behind, of course, since it should have been completed earlier in 2018. Given a history of squabbling over responsibilities and rights among the custodial groups, I find it surprising the long-deferred repairs and renovations ever began – in fact, a deadlock over who would

---

[77] Much of the preceding, and some of the following, was derived from a slim volume about the basilica: Garo Nalbandian and Fred Strickert, *The Church of the Nativity* (Bethlehem: Diyar Publisher, 2013), esp. pp. 5-7.

pay for the roof repair was only broken by UNESCO stepping in, declaring it a World Heritage Site, and putting up the money.

Just visible to the left, above the roofline of the façade of the Franciscan monastery, we could see the peak of a second church, another part of the "complex" of the Basilica of the Nativity. St. Catherine of Alexandria is said to have received a visitation on that spot from an angel predicting her martyrdom during the Great Persecution which preceded Constantine's legalization of the Church. The Catholic church dedicated to her is of more recent construction, beginning with a small chapel built by the Franciscans in 1347, which was rebuilt and expanded into the present full-scale church in 1880. This is where the Latin Patriarch of Jerusalem celebrates Midnight Mass on Christmas Eve. St. Catherine's is also Sana's parish church, and she did not hesitate to take us where we needed to be and make needed changes on the fly. At one point, taking us out a door clearly marked "Entrance Only," she declared as much: "This is my church – I can take you where I want!"

Making itinerary changes "on the fly" continued. We were supposed to have Mass at 11:00 in the cave where St. Jerome lived and translated the Vulgate Latin Bible in the fourth century. So, from Manger Square, Sana led us through Nativity Square and through the famous "Door of Humility" that stands only about four feet tall, some say to make everyone who passes through it abase themselves before this holy place, others say to keep mounted knights from entering on horseback (!); cutting through the left back corner of the basilica itself and through the cloistered Franciscan courtyard with a statue of St. Jerome at its center, into St. Catherine's Church and downstairs to the Grotto of St. Jerome. Making our way through the caves, we passed mosaic or mural memorials to St. Jerome and two of his disciples, the mother and daughter Sts. Paula and Eustochium, who may be entombed there. We were just settling in for Mass when Sana entered into an animated conversation with what I presume to have been a sacristan; there was obviously some issue, but Sana quickly secured us a side chapel of the main church and Mass proceeded.[78] Father's theme was, again, emphasis on the fact that *it was here, in this place*, that the infinite God of the Universe revealed His face as that of a helpless child, assuming humanity in humility. We, too, must assume humility if we are to be like him.

---

[78] As was proclaimed several times while we were in Bethlehem, "In Bethlehem, every day is Christmas." The Mass according to the Custody Missal was that of Christmas: Isaiah 9: 1-6; Psalm 96; Luke 2: 1-14.

Although the Church of St. Catherine was not as thoroughly post-Vatican II "ugly" as some pictures I had seen suggested, the results of its post-Conciliar renovation nonetheless contrasted sharply with the glorious basilica which we entered next, retracing our steps back through the cloistered courtyard of St. Catherine's. The Basilica of the Nativity of Our Lord Jesus Christ - announced by a mosaic above the door through which we now returned, "*Ingressus Basilicae Nativitatis D.N.J.C.*," beneath a Jerusalem cross - reeks of glorious antiquity. It certainly is more what I envisioned for the churches of the Holy Land than any church we had seen thus far. The current renovation meant that there was a lot of construction equipment and debris in the nave. But remnants of magnificent murals lined what would be termed the gallery or perhaps the clerestory - if those western church architectural terms even apply. The Greek Orthodox sanctuary was magnificent with its great iconostasis covered in icons with a myriad of lamps, which also filled the right-side aisle leading to the entrance to the grotto. The massive pillars that line the nave bear faded and often illegible paintings of some of the great saints, both eastern and western - Sts. Sabas and Theodosius stand immediately adjacent to Sts. Olaf of Norway and Cnut of Denmark! These pillars date from the era of the Crusades when the church was under the control of western Catholics. All in all, the impression with which I came away was of murals and icons and mosaics and metalwork and lamps in a wonderful mix of styles reflective of the various Catholic and Orthodox groups which have held custody of the church over its long history. Nevertheless, the dominant character was Orthodox.

An incredible number of people were there. Here we first encountered the truly claustrophobia-inducing crowds that characterize the most important pilgrimage sites. We fought - generally successfully - a standing-room-only mass of people for about an hour to get through to the Grotto of the Nativity and the place where the Manger was. As we got closer, Sana warned us that others would shamelessly push their way in front of us if we let them and insisted that we lock ourselves into an impassible wall spanning the gap. I imagined Uhtred, son of Uhtred, bellowing out "*Shield - WALL!*" as in TV's *The Last Kingdom*.

It worked - mostly. Some other pilgrims still bull-dogged around or even between us, pressing toward the entrance to the grotto. We thus had a taste of how enthusiasm to be in the presence of such a holy place could drive the passions of the competing religious groups that make the Status Quo an unfortunate necessity. In any case, we did finally make it through the narrow entrance and down the narrow steps into the Grotto of the Nativity, cave-stable in which Our Lady gave birth to Our Savior.

> And while [Joseph and Mary] were [in Bethlehem], the time came for her to be delivered. And she gave birth to her first-born son and wrapped him in swaddling clothes, and laid him in a manger, because there was no place for them in the inn. (Luke 2: 6-7)

A fourteen-pointed silver "Star of Bethlehem" marks the spot, which we were able to kiss or touch as millions of other believers have before us. Only feet away was the place where the Manger was. I say "was" because the Manger itself was taken away long ago; I do not remember if it was by St. Helena the mother of Constantine the Great or by Latin Crusaders, but I had actually seen it before, in Rome, in the grotto beneath the altar of the Basilica of St. Mary Major.[79]

(As an aside, the lack of a place in the inn may not have been for the reasons usually assumed, either because of vast crowds of visitors or indifference on the part of the innkeeper. Michael Hesemann, in his *Mary of Nazareth: History, Archaeology, Legends*, suggests that it may have been because of Mary's imminent birthing, which would have rendered anyone encountering her immediately afterward ritually impure. He considers that to have been of particular concern because he believes Jesus' birth to have been most likely just before Passover[80] – an interpretation I do not share, but it seems to me that the issue would have been of concern before any feast, for instance, *Hanukkah* at the more traditional season for Jesus' birth in mid-winter.)[81]

---

[79] As noted above, p. 41, n. 24, part of this relic has been returned to Bethlehem as of November 2019.

[80] Michael Hesemann, *Mary of Nazareth: History, Archaeology, Legends*, trans. Michael J. Miller (San Jose, California: Ignatius Press, 2016), Kindle edition, loc. 2242.

[81] Although it is not specifically relevant to this book, my personal theory regarding the eternally-debated question of when Jesus was born, i.e., "Was the First Christmas on 25 December?," is that the date is tied to the beginning of Hanukkah, the Festival of the Dedication mentioned in John 10: 22. Hanukkah commemorates the Maccabean rededication of the Temple on the 25th day of the Jewish month Khislev, 164 BC, after its profanation by the Seleucids exactly three years earlier by the Jewish reckoning. The Jewish calendar is a lunar calendar, making a consistent correspondence of dates with the solar-based Roman calendar from year to year impossible. That is part of the reason Easter moves around. In the case of Easter, the calculation is further complicated by the compulsion to celebrate the Resurrection on Sunday as well as account for the connection to Passover and hence the Vernal. Without those complications, I believe it would have been easier for non-Jewish Christians simply to conceptualize "25 Khislev" as "25 December," hence the (demonstrably early, contrary to popular belief) traditional dating of Christmas to 25 December. Note that I am not

During a short drive from the Church of the Nativity to Shepherds' Fields, located in an immediately adjacent town, Beit Sahour, Tony described what herding and shepherding sheep and goats entailed. They require entirely different techniques. For instance, the shepherd's crook is used to train and control an alpha male sheep, and the others will follow that alpha male; on the other hand, herding goats sounds like herding cats, requiring with great skill with a slingshot, *not* to hit and injure the goat (which would be a blemish rendering it unusable in the Temple Sacrifice), but rather to plant one right in its path and thus deflect it the direction you want it to go. Quiz: What kind of herder was King David?

At Shepherds' Fields, while Sana went into the restaurant at which we would be eating to arrange our lunches, we passed through a large gate over which arch in red the words of the angels announcing the birth of their Lord, "*GLORIA IN EXCELSIS DEO* – Glory to God in the Highest." A long, shaded path brought us into a courtyard garden where Tony continued his discourse on herding in ancient Israel, which was primarily to supply the Temple, where the daily sacrifices required a steady supply of sheep and goats.

> And in that region there were shepherds out in the field, keeping watch over their flock by night. And an angel of the Lord appeared to them, and the glory of the Lord shone around them, and they were filled with fear. And the angel said to them, "Be not afraid; for behold, I bring you good news of a great joy which will come to all the people; for to you is born this day in the city of David a Savior, who is Christ the Lord. And this will be a sign for you: you will find a babe wrapped in swaddling cloths and lying in a manger." And suddenly there was with the angel a multitude of the heavenly host praising God and saying, "Glory to God in the highest, and on earth peace among men with whom he is pleased!" When the angels went away from them into heaven, the shepherds said to one another, "Let us go over to Bethlehem and see this thing that has happened, which the Lord has made known to us." (Luke 2: 8-15)

---

arguing that Jesus was indeed born on 25 Khislev specifically, but I do believe the connection with Hanukkah is crucial. Why I believe so would require lengthier explanation that is well beyond the scope of this book, but if nothing else the connection of the coming of the Light into the world with Hanukkah – popularly known as the "Festival of Lights" – would have been considered fitting.

A small round chapel designed by Antonio Barluzzi to resemble a Bedouin's tent had fantastic acoustics. Jennifer and I spontaneously chanted the *Gloria* from *Missa VIII de Angelis*. Then we took a quick look into a typical cave such as would have been used by the shepherds to shelter their sheep. Pilgrimage groups use a couple of such at that location for Mass, although we did not. Behind a fence, we could also see ongoing excavations of a fourth- to sixth-century Byzantine monastery and church.

The Shepherds' Nai Restaurant, directly across the street from the Shepherds Fields, served us another in the series of consistently excellent lunches we enjoyed in Israel. In this case, in addition to the customary salad dishes, abundant pita bread, and a variety of sauces and dips, especially hummus, the main course (served "family style) was a form of "barbecue" which was very good. At least that is what Tony called it - "barbecue" - although it was like no barbecue *I* ever had. There was chicken, which was basically kabobbed (without the stick) and tastily seasoned - but it was not "barbecue." There was also something that tasted much more like our barbecue. It was some form of ground meat - a mixture of beef and lamb, I believe - formed into a roughly conical shape about four inches long on some sort of skewer. That was quite good.

At the end of our meal, Sana bid us farewell as we did what she, as a "Palestinian" Christian of Bethlehem, cannot do under Israeli law. We passed through the Wall back into Israel. Tragically, the Christians of Bethlehem cannot make the easy day trip to visit the holy sites just a few miles away in Jerusalem that we came thousands of miles to experience.

Tony did not tell us, but I discovered independently just how personally this situation has affected him. His Jerusalem-born - Israeli - brother was married to a Bethlehemite girl. He smuggled her into Israel. But after she gave birth, her "Palestinian" status was discovered, and she was deported - separated from husband and baby. Israeli law forbids marriage between Israeli citizens and Palestinians. The fact that, as mentioned before, "Palestinian" is a Muslim political neologism and Christians in Israel and the Palestinian Authority mostly identify as "Aramaeans" matters not. As of 2015, at least, the situation had not been resolved.[82]

---

[82] Nancy Hoefer, "A land of calm, chaos and other Holy Land observations," *Diocese of Oakland: The Catholic Voice Online Edition*, vol. 53, no. 7 (06 April 2015) [https://www.catholicvoiceoakland.org/2015/04-06/inthisissue15.html].

We made our way to Mount Zion, perhaps the most important hill of the traditional seven that make up Jerusalem, the one whose name became synonymous with the city itself ... and which is ironically outside walls of the Old City! It is a somewhat funny story. Soon after the Ottoman Turks took over Jerusalem in the early sixteenth century, Suleiman the Magnificent ordered built what still stand as the Old City walls. Unfortunately, his architects messed up and left Mount Zion out. Unfortunately – for them. The way the story goes, their heads are now inside the walls.

I imagine they would not have thought the story is that funny.

In subsequent reading, I discovered an answer to something that had long mystified me. Tony never addressed it, either. If the original settlement of Jerusalem, what became the original Jebusite city that David captured and then made the capital of his kingdom, was on Mount Zion, as implied by the name – why then has archaeology found David's city on the smaller hill directly south of the Temple Mount? The reason appears to be that until the nineteenth century, local tradition had David's city on the western hill south of the Old City, beneath sites we were headed to see that afternoon, and hence called that hill by the name, "Mount Zion." It appears to be another rare case of ancient tradition leading us wrong, as was discovered when archaeologists uncovered the *real* Jebusite/Davidic city to the east. By that time, however, the name "Mount Zion" for the western hill was too ingrained to be displaced. A relic of this confusion may be, however, the presence of the so-called Tomb of King David, which we would visit later on the "western" Mount Zion.

Wael dropped us a short distance away from our destination, and we walked the rest of the way, past the "Belvedere Scenic View" of the Old City, the Kidron Valley, and the Mount of Olives, to arrive at the Church of St. Peter in Gallicantu. The name means "the Cock Crowing" and commemorates where Peter, after having promised Jesus he would follow him even unto death and been rebuked for it, with Jesus predicting he would betray him three times ere the cock crowed, did just that.

There are a couple of notable iconographic features on the great bronze double door to the church that Tony brought to our attention. First, Christ's finger, at first glance pointing toward Peter as he predicts the latter's threefold denial, can on closer examination be seen to be raised to point outward – at the viewer. We all deny Christ through our sins. Second, Christ's left hand holds up his index, middle, and ring fingers to indicate "three times" – and is a dead giveaway that the door was designed and executed by a westerner (which it was, although not by the ubiquitous Antonio Barluzzi) because the Middle Eastern way of indicating "three" is by means of the thumb plus the index and middle fingers. I had already, in fact, noticed that was the way Tony himself indicated "three."

Tony's experience excavating beneath the Church of St. Peter in Gallicantu made his exposition at this site especially effective. The church occupies the grounds where once stood the house of the High Priest Caiaphas where Jesus was taken directly from his arrest in the Garden of Gethsemane. The path from the Garden of Gethsemane on the slope of the Mount of Olives, down the Kidron Valley, across the Lower City of first-century Jerusalem and up Mount Zion, culminates in steps ending at the courtyard immediately adjacent to the church. Most likely having earlier in the evening descended those steps after the Last Supper only a short distance away, Jesus was dragged back up them in chains to face Caiaphas and the hastily assembled Sanhedrin in the High Priest's house. Below that courtyard are cisterns which also served as a dungeon where, although the Gospels do not mention it explicitly, Jesus would likely have spent several hours overnight at the mercy of the high priest's guards. Tony took us down into that dungeon where he talked us through the evidence he helped unearth, describing the tortures which archaeology suggests would have been inflicted on Our Lord between the preliminary trial before Caiaphas and dawn when he would go before the Roman governor, Pontius Pilate.

> Then those who had seized Jesus led him to Caiaphas the high priest, where the scribes and the elders had gathered. But Peter followed him at a distance, as far as the courtyard of the high priest, and going inside he sat with the guards to see the end. Now the chief priests and the whole council sought false testimony against Jesus that they might put him to death, but they found none, though many false witnesses came forward. At last two came forward and said, "This fellow said, 'I am able to destroy the temple of God, and to build it in three days.'" And the high priest stood up and said, "Have you no answer to make? What is it that these men testify against you?" But Jesus was silent. And the high priest said to him, "I adjure you by the living God, tell us if you are the Christ, the Son of God." Jesus said to him, "You have said so. But I tell you, hereafter you will see the

Son of man seated at the right hand of Power, and coming on the clouds of heaven." Then the high priest tore his robes, and said, "He has uttered blasphemy. Why do we still need witnesses? You have now heard his blasphemy. What is your judgment?" They answered, "He deserves death." Then they spat in his face, and struck him; and some slapped him, saying, "Prophesy to us, you Christ! Who is it that struck you?"

Now Peter was sitting outside in the courtyard. And a maid came up to him, and said, "You also were with Jesus the Galilean." But he denied it before them all, saying, "I do not know what you mean." And when he went out to the porch, another maid saw him, and she said to the bystanders, "This man was with Jesus of Nazareth." And again he denied it with an oath, "I do not know the man." After a little while the bystanders came up and said to Peter, "Certainly you are also one of them, for your accent betrays you." Then he began to invoke a curse on himself and to swear, "I do not know the man." And immediately the cock crowed. And Peter remembered the saying of Jesus, "Before the cock crows, you will deny me three times." And he went out and wept bitterly.

When morning came, all the chief priests and the elders of the people took counsel against Jesus to put him to death; and they bound him and led him away and delivered him to Pilate the governor. (Matt. 26: 57 - 27: 2)[83]

What occurred to Jesus between the Sanhedrin's outraged judgment, "He deserves death!," and the statement, "When morning came...," is summed up as, "Then they spat in his face, and struck him; and some slapped him, saying, "Prophesy to us, you Christ! Who is it that struck you?" Tony's graphic explanation describing his analysis of anchor points for shackles holding a prisoner spread-eagle and helpless between two pillars – with traces of blood all around – and areas worn by ropes bearing the heavy burden of a human body suspended in darkness, suggests that to be quite understated. Jesus likely suffered flogging while shackled between those pillars, then being beaten while hanging helpless, suspended by a rope through a small opening in the

---

[83] The detail that Peter was warming himself at a charcoal fire, later recalled by the Sea of Galilee at the *mensa Christi* as related by John in chapter 21, is supplied in the Passion narrative by that same Evangelist at 18: 18.

ceiling – all within earshot of the courtyard above, where Peter stood, hearing it all. Tony expressed great understanding and sympathy for Peter. *Anyone* would have lost their nerve hearing their Lord screaming in agony, as Tony says any man would if his interpretation is correct – and Jesus was fully man as well as fully God.

In the dungeon itself, in deference to his own spoken English being heavily accented, Padre Emilio offered me the privilege of reading Psalm 88 aloud:

> O Lord, my God, by day I cry out,
> at night I clamor in your presence.
> Let my prayer come before you;
> incline your ear to my call for help,
> For my soul is surfeited with troubles
> and my life draws near to the nether world.
> I am numbered with those who go down into the pit;
> I am a man without strength.
>
> My couch is among the dead,
> like the slain who lie in the grave,
> Whom you remember no longer
> and who are cut off from your care.
> You have plunged me into the bottom of the pit,
> into the dark abyss.
> Upon me your wrath lies heavy,
> and with all your billows you overwhelm me.
> You have taken my friends away from me;
> you have made me an abomination to them;
> I am imprisoned, and I cannot escape.
>
> My eyes have grown dim through affliction;
> daily I call upon you; O Lord;
> to you I stretch out my hands.
> Will you work wonders for the dead?
> Will the shades arise to give you thanks?
> Do they declare your kindness in the grave,
> your faithfulness among those who have perished?
> Are your wonders made known in the darkness,
> or your justice in the land of oblivion?
>
> But I, O Lord, cry out to you;

with my morning prayer I wait upon you,
Why, O Lord, do you reject me;
why hide from me your face?
I am afflicted and in agony from my youth;
I am dazed with the burden of your dread,
Your furies have swept over me;
your terrors have cut me off.
They encompass me like water all the day,
on all sides they close in upon me.
Companion and neighbor you have taken away from me;
my only friend is darkness.[84]

After a few minutes for pictures, including the spectacular stained-glass cross in the dome of the main church, we walked back up to where Wael waited with the bus, which took us just a short distance to drop us near the Zion Gate, near the western end of the southern wall of the Old City. Our destination was nearby Dormition Abbey, but first, we stopped to contemplate the rather battered appearance of the gate.

The stone walls all around the Zion Gate took their beating from Israeli artillery during the Six Days War of 1967, in a diversionary assault which left the rest of the Old City virtually undefended when Israeli paratroopers dropped in and secured Jewish access to the holy sites for the first time in nineteen years. Hitherto, ever since the end of the 1948 War, the Old City and East Jerusalem, as well as the West Bank, had been under the control of the Kingdom of the Transjordan,

---

[84] The text of Psalm 88 supplied at the Church of St. Peter in Gallicantu is, interestingly enough, Psalm 87 (traditional numbering) in the mid twentieth-century Confraternity Version, an abortive translation of the Bible published in parts between 1941 and 1969, still incomplete at that time when the project was pre-empted by the appearance of the New American Bible. Generally speaking, the Confraternity translation would have implemented the vision of Pope Pius XII as expressed in his 1943 encyclical, *Divino afflante Spiritu*, incorporating for the first time the fruits of studies of the scriptures in their original languages, Hebrew, Aramaic, and Greek, into a new translation of the Latin Vulgate, while the New American Bible, implementing the vision of the Second Vatican Council, translated directly from those original languages while only making reference to the Latin Vulgate. The Psalms – again, interestingly enough – actually appeared in two different versions: 1950, then revised in 1955; I do not know how extensive the 1955 revision was, although I have read that it can be easily distinguished by the first word of Psalm 1, which is changed to "Happy" from the 1950 "Blessed." For what it is worth, the wording here, confirmed by multiple YouTube videos of pilgrims reading it as did I, matches exactly that appearing in the Catholic Press edition of the Holy Bible, dated 1950, and presented to or purchased by my wife's parents for Christmas 1951.

modern Jordan, and Jews had been barred entry at all. Henceforward, Israel would control the city in its entirety but would allow Muslim entry to the Temple Mount and the Dome of the Rock – for all the thanks it has ever gotten them.

We then walked through narrow streets to the Abbey of the Dormition of Our Lady, where the Blessed Mother of Our Lord is said to have "fallen asleep" before being assumed into heaven. Although definition of the Assumption of Mary as a dogma came only late, in 1950, it was believed consistently from the earliest days of the Church and, like other such late definitions or decrees, only required formal definition as such when called into question. Whether she died first or was taken up alive into heaven like Enoch and Elijah (and Moses, according to Jewish legend) has, however, never been definitively stated by the Church. In general, I believe, the formal western (Catholic) position is that either could be the case, and either would be equally fitting. Sinless from the instant of her Immaculate Conception, she was not subject to death; a general preponderance of tradition, however, suggests that she freely chose to die in union with her Son. The eastern (Orthodox) tradition is more definite, holding that she did indeed perish but was not subject to the *pains* of death, and so merely fell asleep, peacefully – hence, "Dormition" – to be received body and soul into heaven. Catholics and Orthodox believe in common, therefore, that Mary now resides bodily on high, reigning as Queen of Heaven beside her Son, Christ the King.

Early legend adds detail to the story, of course. In general, it describes how all the apostles were either summoned or miraculously transported to attend the Mother of God as she approached the end of her life – except for St. Thomas, who arrived too late. Thomas arrived to find that her body had already been entombed on the Mount of Olives (which church we did not visit). Desiring to see her one last time – or, in some accounts, doubting that she had died – Thomas insisted that the tomb be opened – and it was found empty. As they faced another empty tomb, the apostles concluded that the Blessed Mother had been indeed taken up into heaven, body and soul.

Incidentally, as in so many of these traditional sites, there is a competing location for the site of Mary's Assumption. Another ancient Catholic tradition – given currency because it accords with the visions of German seer Blessed Anne Catherine Emmerich[85] – has it that she died and was buried near Ephesus in Turkey, where she had lived out the rest of her life on earth with John, the Beloved Disciple, after being entrusted to him by her dying Son on the Cross, with the tomb being found empty three days later. This version plays a role in Michael D. O'Brien's novel *Father Elijah*.[86]

A beautiful mosaic floor adorns the main church, depicting three interlocking circles representing the Holy Trinity within a starburst at the center of concentric rings, depicting first the twelve apostles and then, further out, the twelve signs of the zodiac. Alcoves around the church, which is inspired in its design by the Carolingian cathedral in Aachen, Germany, depict various other imagery from the life of Our Lady and Our Lord. Downstairs is, however, the most distinctive feature I remember from the Church of the Dormition – besides the tower visible outside, surmounted by a highly stylized Second Reich-era military helmet (the modern church was funded by Kaiser Wilhelm II between 1898 and 1910). Centered in the crypt is a columned bier with a life-size effigy of Our Lady in the sleep of death. In the muted light of the crypt, it was quite moving. There, as in so many other places in the Holy Land, I lit a candle for the intentions of my friend Angel back home.

I *think* it was immediately after Dormition Abbey, specifically, in its gift shop across a small courtyard, that I earned the dubious distinction of being our first "goat." I tarried a little overlong trying to procure an item that Angel had asked me to bring her, a large panoramic poster of Jerusalem, as seen from the Mount of Olives. She has not been home in almost thirty years; the poster she has is tattered and worn. As I talked with the proprietor, I did not realize that my Whisper was off. Someone from our group came in and asked me if that were the case because the group was ready to move on. As I hot-footed it out

---

[85] Blessed Anne Catherine Emmerich, *The Life of the Blessed Virgin Mary*, trans. Sir Michael Pelairet (London: Catholic Way Publishing, 2013), 18: 12-14; 19; Kindle edition locs. 78% ff. Also available online [https://www.ecatholic2000.com/anne/lom177.shtml, to - lom180.shtml], accessed 29 November 2019.

[86] The question, "Where did the Assumption take place?," was examined by Mark Alessio in his article bearing that title published in *The Angelus* (July 2003), reprinted by the Society of Saint Pius X (14 August 2014) [https://sspx.org/en/news-events/news/where-did-assumption-take-place-4650]. The Ephesus tradition did not, as is sometimes suggested, originate with Anne Catherine Emmerich; Pope Benedict XIV (r. 1740-1758) wrote in his *Treatise on the Feast of the Assumption*, "John amply fulfilled Christ's order; in every way he forever cared for Mary with a sense of duty; he had her live with him while he remained in Palestine, and he took her with him when he departed for Ephesus, where the Blessed Mother at length proceeded from this life into heaven" (quoted by Alessio).

and back to the group, turning on my Whisper, I heard Tony's voice calling me: "*Keh-eh-eh-eh-eh-ehnt! Keh-eh-eh-eh-eh-ehnt!*"[87] - like a goat braying. Well played, sir, well played. I would not be the last goat, however. If I recall correctly, the next day at the Dead Sea, Tony was himself the last to board the bus, to calls of "*Toh-oh-oh-oh-ony! Toh-oh-oh-oh-ony!*"

From there, we proceeded a very short distance and up several discontinuous flights of stairs into the Cenacle or Upper Room of the Last Supper.

> And on the first day of Unleavened Bread, when they sacrificed the passover lamb, his disciples said to him, "Where will you have us go and prepare for you to eat the passover?" And he sent two of his disciples, and said to them, "Go into the city, and a man carrying a jar of water will meet you; follow him, and wherever he enters, say to the householder, 'The Teacher says, Where is my guest room, where I am to eat the passover with my disciples?' And he will show you a large upper room furnished and ready; there prepare for us." And the disciples set out and went to the city, and found it as he had told them; and they prepared the passover. (Mark 14: 12-16)

The present construction, called the "Cenacle" or *Coenaculum* (little dining hall - although it is by no means little) is not at all how it would have appeared in Jesus' time, however, with vaulted ceilings and columns surmounted by obviously medieval carvings. It dates from the era of the Crusades and has been at times both a synagogue and a mosque. Despite which - and despite efforts to erase it - the essential Christian character of the room survives in some of the iconographic stonework. Not in this building, granted, but in this spot, two of the great events of salvation history took place, the Last Supper and the first Pentecost - the institution of the Eucharist and the Sacramental Priesthood and the descent of the Holy Spirit 54 days later.

> And when the hour came, he sat at table, and the apostles with him. And he said to them, "I have earnestly desired to eat this passover with you before I suffer; for I tell you I shall not eat it until it is fulfilled in the kingdom of God." And he took a cup, and when he had given thanks he said, "Take this, and divide it among yourselves; for I tell you that

---

[87] He always pronounced my name with the proper "eh" vowel sound, not the "ih" I usually hear - or worse, a diphthongized "yi" ("ee-ih") - "*Keyint!*" No. Just ... no.

from now on I shall not drink of the fruit of the vine until the kingdom of God comes." And he took bread, and when he had given thanks he broke it and gave it to them, saying, "This is my body which is given for you. Do this in remembrance of me." And likewise the cup after supper, saying, "This cup which is poured out for you is the new covenant in my blood." (Luke 22: 14-20)

Among the various carvings, we found, atop columns near the exit, those of pelicans, an ancient symbol of the Eucharist. According to medieval lore, the mother pelican would tear her breast with her beak to feed her chicks with her flesh and blood. Of course, Tony knew the legend. But he did not know the special significance of the pelican for our home state of Louisiana, so for once, we got to tell Tony something new.

When the day of Pentecost had come, they were all together in one place. And suddenly a sound came from heaven like the rush of a mighty wind, and it filled all the house where they were sitting. And there appeared to them tongues as of fire, distributed and resting on each one of them. And they were all filled with the Holy Spirit and began to speak in other tongues, as the Spirit gave them utterance. (Acts 2: 1-4)

Unfortunately, the varied history of the site has left its mark in a modern agreement that no religious activities can take place in the Cenacle. Someone proposed praying the *Come Holy Spirit*, but Tony dissuaded us, cautioning us that we could not chant it aloud because of that agreement.

Exiting the Cenacle, we went down and around to what I did not know at the time was the lower floor of the same building, and into a synagogue at what is celebrated (incorrectly, Tony said) as the Tomb of David. It was an interesting experience. Being the Sabbath, it was filled with Orthodox Jews rocking back and forth and chanting individually, creating a cacophony of noise. It was segregated by sex, of course, so the ladies had to go to the women's side. I do not know what their experience was, but I, Fr. Emilio, and Br. Miguel did not spend much time on the men's side. We donned the cheap disposable yarmulkes before entering, but we – I – felt like we stuck out like a sore thumb and that we were not welcome there. To be fair, however, I understand;

I know how I feel when tourists barge into the Minor Basilica back home during First Friday Adoration of the Most Blessed Sacrament.

On the way back to our hotel, Tony again expressed his admiration for those Bethlehem Christians, such as Sana, who are courageous and tough and determined not to give in. She is one of only a few female guides in Bethlehem, but he considers her the best.

Back at the hotel, we had about an hour's happy hour in the bar before 19:00 dinner. Once again, I enjoyed two excellent Taybeh beers. This evening, with most of our group congregated in the bar's lounge area, Tony joined us and regaled us with various stories of the local culture that some in the front of the bus had heard already, but we toward the back had not. I remember being quite entertained as well as fascinated by how different the underlying culture is from our own – but I, unfortunately, remember none of his tales well enough to relate them here.

After supper, I returned to my room and once again worked on the blog until almost 22:00. By that point, I had reached something of a rhythm, successfully balancing my need to get something in place to work with later with the real point of pilgrimage, which is *not* blogging. Having that balance, *having* something established that I knew I could go back and flesh out later, relieved me of a sense of leaving something undone and allowed me to enter more fully into the experience of the moment.

Sunday 19 August 2018 – Holy Land Day Seven: *Ein Karem, Jericho, the Dead Sea*

It was a pretty normal morning – up, dressed, breakfast, then heading out for another full day. One perceived difference was that it was pleasantly cool when we boarded the bus to head out and remained so for most of the morning. The afternoon would make up for that respite, however!

We departed Bethlehem, passed through the Wall checkpoint again without incident, driving up and around the west of Jerusalem toward Ein Karem, the birthplace of John the Baptist. Along the way, Tony expanded on his family's deep Christian roots in the Holy Land. Among his ancestors, he claims Maltese Crusaders as well as a direct line of descent from the native Christians of the Holy Land as far as records will carry him – which is 1400 years, all the way back to the devastating Persian conquest of 614 when a lot of records were lost. His family name, Azraq, is Arabic; meaning "blue," it is a legacy of the seventh-century Muslim conquest of the Holy Land when his ancestors were forced to wear blue belts to identify them as Christians. So, his family name, in context, literally marks him as an Israeli Christian.

Along the way, we passed the large Israeli Holocaust Memorial complex, Yad Vashem, on the forested western slope of Mount Herzl, the Mount of Remembrance. It is more than just a museum. It includes a school, as well as archives and a library. There is also a section of train track and one of the cattle cars that transported victims to the death camps.

Our first stop in Ein Karem was the Church of the Nativity of St. John the Baptist, also known as "St. John ba Harim" (in the Mountains) because it is located in the hill country of Judah to which Our Lady is said to have traveled soon after the Annunciation (Luke 1: 39). We saw the very place of the Baptist's birth, downstairs in another grotto, under an altar where it is marked by what I believe Tony said is the oldest Jerusalem Cross ever found. Besides the Basilica of the Nativity in Bethlehem which we had seen before, and the Church of the Holy Sepulcher which we would see the next day, this was one of the few really old churches we saw; compared to those two ancient edifices, it is a relative newborn, however, dating back to the seventeenth century. Like the many newer churches that we saw, however, it rested on foundations of much older Byzantine and Crusader churches.

Outside the church, there are a series of tile-plaques around the shaded courtyard, each bearing in a different language the text of the *Benedictus*, the Canticle of Zechariah (Luke 1: 66-79), first proclaimed when the priestly father of John regained the use of his voice after the birth of his son. We found the one in English and recited it together:

> **Blessed be the Lord, the God of Israel!**
> **He has visited his people**
> **and redeemed them.**
> **He has raised up for us a mighty saviour**
> **in the house of David his servant,**
> **as he promised by the lips of holy men,**
> **those who were his prophets from of old.**
> **A saviour who would free us from our**
> **foes, from the hands of all who hate us.**
> **So his love for our fathers is fulfilled**
> **and his holy covenant remembered.**
> **He swore to Abraham our father**
> **to grant us, that free from fear,**

> and saved from the hands of our foes,
> we might serve him
> in holiness and justice
> all the days of our life in his presence.
>   As for you, little child,
> you shall be called a prophet of God,
> the Most High.
> You shall go ahead of the Lord
> to prepare his ways before him.
>   To make known to his people
> their salvation
> through forgiveness of all their sins,
> the loving-kindness of the heart of our God
> who visits us like the dawn from on high.
>   He will give light to those in darkness,
> those who dwell in the shadow of death,
> and guide us into the way of peace.[88]

Then we took a long half-mile walk, ("many steps"!), up the side of a hill to the Church of the Visitation. To our right was a spectacular view of the rugged, forested hills of Judah. As we climbed, we recited the Rosary. I led the last decade ending at the gate into the courtyard right outside the church; instead, however, of concluding in English, I continued without pause directly into chanting the *Salve Regina* in Latin. Almost everyone joined in, I believe.

We entered right at 10:00, time for Mass in the main Church of the Visitation, commemorating when Mary, newly pregnant with the Son of God, came to her aged cousin Elizabeth, six or more months along in her own miraculous pregnancy:

> And the angel said to [Mary] ... "And behold, your kinswoman Elizabeth in her old age has also conceived a son; and this is the sixth month with her who was called barren. For with God nothing will be impossible." And Mary said, "Behold, I am the handmaid of the Lord; let it be to me according to your word." And the angel departed from her.

---

[88] These plaques were donated by organizations in many different countries, mostly from the late 1980s, it seems. The one in English came from the Commissary of the Holy Land, London, in 1989. The Wikipedia article on the *Benedictus*, s.v. "Benedictus (Song_of_Zechariah)," shows a selection of the other plaques in Hebrew, Esperanto, Russian, Greek, Arabic, and Latin.

The text quoted here was transcribed from my own photograph.

> In those days Mary arose and went with haste into the hill country, to a city of Judah, and she entered the house of Zechariah and greeted Elizabeth. And when Elizabeth heard the greeting of Mary, the babe leaped in her womb; and Elizabeth was filled with the Holy Spirit and she exclaimed with a loud cry, "Blessed are you among women, and blessed is the fruit of your womb! And why is this granted me, that the mother of my Lord should come to me? For behold, when the voice of your greeting came to my ears, the babe in my womb leaped for joy. And blessed is she who believed that there would be a fulfilment of what was spoken to her from the Lord." (Luke 1: 35-45)

Mary as the Ark of the New Covenant explains why the preborn John the Baptist leaped in his mother's womb. In the Old Testament, the Ark of the Covenant was the dwelling-place of God Himself, before which King David danced as it entered Jerusalem (2 Samuel 6: 11-16). In conceiving Jesus, Mary became the dwelling-place of God Himself. When Mary approached Elizabeth, the older woman felt John leap within her, dancing before his God.

Why is the Church of the Nativity of St. John the Baptist at the bottom of the hill while the Church of the Visitation is at the top? Legend has it that the priest Zechariah had both a main home in the valley and a "summer home" where the elevation would make it cooler.

We proceeded directly to the upper church for Mass.[89] In his homily, Padre's theme was: Mary came *here* in haste, from Nazareth on foot, a journey comparable to our own a couple of days before which had taken us a couple of hours driving all told, in air-conditioned comfort. Hers was much longer, much more difficult, much less comfortable. (An amusing, albeit embarrassing, story: I had offered after the first day to start chanting the Responsorial Psalms, which I then did at every Mass. Just the day before, I had proposed to Padre that we chant the simple Latin Mass Parts at least for Sunday, which he had okayed as well. And then I proceeded to mess it up. For whatever reason, I zoned out after the Creed if we said it at all this particular Sunday; I may even have dozed off for a moment sitting up – by this point in the pilgrimage, I was dragging a bit. Whatever the reason, I suddenly zoned back in and heard Padre say something about, "and we say...." I thought it was time for the *Sanctus* and launched into it. Others joined in after a

---

[89] The readings for the Church of the Visitation according to the Custody Missal are: Zephaniah 3: 14-18; Responsorial, Isaiah 12; Luke 1: 39-56.

moment, but since I was not looking directly at him, I did not see what others reported to be an amused smile on Padre's face – because he had *actually* been introducing the Intercessions! I only realized my blunder when Br. Miguel took up with the Intercessions immediately upon us finishing the *Sanctus*. All I could do was a quiet face-palm. So, in my mind, at least, our Mass at the Church of the Visitation became the "Mass of the Double *Sanctus*." And, of course, I was wide awake from that point; sudden humiliation with a side of adrenaline kind of does that.)

The upper sanctuary of the Church of the Visitation contains magnificent paintings of scenes both from the Bible and from Christian history. Above the main altar is what I take to be Mary arriving in Ein Karem. Along the sides: Mary and Jesus at Cana; the 431 Council of Ephesus where the question of Mary's status as *Theotokos*, "God-Bearer," Mother *of God*, was definitively decided; Duns Scotus, the great Franciscan philosopher who advocated for the understanding that Mary was not just born and lived without sin, but was indeed *conceived* without sin through the prevenient grace of God; the 1571 Battle of Lepanto, a great victory over the Turks through the intercession of Our Lady and the prayers of the Rosary, on 07 October (formerly Our Lady of Victory, now commemorated as the Feast of Our Lady of the Rosary)[90]; Mary being crowned Queen of Heaven – and of course, the Visitation itself. High on the back wall of the church, above a pipe organ is one of the most strikingly beautiful paintings of the Virgin and Child I have ever seen, modern though it be.

Descending an exterior staircase, we entered the lower church – somewhat plainer but still filled with beautiful paintings high on three sides: Zechariah serving at the altar; the Visitation; and the Slaughter of the Innocents, while an angel hides Elizabeth and the infant John. Inset into the wall below that latter painting is a large boulder said to be the one illustrated in the painting, behind which the angel hid the mother and child. That John would have been endangered by Herod the Great's order that all male children less than two years of age be slain is possible, indeed likely. Ein Karem was close to Jerusalem (it is part of expansive west Jerusalem now) and would have been under Herod's jurisdiction. Interestingly, the altar is somewhat offset in the

---

[90] Don John of Austria, commander of the Christian forces, had on his flagship one of the earliest known copies of the image of Our Lady of Guadalupe, a mere forty years after the apparition to Juan Diego.

lower church – balanced along the eastern wall by the entrance to an ancient cistern.

In the courtyard outside, like in the Church of John the Baptist at the bottom of the hill, many tile plaques display the words of Mary's song which followed immediately from the Visitation quoted above – The *Magnificat* (Luke 1: 46-55):

> MY SOUL MAGNIFIES THE LORD AND MY SPIRIT REJOICES IN GOD MY SAVIOR, BECAUSE HE HAS REGARDED THE LOWLINESS OF HIS HANDMAID. FOR BEHOLD, HENCEFORTH ALL GENERATIONS SHALL CALL ME BLESSED, BECAUSE HE WHO IS MIGHTY HAS DONE GREAT THINGS FOR ME, AND HOLY IS HIS NAME. AND FOR GENERATION UPON GENERATION IS HIS MERCY TO THOSE WHO FEAR HIM. HE HAS SHOWN MIGHT. WITH HIS ARM HE HAS SCATTERED THE PROUD IN THE CONCEIT OF THEIR HEART. HE HAS PUT DOWN THE MIGHTY FROM THEIR THRONES AND HAS EXALTED THE LOWLY. HE HAS FILLED THE HUNGRY WITH GOOD THINGS AND THE RICH HE HAS SENT AWAY EMPTY. HE HAS GIVEN HELP TO ISRAEL HIS SERVANT, MINDFUL OF HIS MERCY – EVEN AS HE SPOKE TO OUR FATHERS – TO ABRAHAM AND TO HIS POSTERITY FOREVER.[91]

We walked back down the hill. Halfway, we stopped at another religious articles store vouched-for by Tony. I think it may have been connected with the Sisters of the Rosary, who also run a guest house for pilgrims. At the bottom of the walk, we took a break at a gelato shop!

Then we took a long bus ride into the Judaean Wilderness to the east, to Jericho, descending from Jerusalem's altitude of about 2500 feet above sea level to about 850 feet below sea level. We dropped altitude so fast that my ears popped. The thicker air plus temperatures pushing 100°F were, moreover, not nearly so pleasant as the morning had been. Along the way, the stark contrast with the western approaches to Jerusalem was impressive. There is pretty much *nothing* to the east but rocks. Whitish-grey rocks with just a hint of beige, against a deep blue, cloudless sky – harshly beautiful ... but *rocks*, and how anything could live there was beyond me. And yet we passed

---

[91] The plaques listed no provenance, but I suspect it is much as with the *Benedictus* plaques down the hill, that they were individually donated by various organizations. This text I also transcribed from my own photograph, retaining the "SMALL CAPS" presentation of the plaque.

ramshackle Bedouin camps as well as the goats they herd, nipping at the rocks as if finding some sustenance. Amazing.

Jericho is, on the other hand, an oasis – literally – with gardens and groves and orchards (bananas are a major product), by comparison with the surrounding landscape downright lush and green. As we drove through the town, Tony pointed out a lone sycamore tree, which he pointedly said is *not* the very tree climbed by the tax collector Zacchaeus (Luke 19: 5-9) – although some tour guides apparently try to pass it off as such, it is not *that* old, but it *is* the oldest sycamore tree in the world. It is in fact only about a thousand years old....

As Wael pulled the bus into a small parking area, Tony pointed out in the distance his own vacation home. Then, as we descended out of the bus, we beheld, looming over us, the Mount of Temptation, where Jesus spent forty days and forty nights fasting immediately after his Baptism in the nearby Jordan River.

> **Jesus was led up by the Spirit into the wilderness to be tempted by the devil. And he fasted forty days and forty nights, and afterward he was hungry. And the tempter came and said to him, "If you are the Son of God, command these stones to become loaves of bread." But he answered, "It is written, `Man shall not live by bread alone, but by every word that proceeds from the mouth of God.'"**
>
> **Then the devil took him to the holy city, and set him on the pinnacle of the temple, and said to him, "If you are the Son of God, throw yourself down; for it is written, `He will give his angels charge of you,' and `On their hands they will bear you up, lest you strike your foot against a stone.'"**
>
> **Jesus said to him, "Again it is written, `You shall not tempt the Lord your God.'"**
>
> **Again, the devil took him to a very high mountain, and showed him all the kingdoms of the world and the glory of them; and he said to him, "All these I will give you, if you will fall down and worship me." Then Jesus said to him, "Begone, Satan! for it is written, `You shall worship the Lord your God and him only shall you serve.'"**
>
> **Then the devil left him, and behold, angels came and ministered to him. (Matt. 4: 1-11)**

Tony pointed out that, given the proximity of mount and oasis, during his long fast culminating in the Temptations for which the mountain is named Jesus could have seen looming below him immediate relief from the torments of hunger and thirst, doubtless making the first Temptation all the more tantalizing to his human nature. Small against the side of the mount, we could see tiny structures – a Greek Orthodox monastery hanging off the sheer rocky face.

Sunday afternoon became something of a play day at that point, however. Near where Wael parked the bus was a large bazaar, Temptation Gallery, as well as an area where a man, a little boy, and their camel were set up. The man was taking the money, the boy was leading the camel, and the camel was giving rides – around the open area in front of the busses, up the short street in front of the bazaar, and back again. A few of our group took advantage of this stereotypical Holy Land tourist activity. Brother Miguel went full-on Lawrence of Arabia, procuring a white robe and the *kaffiyeh* headdress popular among the Bedouin before mounting up.

I did not ride the camel, but after Kristal's turn, she and I walked first up the street to where I had spied an adjunct of Temptation Gallery advertising Dead Sea cosmetics, and so I was able to procure for my wife some of the cosmetics and soap products that I had seen but passed up at the Nativity Souvenir Co-op the day before. We then walked back up and through the main Temptation Gallery where many kinds of souvenirs (including a variety of camel-leather goods), as well as various dried nuts and dates, were available for sale.

Regrettably, we did not visit *Tel es-Sultan*, the sizeable archaeological mound, which represents about ten thousand years of near-continuous settlement. Long considered the oldest city in the world, Jericho remains in the running for that title. The historian in me would have liked to see this with my own eyes, but it was not to be. Nor, it turns out, did we see a couple of other things that had been on our initial agenda. I had long since (well, since Friday) abandoned what had begun as constant comparison of our schedule with that sent to us by Nativity Pilgrimage a couple of months before in favor of simply going with the flow (as if I had any choice in the matter). So, I did not fully comprehend that we were squeezing a full day's scheduled itinerary into an afternoon. Things had to give.

As we departed Jericho, Tony presented us with the options. There were three more sites we were supposed to visit in the excursion to the east of Jerusalem. Having taken in Jericho, we still had the Baptism Site at Qasr al-Yahud on the Jordan River, the location where the Dead Sea Scrolls were found near Qumran, and the Dead Sea itself. Although it was still before midafternoon, we knew we had to be back to the Saint Gabriel Hotel by 17:00 to allow plenty of time to freshen up for the traditional end-of-pilgrimage "farewell" dinner at a restaurant outside the hotel – a night early. As it was terribly hot, we knew we would need those couple of hours.

As to Qasr al-Yahud, the reputed site of Jesus' Baptism, Tony argued that at this time of year, we would only see a bare trickle of muddy water through a narrow ribbon of mud in a mostly dry riverbed. We opted out.

We did see Qumran and the caves where the Dead Sea Scrolls were discovered in 1947, however – after a fashion. Tony told us the story of the most important archaeological discovery of the twentieth century. A young Bedouin goatherd, seeking a stray, cast a stone into one of the many caves dotting these cliffs. He was startled to hear clay pottery shattering. Hoping to find treasure, he did, just not the kind he expected or even recognized as such. Some of the many clay jars stored in that cave contained old scrolls, most in fragments. As it turned out, some were copies of Hebrew scriptures a thousand years older than any existing Biblical manuscript. The result was a revolution in Biblical studies that is still ongoing.

But we did not stop there, either. Tony said it was not worth the time it would take. As he told us the story of the Qumran community of Jewish "monks" called Essenes, he had Wael drive up and make a circle through the bus lot of the Qumran welcome center while he pointed out, far up the side of the cliff, the caves in which the scrolls were discovered. We continued onward.

And so, little more than an hour after pulling up in Jericho, we were making the turn off the road toward Kalia Beach, near the northern tip of the Dead Sea. As we approached, Tony described the process of "bathing" in the highly salinized and mineral-laden waters and benefiting from the unique chemicals to be found in the dark grey-brown mud (from which are formulated the Dead Sea cosmetics mentioned above). It involved some process of taking a dip in the water, slathering the mud all over the body, baking in the hot sun for ten or fifteen minutes, and then taking another dip to wash it off as best as possible. Or something like that. I did not pay close attention because, as he started his discourse, Tony had caught himself and pointedly said to me, "Not you, Kent." Not with the recent pacemaker implantation. And, as it happened, as I walked down toward the water's edge for a few minutes to take pictures, I spied a rather amusing sign written in Hebrew, English, and Russian – transcribed accurately as:

> Dead Sea bathing dangerous
> heart patients and owners
> of high blood pressure

This below a similar warning, in Hebrew, English, and *Arabic*, reading:

> Swimming on the stomach
> is strictly prohibited

I guess Arabs do not have high blood pressure, and Russians do not swim on their stomachs...?

Having trudged down to the beach, watched most of our number availing themselves of the opportunity to float like corks and follow the rest of Tony's prescription, and taken a few pictures, I trudged back up about halfway to the main strip, to "The Lowest Bar in the World." There I enjoyed a wonderfully chilled Goldstar Dark Lager at about 1300 feet below sea level. It was quite lovely, especially since I snagged a table by an evaporation air cooler. After a while, most of our "floaters" having passed by on their way back up to shower and change back into their street clothes, I trudged (it was *so* hot, the air was *so* thick – and humid to boot, right there by the Dead Sea, which gains its highly concentrated mineral content through evaporation into the surrounding air trapped in the "bowl" of the Dead Sea basin – yes, "trudged" is *exactly* the right word!) the long walk back up to the main strip, where I found most of our number had gathered in an open-air cantina at a table directly facing another evaporation air cooler. We shared a late, light lunch of a pizza, and I had another Goldstar.

About 16:00, we set forth back toward the hotel, retracing our path through the Judaean wilderness, ascending rapidly from 1300 feet below sea level to Bethlehem's 2530 feet above sea level. Bethlehem is actually slightly higher in elevation than Jerusalem. We arrived a bit after 17:00. We had some free time to freshen up and rest, until 19:00.

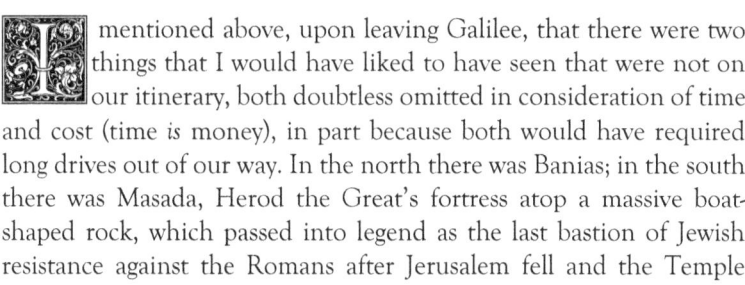 mentioned above, upon leaving Galilee, that there were two things that I would have liked to have seen that were not on our itinerary, both doubtless omitted in consideration of time and cost (time *is* money), in part because both would have required long drives out of our way. In the north there was Banias; in the south there was Masada, Herod the Great's fortress atop a massive boat-shaped rock, which passed into legend as the last bastion of Jewish resistance against the Romans after Jerusalem fell and the Temple

burned in AD 70, at the end of the Jewish War. It was less Roman military force than Roman military engineering that brought the fall of Masada – the remains of a great ramp built by the Tenth Legion under General Flavius Silva stand even today in remembrance of how the Romans moved their siege engines into place 1300 feet above the desert floor (therefore, pretty much at sea level...), against the walls of the fortress, and breached them ... to find that a thousand Jewish rebels had committed mass suicide rather than be slaughtered or taken. That happened in either AD 73 or 74. Amazingly, we are not certain which year it was, but then the Jewish-Roman historian Flavius Josephus could be disconcertingly careless with his chronology. Masada continues to loom over the Jewish psyche, a rallying cry more powerful by far even than Texans' "Remember the Alamo!" or the Greatest Generation's "Remember Pearl Harbor!"

For dinner Sunday night, we went out of the hotel back out by Shepherds' Fields, to the Grotto Restaurant across from the Shepherds' Nai where we had lunch the day before. At the Grotto, we had, a night early, our semi-formal "farewell dinner." It was virtually the same menu as lunch at Shepherds' Nai, but maybe even better. Hatem, the local head of Nativity Pilgrimage, joined us. There were thank yous and testimonies all around. Hatem joined Tony in making a strong case for Nativity Pilgrimage and the work it does, as not just another tour company, not even just another pilgrimage company, but indeed a ministry or apostolate to, among other things, support the native Christians of the Holy Land, especially those misidentified as "Palestinians" and trapped in Bethlehem. That is one of the most important things I think I learned and experienced on my pilgrimage to the Holy Land, that there is a dwindling population of essentially original Christians whose story is not told, or even worse, is *misrepresented*. There are indeed many Arab Christians who self-identify as "Palestinian Christians," but there are also those who, like Tony and Sana, proudly claim a heritage going back to before the arrival of the Arabs in the seventh century. "Palestinian" is, as I said, a modern political neologism rather than a historical ethnic description. The other topic of conversation was the role and value of Radio Maria, and the vital role almost everyone in attendance played in supporting that apostolate. I think every one of our pilgrims from Alexandria proper works to one degree or another as a volunteer; Kathie, in fact, hosts a show, *Sacred Treasures*.

It would have been an excellent way to end the pilgrimage. But we had one more day, a day that would bring us to the *sine qua non* of every Catholic pilgrimage to the Holy Land.

Monday 20 August 2018 – Holy Land Day Eight: *JERUSALEM*

Once again, the morning began with an excellent breakfast at the Saint Gabriel Hotel, then we were on the bus, out of Bethlehem and on the road toward Jerusalem. We drove around the western and northern walls of the Old City, past the Jaffa, New, and Damascus Gates. As we came upon the latter, Tony pointed out his "house" to us visible above the wall – a large building which he called an *insula*. I am amazed at how the Romans' name for a tenement or apartment building has survived through two millennia! Located just to the west of the Damascus Gate, at the edge of the Christian Quarter, it faces across the El-Wad street directly toward the Muslim Quarter. Three hundred years old, built on the foundation of an earlier structure going back to the 1200s, it is "his" house in the sense that all of the residents are members of his family, of which he is, as I understand, the head since the death of his father. As I discussed with him at lunch later that day, the Middle Eastern conception of "family" is quite different from our own. It is very much an extended family, virtually a clan or small tribe, including brothers, cousins, in-laws, and so forth. If I remember correctly, Tony's "immediate" family numbers six hundred, all living together in the building we saw. Coming from a culture whose families are much smaller (conceptually not extending further than the immediate nuclear family, grandparents and -children, and generally including cousins only to the first and second degree) and scattered to the four winds (besides my mother, residing in a nursing home near me, my nearest blood-relatives are my son, now living several hours away in another state, and my brother and his family, several hours away in pretty much the opposite direction), I find that mind-boggling. Our fast-paced, consumer-driven, highly mobile culture has lost something precious, I believe.[92] (And, "my mother, residing in a nursing home…"? – such is not part of Tony's culture, where elderly parents are cared for by the extended family within the home.)

---

[92] For an eye-opening account of rediscovering the value of close-knit community, see Rod Dreher's *The Little Way of Ruthie Leming: A Southern Girl, a Small Town, and the Secret of a Good Life* (New York: Grand Central Publishing, 2013).

Wael dropped us at the peak of the Mount of Olives, the highest of the hills of Jerusalem, the ridge facing the eastern wall of the Old City, the height of which is one of the sites associated with the Ascension of Our Lord into heaven, forty days after His Resurrection:

> And when he had said this, as they were looking on, he was lifted up, and a cloud took him out of their sight. And while they were gazing into heaven as he went, behold, two men stood by them in white robes, and said, "Men of Galilee, why do you stand looking into heaven? This Jesus, who was taken up from you into heaven, will come in the same way as you saw him go into heaven."
>
> Then they returned to Jerusalem from the mount called Olivet, which is near Jerusalem, a sabbath day's journey away.... (Acts 1: 9-12)

A mosque marks the site today. Standing within a large courtyard defined by an octagonal wall, all that remains of a fourth-century Byzantine church, the twelfth-century octagonal Crusader chapel once open to the sky has been covered by a dome and served as a mosque since the fall of Crusader Jerusalem to Saladin in 1187. Muslims do revere *Issa* – Jesus – as a prophet, although their beliefs about him are hugely different from our own. For instance, they regard him *only* as a prophet, inferior to *The* Prophet, for all that he was conceived virginally (by Mary or Miriam ... the sister of Moses!? – *Quran* Suras 19: 27-28 and 66: 12) and ascended to heaven from that very spot. He did so without having resurrected from the dead, however, because he did not die on the cross but was instead miraculously replaced by a lookalike. It could be considered a scandal that Muslims control this site, but such is the legacy of the *Status Quo*, which on balance probably is more beneficial to Christians than detrimental; Catholics are allowed to visit freely, and even to celebrate Mass there on the Feast of the Ascension.

Inside the small structure, there can be seen, framed in stone, the "Rock of the Ascension," bearing what is said to be a footprint, that of Christ, left behind when he rose into the heavens. The other print is said to have been cut out and moved to the al-Aqsa Mosque on the Temple Mount sometime in the Middle Ages. I looked hard. I squinted sideways. I could see no footprint.

A merchant was set up with a portable kiosk within the enclosure, just outside the door to the shrine. There I found precisely the panoramic poster view of Jerusalem my friend Angel had requested. I bought two.

We started our descent of the Mount of Olives, joining the path that Jesus would most likely have trodden, coming from Bethany to Jerusalem over the peak of the Mount of Olives, most notably on Palm Sunday. We proceeded to the Eleona, the "Olive Grove," the site of a church built by St. Helena in the early fourth century – but destroyed by the Persians in the seventh. It was rebuilt during the Age of the Crusades, but once Saladin took Jerusalem in 1187, the church fell into desuetude and ruin.

Rebuilding of the Eleona as the Church of Paternoster commenced in the mid-nineteenth century when a French princess acquired the spot, founded a Carmelite monastery, and built a chapel encompassing a cave where Jesus may have taught his disciples, at their behest, the only prayer he is recorded to have given them. Later, an attempt was made to rebuild the entire old Byzantine church of the Eleona, but funding ran out, and it remains unfinished. The walls define a large enclosure with the classic basilica floor plan still discernable.

Tony put Jesus' teaching of the Our Father into the context of the aftermath of the raising of Lazarus from the dead, which probably happened only a short time before Palm Sunday, at nearby Bethany, just to the east of the Mount of Olives. That is not precisely how the Bible presents it. Matthew has the Our Father (Matt. 6: 9-13) as part of the Sermon on the Mount (Matt. 5-7); Luke does not, however (Luke 11: 1-4), although neither does Luke present it so late in his Gospel, so soon before the Passion Narrative, as Tony would have it. I do not see any reason why Jesus could not have given this teaching more than once over the most likely three years of his ministry, including a final time on the Mount of Olives as events unfolded rapidly at the end. In any case, the site is overseen by Carmelite nuns, whose monastery is immediately adjacent to the church. Just outside the cave, Tony explained why, for simple acoustical reasons, the entrance of a cave, its *mouth*, formed a natural spot for a man to address a crowd. We then stepped inside where Fr. Emilio led us in praying the Lord's Prayer, after a short homily pointing out that for all the things we ask of God in this prayer ("Give us ... our daily bread; ... Lead us not into temptation, but deliver us from evil") we make only one promise: "Forgive us our trespasses, *as we forgive those who trespass against us.*"

Visitors to the Eleona, such as we, often leave notes and petitions in the cave to be prayed over by the cloistered nuns. Tony had told us about this more Catholic custom the day before, considering having the nuns praying over the petitions preferable to the more widely known custom of stuffing notes between the rocks of the Western Wall. In that latter place, he said, they are eventually just thrown away. He gathered our slips of paper from us and deposited them through a little window.

The unfinished walls of the abortive reconstruction of the Eleona display scores of large ceramic tile plaques bearing the words of the Our Father in the various languages of the world. Fired in the Armenian Quarter, each bordered by an elaborate uniform floral design, the tiles are works of art in themselves. They were everywhere; expansive though it was, there were more than could be contained in a single courtyard, and plaques were to be found in smaller nooks and crannies here, there, and yonder, including inside the church, to the tune (I believe) of 178! Finding the one in Hebrew, Tony explained why he believes that Jesus would have taught the Our Father to the disciples in that tongue, the liturgical language of Judaism, rather than, as commonly believed, in Aramaic – and read it to us in Hebrew;[93] in a

---

[93] Back home, I decided to use Tony's recitation, which I had recorded, to learn for myself the Our Father in Hebrew. In order to nail down the vowels – which are often not represented in Hebrew and are not on this plaque – I started doing a little research and found that no two versions of the "Hebrew Our Father" available today are the same. In fact, examining my pictures, which include a large concrete plaque from the Church of Paternoster bearing the prayer in both Hebrew and Aramaic, I saw that the two Hebrew versions displayed *in that very church* do not match each other! On reflection, it makes sense. Whether or not the Gospel of Matthew, our primary source for the prayer, was indeed first written in Hebrew as the early Church historian Eusebius states [*Historia Ecclesiastica* 3.24.6], and then translated into Greek, or was indeed first written in Greek as it comes down to us, we do not possess that purported Hebrew original. The case for the 14th-c. Rabbi Shem Tob's version, included in his anti-Christian polemic, *Eben Bohan*, going back to such a Hebrew original, made by George Howard, *The Gospel of Matthew according to a Primitive Hebrew Text* (Macon, Georgia: Mercer University Press, 1987), is opposed by Petri Luomanen, *Recovering Jewish-Christian Sects and Gospels* (Leiden: Brill, 2011), p. 3, n. 12, who finds Howard "convincingly" refuted by William L. Petersen in his review in *Journal of Biblical Literature* 108 (1989): 722-726. Any Hebrew version of the Our Father that exists today is almost certainly translated from Greek into Hebrew. Assuming that Jesus did indeed teach the prayer in Hebrew, and that Matthew remembered it exactly word for word in recording it first in that language, and even if he was the one who then translated it into Greek, such a translation even by the original author requires judgment calls in how best to represent the meaning of the original language in a second language. There is never a one-to-one correspondence of words and their meanings and connotations. A second person translating the same text into the same language will almost never choose exactly the same words, phrases, and idioms. It is therefore not surprising that the process of translating the prayer from (maybe) Hebrew to Greek then (definitely) to Hebrew yields different results. There is, consequently, no single "standard" Hebrew Our Father. Which is more authoritative? Having no clear answer to that question,

different area, he pointed out that Chaldean, one of the world's oldest languages still spoken, is placed directly opposite one of the world's newest languages – English – and proceeded to read the Chaldean to us!

I took a couple of quick pictures of those and a couple of other languages that have special meaning to me – Latin, of course, as well as Armenian. I wish I there had been time to get more, but the group was ready to move on.[94] Departing from the Eleona, most of us purchased olive sprigs and palm fronds from a young man recommended by Tony.

Proceeding a little further down, we entered the expansive Jewish cemetery. The Mount of Olives is a coveted place of burial because the Jews, still awaiting the Messiah, expect that when he comes, those buried on the Mount of Olives will resurrect first.

The spot provides a striking view of the Old City. Tony recruited one of his friends (he seemed to have them wherever we went) – a seller of scarves from whom he had already recommended we make our purchases (and we would, albeit later) – to use Ingrid's camera to take what would be our official group photo. There were also a number of individual and smaller-group photos taken before we continued down a steep grade to a first- or second-cemetery necropolis where, behind a grill, we could see the niches where bodies would be interred. After a year, the bones would be removed and placed into ossuary boxes, which we could also see there.

That was near the Church of *Dominus Flevit*, "the Lord wept":

> As he was now drawing near, at the descent of the Mount of Olives, the whole multitude of the disciples began to rejoice and praise God with a loud voice for all the mighty works that they had seen, saying, "Blessed is the King who comes in the name of the Lord! Peace in heaven and glory in the highest!" And some of the Pharisees in the multitude said to him, "Teacher, rebuke your disciples." He answered,

---

I therefore took the one displayed on the large plaque at the Church of Paternoster, as recited by Tony, as my own, worked out the vowels as best I could by listening to him, and have indeed learned it.

[94] Astonishingly enough, I can find no evidence of any kind of large format picture-book bearing the images of the tiles, nor can I find a complete online repository of images. One reason may be that the collection is ever growing and will be quickly rendered incomplete. Neither can I find an authoritative source for a current number; I have seen figures ranging up from "over sixty" to "well over one hundred," to "140," in addition to a vague "dozens upon dozens" .... The frequently repeated figure "62" seems low to me. "178," while high, is the number that I jotted down when we were there, although I did not count them....

"I tell you, if these were silent, the very stones would cry out."

And when he drew near and saw the city he wept [*flevit*] over it, saying, "Would that even today you knew the things that make for peace! But now they are hid from your eyes. For the days shall come upon you, when your enemies will cast up a bank about you and surround you, and hem you in on every side, and dash you to the ground, you and your children within you, and they will not leave one stone upon another in you; because you did not know the time of your visitation." (Luke 19: 37-44)

The church is very new, built by Antonio Barluzzi for the Franciscan Custody in the 1950s on a traditional site associated with the event, where hitherto there had been a small chapel. Dominus Flevit is the other Catholic church in Israel facing toward the west, across the Kidron valley toward Jerusalem because that is the direction Jesus was facing, toward the Temple, when he wept. The shape of the church, an elongated dome, is said to evoke those tears, although I am not sure I would see that without it being pointed out to me. While digging the foundations, workers uncovered remains that inspired a wholesale excavation of the site, unearthing ancient Canaanite as well as more recent Byzantine tombs. They also found a Byzantine monastery containing mosaic floors that Barluzzi incorporated into the church. In the altar is a mosaic roundel of a hen and her chicks, surrounded by the words, "*IERVSALEM IERVSALEM QVOTIES VOLVI CONGREGARE FILIOS TVOS QVEMADMODVM GALLINA CONGREGAT PVLLOS SVOS SVB ALAS*"; inside the roundel, below the nest, is the question, "*ET NOLVISTI?*" - "Jerusalem, Jerusalem, how I have wanted to gather your children like a hen gathers her chicks under her wings"; "And you would not?" - all recalling Our Lord's lament over Jerusalem:

> "O Jerusalem, Jerusalem, killing the prophets and stoning those who are sent to you! How often would I have gathered your children together as a hen gathers her brood under her wings, and you would not!" (Matt. 23: 37)

Rendering that last as a question is interesting. The leaders of Jerusalem had just rejected Jesus as their Messiah ... and would soon do so again, definitively. Here it becomes a final plea.

Behind the altar, a large picture window incorporating a host-and-chalice design gives a panoramic view of the city. When one stands dead center in the church, and a typical altar-cross or crucifix sits centered on the altar, it transfixes the golden Dome of the Rock precisely.

... None of which did we see, however, except obliquely, through a side window on the northern wall as another group's service was taking place. We had expected to have Mass at 10:30 inside the church. Unfortunately, as we arrived, I overheard Tony tell Padre that larger groups take precedence and that our small group was being bumped into an adjacent outdoor chapel (there seemed to be two).[95] Padre's theme was, as usual, that Jesus came *here* - knowing what was about to happen to him. "He suffered, and he cried here *in this place*. ... One of those tears is *for you*. ... Let us be thankful to God for the blessings He has given us *here* in the Holy Land."[96]

In a large courtyard adjacent to the Church of *Dominus Flevit*, overlooking the city, Tony described what we could see from the Mount of Olives: from the earliest Jebusite city which became the City of David at left, in the south; across to the massive extension of Mount Moriah created by Herod the Great which became the Temple Mount, now dominated by the Muslim Dome of the Rock shining brilliantly golden, beyond which could be seen the grey domes of the Church of the Holy Sepulcher; the walled-up Golden Gate through which (an earlier incarnation of course, since the present walls date only from the sixteenth century) Jesus passed on Palm Sunday, through which the Jews believe the Messiah will arrive when he comes and Christians believe Jesus will arrive when he comes again - for which reason the gate has been repeatedly walled up, even by Suleiman the Magnificent shortly after rebuilding the walls with an open gate!; to St. Stephen's Gate through which the first martyr was dragged out into the northern part of the Kidron Valley and stoned to death. We could also see, further down the slope of the Mount of Olives, such other landmarks as the golden spires of the Russian Orthodox Church of St. Mary Magdalene.

Leaving *Dominus Flevit*, we caught up with one of the scarf vendors that Tony recommended - in fact, it was his friend Karkash whom

---

[95] Ironically, when I took my pictures through the window, after our Mass had ended, the group that was currently there numbered only six. We were thirteen. Perhaps we were into the next time slot by that time, and the larger group that had evidently bumped us had departed.

[96] Per the Custody Missal, the Mass at *Dominus Flevit* had the readings: Jeremiah 14: 17-21, Psalm 79, and Luke 19: 41-44.

Tony had corralled to take our group picture a little while earlier. Kristal and I went in together to buy several elegant pashmina shawls and scarves to take home as gifts: for my wife, her sisters (Kris' sisters-in-law), Kris' daughters, and my son's girlfriend.

We continued our walk down to the bottom of the Mount of Olives, arriving at Gethsemane, the "place of the olive press," the garden to which Our Lord retreated after the Last Supper, where he suffered the agony of knowing every detail of his coming Passion; where his disciples could not watch with him even one hour; where Judas would appear, betraying him to the Temple Guard, and where his disciples would flee, abandoning him. Most of the trees from which the Mount of Olives takes its name are long gone, victims of various wars through the centuries starting with the Romans – who pitched their camps there during the Jewish War and cut down every tree. So, although it is often said that some of the trees in the small enclosed garden we entered are "witness trees," that is, that they beheld Jesus' agony in the garden forty years earlier, that is probably not the case ... for the most part.

On the other hand, olive trees are among the longest-lived trees there are and can grow back after being cut down to their roots, so it would not be surprising if the progenitor of one of these trees *did* stand in mute witness ca. AD 33, when God Incarnate willingly took upon Himself the sins of the world, becoming as the Scapegoat of Yom Kippur.

> Then Jesus went with them to a place called Gethsemane, and he said to his disciples, "Sit here, while I go yonder and pray." And taking with him Peter and the two sons of Zebedee, he began to be sorrowful and troubled. Then he said to them, "My soul is very sorrowful, even to death; remain here, and watch with me." And going a little farther he fell on his face and prayed, "My Father, if it be possible, let this cup pass from me; nevertheless, not as I will, but as thou wilt." And he came to the disciples and found them sleeping; and he said to Peter, "So, could you not watch with me one hour? Watch and pray that you may not enter into temptation; the spirit indeed is willing, but the flesh is weak." Again, for the second time, he went away and prayed, "My Father, if this cannot pass unless I drink it, thy will be done." And again he came and found them sleeping, for their eyes were heavy. So, leaving them again, he went

away and prayed for the third time, saying the same words. Then he came to the disciples and said to them, "Are you still sleeping and taking your rest? Behold, the hour is at hand, and the Son of man is betrayed into the hands of sinners. Rise, let us be going; see, my betrayer is at hand."

While he was still speaking, Judas came, one of the twelve, and with him a great crowd with swords and clubs, from the chief priests and the elders of the people. Now the betrayer had given them a sign, saying, "The one I shall kiss is the man; seize him." And he came up to Jesus at once and said, "Hail, Master!" And he kissed him. Jesus said to him, "Friend, why are you here?" Then they came up and laid hands on Jesus and seized him. And behold, one of those who were with Jesus stretched out his hand and drew his sword, and struck the slave of the high priest, and cut off his ear. Then Jesus said to him, "Put your sword back into its place; for all who take the sword will perish by the sword. Do you think that I cannot appeal to my Father, and he will at once send me more than twelve legions of angels? But how then should the scriptures be fulfilled, that it must be so?" At that hour Jesus said to the crowds, "Have you come out as against a robber, with swords and clubs to capture me? Day after day I sat in the temple teaching, and you did not seize me. But all this has taken place, that the scriptures of the prophets might be fulfilled." Then all the disciples forsook him and fled. (Matt. 26: 36-56)

We could perhaps have gone directly from the Garden into the adjacent Basilica of the Agony, but we did not. Instead, we went back out the gate whence we had entered, around the corner, and entered that church from the front – approaching one of the most oft-photographed landmarks in Jerusalem, the iconic triangular mosaic surmounting the Romanesque façade of that church. Designed by Barluzzi, built in 1924, also called the "Church of All Nations" because contributions from around the world financed its construction, the Basilica of the Agony incorporates design elements from all the churches that have occupied this site, back to the Byzantine church of the fourth century. Its central feature, directly before the altar, bordered by a wrought-iron "crown of thorns," is the Rock of the Agony upon which Our Lord is said to have poured out his entreaties that, if possible, the cup of his coming Passion might pass from him. Stained-glass windows admit only a muted, violet light that, along with other design elements, purposely evokes the darkness and gloom of that Holy Thursday night two thousand years ago.

From there, it was only a short walk to where Wael could pick us up to take us to lunch, which was at the Notre Dame Centre just north of the New Gate, the westernmost gate in the northern wall of the Old City. The Notre Dame Centre is a picturesque castle-like structure owned by Vatican City. It was conceived in the nineteenth century to minister to pilgrims, a mission which it has maintained through good times and bad. Part of the complex is a hotel (which Steve Ray's pilgrims use). Flanking the lobby were two dining establishments, a restaurant at left, and a buffet at right. Somehow Kristal and I got separated from the group – we went through the buffet line, but then could not find them in that area. Tony and Wael were there, however, and waved us over to their table where we had a nice visit. Later, we found Fr. Emilio and pretty much the rest of our group across the way in the restaurant, finishing up their meal.

I believe it was Fr. Emilio who pointed out that the Notre Dame Centre hosts a permanent exhibit of the Shroud of Turin, almost certainly the authentic burial cloth of Jesus when he was taken from the Cross and entombed until the third day. Knowing we had about a half an hour, several of us went across with Padre, who referred to a life-size facsimile of the Shroud mounted on one wall as well as a life-size effigy of the Man on the Shroud in death as he explained how perfectly – and graphically – the ghostly image on the Shroud testifies to the sufferings of Our Lord as described in the Gospels.[97]

After lunch and that short excursion, the bus took us around and back up the street paralleling the northern wall of the Old City, dropping us near the northeastern corner. We then walked south through a Muslim graveyard, which does not appear nearly so well maintained as the immaculate Jewish cemetery on the Mount of Olives. We generally paralleled the eastern wall of the Old City until we came to the northernmost gate, variously called "Lion's," "St. Stephen's," "Sheep," or even "Lady Mary's" (for the church we were about to visit).

---

[97] Little did I know then, August 2018, that within just a few months the Cathedral of St. John Berchmans in Shreveport, Louisiana – just 75 minutes north of Natchitoches – would come into possession of a collection of Shroud-related materials that will, once it is properly displayed, dwarf the exhibit at the Notre Dame Centre of Jerusalem. See below in Chapter Five.

Entering that particular gate, which is flanked by bas-reliefs of two small lions (hence the name, although, as I understand, they are leopards), brought us into the Muslim Quarter of the Old City.

The Old City, which is not contiguous with the city of Jerusalem as it was in the time of Jesus but instead as it developed in the later Middle Ages and more recent centuries, is (very) roughly a square, oriented (very) roughly north-south-east-west, and divided culturally, religiously, and even historically into four unequal quarters – with the Temple Mount cutting into the eastern two quarters. The Muslim Quarter (the largest) is in the northeast, then clockwise there are the Jewish Quarter (the smallest) in the southeast, the Armenian Quarter where my friend Angel Kitishian grew up in the southwest, and the generically named Christian Quarter in the northwest. The present Old City is shifted north from the city of two thousand years ago, when Mount Zion and the City of David, presently outside the sixteenth-century Ottoman walls to the south, were within the city while much of the Christian and Muslim Quarters lay outside the walls to the north. Most obviously, of course, the location of the Church of the Holy Sepulcher, now in the heart of the Christian Quarter, was at that time outside the walls.

From the gate, we walked fifty or seventy-five yards up Lion's Gate Street and turned right under a lintel bearing the words, "BIRTH PLACE *of the* VIRGIN MARY." We passed from a crowded, busy street (mainly pedestrian, few vehicles, but narrow) through a short passage into a quiet, peaceful, shaded courtyard in front of St. Anne's Church, named for the mother of Our Lady who, tradition says, gave birth here, in this place.

The idea that this church, considered the best surviving example of a Crusader-era church, located just north of the Temple Mount, actually marks the birthplace of Mary, engendered a bit of debate among our number, given the fact that Luke places her in Nazareth at the time of the Annunciation thirteen to fifteen years later. I, for one, have no problem with the tradition. Michael Hesemann, in his *Mary of Nazareth*, makes a strong case based on ancient tradition recorded in the apocryphal *Protoevangelium of James* and the *Gospel of Pseudo-Matthew* that Our Lady may well have been born here, in the shadow of the Temple.[98] He reports an ancient name for the nearby gate today called "Lion's" as, in Arabic, preserving the Byzantine-era name, "*Bab*

---

[98] Hesemann, loc. 901 ff.

Sitti Maryam – Lady Mary's Gate."[99] Much more speculatively, if Jesus had kinfolk there in northeastern Jerusalem, such might help explain his movements described in the early part of the Gospel of John:

> ... John was standing with two of his disciples [at Bethany beyond the Jordan, where he was baptizing[100]]; and he looked at Jesus as he walked, and said, "Behold, the Lamb of God!" The two disciples heard him say this, and they followed Jesus. Jesus turned, and saw them following, and said to them, "What do you seek?" And they said to him, "Rabbi" (which means Teacher), "where are you staying?" He said to them, "Come and see." They came and saw where he was staying; and they stayed with him that day, for it was about the tenth hour.
>
> One of the two who heard John speak, and followed him, was Andrew, Simon Peter's brother. He first found his brother Simon, and said to him, "We have found the Messiah" (which means Christ). ....
>
> The next day Jesus decided to go to Galilee [where] On the third day there was a marriage at Cana in Galilee.... (John 1: 35-39, 43; 2: 1)

Two disciples follow Jesus from where John the Baptist sees him, presumably in the morning, at Bethany beyond the Jordan. By the tenth hour – by Jewish reckoning, from sunrise about 06:00, about 16:00 – they are "**where [Jesus] was staying**" (John 1: 39). It is about ten hours walking from Bethany beyond the Jordan to what is now St. Anne's Church. If, as Hesemann, speculates, the site remained in the hands of Our Lady's relatives, Jesus may have gone to stay there overnight. Wherever he went, it was not in the middle of nowhere; Andrew's brother Simon was in the area, which implies it was some

---

[99] Ibid.

[100] Bethany beyond the Jordan, identified with a short (1.5 miles), spring-fed tributary of the Jordan River, the Wadi Kharrar, located almost directly across the Jordan from Qasr al-Yahud, is the rival pilgrimage "Site of Jesus' Baptism." Qasr al-Yahud being in Israel, the Wadi Kharrar being in Jordan, the former sees a lot more pilgrimage traffic, to Israeli delight and Jordanians' chagrin. Which was the actual site of Jesus' baptism will probably never be determined. They are so close together John probably baptized at both locations, and probably many more. Interestingly enough, however, the last three Popes have each visited the latter, in Jordanian territory, during their highly publicized pilgrimages. – William Booth and Taylor Luck, "Pope picks one of dueling baptism sites in visit to Holy Land," *The Washington Post* (20 May 2014) [https://www.washingtonpost.com/world/middle_east/pope-picks-one-of-dueling-baptism-sites-in-visit-to-holy-land/2014/05/20/7cd22336-e00a-11e3-9442-54189bf1a809_story.html]

population center; otherwise, the coincidence seems unlikely. Then, on the third day after that, "**there was a marriage at Cana,**" at which Jesus and the disciples were present. From Jerusalem to Cana is about 96 miles, 32 hours of walking, or three days walking ten-plus hours per day. Jesus and his first disciples would, therefore, have walked a long distance in just a couple of days, arrived at the wedding, and then (as the King James Version translates it bluntly), "They wanted wine." I bet they did!

Family just north of the Temple is not necessary as a solution to where Jesus was staying. If he in fact already had friends at Bethany in Judaea, just beyond the Mount of Olives (Lazarus and his sisters Mary and Martha), they could just as well have provided him lodging. It seems less likely, in that case, that Simon would just happen to be nearby.

Its mostly intact twelfth-century architecture today distinguishes Saint Anne's Church – late Romanesque, just before the explosion of the Gothic style. It was one of the first churches built in Jerusalem after the First Crusaders captured the city in July 1099. But the Crusaders were, in actuality, *rebuilding* a former church on the site. They rebuilt it as St. Anne's Church, after the mother of Mary, but until ninety years before and for at least six hundred years before that, the oldest church in Jerusalem stood there, a Byzantine church dedicated to Mary herself. Remnants of that church's mosaic floor are still visible, decorated with crosses. Such a design feature dates the floor to before 427, because in that year Emperor Theodosius II forbade crosses in floor mosaics because of the impiety of walking on the image of the holy instrument of our Salvation. That first St. Mary's, perhaps the first church dedicated to Our Lady after the legalization of Christianity in the 300s, was damaged but not destroyed in the 614 Persian invasion, and continued in use until the "Mad Caliph" destroyed both it and the Holy Sepulcher in 1009.[101]

Besides its rich history and noble Romanesque simplicity, what has stood for near a thousand years as St. Anne's church is famed for its acoustics. Another group of pilgrims was present when we entered, among them a small group chanting a beautiful rendition of, I believe, the *Te Deum*. Once they had departed, I was privileged to chant the *Salve Regina* along with Padre Emilio. Kathie and I were discussing getting the group together since most of them knew it when Padre, who was not party to our hushed conversation, appeared from across the

---

[101] Hesemann, *Mary of Nazareth*, loc. 917 ff.

nave and started chanting – so I joined in. Great minds obviously think alike. Although I did not perceive it at the time, a video that Kristal took sounds like others joined in as well. And the acoustics were indeed remarkable, especially then and there, in the moment.

A little later, after exploring the crypt where Our Lady may well have been born, I returned to the nave and, just before we left the church, stood right on top of a star on the floor in front of the altar, across which Padre and I had faced each other as we sang, and chanted one *Non Nobis Domine*[102] (Patrick Doyle's from Kenneth Branagh's *Henry V*) – and that was, indeed, as I had read, the sweet spot. I got no recording, unfortunately, but I do have the memory.

Not far from St. Anne's, further back in the courtyard, can be seen the remains of the Pool of Bethesda, renowned as where Jesus healed on the Sabbath:

> After this there was a feast of the Jews, and Jesus went up to Jerusalem. Now there is in Jerusalem by the Sheep Gate a pool, in Hebrew called Bethzatha, which has five porticoes. In these lay a multitude of invalids, blind, lame, paralyzed, waiting for the moving of the water; for an angel of the Lord went down at certain seasons into the pool, and troubled the water: whoever stepped in first after the troubling of the water was healed of whatever disease he had. One man was there, who had been ill for thirty-eight years. When Jesus saw him and knew that he had been lying there a long time, he said to him, "Do you want to be healed?" The sick man answered him, "Sir, I have no man to put me into the pool when the water is troubled, and while I am going another steps down before me." Jesus said to him, "Rise, take up your pallet, and walk." And at once the man was healed, and he took up his pallet and walked. **Now that day was the sabbath.** ... (John 5: 1-9)

Of course, Jesus healing on the Sabbath was, to the Jewish authorities, worse than the sick man's lifetime of suffering which Jesus alleviated.

What is now called the Lion's Gate or St. Stephen's Gate was then called the Sheep Gate (as does John), because the market for procuring sheep for the Temple sacrifices was just beyond it. Hesemann

---

[102] "*Non nobis, Domine, non nobis, / sed nomini tuo da gloriam*" – "Not to us, O Lord, not to us, but to thy name give glory" (Psalm 115: 1 [113: 9 traditional]).

speculates the proximity of the market to have indeed been why St. Joachim, the husband of Anne and father of Mary. According to the *Protoevangelium*, Joachim was a wealthy dealer in cattle, which would have included sheep for the Temple sacrifices.[103]

Exiting Bethesda through the courtyard fronting St. Anne's, we went a short distance further up Lions' Gate Street, and began the *Via Dolorosa*, the Way of Sorrows, an extended walk of about a quarter-mile which is obviously not a "site" per se, but rather a route through the narrow streets of the Muslim Quarter into the Christian Quarter, with various individual locations traditionally associated with the Stations of the Cross formally marked by black disks bearing Roman numerals mounted to the walls of buildings. Other identifications ranging from simple to ornate often accompany those formal disks.

Historically speaking, most scholars consider it doubtful that the traditional "pilgrims' route" of the *Via Dolorosa* traces the actual route upon which Our Lord carried the Cross to his place of execution. Jerome Murphy-O'Connor sums up the case quite well.[104] For one thing, it is far more likely that the "Praetorium" in which Pilate would have judged Jesus should be identified with the palace built by Herod the Great, the modern Citadel just inside the Jaffa Gate, than at the Antonia Fortress overlooking the Temple, which was a military barracks and base focusing on keeping a close eye on the troublesome Jews. An abundance of ancient evidence places the Jerusalem residence and headquarters of the Roman procurators at Herod's Palace, including contemporary Philo of Alexandria, who puts Pilate there on the occasion of an earlier dispute with the Jews, the matter of the golden shields.[105] Condemned there, on the opposite side of the Old City from the traditional spot, Jesus would have carried his Cross on a path coinciding with the traditional route only toward its end – converging on Calvary or Golgotha, now inside the Basilica of the Holy Sepulcher. Secondly, the tradition placing the Way along its present path only

---

[103] Hesemann, *Mary of Nazareth*, locs. 841, 977.

[104] Jerome Murphy-O'Connor, "Tracing the Via Dolorosa," Chapter 5 in *Jesus: The Last Day – A Collection of Essays Published by the Biblical Archaeology Society*, ed. Molly Dewsnap Meinhardt (Washington: Biblical Archaeology Society, 2003), pp. 71-89, which forms the major source for what follows here.

[105] Pilate displayed, inside the Roman headquarters and therefore out of sight of the Jews, golden shields honoring the Emperor Tiberius. Out of sight, he doubtless thought the Jews would have no complaint. He was wrong. Although he seems to have purposely left off the image of the emperor that was customary on such mementos, Pilate did include the usual inscriptions with their clear implication of imperial divinity. Such an affront against the First Commandment, within the very precincts of Jerusalem, was all it took to incite the Jews to formally protest, eventually to the emperor himself.

developed during the fourteenth century, as the Franciscans formalized an overall systematic circuit of the holy places that was based more than anything else on servicing the pilgrimage industry most efficiently. Nevertheless, Murphy-O'Connor concludes, "The Via Dolorosa is defined not by history but by faith."[106] That faith itself – of millions, at least, who have through the last seven centuries walked the present route, which is, even if modern scholars are correct, nonetheless within a few hundred yards of the historical route and ends at the same destination – hallows the religious exercise *qua* religious exercise. For simplicity's sake, going forward, I refer to various Stations as "marking the spot where such-and-such happened" and ask that the reader bear in mind the problematic state of such identifications, which I will belabor no further.

The Pilgrims' *Via Dolorosa*, as well-walked as it is, is nevertheless not a dedicated way, by which I mean that the streets are part of the everyday life of the Old City, with all the hustle and bustle of the inhabitants going about their business even as pilgrims make their way along it. Shops, markets, and so forth open directly onto the streets. It is as if a way were marked through the middle of Natchitoches, and we were able to walk it devotionally – which we do, of course, every Good Friday – but without the police blocking traffic for us and with considerably narrower streets and greater crowds than we experience back home. In the midst of it all, we walked, carrying small crosses to remind us of the Cross He bore, praying the Rosary, stopping at each Station as Padre led us in the meditations as written by St. Alphonsus Liguori, and praying, "We adore you O Christ, and we praise you, – because by your Cross you have redeemed the world...":

I. Station: Pilate Condemns Jesus to Death – A further hundred yards or so along the Lion's Gate Road from the entrance to St. Anne's Church, to the left, the First Station is commemorated in the courtyard of the El-Omariya Elementary School for Boys.

> **And as soon as it was morning the chief priests, with the elders and scribes, and the whole council held a consultation; and they bound Jesus and led him away and delivered him to Pilate. ... And having scourged Jesus, [Pilate] delivered him to be crucified. (Mark 15: 1, 15)**

Established in the early twentieth century and named for the seventh-century Muslim conqueror of Jerusalem, the El-Omariya School

---

[106] Murphy-O'Connor, "Via Dolorosa," p. 88.

rest atop the site of the Antonia Fortress. It is not often open to pilgrims, never when students are present, and otherwise only at the sufferance of the caretaker, so instead, we turned to the right ...

II. Station: Jesus Takes Up His Cross – Across the street from the El Omariya School is a Franciscan Friary. We passed into a courtyard which gave access to two chapels, dedicated respectively to the Flagellation and Condemnation of Jesus.

> **Then Pilate took Jesus and scourged him. And the soldiers plaited a crown of thorns, and put it on his head, and arrayed him in a purple robe; they came up to him, saying, "Hail, King of the Jews!" and struck him with their hands. ... [T]hey took Jesus, and he went out, bearing his own cross, to the place called the place of a skull, which is called in Hebrew Golgotha.** (John 19: 2-3, 17)

In the Chapel of the Flagellation, colorful stained glass depicts the Flagellation and the Crowning with Thorns, Pilate presenting Jesus to the Jews and Barabbas going free, and Pilate washing his hands; the Chapel of the Condemnation marks the spot where Jesus is said to have taken up his Cross. It also contains the *"lithostratus,"* long assumed to be the flagstone pavement on which Jesus stood. In reality, the flagstones date from about a century later, a product of the same building program as produced a landmark that is not explicitly one of the stations but is associated with the Passion. The flagstones are of direct interest to the Passion, however, in that they contain scratched game-marks inscribed by Roman soldiers such as those who "cast dice" for Our Lord's seamless garment as he suffered on the Cross (John 19: 23-24).

Perhaps somewhat out of sequence, a bit further along the street is one of the iconic images of the Via Dolorosa, the *Ecce Homo* arch, commemorating when Pilate presented the scourged Jesus – beaten and bloodied, crowned with thorns – to the Jews ("Behold the man!") and gave them the choice to free Jesus or Barabbas. They chose Barabbas. We passed under the arch, which is commonly misrepresented as surviving from the Antonia Fortress but was really built by the Emperor Hadrian a century later, in AD 135, after the Second Jewish War (the "Bar Kochba War" of 132-135) left the Jews utterly crushed and expelled from Jerusalem for good, the city being rebuilt as a Roman city, Aelia Capitolina. We continued slightly downhill as the street became very congested with vendors and shops on both sides.

We turned sharply to the left (south) onto El-Wad Street, which to the north leads through dense markets to the Damascus Gate, and to the south generally parallels the western edge of the Temple Mount. At that turn, we saw a small Israeli Security kiosk, manned by (I believe) three heavily armed police, although they seemed at ease. At the time, I thought visible security at that intersection would make sense because I was under the impression that we were passing from the Islamic Quarter to the Christian Quarter, that El-Wad indeed marks the boundary. It does not. So, I am not sure what garners that intersection special attention that is even visible on Google Maps' Street View (date-stamped Sep 2011) in the form of barricades stacked against the wall, ready for use.

III. Station: Jesus Falls for the First Time – Immediately after turning right onto El-Wad Street, we hooked back to the left into a small Armenian Catholic chapel, passing under a stone relief of Jesus falling. Then, in the entrance hallway, we beheld a stunningly crafted shrine with basically the same image in statue form, backed by a painting of ranks of angels watching and praying in grief. I imagine them waiting and ready for a command to intervene that would not be given.

The Third Station is the first of several traditional Stations of the Cross which are not backed up by Scripture. That is not to say that they did not happen, of course. There is robust and early tradition for some; there is the quite simple human likelihood in the case of others, such as this one. Beaten, scourged, abused, doubtless sleep-deprived, by this time undoubtedly dehydrated and weakened by loss of blood – and bearing upon himself the burden of mankind's sin – now forced to carry, very likely, a crossbar weighing close to a hundred pounds – it is near certain that Jesus would have fallen, probably several times. If not there, then somewhere along the route.

IV. Station: Jesus Meets His Afflicted Mother – Although this next station was long commemorated a few dozen yards further along the street, it has, in recent years, been moved to the immediately adjacent Armenian Catholic Church of Our Lady of the Spasm. We observed this Station in a courtyard below an elaborately carved monument with a cross, "In Memory of the Armenian martyrs of 1915."

"Spasm" refers to the intensely emotional sob of grief any mother would suffer at the sight of her child so abused. As prophesied by Simeon in the Temple so many years before (Luke 2: 34), a sword of grief did pierce Our Lady's heart as she accompanied Jesus to his death....

V. Station: Simon of Cyrene Helps Jesus Carry His Cross – Twenty-five yards further on, the Way of the Cross turned to the right, onto Via Dolorosa Street. Immediately on the left, a Latin inscription on the lintel above a door marked the Fifth Station: "*SIMONI CYRENAEO CRUX IMPONITUR* - THE CROSS IS PLACED UPON SIMON THE CYRENEAN." All four Gospels record this event, but here I quote only one:

> And as they led him away, they seized one Simon of Cyrene, who was coming in from the country, and laid on him the cross, to carry it behind Jesus. (Luke 23: 26)

The door enters the first Franciscan house in Jerusalem, dating to 1229. Having turned the corner, we began the gradual ascent to Golgotha along the stepped street, which got narrower and was covered in areas by awnings and arches. We proceeded about a hundred yards or so....

VI. Station: Veronica Offers Her Veil to Jesus - A wooden door with studded metal bands marks the Greek Melkite Catholic Church of St. Veronica. Another of the several Stations based on tradition rather than Scripture, this church commemorates the brave woman who stepped out of the crowd and wiped Jesus' face, by this time battered, bloodied, dirty, giving him what comfort she could in the instant before the Roman soldiers would doubtless have shoved her back from the procession. The cloth she still held was then found to bear the imprint of Jesus' face. The "legend" of St. Veronica and the Holy Face of Jesus long predates the fourteenth-century development of the Stations of the Cross; the Cloth of St. Veronica has been in the Basilica of St. Peter in Rome since the eighth century. Rationalists have long taken the "coincidence" of the name "Veronica" with the Latin *vera* "true" plus Greek *icon* "image" to indicate the legendary status of the tale, but such a bilingual "folk etymology" makes no sense, and the name could just as easily be a Latinized Hellenistic Jewish form of the Greek name Berenice - which was borne by other Jewish women of the age, most famously the sister of King Herod Agrippa II who became the concubine of the Roman general Titus during the Jewish War a generation later.

VII. Station: Jesus Falls for the Second Time - Seventy-five yards further uphill, at the junction of the Via Dolorosa with the Souq Khan al Zeit (the Oil Market - and the *real* boundary between the Christian and Islamic Quarters), we paused at what was in the first century the site of the Gate of Judgment, passing through the western wall of the city in the north. It was called the Gate of Judgment because the names of the accused and their sentences were posted here for all to see. The marker appears by an intricately designed red and black door entering a pair of chapels, one above the other. Although we did not go in, the lower chapel is open; the upper chapel is closed to the public. There we commemorated the Seventh Station.

At this point, as I understand it, the traditional pilgrims' Via Dolorosa we were walking converged with the more likely historical way of the Cross argued by scholars. Either way, Jesus would have passed through the Judgment Gate. Perhaps, and I am just guessing, the *titulus* bearing the statement of his crime would have been posted here –in this case with a duplicate being given to affix to the Cross itself.

VIII. Jesus Speaks to the Women of Jerusalem – Twenty yards further along, outside the city wall of Jesus' time but still passing through a dense mass of humanity seemingly oblivious to the significance of the events that played out here, in this place, near two thousand years ago, we found the eighth station via a round stone embedded in the rough-hewn stone wall of the Greek monastery of St. Charalambos, an early martyr. Below the marker, a Latin cross with the letters *IC XC NI KA* in the four quadrants proclaims via an abbreviation for the Greek, "Jesus Christ Conquers." Such an outcome would not have seemed likely when the women wailed and lamented him....

> But Jesus turning to them said, "Daughters of Jerusalem, do not weep for me, but weep for yourselves and for your children." (Luke 23: 28)

At that point, for some reason that was not explained,[107] we backtracked a short way, then followed what was long ago the Roman Cardo Maximus, the "Main Street" integral to every planned Roman settlement from army camps to full-blown planned cities, such as Roman Jerusalem was after the Jewish city suffered utter destruction in the First and Second Jewish Wars (AD 66-70 and 132-135). We did not go all the way to the excavated portion of the Roman street, only so far as a flight of 28 steps to the right, then up a winding lane to what then would have been within sight of Golgotha, today is a Coptic chapel marked with a column built into the door –

---

[107] It was not explained, but I have a theory. The present walking path must adhere to streets and paths weaving around buildings that were obviously not there at the time of the Crucifixion. Assuming that, whether the full Way of the Cross started at the Antonia or Herod's Palace, it passed through a gate where is the Seventh Station, Jesus would almost certainly have carried his Cross from that point to the peak of Calvary directly past the points where are the Eighth and Ninth Stations.

IX. Jesus Falls for the Third Time – The Coptic chapel of St. Helena, the mother of Constantine.

Then, again, we backtracked, made our way a few more yards up the street, then turned right once more and were on St. Helena Street, leading to the courtyard of the Basilica of the Holy Sepulcher, rightfully called the holiest place in Christendom. The last five of the fourteen Stations are inside that massive church, which encompasses what remains of the mount of Calvary on which Jesus "was crucified [and] died," as well as the Tomb in which he "was buried ... [and] On the third day, ... rose again from the dead..." (The Apostles' Creed). The sites of the Crucifixion and the Resurrection are really within just a few yards of each other (contrary to most people's – and my own, until recently – mental image), and all beneath one roof within the walls of this great church.

Speaking historically, it is as certain as certain can be that this is indeed the site of Golgotha/Calvary and the Tomb. It was revered as such from a very early period – at least the second century, when, according to the early church historian Eusebius, the Roman Emperor Hadrian built a temple dedicated to the goddess Venus atop the site to preempt Christian worship there. Two hundred years later, the first Christian Emperor Constantine the Great ordered the temple to be replaced by a church – during which construction his mother, St. Helena, is said to have rediscovered the tomb and the True Cross, celebrated on 03 May as the Feast of the Finding of the Holy Cross. Much of the rock of Calvary and around the tomb was removed to isolate the two sites and level the ground. Constantine's church (actually two adjacent chapels in one complex) was damaged by wars, attacks, and earthquakes through the subsequent centuries: the Persians in 614 when they captured and carried off the True Cross (recovered and restored by the Emperor Heraclius in 630, commemorated in the 14 September Feast of the Exaltation of the Cross); long centuries of Muslim rule from 638 – until 1009 when the Mad Caliph Al-Hakim ordered it destroyed completely and helped provoke the First Crusade before the end of the eleventh century despite a meager rebuilding negotiated by the Byzantine Emperor and Al-Hakim's son at mid-century.

The current building is perhaps the most magnificent monument to the First Crusade, called in 1095, at least in part to restore the Holy Sepulcher. Their capture of Jerusalem on 15 July 1099 inaugurated most of a century, the twelfth, of Christian rule over the Kingdom of

Jerusalem. By 1187 when Saladin took the city, the great church as it exists today was more or less in place although there have, of course, been extensive repairs, renovations, and even expansions through the following centuries. Like the Basilica of the Nativity, management of the Holy Sepulcher is a complicated "cooperative" between religious communities – Catholic and multiple Orthodox – with even more jealously guarded claims, rights, and privileges giving rise to sometimes ridiculous oddities such as the workman's ladder which has stood in one place beneath a window overlooking the courtyard for over a century and a half because to remove it would violate one or the other denomination's rights!

(As an aside, in this case also, there is an "alternative," however. Protestants generally prefer what is known as "the Garden Tomb" some distance away, "rediscovered" in the nineteenth century by British Major-General Charles Gordon. No reputable scholar today, Catholic *or* Protestant, disputes the location of the Holy Sepulcher, however. Even the Protestant trust overseeing the Garden Tomb refrains from promoting it as the very site, instead emphasizing it as a better representation of the site described in the Bible. Perhaps it is. But it is *not* the spot.)

Inside the Holy Sepulcher, one can ascend to the top of Golgotha and the site of the Crucifixion and touch the actual rock; one can venerate the Stone of Unction, where Jesus' body was laid out for hasty preparation before entombment; and one can view the Tomb, which underwent renovation to much fanfare in 2016. But one cannot do these things quickly. We were in the Church for a long time just standing, awaiting our turn to do these things.[108] Our praying of the last five

---

[108] In actuality, we were not in the Church of the Holy Sepulcher as long as it seemed. Time seemed to slow down. I was astonished later, after returning home, to examine the time stamps of photographs that I took, allowing me to reconstruct a time-line for our afternoon in the Old City, walking the *Via Dolorosa*, and our time in the Holy Sepulcher, from our entry through the Lions' Gate to our exit through the Jaffa Gate, to see how short a time it really was. Note that the following are not arrival times; they are the minutes when I snapped certain photographs:
    14:51 We were at the Lions' Gate
    15:08 We were in the Church of St. Anne
    15:44 We were on the *Via Dolorosa*
    16:09 We were at the Armenian Holocaust Memorial
    16:29 We were in the courtyard outside the Holy Sepulcher
    16:48 We were at the Greek Orthodox Chapel of Calvary
    16:56 We were back down at the Stone of Unction
    16:59 We were in the line around the back of the Rotunda
    18:58 We were about to be allowed into the Edicule

Stations of the Cross broke down simply because of the press of people, the bustle and the noise. There was no way for us to stay together as a group and pray. Or rather, we did pretty much stay together, but there was no way to pray as a group. We all therefore prayed the remaining Stations individually. Those Stations do, however, make a good organizing scheme for our time in the Church. So, to continue ...

X. Jesus is Stripped of His Garments - We made our way in through the left door - the right is sealed shut - noted the people crowded around, kneeling, and venerating the large flat Stone of Unction set into the floor beneath a half-dozen ornate hanging lamps, turned right, and entered a steep, narrow curving staircase up to a cluster of small chapels on Golgotha, Calvary itself. The first we entered, in the custody of the Franciscans and named for its place in the sequence of events during the Passion, was the "Chapel of Divestiture."

And when they had crucified him, they divided his garments among them by casting lots. (Matt. 27: 35)

From this point, it was slow progress, moving with the crowd of pilgrims from all over the world. But, straight ahead, we could see a sizable mosaic dominating the far wall behind an altar, depicting:

XI. Jesus is Nailed to the Cross - The ceiling of this "Chapel of the Nailing to the Cross," which is also in the custody of the Franciscans, contains the only surviving Crusader-era mosaic in the Church of the Holy Sepulcher, depicting the Ascension.

Passing through an arch and by a Catholic altar and statue of Our Lady of Sorrows, with a sword piercing her heart, we entered the Greek Orthodox custody and were standing atop Calvary, Golgotha.

XII. Jesus Dies Upon the Cross - Before a large depiction of Christ on the Cross, flanked by the Beloved Disciple on his left, his grieving Blessed Mother on his right, mostly of silver except for the depictions of flesh and wood, there stands an ornate altar, itself flanked by glass boxes on the floor. These latter allow viewing of the rock of Calvary. Through the glass on the right a fissure is visible, said to be the crack left by the earthquake that occurred when Our Lord died.

19:20 We were leaving through the Jaffa Gate

Of our slightly less than three hours in the great church, almost precisely two were occupied awaiting entry to the Holy Sepulcher. It all seemed longer.

> And Jesus cried again with a loud voice and yielded up his spirit. And behold, the curtain of the temple was torn in two, from top to bottom; and the earth shook, and the rocks were split. (Matt. 27: 50-51)

Each pilgrim, in turn, knelt beneath the altar which covered a narrow shaft down which one could stick one's arm pretty much up to the elbow – and touch the naked rock of Golgotha.

It was a powerful moment.

The Greek Chapel of Calvary is open at the rear, overlooking the entranceway we had come through a half an hour earlier (it seemed longer), the Stone of Unction, and the entrance to the Rotunda where is the Holy Sepulcher itself.

XIII. Jesus is Taken Down From the Cross – Descending stairs at the rear of the chapel opposite where we had ascended, we paused a moment to venerate the Stone of Unction beneath a long mosaic depicting three scenes in order, from right to left: Jesus' Body being taken down from the Cross; the Blessed Mother and her companions washing and anointing His Body; and His Body being carried into the tomb.

> When it was evening, there came a rich man from Arimathea, named Joseph, who also was a disciple of Jesus. He went to Pilate and asked for the body of Jesus. Then Pilate ordered it to be given to him. And Joseph took the body, and wrapped it in a clean linen shroud, and laid it in his own new tomb, which he had hewn in the rock; and he rolled a great stone to the door of the tomb, and departed. Mary Magdalene and the other Mary were there, sitting opposite the sepulchre. (Matt. 27: 57-61)

XIV. Jesus is Placed in the Sepulcher – Finally, we continued into the large Rotunda, at the center of which is the cubical Edicule in which are two tiny chapels – the Chapel of the Angel and that of the Tomb itself. A marble slab now covers the shelf on which His Body would have lain, but we were allowed in to pray before it ... after a wait for almost exactly two hours in what can only very generously be called a "line"; it was, in reality, a mob inching around the periphery of the Rotunda, a mass of people pressing to get through a small door for a few seconds in that holiest place in Christendom, where Our Lord was dead and rose again to life. It was hot; people were rude (especially a group of Russians, one woman of which kept pressing to push me out of the way, and when I held firm she looked at me and either hissed or spat; I looked back at her and retorted, "*Pfft* to you too!" Not my finest moment, but tempers were short all around). Our slow progress stopped entirely twice, once when the Franciscans sang what we took to be Vespers,[109] and once to accommodate a group of Knights of the Holy Sepulcher who can show up unannounced and immediately gain precedence and private access to the tomb for thirty minutes. But Tony assured us we were actually lucky – imagining the circuit of the Edicule as a clock with the entrance at twelve o'clock, we began our wait at about four o'clock; Tony said he had seen the "line" filling the Rotunda, extending out through the plaza and into the street, with a wait lasting many hours. When I commented that Disney World could give them some pointers on crowd flow management, he replied that the various groups sharing custody of the church would never be able to agree on it.

At about six o'clock of the circuit, I – or rather Jennifer, because there was no way I could maneuver my way there in the crowd! – lit the last of the many candles I set all across the Holy Land for my Jerusalem-born friend Angel and her family, in a small chapel at the opposite end of the Edicule from the entrance to the Holy Sepulcher. It was incredibly ornate, filled with candles. At the time, I was given to believe the chapel was Armenian. Every reference I have seen since, however, lists it as a Coptic chapel. Oh well. It is the same God.

At last, we were allowed to enter through the single small door to the Edicule, passing through the outer chapel and into the Tomb to pray for a few seconds kneeling before a marble slab covering the rock-hewn shelf whereon lay Our Lord's Body in death through Friday evening, Saturday, and into Sunday – then to be herded back out by one of the friars, who was young but very no-nonsense. *That* was a thankless job, I'm sure!

---

[109] On further research, I am not sure this was Vespers. I discovered, at the Franciscan Custody website for the Holy Sepulcher, a page, "Time at the church and of the services" [http://www.sepulchre.custodia.org/default.asp?id=4128] accessed 19 September 2018, which lays out the schedule along with the fascinating fact that inside the Church it is always "winter time" – "as the agreed rules do not allow for changing to 'summer time'. As a result, times of summer services are one hour later (by the watch) than in the winter." In the afternoon, "at 16.00 the Franciscan community leads a procession throughout the Church of the Holy Sepulcher, departing from the Chapel of the Blessed Sacrament and stopping in each of the chapels along the eastern ambulatory, descending also to the Chapel of the Finding of the Cross and exiting from Calvary to rejoin the Edicule of the Tomb. The procession concludes with the Eucharistic Blessing at the point of departure." This sounds like what we saw, which would have been at 17:00 by my watch, I think.

Those few seconds were, however, a spiritual highlight of our pilgrimage. We were *there* – in that *place* – where occurred the most significant single event in history – the Resurrection.

> **Now after the sabbath, toward the dawn of the first day of the week, Mary Magdalene and the other Mary went to see the sepulchre. And behold, there was a great earthquake; for an angel of the Lord descended from heaven and came and rolled back the stone, and sat upon it. His appearance was like lightning, and his raiment white as snow. And for fear of him the guards trembled and became like dead men. But the angel said to the women, "Do not be afraid; for I know that you seek Jesus who was crucified. He is not here; for he has risen, as he said. Come, see the place where he lay. (Matt. 28: 1-6)**

That we did.

Exiting the Holy Sepulcher, we were to gather in the courtyard. Passing by the Stone of Unction we found that the crowd had thinned considerably, and some of our number venerated it again without the hustle and bustle.

Once we came out of the Church, our agenda had us walking across to the Western or "Wailing" Wall, the sole surviving remnant of the Second Temple, rebuilt and greatly expanded by King Herod the Great, the Temple that the young Jesus called "His Father's House" (Luke 2: 49). Given the lateness of the hour (it was past 19:00), the length of the walk in pretty much the opposite direction from where Wael would be waiting with our bus, and Tony's advice, we ended up walking instead through the winding streets of the Christian Quarter and ultimately out the Jaffa Gate to meet up with Wael to be taken back to Bethlehem and our last night in the St. Gabriel Hotel. Along the way, we passed by the Razzouk Tattoo Parlor; I asked Tony, "Is that the famous tattoo parlor?" He confirmed that it was and that it was where he got his tattoos. At one time, I had hoped to come away with a traditional pilgrim's tattoo of a Jerusalem Cross on my right wrist, but time did not allow. And once I got the Jerusalem Cross ring at the Nativity Souvenirs Co-op that was off the table anyway.

As we arrived back at the St. Gabriel, another bus was leaving a new group of pilgrims, a couple of dozen Ethiopians, and suddenly that hotel which had been very quiet for several days got very busy, with a full buffet laid out for both parties, them and us.

After supper, Kristal and I took the opportunity to go down to the bar one last time to bid Tony farewell, although we did not order anything. Both of us had a lot of packing to do to get to bed at a decent hour because we were told to have our suitcases outside our doors no later than 05:15 for a planned departure at 05:45.

And so ended, for all intents and purposes my (hopefully just the first) pilgrimage to the Holy Land.

Tuesday 21 August 2018 – Holy Land Day Nine: *Departure*

There is not much to say in this regard. An early alarm, a drive to Ben-Gurion Airport, a long couple of flights once again connecting through Istanbul and we were back in the United States. It was late in the evening of the same calendar-day, Tuesday 21 August, when we landed back in Houston. As I had feared, we were all suddenly going our separate ways, and I never got a chance to properly bid farewell to some of my companions, my fellow pilgrims, my newfound friends. Later, I sent a general WhatsApp text message to the group:

> *As I knew would happen, in the rush of deplaning and getting thru the Houston airport, I did not get a chance to say proper farewells to some of you. This past week has been a pleasure and a privilege. I especially thank all of you who were so solicitous of me in my debilitated state. Fr. Emilio, thank you for putting this pilgrimage together. I hope all our paths will cross again sooner rather than later. Kent*

Owing to our east-to-west route, it was over 24 hours since we rolled out of Bethlehem, so Kathie and Robert and I opted to find a hotel as soon as we got out of Houston rather than face the four-hour drive back to central Louisiana. Hence, I did not get back home until Wednesday. They were kind enough to swing north to Natchitoches, somewhat out of their way, and take me directly home so that I did not have to call my wife to take off work to come to retrieve me from Pineville.

Sometime shortly after noon, we arrived at my house, and my pilgrimage to the Holy Land came to its official end. As a small token of thanks to them for transporting me to and fro, and for so much more, I was able to give Robert and Kathie a print of a photograph I had taken in the church in Cana and which Anne had framed, from immediately after the marriage blessing they received in the place where Our Lord consecrated the Sacrament of Matrimony.

HOLY RAMBLINGS

And then they departed, and it was indeed over.

Addendum One: Counting the Cost...

I did not track the cost of the Pilgrimage to the Holy Land as carefully as I did for previous trips, but I did keep PDF copies of the essential payments. When I first signed on, I opted to hope for a fellow male pilgrim also looking to share a room, so I paid just the base price of $2,990.00, which covered double-occupancy as far as lodging went. I was cautioned that it was unlikely there would be such – apparently unaccompanied female pilgrims are far more common than unaccompanied males – and in the end, there was not. As I understand it, Fr. Emilio and Br. Miguel roomed together, and the only other man on this trip was Robert. He already had a roommate. However, long before any of that was clear, my wife had prevailed on me to go ahead and pay the upgrade for a single room, which was another $440.00.

The base price included limited travel insurance, but I opted from the beginning for "Cancel-For-Any-Reason" (CFAR) insurance, at $258 (up to $3,000.00 trip cost – we slid in just below that). Upgrading to the single room bumped me up into the next bracket on CFAR premiums, so I paid another $105 for that.

Adding all that up came to a Single-Room, Base Price, CFAR total cost of $3,793.00.

Beyond that, there were plenty of other associated costs, but I did not tally them along the way and thus have no way of properly including them. Suffice it to say that some of the lighter, hot-weather clothing I had acquired, as well as a new backpack/carry-on bag, were rendered unusable by the pacemaker implantation, which left me unable to manage donning and doffing certain types of clothing or maneuvering such a thing as a backpack due to my left arm being effectively incapacitated until the day we returned – two weeks after the surgery. So, during that weekend between the pacemaker surgery and departure – when I did not know for sure I would be going at all – Anne was reconfiguring my meticulously planned wardrobe and baggage situation with a whole new set of purchases.

Nor am I able, sometime later, to tally the purchases I made along the way, including the "souvenirs" I brought back. I *think* that the bottle of wine I bought that first night in Tiberias was about $80.00. The items from Bethlehem Nativity Souvenirs totaled ... well, I think that is better left unsaid. There were various other expenditures, including between ten and twenty dollars each day for lunch, but there is no way I can reconstruct them now.

Except to say that, all told, the cost for the pilgrimage to the Holy Land was $3,793.00 plus ... quite a bit. Just for me. Had my wife gone with me, double the base amount including CFAR, with no need for the $545.00 upgrade to single occupancy that I paid for, because had she gone, then *I* would have "already had a roommate".... So, $6,496.00 ... plus some.

Addendum Two: Reflections

Once I had returned from my pilgrimage to the Holy Land, almost immediately, people started asking me how it was. I did a lot of reflecting on the experience. Going back and filling out the placeholder blog entries was only the beginning. I put together a couple of photo books; gave a couple of presentations; guested on Kathie's radio show spending an hour with her reminiscing about the trip, then inadvertently did a repeat when she had scheduled Tony for the show via Skype and the connection failed – and I was waiting on the call-in line; and put together *another* photobook incorporating a basic narrative of the pilgrimage. I have never gotten far away from the pilgrimage even though it is now over a year later. The desire to share the experience ultimately gave birth to this book.

Long and short: I have contemplated the experience a great deal. It will always be a milestone in my life. Trying to distill all that thought into some meaningful, comprehensive form is difficult. Luckily, I had made a beginning just a couple of weeks after returning, and I can use that as a foundation. So, as I did there, I will begin with a couple of the most frequent questions I got upon my return: *Did you feel safe?* And, *What did you like best?*

As to the first of those questions, the answer is a resounding *Yes* – at no time during the six days we were on the ground in Israel or the Palestinian Territory – did I feel unsafe. That is said with the given, of course, that I was part of a group and therefore not "on my own," I still say with all sincerity that even more so than Mexico when we were there in 2016, the reality on the ground is very different than the impression given by the news media. I was perhaps a bit more expectant of what turned out to be the reality since I did watch through the entirety of a couple of Steve Ray's video-blogged pilgrimages from earlier in the year – one before and one after the uptick in tensions and reported violence in May 2018 as Palestinians (and their sympathizers) took out their frustration that the United States had followed through on its long-delayed recognition of Jerusalem as the capital of Israel. There I perceived no effect on a pilgrimage group much like our own, just larger. I also started pulling in feeds from Israeli news media on the private news aggregator I long ago set up just for myself. Although there had been of late a good bit of frank discussion of the ongoing tensions and related issues, as well as the perennial unrest churning down on the Gaza Strip, by and large the impression I got was of a peaceful country in which the people went about their daily lives with a feeling of security, not in constant fear for their lives that western media reports would seem to indicate *must* be the situation. And that security did not seem to come at the cost of a visibly ubiquitous police/military presence. Contrary to my expectation based on what friends and colleagues who had traveled to Israel told me, we did *not* see an armed security presence everywhere. To be sure, there probably was more of a presence than I perceived; I imagine they would not *want* to be seen, that they would want to be discreet, however vigilant and ready to act quickly and decisively they were. But the fact is that, from what I observed, whatever security presence there was in Israel was considerably less visible than it was in Mexico. Excepting the checkpoint agents at the Security Wall going into and out of Bethlehem, I noticed armed security on just three occasions. Most notably, there was the small security station on the *Via Dolorosa* right where it turned from Lions' Gate Street onto El-Wad. I do not specifically remember where the others were, but they did not seem to be in any specifically memorable positions other than that.

But to make a long answer short: Yes, *I felt absolutely safe the entire time*. That was the case even in Bethlehem, although I must also say that Tony made it crystal clear that, whatever the politicians might say, Bethlehem and the West Bank – the Palestinian Territory – is not Israel and is a different situation entirely regarding safety. We took him seriously, were vigilant any time any of us were not with him and the full group and were just fine.

But that is way too much space given to an issue that was no issue. Yes, *I felt safe*.

Answering the other common question is more difficult: *What did you like best?* How to decide? There were so many wonderful moments of deep spiritual intensity. The answer also depends on exactly what is meant by that question. I am taking it as, *What specific holy place or sight, in general, did you find the most moving?* ... Yeah, it's *still* a conundrum!

I have given different answers to these questions at different times, simply because it *is* so hard to decide. But there are moments which always come to mind first: 1) The Noon Procession and *Angelus* at the Basilica of the Annunciation in Nazareth. I heard them come out chanting *Ave Maris Stella* (I believe) and for the next ten minutes or so I was in hog heaven. I really did turn to Ingrid at the end and say, "*Tell me it's not better in Latin!*" ... That is what came to mind first the first time I was confronted with the question "cold," which tells me it made even more of an impression on me than I would have thought, given the other two things that come to mind – both in the last hours of the pilgrimage, both within the Church of the Holy Sepulcher: 2) Reaching down the shaft under the altar in the Calvary Chapel, touching the bare rock of the Place of the Skull, Golgotha, where my God gave everything for me – and for you. ... And, 3) My few moments in the Edicule, kneeling beside two or three others (I do not remember precisely who, or even if they were from our group or were others from the crowd with whom we had slowly made the circuit of the Rotunda over the past couple of hours, waiting for that moment) before the marble slab covering the hewn rock shelf upon which the Body of Christ was dead, then alive – was bound by the physical laws of the Universe, then was Transfigured. At that latter moment, if scientific reconstructions based upon the Shroud of Turin have any validity (and I believe they do), there would have been an intense burst of light and radiation – an instant, less than one forty-billionth of a second in duration; on the order of several billion watts[110] – Light as of Creation itself, because this was the New Creation. Is it any wonder that the earth shook? The wonder is that it was not annihilated!

Identifying those three moments as most meaningful to me is not to denigrate in any way all the other holy places we saw, holy spots I *touched* – each of which had its own profoundly wondrous appeal just from the knowledge that I was seeing – *touching* – places where heaven had in one way or another come down to touch the earth. As Fr. Emilio refrained, again and again, in his homilies, *It was here, in this place*.

And *I was there, in that place*.

There is no way to describe how moving those moments were, so I seldom try. But I always recommend them. Take it from me: There is no place like *place*.

---

[110] Robert J. Spitzer, S.J., "Science and the Shroud of Turin" (May 2015), *Magis Center of Reason and Faith*, p. 29 [https://2i7i0l43ftgic4pas6ndtk6b-wpengine.netdna-ssl.com/wp-content/uploads/2017/07/Science_and_the_Shroud_of_Turin.pdf], accessed 06 October 2019.

There was, however, something else I took away from this pilgrimage. Not so much an experience as a realization. I do not recall ever getting it as a specific question – *What was the most important thing that you learned on your pilgrimage to the Holy Land?* But I will go ahead and answer it now, anyway: Perhaps the most important thing I learned was how blind we Christians in the west are to the dire state of our brethren in the east. Yes, we have heard about the persecutions of Christians by various Middle Eastern Islamist groups, specifically the so-called "Islamic State" in Iraq and Syria. We have been outraged by our own governments' preferential treatment of Islamic "refugees" over the many, many Christians who are being systematically eradicated from Islamic lands. But we never hear about the lamentable conditions being endured by dwindling numbers of Christians in the very birthplace of our Faith – in Bethlehem itself. I wrote about this already in a couple of places, and will not repeat the details, but I would sum it up succinctly: They do not even receive the dignity of being correctly identified as "Aramaean Christians," what they have long called themselves as natives of the land from which Christianity sprang, but rather have been lumped in with their Muslim Arabic neighbors under a new "national identification" based solely on geography, as "Palestinians," and are caught in the middle, with the Israelis considering them "Palestinians" and the Muslims considering them Israeli collaborators. Trapped in enemy territory, behind the "West Bank Security Wall," their straits are desperate. Given what Tony said about the implosion of Christianity in Bethlehem since 2000, I fear we are just one Intifada away from losing Bethlehem altogether, a tragedy for those poor people far and away beyond the tragedy it would be for the Church as a whole.

These are perceptions, I believe, that one cannot gain by reading, by watching videos, or in any other way, but only by being there. Hopefully, I have conveyed how wonderful and enriching my pilgrimage to the Holy Land was. I would therefore like to repeat here the first words I said to a friend whom I urged to come with me on this journey, but who passed, when first I saw him upon my return – "If you ever get a chance to go to the Holy Land again, *don't pass it up!*"

I certainly will not. Because for all we saw, there is so much more to see. Billed as a "Nine-Day Pilgrimage," two days at the beginning and one (exceptionally long) day at the end being swallowed whole by travel, meant that we spent only six days on the ground. Thanks to Tony and Nativity Pilgrimage, we accomplished an amazing amount in those six days, which will stay with me forever. But we could not do everything. Besides the major sites I highlighted in the foregoing account, the most significant lacuna came right at the end.

One day in Jerusalem is not at all enough. The morning on the Mount of Olives, the afternoon and early evening on the *Via Dolorosa* and in the Church of the Holy Sepulcher made up one full day that barely scratched the surface. My wife always says that a guided tour such as this one shows you mainly what you want to go back and properly *see* – and that was nowhere more the case than in Jerusalem. There is so much more that I want to see and to do. I could easily fill a week. Or a month.

We saw only a fraction of the Church of the Holy Sepulcher; I want to spend a day there. I want to attend Mass there. I would like to see the Tower of David Museum and the Jerusalem Archaeological Park, the Old Testament City of David. I want to walk around the Old City walls from the Jaffa Gate to the Lions' Gate. I would like to spend a day or two in the Christian and Armenian Quarters – there are plenty of churches! Most of all, I just want to spend time there, *taking* my time. I want to pay my respects at the Western Wall – it is, after all, all that remains of what Our Lord called, "My Father's House" – and see the Dome of the Rock in person.

And that is all just in the *Old City* of Jerusalem. There is the *rest* of Jerusalem. The Tomb of the Virgin Mary – we walked right past it and did not take note of it. The Shrine of the Book. The Bible Lands Museum. And there are, of course, those things I highlighted in the rest of Israel, primarily Banias and Masada. God willing, I will make it back someday.

And so, to echo a sentiment repeated for hundreds of years before finally being fulfilled, yet continuing to be repeated as an eternal ideal, I conclude with the fervent hope, the *prayer* ...

לשנה הבאה בירושלים
"Next year, in Jerusalem!"[111]

---

[111] The traditional conclusion to the Seder.

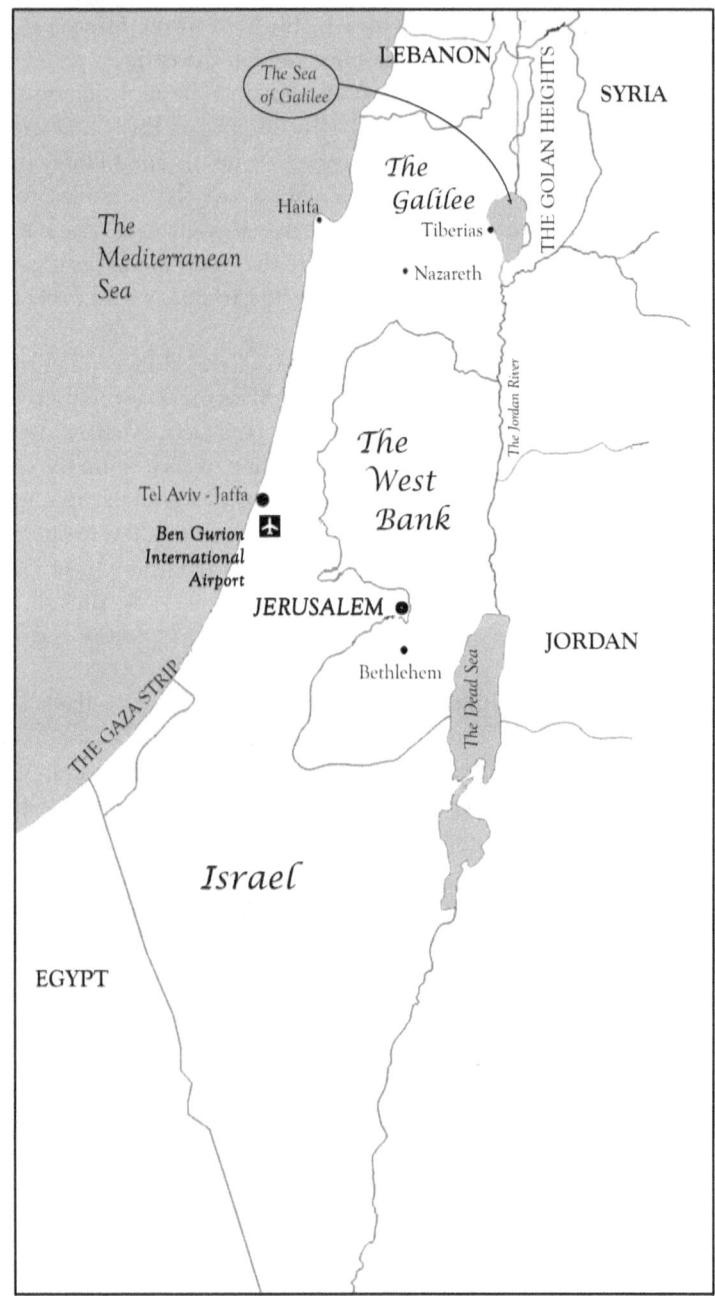

Figure 25: Map of Israel

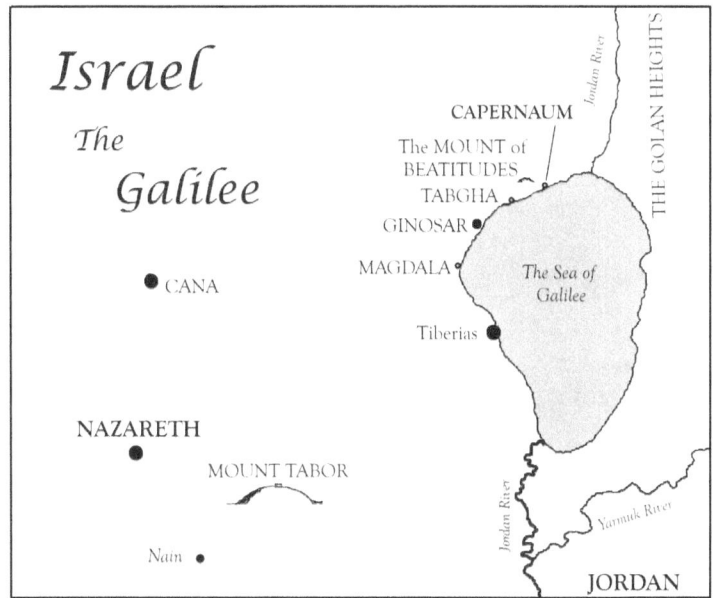

Figure 26: Map of the Galilee

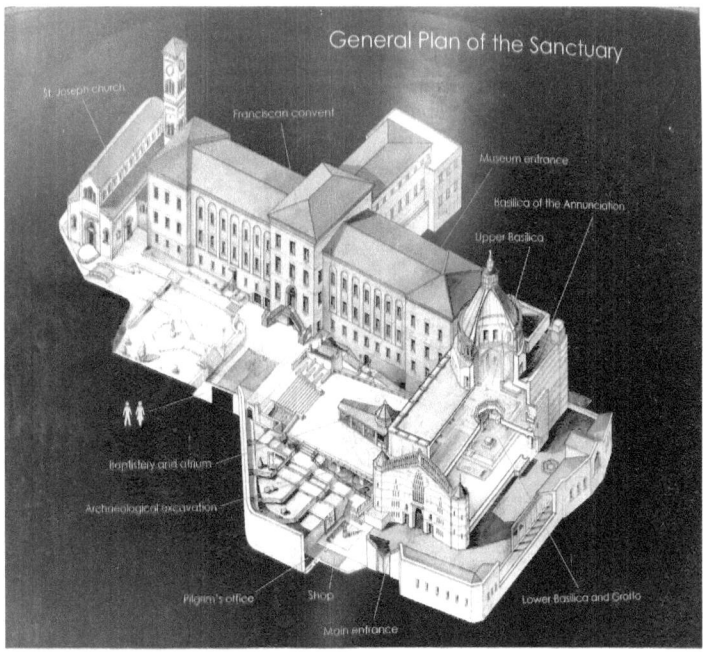

Figure 27: Layout of the Sanctuary of the Annunciation, Nazareth
Photo of signage on site, taken by author.

Figure 28: The Grotto of the Annunciation, Nazareth.
Photo by author.

Figure 29: Derelict trucks from 1948 Israeli attempt to relieve besieged Jerusalem. See p. 178. Photo by author.

Figure 30: Br. Miguel and Tony, our guide. Photo courtesy of Kathie Duggan.

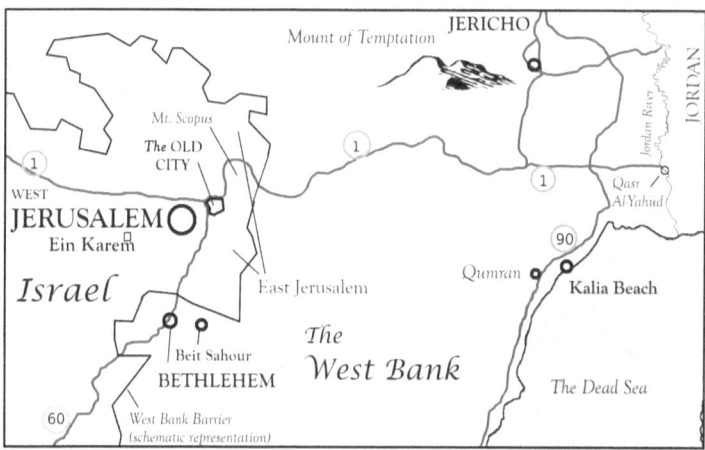

Figure 31: Map of Jerusalem, Bethlehem, and the Dead Sea.

Figure 32: Restored Byzantine murals inside the Church of the Nativity. Photo by author.

HOLY RAMBLINGS

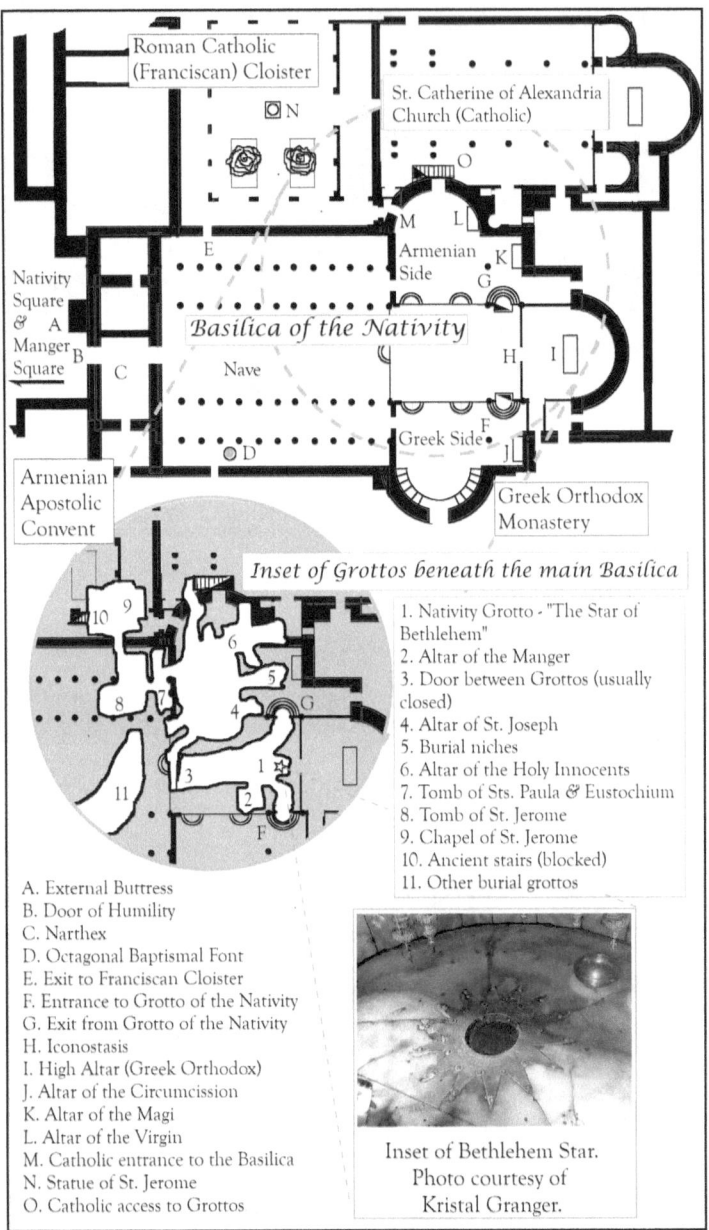

Figure 33: Layout of the Basilica of the Nativity

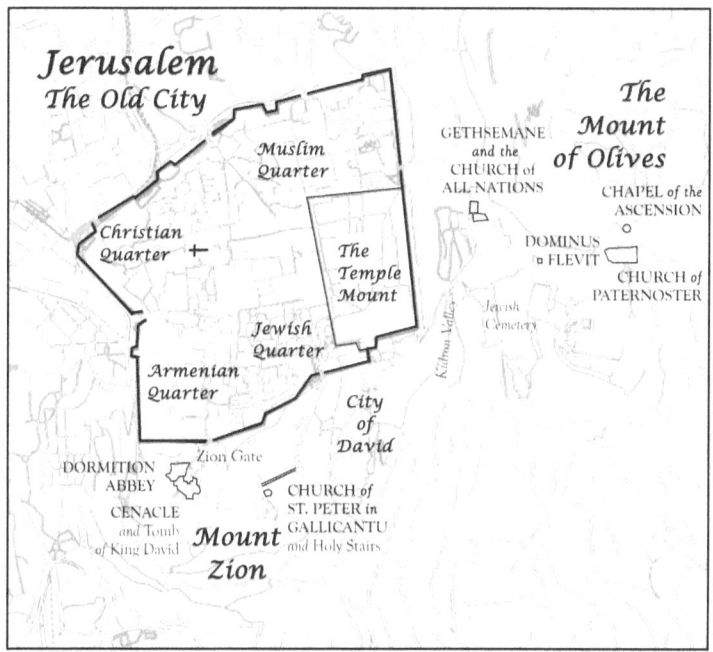

Figure 34: Map of Jerusalem: The Old City and the Mount of Olives

Figure 35: Praying at the VIII. Station of the Via Dolorosa.
Photo by author.

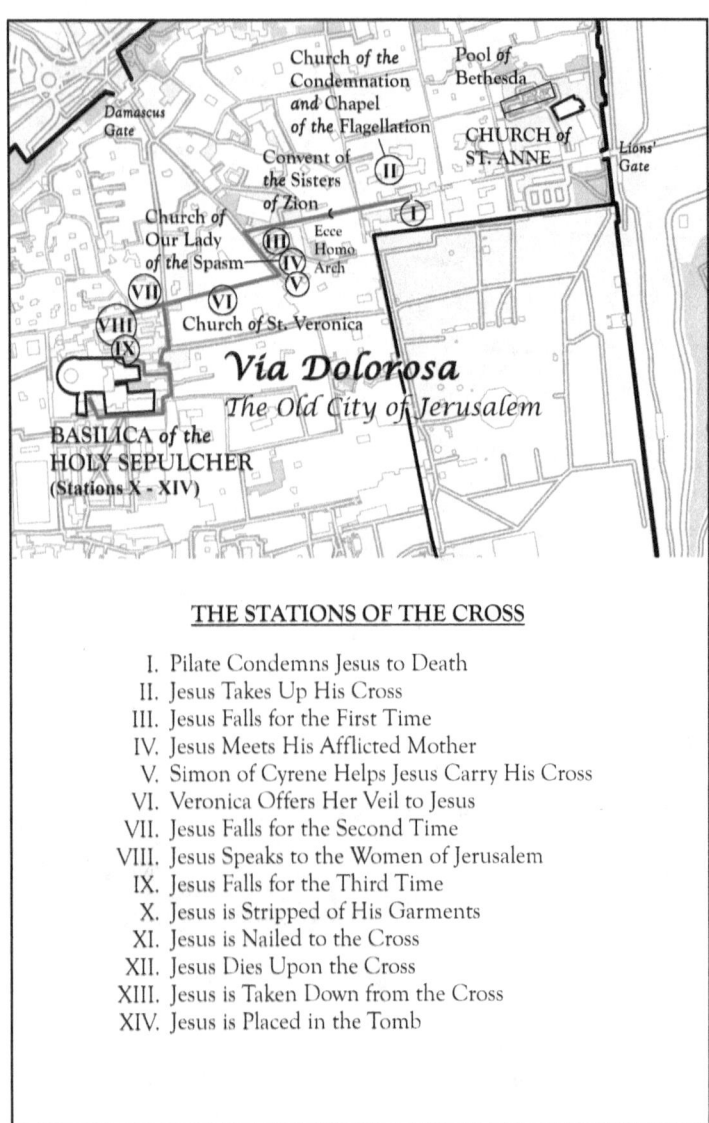

THE STATIONS OF THE CROSS

I. Pilate Condemns Jesus to Death
II. Jesus Takes Up His Cross
III. Jesus Falls for the First Time
IV. Jesus Meets His Afflicted Mother
V. Simon of Cyrene Helps Jesus Carry His Cross
VI. Veronica Offers Her Veil to Jesus
VII. Jesus Falls for the Second Time
VIII. Jesus Speaks to the Women of Jerusalem
IX. Jesus Falls for the Third Time
X. Jesus is Stripped of His Garments
XI. Jesus is Nailed to the Cross
XII. Jesus Dies Upon the Cross
XIII. Jesus is Taken Down from the Cross
XIV. Jesus is Placed in the Tomb

Figure 36: Map of The Via Dolorosa

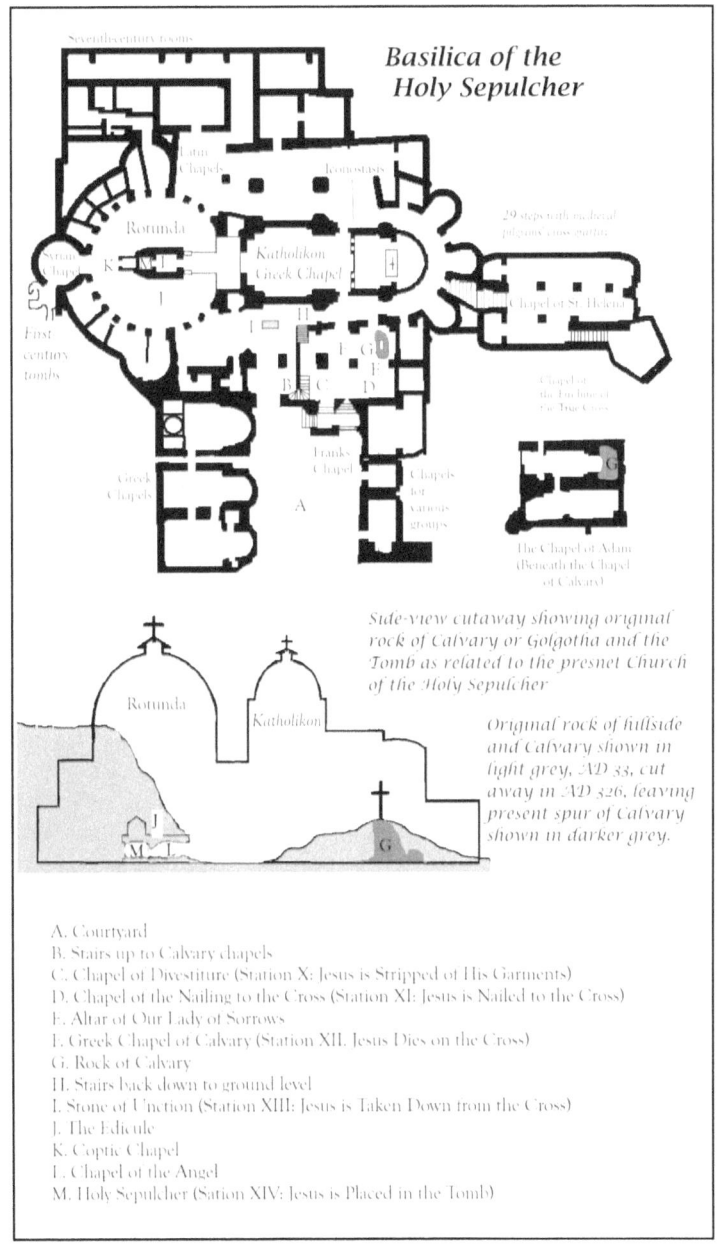

Figure 37: Layout of the Holy Sepulcher

Figure 38: Golgotha or Calvary Chapel, Church of the Holy Sepulcher.
Photo by author.

PART TWO

PILGRIMAGES FUTURE AND PRESENT

CHAPTER FOUR

PILGRIMAGES FAR ...

In previous chapters I detailed, from conception to return, three major pilgrimages, in order: 1) to the heart, the capital, of our Holy *Roman* Catholic Church; 2) to the most heavily visited pilgrimage destination in the world, the Shrine of Our Lady of Guadalupe; and 3) to the Holy Land, where it all started. One more "minor" pilgrimage is told more briefly and is more relevant to the subject of the next chapter. In just the last five years, I have, by the grace of God, been able to visit the top three pilgrimage destinations in the world. But there are many others. Here follows a list of the top *ten* pilgrimage destinations in the world, followed by a quick discussion of each beyond the first three, for which I have probably written quite enough. Generally, I will discuss the origins of the site, its development and status within the Church, and any controversies that surround it. I may touch on in what ways that the site or its associated devotions have affected my own life and faith. Be aware that as of this writing, I have visited not even one of these, so none of this information is firsthand. What follows is, instead, the beginning of my "prep" for eventual pilgrimages – God willing – to some of or all these destinations. Finally, note that although I am assessing the status of "top" pilgrimage destinations by the number of Catholic visitors annually, I nonetheless count the Holy Land first, for reasons I believe to be obvious but will state anyway – its importance transcends the quantifiable. All numbers are rounded; more specific details can be found in the associated notes.

The Top Ten Catholic Pilgrimage Destinations in the World
The Holy Land – approximately 1 million.[112]

---

[112] 1.06 million Catholics in 2011, 0.91 million in 2013, per the Israeli Ministry of Foreign Affairs, "Christian Tourism to Israel," *About Israel* (23 December 2014), [https://mfa.gov.il/MFA/AboutIsrael/Spotlight/Pages/Christian-tourism-to-Israel.aspx]. This is the most recent data I find specifically on Catholic pilgrims. The Holy Land is, of course, a "religious tourism" destination for more than Catholics; the IMFA lists total Christian visitors to Israel at 3.36 million in 2011, and 3.54 million in 2013, noting a six-point

Guadalupe, Mexico City – approximately 20 million.[113]
The Vatican City – approximately 18 million.
Our Lady of Lourdes, France – 8 million.
Padre Pio, San Giovanni Rotondo, Italy – 7 million.
Our Lady of Aparecida, Brazil – 6.6 million.
Our Lady of Fatima, Portugal – 4-5 million
St. Joseph's Oratory, Montreal, Quebec – 2 million.
Medjugorje, Bosnia-Herzegovina – 1-2 million.[114]
El Camino de Santiago de Compostela, Spain – over 300,000.[115]

The Sanctuary of Our Lady of Lourdes, Lourdes, France
Nestled in the northern foothills of the Pyrenees mountains that separate France from Spain, Lourdes was a quiet, virtually unknown market town until 1858. Today, while home to only 17,000 citizens, the town welcomes millions of pilgrims each year seeking the graces of Our Lady in conversion and physical and spiritual healing.

The change came on 11 February 1858, when a young girl of barely fourteen, Marie Bernadette Soubirous, while searching for firewood by the River Ousse at the grotto of Massabielle, witnessed the appearance of a beautiful Lady. The one whom Bernadette always

---

drop in percentage Catholic from 32% to 26% in the same period. Not seeing any more data than these isolated numbers, I make only the following comments: 1) The fall in percentage by itself could be attributed to a dramatic uptick in the number of evangelical Protestants visiting Israel, as noted by multiple articles, most notably this, "Christian evangelicals from the US flock to Holy Land in Israeli Tourism Boom," *The Independent* (06 April 2018); 2) The drop in actual numbers of Catholics by approximately 150,000, is troubling, however, *if that is a trend that has continued*. Further research would be interesting.

[113] For numbers 2 through 8, estimates are taken from a list of "approved Catholic sites of pilgrimage" at *Catholic Doors Ministry*, "Frequently Asked Questions regarding The Most Visited Catholic Sites" [https://www.catholicdoors.com/faq/1000/qu1222.htm], accessed 29 August 2019. The list includes the following as well: "1.7 million participants at the World Youth Day," "1 million pilgrims at St Anne de Beaupre, Quebec, Canada," and "350,000 pilgrims at the Basilica of Notre-Dame-du-Cap in Trois-Rivières, Quebec, Canada." I do not consider the World Youth Day a "pilgrimage destination," although attendance does share elements of retreat and pilgrimage. Keeping my list to ten, my sense is that Medjugorje (despite its ambiguous status as discussed below) and the Camino de Santiago are more significant and well-known than either of the latter two.

[114] The estimate of one million comes from "How many Tourists visited Medjugorje last Year?," *Sarajevo Times* (19 April 2018) [https://www.sarajevotimes.com/how-many-tourists-visited-medjugorje-last-year/]; the *Sarajevo Times* does not distinguish between "tourists" and pilgrims, but I assume the vast majority of visitors to Bosnia-Herzegovina are of the latter variety.
The estimate of two million is rounded from "About 2 200 000 (source: BH INFO / 2011)" per "Medjugorje: All the Statistics," *Medjugorje: Le Cri du Ciel vers La Terre* (20 August 2014) [http://marie-oasis.eklablog.com/medjugorje-all-the-statistics-a109071380].

[115] Per Wikipedia, *s.v.* "Camino de Santiago," accessed 29 August 2019.

called simply "the little Lady" would only later identify herself as "the Immaculate Conception."

It was then just slightly more than three years since Pope Pius IX had, on 08 December 1854, infallibly declared as binding dogma the Catholic Church's consistent teaching that the Mother of God was conceived immaculately, without any stain of Original Sin on her soul. In so proclaiming, the Holy Father put an end to a debate that had arisen only recently in the history of the Church. That the Blessed Virgin was personally free from sin had been believed from the beginning and went long unquestioned. Exactly how that worked in practice, and from what point she was without sin, were not issues either until the explosion of Scholastic Theology in the twelfth and thirteenth centuries. At that time, an intense debate arose between the Franciscans and the Dominicans. The former favored the idea that the Mother of God was preserved free from even Original Sin by the prevenient graces of her Son's Sacrifice on the Cross being applied to her at the very instant of her conception in her mother's womb. The Dominicans, on the other hand, considered that she had to have been touched by Original Sin, however fleetingly, to be redeemed from it as are all the children of men. Even St. Thomas Aquinas seems to have waffled on the issue. The consensus of the Church, however – the *sensus fidelium* – never doubted what Pius IX confirmed in 1854, that not even the least hint of sin ever touched Mary. Concentrating on such debates that so exercise scholars and theologians at the highest levels of the Church's intelligentsia obscures the fact that (especially in earlier ages) such questions are not part of the daily religion of the vast majority of the Faithful. That an illiterate provincial girl such as Bernadette would, therefore, even know the term seemed so outlandish as to convince the local priest of the veracity of her claims.

In the course of eighteen apparitions over the next five months,, increasing numbers of people – ultimately thousands – attended to witness Bernadette in ecstasy, praying the Rosary, performing penances, sometimes reporting requests from the Lady to the clergy and the people, exhorting them to prayer and penance. Perhaps the strangest thing those witnesses beheld was when, at the behest of the Lady, Bernadette started scratching at the ground with her bare hands in a certain spot before the grotto and proceeded to drink from a small spring of muddy water that began to bubble up. They took it as a sign she was mad. Within days, however, the first of what would become a vast number of cures were claimed by those who similarly drank, or simply bathed in, the effluent which increased until today thousands of gallons of crystal-clear water gush forth each day. First was a woman's dislocated shoulder - cured - followed by more spectacular claims of cancers, paralysis, nervous disorders, and even blindness - cured. The Lourdes spring water tested - and tests - normal; claims of cures continue. The Catholic Church has rigorously investigated the thousands of cures claimed and officially deemed only a relative handful - 68 - as authentically miraculous. The prospect of such a cure nonetheless has drawn many desperate individuals among the millions of pilgrims over the years since, seeking relief from every type of malady known to man, and reports of cures number many times over the Church's approbation.

Within four short years, following an intense investigation, the local bishop declared the apparitions to be authentic, that the Blessed Virgin Mary, the Mother of God, the Immaculate Conception, had indeed appeared to Bernadette. Such is the normal procedure - the local ordinary has primary jurisdiction, investigates claims regarding the miraculous, and renders a judgment which is typically one of three: 1) the claimed miracle may be "not worthy of belief" (i.e., condemned); 2) it may be "not contrary to the faith" (i.e., neutral); or 3) it may be "worthy of belief" (i.e., authentic). Within a couple of decades, the chapel built at the grotto, rebuilt as a church, was consecrated a basilica. By that time, Bernadette, having entered a religious life of penance and suffering, had died of tuberculosis - but her body remains incorrupt to this day.[116] She was canonized in 1933.

The Sanctuary of Our Lady of Lourdes, also called "the Domain," is today a substantial religious complex which includes *three* basilicas, dedicated respectively to the Immaculate Conception, Pope St. Pius X, and Our Lady of the Rosary. Other notable sites are the Church of St. Bernadette, the Crypt on the Rock of Massabielle, and the Grotto beneath it, whence flows the spring into the town's baths, pools, and fountains. There are also countless hotels, hostels, and gift shops.

I was forced to pass up an opportunity to visit Lourdes in 2016. Two years after his first "Basilican Pilgrimage," to Italy as chronicled in Chapter One, Fr. Ryan Humphries led a second, to Fatima, Santiago de Compostela, and Lourdes. It was also in October. As much as I would have liked to go, there was no way I could justify another two-week absence from my teaching duties only two years after the last. Nor could I make a persuasive case for any direct relevance of these

---

[116] It is not at Lourdes, however. The incorrupt body of St. Bernadette Soubirous may be viewed in the chapel of the Monastery at Nevers, where she died in 1879.

destinations to my teaching or research as I could for Rome. Perhaps someday, however.

The Sanctuary of St. Pio of Pietrelcina, San Giovanni Rotondo, Italy

Saint Pio of Pietrelcina, almost twenty years after his 2002 canonization, remains more popularly known simply as "Padre Pio." One of the most beloved holy men of the twentieth century, he is famous for bearing the stigmata (the wounds of Jesus Christ's Passion), his visions, his gifts of healing and the reading of souls, and even levitation and bilocation. Rumors of these prodigies brought unwanted fame as well as savage hostility from certain quarters even within the highest echelons of the hierarchy.

Born in 1887, given the name Francesco Forgione by his devoutly religious parents, he took the name "Pio" (the Italian form of the Latin "Pius") when he entered religious life as a Capuchin at Morcone in 1903. Raised to the priesthood in 1910, he became well-known as an insightful confessor who could read the heart of a penitent and know if they held back or minimized a sin. He spent hours in ecstatic adoration of the Most Blessed Sacrament, during which time observers noted him floating a few inches off the floor. On multiple occasions, unimpeachable witnesses saw him in two places at once. He also suffered greatly from headaches, insomnia, exhaustion, and chronic indigestion. Sent to the commune of San Giovanni Rotondo in the Gargano Mountains in 1916 for rest and recuperation, he requested and received permission to remain there in the Monastery of St. Mary of Grace. In 1918, after offering his sufferings to hasten the end of the World War, he was stricken with the stigmata, which caused him constant pain to the end of his days.

As word spread, the faithful traveled great distances to confess to Padre Pio, to receive his blessing, to hear him say Mass. Convinced that he was cultivating a personality cult, the Vatican imposed sanctions on him in the 1920s, forbidding him to say Mass publicly, to hear Confessions or bestow blessings, or to display his stigmata. He was subjected to physical and mental examinations, official visitations and wiretaps in his cell, slanderous charges of inflicting the wounds of Christ to himself, of being a simpleton, even of engaging in indecent relations with his followers – all the while being attacked directly by the devil, both physically and spiritually. The investigations found only a simple, devout, gifted priest; the calumnies were determined to be baseless. Despite vociferous opposition by some in the hierarchy who remained utterly opposed to him, all his priestly faculties had been restored by the 1930s, and by 1939 the newly elected Pope Pius XII was encouraging the faithful to visit Padre Pio. The Monastery of St. Mary of Grace, where Padre Pio lived from 1916 until his death a half-century later, became a pilgrimage destination while he yet lived. He turned his fame to good works raising funds and founding a world-class scientific research hospital, the *Casa Sollievo della Sofferenze*, Home for Relief of Suffering, in San Giovanni Rotondo.

Even as his health deteriorated in the 1960s, Padre Pio maintained a rigorous regimen of Mass, Confessions, spiritual works, and mystical contemplations to the very end. During his last Mass on 22 September 1968, his voice was so weak his attendants could barely hear him to make the responses. Early the next morning he made his last Confession, shortly after which he died with the name, "Maria!" on his lips. When his body was exhumed years later during the process of investigation accompanying the prosecution of his cause for sainthood, it was found incorrupt, and is today displayed in a crystalline sarcophagus in the crypt of the Sanctuary of St. Pio of Pietrelcino, built in 2004 beside St. Mary of Grace at San Giovanni Rotondo.

The Basilica of the National Shrine of Our Lady of Aparecida, Brazil

Aparecida is a municipality in São Paulo, Brazil, named for *Nossa Senhora da Conceição Aparecida*, literally "Our Lady of the Conception Who Appeared." In 1717, three fishermen on the Paraná River, desperate for a good catch to provide a worthy feast to honor a visiting dignitary, prayed to the Blessed Mother and immediately drew forth from the water a small black clay statue of Virgin – followed by the largest catch any of them had ever seen. One of the fishermen set up a shrine in his home where locals came to venerate the little statue. Miracles were soon reported, drawing more and more pilgrims from a wider area. The fisherman's family built a chapel to accommodate them. Over time, a larger church was necessary; then in 1834, a popularly-proclaimed basilica replaced it, to be replaced in its turn by the present building, the Basilica of the National Shrine of Our Lady of Aparecida, dedicated in 1955 as the largest Marian shrine in the world with a capacity of 45,000 worshippers. At first regarded as a basilica as had been its predecessor, by popular acclaim rather than Papal proclamation, the National Shrine was finally and formally granted that status by Pope John Paul II in 1980.

After its initial discovery, inquiries were made. and the most likely origin for the statue was determined to be that it was a long-lost clay statue of Our Lady of the Immaculate Conception either brought from Portugal or made in Brazil by the monk Frei Agostinho de Jesus in the middle of the seventeenth century. Painted initially with lifelike colors, a half-century or more in the river water leached away the pigments, leaving the dark greyish-brownish color of the clay. A dark blue robe, richly embroidered with the flags of Brazil and the Vatican City, presently adorns it along with an imperial crown signifying Our Lady of the Immaculate Conception's status (since 1904) as the patroness of Brazil.

As evidenced by the millions who make a pilgrimage to it each year, much of Brazilian Catholic religious devotion revolves around Our Lady of Aparecida in a manner reminiscent of Our Lady of Guadalupe in Mexico. The statue has, however, become a source of controversy as Protestantism has made inroads into the once solidly Catholic country. In 1978, a Protestant fanatic attempted to steal the statue, which ended up shattered in the ensuing scuffle. Devotees carefully collected the pieces and pieced them together again; in 1995, on the 12 October Feast of Our Lady of Aparecida, a national holiday in Brazil, a Protestant minister and televangelist publicly insulted a replica of the statue, kicking it and proclaiming it an idol that "can do nothing for you." The outcry and mass protests outside their churches compelled the elders of that minister's sect to transfer him out of Brazil altogether. Catholicism continuing to be the majority religion in Brazil, devotions at and pilgrimages to the National Shrine remain high.

The Shrine of Our Lady of Fatima, Fatima, Portugal

In the summer of 1916, an angel appeared to three shepherd children at the Cova da Iria, a field outside the village of Fatima in Portugal. Identifying itself as the Angel of Portugal, the angel taught them prayers and urged them to spend time adoring God. Less than a year later, on 13 May 1917, those same three children – ten-year-old Lucia dos Santos and her younger cousins, Francisco and Jacinta Marto, aged nine and seven respectively – received the first of a series of six more visitations, this time seeing a Lady they described as "more brilliant than the sun." She bade them pray for an end to the war raging across Europe and promised to return on the thirteenth day of the next five successive months, revealing prophecies, her own identity, and finally, a miracle, "so that all might believe." Word spread, and subsequent months brought increasing numbers of people to witness the children as they purported to see and hear the Lady. During the July apparition, the children were visibly disturbed, although they would not speak of what they saw. The next month, local representatives of the anti-religious government of Portugal kidnapped the children and attempted to coerce them into admitting it to be all made up; threatened even with death, the children would admit no such thing. Missing the 13 August visitation at the Cove da Iria because of their abduction, they nonetheless were graced with a late visitation once they were returned to their homes. The people's outrage at the treatment of the children – and growing anticipation of the promised miracle – swelled the numbers in attendance to a reported 70,000 believers and skeptics alike on 13 October. These did not, of course, see the Lady when she appeared again to the children and revealed herself to be the Virgin Mary; but then, *all of the people, 70,000 believers and skeptics alike*, witnessed the promised miracle, as the sun danced in the sky. More than those present, people miles away saw the phenomenon. It has been called (by Taylor Marshall, multiple times on his podcast) the miracle directly witnessed by more people than any since the Exodus. Skeptical, atheistic newspaper writers who were present to debunk the children's claims, characterized what they saw as "Amazing Things! How the Sun Danced at Noon in Fatima!"[117]

Within a couple of years, both Francisco and Jacinta would be dead, victims of the great influenza epidemic that followed close on the heels of the end of the First World War. Lucia entered a convent and, under obedience, would eventually reveal certain things that were shown and told to them by the Mother of God – the famous Three Secrets of Fatima. The First Secret was a vision of hell and the lost souls in torment, as they had witnessed on 13 July. The Second Secret was multifold, but generally had to do with the end of the Great War raging across Europe at the time, while warning of a worse war if people did not perform penance and prayers, including the daily recitation of the Rosary. Without such reparations, the "errors of Russia" would spread, bringing wars and persecutions. Bear in mind that Russia was at this time in chaos, still months away from its Communist Revolution that would unleash hell upon the earth for most of the twentieth century. Nevertheless, the Blessed Mother promised that, in the end, her Immaculate Heart would triumph. Although Sr. Lucia stated that

---

[117] *O Seculo* (15 October 1917). The cover of the newspaper is available in many places across the Internet, including with an English translation of the title, quoted here, and the full story, at Franciscan Friars, "How the Sun Danced at Noon in Fatima!" *Fatima* (17 June 2016) [http://livingfatima.com/how-the-sun-danced-at-noon-in-fatima/].

the Third Secret should be made public sometime around 1960 (sources differ – in? by? after?), that was not done. Rumors and speculations abounded until the belated revelation of the Third Secret in 2000 – a prophesied persecution of the Church and the apparent assassination of a Pope, which the hierarchs revealing it promptly equated with the *attempted* assassination of Pope John Paul II in 1981 – on 13 May, the 64th anniversary of the first apparition. John Paul II always attributed his survival of life-threatening wounds to the intercession of Our Lady of Fatima.

Our Lady's interactions with Sr. Lucia did not end on 13 October 1917 but instead continued with periodic visitations. In 1925, the Virgin conveyed to her the First Saturday Devotion to the Immaculate Heart of Mary; In 1929 and 1931, she requested a Papal Consecration of Russia to her Immaculate Heart and warned of the example of France, which ignored Our Lord's request for a royal consecration to His Sacred Heart and precisely one hundred years later suffered the beginning of the French Revolution; there were perhaps other private and unrecorded visitations as well. Eventually entering the Discalced Carmelite Order, Sr. Lucia lived long enough to see her cousins beatified in 2000 before she herself died at age 97 in 2005.

Despite the efforts of the secularist government, once the 13 October Miracle of the Sun was witnessed and reported so widely, there was no stopping an explosion of pilgrimages to Fatima – two million within the first decade of the Event. Against the orders of the government, the local people erected a chapel, although the Catholic Church as yet took no stance. But the local Bishop investigated and concluded in 1930 that the apparitions of Our Lady at Fatima were "worthy of belief." Such is the Church's cautious way of affirming private revelations that are not part of the deposit of faith that must be believed. Nevertheless, the date of the first apparition is now commemorated liturgically on 13 May, the Feast of Our Lady of Fatima; a succession of Popes have, by their example of repeated pilgrimages to Fatima, given their personal approval to the growing shrine; and the pilgrims' devotions that grew in scope year by year have become "mainstream" Catholic culture (e.g., the "Fatima Prayer" ending each decade of the Rosary); and now, in the 21st century, there can be seen several million pilgrims in attendance each year. During the one-hundredth anniversary of the Fatima Event, in 2017, almost ten million pilgrims appeared.

Interest in Fatima continues unabated even after that much-anticipated centenary came and went in 2017. Two significant reasons arise from two controversies: *Has Russia been consecrated to the Immaculate Heart of Mary in the manner she requested?*; and, *Was the "Third Secret" purportedly revealed in 2000 (and seemingly dismissed as already fulfilled) complete or even authentic?* Even then-head of the Congregation for the Doctrine of the Faith Josef Ratzinger would later, as Pope Benedict XVI in 2010, hint that the Third Secret is of continuing significance. Here is not, however, the place to weigh in on the issues and the questions, only to acknowledge them.

The Sanctuary of Our Lady of Fatima at the Cova da Iria is, like the Sanctuary of Our Lady of Lourdes, a complex of churches and shrines, comprising two basilicas – Our Lady of the Rosary as well as the nearby Basilica of the Holy Trinity; a number of chapels, including at the site of the Lausperene, the holm-oak by which most of the apparitions occurred, and the Chapel of the Apparitions; a Monument to the Sacred Heart of Jesus; numerous support buildings, hostels, retreat facilities, monuments to various Popes and individuals important in the history of the Sanctuary; and even a segment of the Berlin Wall commemorating the Fall of Communism, which many attribute directly to Pope John Paul II's 1984 consecration of "the world" to the Immaculate Heart of Mary, although not all agree.

Regardless of one's stance on the controversies the Fatima Event is, without a doubt, one of the most significant occurrences in modern Church – in world – history. Millions of pilgrims each year agree.

St. Joseph's Oratory of Mount Royal, Montreal, Quebec

Of the top ten Catholic pilgrimage destinations around the world, the Blessed Mother under one or the other of her many titles is the patron of five, or half. Besides the Holy Land, four other historical saints are the focus of one each of the other four sites. Saint Joseph, the foster-father of Our Lord, is one of those other saints, although he arguably shares his fame with a modern saint.

The National Shrine of Canada, found on Mount Royal's Westmount Summit, began in 1904 as a simple oratory (a place of prayer) dedicated to St. Joseph. Its founder, Br. André Bessette or "Frère André," a lay brother of the Congregation of the Holy Cross (C.S.C.), was already famous for thousands of miraculous healings which he attributed to his intense devotion to St. Joseph and prayers to that saint in company with application of a simple oil for which he claimed no miraculous properties other than symbolizing faith in prayers offered and hope for graces solicited. Drawn by his fame and healings, a growing congregation rapidly made a larger chapel necessary, then a full-blown basilica church whose most distinctive feature, a dome claimed to be one of the largest in the world, was completed in 1939, two years after the death of Br. André. Formally granted the status of minor basilica in 1955, it will, by law, always remain the tallest structure in Montreal.

"St. Joseph Oil" remains available, ordinary vegetable oil in which a wick burns a day and a night before a statue of St Joseph, which is then bottled and made available to pilgrims at the Oratory or by mail. Like Brother André, the current rectors of the Oratory make a point of not claiming any miraculous or magical powers in the oil itself. Miraculous healings continue, nonetheless, as pilgrims continue to visit the Oratory in great numbers, now seeking the intercession of, in addition to St. Joseph, St. André of Montreal, who was canonized by Pope Benedict XVI in 2010 and whose heart is enshrined within the Oratory.

Medjugorje, Bosnia-Herzegovina

Like so much else regarding Medjugorje, this is going to be an unusual entry. I debated including pilgrimage to Medjugorje in this list and this book because its recent approval as a pilgrimage destination is only guarded and conditional. The purported visions of the Blessed Virgin Mary at Medjugorje, allegedly occurring daily for nearly forty years now, have *not* been approved by the Church as "worthy of belief." Neither have they, on the other hand, been declared "not of supernatural origin" ... sort of. Actually, they *were* condemned by the local Bishop – and then the Vatican intervened, in a virtually unprecedented action, on the basis that Medjugorje had become a worldwide phenomenon. And so, the mystery that is Medjugorje begins....

The simple facts, if they can be called that, and such as they can be determined, are as follows. Beginning on 24 June 1981, six youths aged ten to sixteen began claiming to receive visitations from the *Gospa*, Croatian for "Our Lady," the Virgin Mother of God, on a hill near Medjugorje, a village in what was then the Bosnia-Herzegovina region of communist Yugoslavia. Now in middle age, forties and fifties, the alleged visionaries continue to claim visitations, although one by one each, having received a total of ten "secrets," have ceased to claim daily visions – although they allegedly will each receive an individual visitation from the Blessed Mother once a year for the rest of their lives.

What the seers have revealed about the purported secrets bears much similarity to those of Fatima, being largely eschatological – but more urgent. Ours is a time of Grace, but the world will soon – within the lifetime of at least one of the visionaries – receive warnings that will bring fear and hope and be unmistakable, providing one last chance for unbelievers who will thenceforth be unable to claim ignorance of God's plan.

Most of the alleged messages received from Our Lady in her daily visitations have not concerned such dire events, however. By and large, they have been vague declarations of her and her Son's love for the visionaries and the world, exhortations to peace, to love one another, to pray the Rosary, to adore her Son in the Eucharist, and the like.

So far, the facts that I do not believe anyone would dispute except those who might quibble over my use of the qualifiers "claimed," "alleged," and "purported." The first few days and weeks after 24 June 1981, however, set forth a microcosm of the controversy that has attended the alleged event to this day. The local priest was at first skeptical; he soon became a fervent believer. The local bishop, who in the normal course of events has the primary responsibility of determining and declaring such a claimed event "worthy" or "not worthy" of belief, was at first cautiously receptive; he soon declared the alleged visions absolutely not of supernatural origin – which has remained the stance of his successor.

Of course, nothing about Medjugorje has proven "normal." Very quickly – especially considering the remote, difficult-to-reach locale, behind the Iron Curtain during what no one at the time could know was the last decade of Soviet communism, but that everyone knew was a period of escalating tensions between east and west – pilgrims from all over the world began making their way to Medjugorje to witness the apparitions. Or, rather, to witness the visionaries, usually promptly at 17:40 each day, go into a state of ecstasy with their eyes fixed forward and up, for some time. But such was not all pilgrims witnessed, according to many accounts. Some reported signs and wonders, mysterious lights on "Apparition Hill," the sun dancing in the sky as was so widely associated with the climax of the Fatima Event – although in the case of Medjugorje never was such a manifestation seen in common by all present. Extraordinary healings, conversions of minds and hearts, vocations to the priesthood and religious life, took place as well, providing fodder for those claiming validation for Medjugorje in the Biblical injunction, "You will know them by their fruits" (Matt. 7: 16).

On the other hand, critics pointed to unprecedented messages alleged to have been given by Our Lady – derogating the local Bishops for their unbelief, seeming to involve herself in a longstanding ecclesial-political feud between the Franciscans who have long held custody of the churches in the area and the diocesan hierarchy which has, now for generations, been attempting to bring local Church structures in line with the Universal Church; most notoriously, perhaps, equating Christianity with Islam (Bosnia-Herzegovina historically has a majority Muslim population, although Medjugorje is so close to the border with Catholic Croatia that the local population there is majority Catholic), and so forth. The lives of the local priests who assumed close oversight of the visionaries once initial skepticism shifted radically to enthusiastic belief have not been exemplary – that very priest who was the youths' first spiritual director was eventually defrocked for alleged sexual improprieties and straying into New Age mysticism; the lives of the visionaries themselves have not fit the pattern that had come to be expected for those meeting the Mother of God face-to-face. Most such through time have ended up dedicating themselves to God as religious; all the Medjugorje visionaries married, raised families, and have lived unremarkable lives ... for celebrities, which they have become. They have reportedly monetized their experiences, owning multiple properties in and around Medjugorje as well as in other countries in Europe and the United States, appearing at "conferences" which charge admission but provide the opportunity to be present when, perhaps, they receive visitations far from Medjugorje, sometimes as if on cue. The village itself has monetized the event, with multiple hotels, support facilities, shops, eateries, bed-and-breakfasts, and so forth opening to accommodate upwards of a million pilgrims each year. In that, to be fair, it is no different than any other pilgrimage site, which must support many times their population in transient visitors, year in and year out. By all accounts, the town retains – despite the bustle – a serenity remarkable to visitors. The same is said of the alleged visionaries. And thousands upon thousands of pilgrims have reported spiritual encounters and come away from Medjugorje with renewed faith, hope, and love for Our Lord.

The above situation developed only over a period of years that extended to decades. From the beginning and through those same years, pilgrimage to Medjugorje was growing and growing. Even the devastating civil war and ethnic cleansings that attended the breakup of the former Yugoslavia after the fall of communism in the 1990s only decreased the number of pilgrims making their way there. It did not stop them. As soon as stability returned, the pilgrimage industry centered on Medjugorje – now part of a new country, Bosnia-Herzegovina – took back up with vigor. The pilgrims would not accept the repeated verdicts of the local Bishops and orders that organized pilgrimages to Medjugorje were not to be undertaken under the presumption of authenticity. Higher Church authorities got involved in the dispute. In 2010, Pope Benedict XVI authorized a Vatican commission to examine Medjugorje. Four years later, the commission reportedly completed its examination ... but although a decision was anticipated to be promulgated the next year – nothing. In 2017, it was revealed that the commission reached a split decision. By a majority of thirteen to one, the commission deemed the first seven apparitions to be of likely supernatural origin, but not subsequent claimed apparitions; they recommended further study. Both critics and supporters read what they wanted from the report. Pope Francis sent a special envoy to Medjugorje to study the pastoral situation and needs of the pilgrims who continued to come ... and in 2019, the Vatican officially authorized pilgrimages to be undertaken – with no explicit statement as to the veracity or not of the claimed apparitions.[118] The situation remains grey, although, at this point, it certainly seems as if the stock of those believing in the Medjugorje phenomenon is in the ascendant.

I certainly do not know what to make of it all. Holy Mother Church herself seems not to know what to make of it! The one thing I can say with certainty is that it is a very polarizing subject. I have been aware of Medjugorje for my entire "Catholic life," having been attracted to the Catholic Church since 1983 and converting formally in 1986. My first exposure to the Catholic phenomenon of "pilgrimage" came within a year or so when a family with whom my wife and myself had become close in our first Catholic parish made a pilgrimage to Medjugorje. They had no doubts as to its authenticity. But at the same time, another parishioner was forwarding me highly skeptical accounts and news stories. I grew intrigued at the dichotomy, and have, off and on over the thirty years since, watched as many thousands of books and articles have emerged ... and, on the whole, shed no more light on the subject. One problem that faces anyone trying to reach an impartial conclusion is that, as far as I can tell, and from the very beginning, not a single one of those many thousands of books and articles (few of which I have actually read, I freely admit, although their stance is

---

[118] "Pope authorizes pilgrimages to Medjugorje," *Vatican News* (12 May 2019) [https://www.vaticannews.va/en/pope/news/2019-05/pope-authorizes-pilgrimages-to-medjugorje.html]

usually quite clear at a glance) approaches the question of authenticity with any objectivity. They are either all-in or all-out, telegraphing their position from virtually the first word and considering the opposition position to be acting at best from ignorance but often enough in obstinate bad faith. There is a troubling lack of charity on both sides. It is therefore hard to get even a simple, reliable, straightforward account of the history of the events or the personalities involved. I know good people on both sides of the issue; I know good *priests* on both sides of the issue – virtually all of whom publicly adopt a "wait and see, let the Church decide" position but who clearly hold strong opinions on the matter when you get them talking.

And that is indeed pretty much my position....

What is the relevance of all that, you might ask? I would respond, first, that without a doubt, Medjugorje merits inclusion in any book on Catholic pilgrimage in the early 21st century. It is a significant destination in and of itself. I believe, moreover, that Medjugorje has contributed to a rise in Catholic pilgrimage overall, including to other destinations. I do not have data to back that belief up, so this is only an impression – except in one respect. One of the major Catholic pilgrimage brokers has its origin and its very name in the Medjugorje phenomenon: "206 Tours" takes its name from the time of the daily apparitions, 17:40 or "twenty minutes to six," in the 1980s when its founder returned from a pilgrimage there with an overwhelming desire to share the experience. Also, among the fruits of Medjugorje I count the very existence of Radio Maria, the sponsoring organization of my pilgrimage to the Holy Land. Radio Maria was founded – and continues, along with much else good that has nothing to do with Medjugorje – to popularize the messages attributed to the "Queen of Peace." It is, as its advertising blurb says, "A Christian Voice in Your Home" – or in my car, which is where I listen to it most of the time.

Nevertheless, there are – just as "without a doubt" – important questions regarding the authenticity of the phenomenon as a whole. The Vatican commission's reported conclusions were hardly a validation except that *perhaps* the entire phenomenon was born in an authentic handful of visitations by Our Lady. Subsequent developments, even the permission finally granted in 2019 for organized, church-sponsored pilgrimages to Medjugorje, were explicitly not intended to be taken as an endorsement for all the claims that have been made through the years, even though there is free acknowledgment of spiritual fruits and benefits arising in that place. Overall, it is rather more about providing for the needs of pilgrims – who had continued to come regardless of former disapproval. In effect, the 2019 permission is, in my view, a capitulation to the reality of the situation as it stands.

So, for what it is worth, here is my summation: If you feel called to make a pilgrimage to Medjugorje, where Our Lady may or may not have appeared or appear today, by all means, *go*. But go informed of the complex questions surrounding this destination, more so than any other of which I am aware. And, as to the authenticity of the apparitions, even at the beginning, my final word is: "Wait and see, let the Church decide." But don't hold your breath.

El Camino de Santiago de Compostela, Galicia, Spain

This final international pilgrimage of the "top ten" described here is known more by the name of the route than by the destination – literally, "The Road of St. James of Compostela," usually known in English as "The Way of St. James" if not merely as the untranslated *El Camino*. The destination is the shrine of the Apostle St. James the Greater in the Cathedral of Santiago de Compostela in Galicia, virtually at the northwestern corner of Spain.

According to ancient legend, James the Greater (*Sanctus Iacobus*, *Sant'iago*), the son of Zebedee, brother to John the Beloved Disciple, probable cousin to Our Lord, evangelized in Spain before returning to Jerusalem to attend the Dormition of Our Lady, ca. AD 42. There, however, he was arrested by King Herod Agrippa and beheaded on the site of the Armenian Orthodox Cathedral of St. James. His disciples later took his bones back to Spain and interred them near the end of the earth. The specific location was lost, however, until the ninth century, when the relics were revealed to a monk by the appearance of a star above a certain field – hence, *Compostela*. Prayers offered at the site resulted in the appearance of St. James shortly afterward to save a beleaguered Christian army from certain destruction by the Moors in the legendary Battle of Clavijo (844) – hence his full Spanish title, *Santiago Matamoros*, the Moor-slayer. As the Reconquista began in earnest after the year 1000, becoming another battlefield of the broader Crusading movement, what had been a trickle of Christian pilgrims from across Europe taking the road to Compostela became a flood. The shrine of Santiago de Compostela developed into the third most popular pilgrimage destination after Jerusalem and Rome. Although traffic on the Pilgrim's Way subsided back to a trickle in the modern age, it never died out and was reborn in the mid-twentieth century to boom in the 1990s and the early 21st century.

What specific route makes up El Camino is, however, somewhat ambiguous. The full Camino is a network of pilgrims' ways spanning most of Europe. Nevertheless, the land routes do pretty much converge just south of the Pyrenees mountains in northeastern Spain, at Puente la Reina, before proceeding westward through Burgos and León before reaching the great cathedral. Common starting points for this most heavily traveled of all the routes are at the border between Spain and France in the Pyrenees mountains, either Saint-Jean-Pied-de-Port on the French side, or Roncevalles on the Spanish side. From the latter to Santiago de Compostela is about five hundred miles.

Whether or not most modern pilgrims do so or not, the archetypal pilgrim on the Way of St. James walks that five hundred miles, taking most of a month to do so; other popular modes of transportation are by bicycle, with some relative few making the journey on horseback or by donkey. In our modern world, there are busses following the journey. Were I to take that expedient, however, I would hesitate to claim to be a "pilgrim of El Camino"! "Pilgrim of Santiago de Compostela," yes, but not "of El Camino." Perhaps more so than any other pilgrimage, the journey is as important as the destination. While "*Es tu Camino* – It is your *Camino*," is indeed the unofficial motto of the pilgrimage, it simply acknowledges that every pilgrim's personal experience of the Road is unique – it does *not* mean, as some of late reportedly take it, "Anything goes!"

Without a doubt, El Camino de Santiago is a significant undertaking, with a substantial support system. With hundreds of thousands reportedly taking to the Way each year, it requires such. Accommodations are plentiful along the main paths, most of them being hostels – some private, some public, some Church-run, some even in a number of monasteries that offer hospitality as one of their works. Those traveling the Road can document their progress by means of a *Credencial*, the Pilgrim's Passport, an official booklet that serves as a modern version of the royal and ecclesiastical warrants provided to medieval pilgrims granting them unhindered passage. The Credencials are meant to be stamped at the various hostels and eateries along the way as both memento and proof of the journey. Those pilgrims who can present such documentation that they have walked the final one hundred kilometers (two hundred if cycling) and state that their motivation in taking the Camino is religious may receive from the Cathedral a *Compostela*, an indulgenced certificate, with all such awards being announced at the two daily Pilgrims' Masses offered there. On Sundays, this ceremony is accompanied by the famous *Botafumeiro*, one of the world's largest censers ("–as big as a Volkswagen!," exulted Fr. Ryan Humphries when he was promoting the 2016 pilgrimage to Fatima, Santiago de Compostela, and Lourdes that I was unable to accompany), in full action.

Although I know that I will never walk those sixty miles to earn a Compostela, I hope one day to be able to walk at least a short distance on El Camino and visit Santiago de Compostela.

In truth, I would like to visit each one of these described destinations – some more so than others, of course, but God willing, and if I am able, I will not allow an opportunity to make a pilgrimage to any one of these pass me by. These international pilgrimage destinations are, however, expensive and time-consuming. What about nearer to home?

CHAPTER FIVE

... PILGRIMAGES NEAR ...

In my account of each of the three major pilgrimages I have been blessed to accompany, I included some tally of the monetary cost, in order to make a point. Pilgrimage to any of the major international destinations is, even today, a significant undertaking. Not on the order of what faced ancient or medieval pilgrims, of course, who would often sell, hock, or mortgage all they had to set forth on a journey which they knew would take months or years to accomplish and return to their homes – if they ever did return home. Pilgrims in the early Church knew that theirs might well be a one-way journey, that they might never see their homes and loved ones again, that they stood a good chance of succumbing to disease, or to the elements, or to bandits, or to any of a score of likely unpleasant deaths far from home that are quite frankly vanishingly *unlikely* to befall a modern pilgrim. Not for nothing was pilgrimage considered a major form of penance during the Middle Ages. A modern pilgrim, on the other hand, can reasonably expect to be safe and snug at home, in his or her bed, a week to ten days (usually) after setting out on their spiritual journey. The cost is, for moderns and relatively speaking, not so high, either – most likely a few months' income, easily budgeted given enough discipline and motivation. Sacrifice is a major part of pilgrimage, but our greatest sacrifices today pale beside those of our forebears!

Nevertheless, an organized, brokered pilgrimage to one of the major sacred destinations such as those I have been lucky enough to make is indeed a significant investment in both time and money. That is true for any of the places described in the previous chapter: the Marian apparition sites at Fatima in Portugal and Lourdes in France, or Medjugorje in Bosnia-Herzegovina; walking the Camino de Santiago de Compostela, the pilgrim's road across northern Spain from the Pyrenees mountains to the Shrine of St. James in the northwest; or beyond that "top ten": following in the footsteps of St. Paul on his three missionary journeys, whether by land, sea, or air (usually a combination of all three, such as will be undertaken by my brother and his wife in the near future in another of their non-Catholic non-pilgrimage *pilgrimages* following the journeys of St. Paul); visiting the holy places of Ireland, Scotland, and England - Knock, Iona, and Lindisfarne or Glastonbury; or countless other destinations around the world, visiting shrines and relics dedicated to any of the many hundreds of major and "minor" saints of our Holy Faith. We can lament all we want that our faith and capacity for sacrifice pales beside our ancestors, but the fact is that not everyone is in a position to make such a commitment, whether because of cost, of job responsibilities, of familial obligations, of health, of age, or any of many other impediments to pilgrimage or international travel for any other purpose.

Nevertheless, the spiritual benefits of pilgrimage are available to those individuals, as well. There are a surprising number of shrines and pilgrimage destinations to be found scattered across these United States, requiring as little as a couple of days or even a couple of hours to visit. Or, one can make a "pilgrimage" on an even smaller scale. In this chapter, I will discuss a range of options that are available and relate my various experiences - or lack of experience - in the case of each.

Lists of pilgrimage sites within the confines of the United States

Should this book somehow come into the hands of someone outside the United States, what is said here will still be true in a general sense, although not in a specific sense. For someone in, say, the United Kingdom, a journey to any of the sites that I am about to discuss would be "international travel." Nevertheless, the point I am making holds for any country. Anywhere you go in the world, there is an abundance of pilgrimage destinations available within the confines of a similar range as represented by the continental United States to a citizen of any one of those states. Similarly, when I narrow my focus to more local options. Especially when it comes to historically Catholic Europe and Latin America, sacred places and shrines may sometimes be found around every corner, at the side of every road. But since I am an American writing almost certainly for a readership in the United States, I am concentrating here.

The renowned pilgrimage sites are, of course, from the United States' perspective, international. They are so well known that producing a list of ten was relatively straightforward. Sitting down to list out ten, I would have listed - probably - pretty much what I ended up discussing, with a couple of exceptions. My list would not have been in the same order but finding data on numbers of pilgrims annually was not difficult. Finding similar information for pilgrimage destinations in the United States proved much more daunting, nor was I able jot down a comparably reliable list off the top of my head. Research revealed that the problem is twofold and at first seemed counterintuitive. There are, on the one hand, too many little places of pilgrimage dotting our great nation. At the same time, however, there are not so many that stand out like, e.g., the Holy Land, or Rome, or Guadalupe, or Fatima, or Medjugorje. So, how was I to produce a manageable and yet meaningful list on which to focus? I checked in turn for guidebooks and the Internet.

Searching Amazon.com yields fewer available – and current – guidebooks describing pilgrimage destinations within the United States than I would have expected. There are a fair number of guides to monastic guesthouses and the like, and I include one of those below. Otherwise, of the books I found, only a couple are less than twenty years old. Perhaps that is to be expected for this type of information. A book cannot easily be kept up to date with ever-changing information. Certainly, a new edition can always be issued, but there will still be many, many copies of the previous edition out there, in which *most* of the information will remain correct, making previous purchasers reluctant to purchase the new edition. The Internet is a wonderful resource in part for this reason – information can be updated instantly, and anyone consulting a well-maintained web page will always have the most up-to-date information. I suspect that to be at least in part the reason for a dearth of more recent hardcopy guidebooks of this type. Nevertheless, for the sake of completeness – and because for certain things I just prefer a real book – here is an annotated list of such books as I found, in more or less order of publication.

National Conference of Catholic Bishops, *Catholic Shrines and Places of Pilgrimage in the United States*, Jubilee 2000 Edition, (United States Conference of Catholic Bishops, 1998).

I include this book first, as much as anything, for its official nature, having been prepared by the USCCB Office of Pastoral Care of Migrants and Refugees for the Jubilee Year 2000. Apparently, "Migrants and Refugees" is the Bishops' committee overseeing pilgrimages. Okay. In any case, this book provides a directory organized geographically. For each entry it includes diocesan affiliation; contact information, a small state map indicating the location of the entry within the state; history; a schedule of Masses and devotions, including special events; a description of facilities and accommodations; and in some cases, even what languages are spoken. All except the historical sections, which are usually a bare two or three paragraphs, appear in list format. There are four indices: an "Alphabetical Listing of Shrines (Using Proper Titles)," followed by three thematic listings of "Shrines and Places Dedicated to the Mystery of Christ," "... to the Blessed Mother," and "... to the Saints."

Theresa Santa Czarnopys and Thomas M. Santa, C.Ss.R., *Marian Shrines of the United States: A Pilgrim's Travel Guide* (Liguori, Missouri: Liguori Publications, 1998).

Over fifty shrines, organized by region of the United States, each introduced with some historical perspective on the shrine and its founding, followed by a prayer from a liturgy associated with Our Lady under that title or attribute, a description of the shrine's appearance, contact information, "tourist information," a map and directions, points of interest purportedly for "first-time pilgrims" (although the information seems useful to any pilgrim), and a list of "factoids" (my term) of particular interest. Some of those sections seem to overlap in their scope and could have been consolidated. The lack of Internet addresses criticized by some Amazon.com commentators I consider somewhat facile – that is what search engines are for – and a URL is something else that could well have changed in twenty-plus years.

Jay Copp, *The Liguori Guide to Catholic U.S.A: A Treasury of Churches, Schools, Monuments, Shrines, and Monasteries* (Liguori, Missouri: Liguori Publications, 1999).

The blurb for this book that appears on Amazon.com asserts "more than five hundred churches, monuments, schools, and monasteries" are included. I did not count, but I can easily believe it. There are a *lot*. There is not a lot of individual information given on most, however – opening up the book to a random two-page spread (pp. 192-193), which happens to be the beginning of the section on Montana, subsection on Western Montana, finds a total of five places described – one with little more than three lines, a couple with several short paragraphs. Coverage varies. Most entries do include basic contact information, a street address and a telephone number. I would say that this book is definitely worth a browse, getting ideas for a given area you might be visiting, but obviously not for in-depth reference. But that is the sacrifice, depth for breadth. The overall organization is first by region of the country, then by state, then as indicated above, by area within the state. There is, however, an alphabetical index of all the sites included as well. This book catches some real obscurities in its net. Immediate kudos are due for the inclusion, on the cover, at top left, of the Rock Chapel at Carmel, Louisiana, just about thirty miles north of where I am sitting as I write. And, frankly, without this book I doubt I would ever have known about what may be the most inaccessible shrine of all: Petoskey, Maine: "At the bottom of Little Traverse Bay is the Skin Diver's Shrine (off US 131). The life-sized figured of Christ stands beneath 60 feet of water" (p. 152).

Robert J. Regalbuto, *Monastery Guest Houses of North America: A Visitor's Guide*, 5th ed. (Woodstock, Vermont: Countryman Press, 2010).

One of the imperatives of monasticism, enshrined in the model *Rule of St. Benedict*, which underlies most monasticism in the western Church, is hospitality, offering a place of refuge to strangers and pilgrims. Weary travelers throughout the Christian era have found themselves welcomed at the once ubiquitous, still numerous monasteries across Catholic Europe. That tradition continues today in American religious houses of the Benedictine tradition. I have availed myself of it on occasion through the years. As I mentioned above, there are many guidebooks to such guesthouses available today. This is the one I found rated highest by Amazon.com users, except for *Sanctuaries, The Complete United States: A Guide to Lodgings in Monasteries, Abbeys, and Retreats*, which is unabashedly ecumenical in making a point that it covers Catholic, Protestant, Buddhist, Jewish, Hindu, Sufi, Quaker.... Preferring to keep this book as Catholic as possible, I chose the next ... And then, examining the Kindle preview introduction, I find that *this* book is "comprehensive, including ... accommodations offered by communities of several denominations: Roman Catholic, Anglican/Episcopal, Eastern Orthodox, Lutheran, [...] Unitarian Universalist, and ecumenical."

As to the book itself, it is basically a catalog organized by state or province (it includes Canada), including for each entry the name, address, religious order, contact information, website and email, accommodations, the availability of meals, costs, directions, public transportation information, a short history, a brief description, a point of interest, and a special note, the latter if applicable. Some also include a black and white sketch. Totaling about 120 lodgings, it seems reasonably complete, as far as I can tell. All the ones I looked for in the table of contents were included, including "my own" monastery as a Benedictine Oblate, St. Joseph's Abbey, St. Benedict, Louisiana.

Julie Dortch Cragon, *Visiting Mary: Her U.S. Shrines and Their Graces* (Cincinnati, Ohio: Servant, 2014)

This book is more devotional than most others listed here. In 28 chapters covering somewhat more than that number of shrines, the author discusses Our Lady in one of her attributes or titles, then describes one or more shrines devoted to her under that particular rubric, ending with a short prayer and meditation on the grace embodied in that title. It is an interesting concept that sets this book apart from a run-of-the-mill guidebook.

Thomas J. Craughwell, *101 Places to Pray Before You Die: A Roamin' Catholic's Guide* (Cincinnati, Ohio: Franciscan Media, 2017).

The title conveys an essential truth. Prayer is central to the practice of pilgrimage. Organized by state, each "place to pray" (or, sometimes, group of closely associated "places to pray") gets about two pages of conversational information, with basic contact information including physical address, telephone number, and Internet information. The author deserves an "attaboy" for including, under Texas, an entry for the "Hill Country: Painted Churches of the Texas Hill Country" (see below, under "Micro pilgrimages").

Of the several books I have detailed here, Craughwell's *101 Places to Pray* strikes me as the most interesting. Copp's *Liguori Guide* appears to be a good bet, as well. Were I more mystically inclined, Cragon's *Visiting Mary* would be on my shortlist as well. The others I would not bother with, either because of age or limited scope, but your mileage may vary.

Turning to the Internet, I found two general types of lists for specifically U.S. pilgrimage and shrine information, what I call respectively, "mega-lists" and "shortlists," usually ranked – explicitly or implicitly – according to some undeclared criterion. The mega-lists typically include dozens or even hundreds of listings, with little information directly available, opting instead for links out to websites for the various entities. In other words, they are basically indexes, usually organized by state. Here is a shortlist of four mega-lists that look most useful:

"Shrines, Basilicas, Cathedrals, Monasteries," *Catholic Shrines and Holy Places* [catholicplaces.org], accessed 26 August 2019.

A state by state listing, each with contact information, a paragraph or two of history and description, and a link to the web site. Despite the rather all-encompassing page title, however, I am not sure how comprehensive it is meant to be. For instance, as I found consulting the entry for my home state, Louisiana, it does lead off with a nice account of my own Minor Basilica of the Immaculate Conception in Natchitoches – but it does *not* include St. Joseph Abbey in St. Benedict, Louisiana, which merits inclusion if only for the striking murals painted by Dom Gregory de Wit, O.S.B in the abbey church and refectory. What it does concisely include, however, is very well done.

"Catholic Shrines, Pilgrimage Sites & Places of Interest in the United States," *The Catholic Travel Guide* [https://thecatholictravelguide.com/destinations/u-s-a/], accessed 26 August 2019.

A lot of links organized by states, multiple links per state. Just links, though.

"Sites by State," *Catholic Pilgrimage Sites* [https://catholicpilgrimagesites.wordpress.com/sites-by-state-2/], accessed 26 August 2019.

Multiple per state, with descriptive blurbs and links.

Shaun McAfee, "These +100 Catholic Pilgrimage Sites in the US are Completely Out of this World," *epicPew* (15 May 2016) [https://epicpew.com/100-catholic-pilgrimage-sites-in-united-states/]

Listing of one hundred – one for each state, with a blurb plus a number of "See alsos." Yes, the inversion of the plus-sign and "100" is transcribed accurately.

Shorter lists usually contain more information on each item. Based on four such lists (one list of twenty, two lists of ten, and one list of seven, I tallied up and extracted one list of "Top Ten" Pilgrimages within the United States[119]:

"20 Pilgrimage Sites Across the United States Worth Visiting" (2018 edition), *Religious Travel Planning Guide* [http://religioustravelplanningguide.com/20-pilgrimage-sites-across-united-states-worth-visiting/], accessed 26 August 2019.

"Pilgrimage Sites in the United States and Canada," *Servants of the Lord and the Virgin of Matara* [https://ssvmusa.org/index.php/catholic-culture/pilgrimage-sites-in-the-united-states/], accessed 26 August 2019.

This is actually a list of twelve because it includes ten from the US and two from Canada. I only consider the ones for the US. They are all concentrated in the northeast.

"10 Top Catholic Shrines in the U.S.," *Religious Planning Travel Guide* [http://religioustravelplanningguide.com/10-top-catholic-shrines-in-the-u-s/], accessed 26 August 2019.

Stephanie Foley, "7 Pilgrimages You Can Make in the United States," *Relevant Radio* (19 April 2018) [https://relevantradio.com/2018/04/7-pilgrimages-you-can-make-in-the-united-states/]

The resulting list of "Top Ten" Pilgrimage Sites in the United States is as follows:

---

[119] For what it is worth, my method was this. In the four source lists, there are 37 unique pilgrimage destinations. There are overlaps - one site appears in all four lists; one site appears in three of the lists, five sites appear in two of the lists. I ranked the latter five according to their implicit ranking in each list as well as the "strength" of each list where something appearing on a shorter, more selective list implied a "stronger" recommendation. That totaled seven, leaving three to be filled. Looking at the remaining 26 unique items, I again selected three, again based on implicit rank and strength in each list. The result was a nice list, fairly well distributed across the United States. Note that I considered as well a list of "Top pilgrimage destinations in the United States" (comprising twelve) which may be found at the Wikipedia entry for "Catholic Church in the United States," *s.v.*, which explicitly cites the article listed above, "10 Top Catholic Shrines in the U.S.," at *Religious Planning Travel Guide*, with two unexplained additions; applying the same methodology described above resulted in no substantial change to the results.

1. Basilica of the National Shrine of the Immaculate Conception (Washington, DC)
2. National Shrine of Our Lady of Częstochowa (Doylestown, Pennsylvania)
3. California Missions Trail (San Diego to Sonoma, California)
4. National Shrine of St. Elizabeth Ann Seton (Emmitsburg, Maryland)
5. Shrine of Our Lady of La Leche (St. Augustine, Florida)
6. National Shrine of St. John Neumann (Philadelphia, Pennsylvania)
7. Shrine of Our Lady of Martyrs (Auriesville, New York)
8. Walk to Mary Pilgrimage (De Pere to Champion, Wisconsin)
9. Ave Maria Grotto and St. Bernard Abbey (Cullmann, Alabama)
10. Franciscan Monastery of the Holy Land (Washington, DC)

Basilica of the National Shrine of the Immaculate Conception (Washington, DC)

A source of occasional confusion is the existence of two major "national" churches in Washington, DC. On the one hand, there is the neogothic medievalesque grandeur of the "National Cathedral," more formally known as the Cathedral Church of Saint Peter and Saint Paul in the City and Diocese of Washington. On the other hand, there is the more ponderous stability of the unique blend of neo-Byzantine and neo-Romanesque that is the Basilica of the National Shrine of the Immaculate Conception. The former is formally Episcopalian, but was conceived, built, and mostly functions as what its popular name implies – a "National Cathedral," hosting state funerals and memorial services for deceased presidents and other nationally prominent figures as well as a host of other events of national import. It is, however, the other, *Catholic* "national" church that concerns us here, dedicated to the patroness of the United States of America.

In discussing Lourdes as a major international pilgrimage destination in Chapter Six, I pointed out that Pope Pius IX's 1854 proclamation of the dogma did not mark the beginning of Catholic belief in the Immaculate Conception of the Blessed Mother. Supporting that point is the fact that seven years before that dogmatic proclamation, in 1847, in response to a unanimous petition by the bishops of the United States of America, the Pope declared the Mother of God to be the patroness of the country under that title. Almost a century in the making, the National Shrine of the Immaculate Conception began construction in 1920 and was only completed with the dedication and solemn blessing of the Trinity Dome mosaic on the Feast of the Immaculate Conception, 08 December 2017. It had long since been raised to the status of a minor basilica by Pope St. John Paul II in 1990.

This massive church - or rather, these massive *churches*, because the National Shrine is like many other major shrine and pilgrimage churches surveyed in this book in that it comprises two churches, the "Great Upper Church" and the "Crypt Church" - now stands as the largest Catholic church in the United States and North America. It is, moreover, the tallest habitable building in Washington, DC. The upper and lower churches host 81 chapels and sacred images, many being mosaic reproductions of traditional European Catholic images, including a rendition of the much-venerated and identifiable *La Purísima Immaculada Concepción* of Bartolomé Esteban Murillo from the Royal Palace of Aranjuez in Spain.

The basilica does not function as a parish church or even as cathedral church of the Catholic Archdiocese of Washington, which honor is held by the Cathedral of St. Matthew the Apostle. Daily services are well attended, however, by students of the adjacent Catholic University of America, the United States Conference of Catholic Bishops, tourists, and pilgrims - besides the numerous services and memorials of national *Catholic* importance that the basilica hosts.

Contact information:
NATIONAL SHRINE OF THE IMMACULATE CONCEPTION
400 Michigan Ave. NE
Washington, DC 20017
(202) 526-8300
info@nationalshrine.org
https://www.nationalshrine.org/

National Shrine of Our Lady of Częstochowa (Doylestown, Pennsylvania)

To understand the origins and significance of this shrine outside Philadelphia, one must consider Poland's long and painful history in European affairs and how central the Catholic Faith and devotion to Our Lady are to the Polish people's national identity.

The rest of Europe today often overlooks how important Poland has been over the centuries. At one time, when in commonwealth with Lithuania, Poland dominated much of Eastern Europe – what is on a modern map Poland plus the Baltic States including Lithuania, along with Belarus, Ukraine, and a wide strip in western Russia. Timely intervention by the Polish King Jan Sobieski on 11-12 September 1683 may well have saved much of Europe from Muslim domination by lifting the Ottoman Siege of Vienna and driving the Turks back down the Danube River. Nevertheless, by little more than a century later, the rising power of Prussia to the west plus the old imperial dynasties of Habsburg Austria in the south and Tsarist Russia to the east had progressively carved up Poland through a series of Partitions, distributing its territory among themselves. The Third Partition finally erased the once-proud kingdom from the map in 1795 – just as the French Revolution and its aftermath sent nationalistic hopes soaring across Europe west and east. The Poles' memories of independence gave urgency to their nationalistic dreams of restoring their kingdom and instigated repeated uprisings that were just as repeatedly crushed.

One comfort that the Polish people took through this long national nightmare of decline was their Catholic Faith. It had long been a strong force in Polish society, perhaps born in their close shave with apostasy and their redemption from a flirtation with Lutheranism in one of the major Counter-Reformation Jesuit success stories, possibly reinforced by the later conflict with Lutheran Prussians and Orthodox Russians. Polish Catholic faith found its focus in Our Lady of Częstochowa. Probably the most famous of many Byzantine-style "Black Madonna" or "Black Virgin" icons across Europe is called by that name and was long ago symbolically crowned as the Queen of Poland. These icons, whose originally more natural tones have darkened over time due to aging or the effects of smoke from centuries of candles lit before them, each one representing a prayer to Our Lady, became a genre all their own, inspiring many copies. The Virgin Mary holds the Child Jesus in the "*hodegetria*" pose of "one who shows the way," her free hand directing the viewer's attention to the Child who, in turn, extends one of his hands outward in blessing while holding a Book of Gospels in the other.

Located for at least six hundred years in the Monastery of Jasna Góra in Częstochowa, Our Lady of Częstochowa is of unknown age and origin. Determining either at this date is rendered near-impossible by a badly botched restoration undertaken after the icon was nearly destroyed in the fifteenth century, suffering severe damage. Despite their best efforts to repair the already precious relic, the medieval craftsmen did not understand the nature of the ancient encaustic method of painting by which the original image had been formed,[120] resulting in the original image being rendered barely discernable to later ages. As hauntingly beautiful as it is, the image as it appears today is fifteenth-century. Art historians nevertheless attribute the underlying original to sometime in the sixth to ninth centuries, somewhere in the Byzantine Empire.

Legend, however, places its origin much further back than that, holding it to be one of the "autograph" icons from the hand of St. Luke the Evangelist, written during time that St. Paul's "beloved physician" (Col. 4: 14) spent talking with the Virgin, learning directly from her the wonders of Jesus' Annunciation, Nativity, Infancy, and Childhood which he would uniquely record in the Third Gospel. Discovered (rediscovered?) in the fourth century, in Jerusalem by St. Helena and sent by her to the court of her imperial son, its path from Constantinople to Częstochowa where it arrived most of a thousand years later and entered history is shrouded in mystery.

Once there, however, several miracles are attributed to Our Lady in conjunction with the image. In 1386, the icon was already in Częstochowa when it was saved by the appearance of a cloud which descended to obscure the chapel currently housing it from marauders ransacking the area. By 1430, it was in the Monastery of Jasna Góra when Hussite raiders sacked the monastery. In a fit of iconoclasm, these proto-protestant rebels against the Church's authority broke the icon into pieces and slashed a sword twice across the Virgin's face before casting it off into a puddle of mud and blood as they made their escape. Divine light shone down to reveal the icon to its rescuers. Although the subsequent efforts of the restorers as mentioned earlier caused perhaps as much damage as the Hussites, obscuring the original image, and the wounds to Our Lady's face would not be covered – again, despite their best efforts – the icon was saved. Miracles continued. In 1655, Protestant Swedish troops were about to overrun the town. The people offered up prayers before the image for the town's deliverance. The town was delivered.

---

[120] Encaustic painting was developed by the ancient Greeks and involves the layered application of hot beeswax mixed with pigments to give a bright, textured effect. It was used extensively in funerary art (the most famous examples are from the Fayum burial portraits from 1st-3rd-c. Egypt). Wood made an excellent medium for encaustic painting, which made it ideal for icons.

Much later, just after the Poles finally regained a state of their own at the end of World War I in 1918, that freedom was almost immediately threatened. In 1920, as the Soviet Red Army massed across the Vistula River from Warsaw, thousands of people walked to Jasna Góra to offer prayers before the icon, to Our Lady of Częstochowa. Our Lady is said to have appeared in the sky above Warsaw – and the Red Army was pushed back by a vastly inferior Polish army. The Soviet defeat at Warsaw is widely credited with blocking the spread of Bolshevism into western Europe. Poland's thanks was to be no less victimized by its German neighbors to the west than its Russian neighbors to the east, then to fall under Soviet domination anyway. Through it all, however – the Nazi and subsequent Soviet occupations, the subsequent Cold War – Jasna Góra became a center of resistance, the icon of Our Lady of Częstochowa, a symbol of that resistance. Once his motherland was freed of the Soviet yoke, the most famous devotee of Our Lady of Częstochowa, the native son of Poland who became Pope John Paul II would credit devotion to the Black Madonna with bringing the Polish people through those dark years with their spirit and Faith intact.

That same intense Catholic culture centered on Our Lady had manifested itself in a Polish diaspora mainly to the United States that had begun over a century earlier, against the backdrop of repeated uprisings and defeats through the first two-thirds of the nineteenth century. What was, however, a trickle of such immigrants before 1870 became a flood after that year due to the same nationalist, social, political, and economic forces driving other central and eastern Europeans to the New World. Arrival in largely Protestant America reinforced these Polish immigrants' ethnic Catholic identity as it did most other such newcomers. Catholic churches and parish schools became central to close-knit ethnic communities in U.S. industrial cities across the northeast from New York City to Chicago.

Nevertheless, the intensely Catholic culture of these immigrant communities was considered alien in the mostly Protestant United States, and there were signs by the mid-twentieth century that second- and third-generation Polish Catholic Americans were losing something of their fervor. For that reason, in 1953, a Polish priest in America, Fr. Michael Zembrzuski, sought and received permission from Philadelphia's Archbishop John Francis O'Hara to construct a chapel near Doylestown, Pennsylvania, dedicated to and to contain a faithful copy of the icon of Our Lady of Częstochowa, blessed by the Pope. Fr. Zembrzuski promoted Our Lady of Częstochowa as a special patroness for Polish Americans. Pilgrimages from local Polish

American parishes began almost immediately and necessitated an expansion within just a few years. In 1966, the thousandth anniversary of the baptism of Duke Mieszko I, the creator of the Polish state, occasioned the Archbishop (later Cardinal) John Krol's dedication of an entirely new facility housing the new Shrine of Our Lady of Częstochowa. In attendance were President Lyndon B. Johnson and his family and other representatives of the Catholic Church and State officials.

In the decades since, Doylestown has hosted Popes and Presidents and has continued expansion and development to accommodate a growing number of pilgrims, including a Lower Chapel housing a faithful replica of the altar at Jasna Góra in Polish Częstochowa. Fr. Zembrzuski lived long enough to see his dream given form, dying in 2003. In 2009 the United States Conference of Catholic Bishops granted "American Częstochowa" the status of "National Shrine."

Contact information:
NATIONAL SHRINE OF OUR LADY OF CZĘSTOCHOWA
654 Ferry Road
Doylestown, PA 18901
(215) 348-0600
info@Częstochowa.us
https://www.Częstochowa.us

California Missions Trail (San Diego to Sonoma)

Stretching more than halfway (540 miles) up the Pacific Coast of California, dotted along *El Camino Real*, The Royal Road, are 21 Spanish missions and five *presidios* (forts) established from San Diego in the south (1769) to Sonoma in the north (1836). Their purpose was threefold: to evangelize the Native Americans along the *Alta California* coast; to extend Spanish royal power; and to preempt rival European powers' settlement in territory that Spain had long claimed but not colonized until the late eighteenth-early nineteenth-century European conflicts that could be considered precursors to the World Wars of the twentieth century brought confrontations extending around the world. Most of the outposts were founded during Spain's rule in Mexico; a couple of missions and the last presidio were set up after Mexico's declaration of independence in 1810 or even after that independence was recognized in 1821. A garrison of troops supported each mission from five major forts or presidios interspersed among them. Because they were founded concurrently and worked so closely together, I include them here.

There are different ways to list them meaningfully, but geographically either north-to-south or south-to-north seems best served by a map, so here I list them in order of foundation – and provide a map (for which, see the end of this chapter, p. 308). One common misconception is immediately apparent as such upon comparison of the list and the map, that the missions were founded in a steady advance northward out of *Baja California* into *Alta California*. Instead, strategic locations were secured first, as far north as possible without infringing on Russian claims, which in 1812 reached their furthest extent southward at Fort Ross in what is now Sonoma County. Then, the large spaces in between were slowly filled in.

California Missions and Presidios – *modern locations in italics*
1769: Presidio of San Diego – *San Diego*
1769: Mission San Diego de Alcala
1770: Presidio of Monterey – *Monterey*
1770: Mission San Carlos Borroméo de Carmelo – *Carmel*
1771: Mission San Antonio de Padua – *northwest of Jolon*
1771: Mission San Gabriel Arcángelo – *San Gabriel*
1772: Mission San Luis Obispo de Tolosa – *San Luis Obispo*
1776: Presidio San Francisco de Asis – *San Francisco*
1776: Mission San Francisco de Asis (Mission Dolores)
1776: Mission San Juan Capistrano – *San Juan Capistrano*
1777: Mission Santa Clara de Asis – *Santa Clara*
1782: Mission San Buenaventura – *Ventura*
1782: Presidio Santa Barbara – *Santa Barbara*
1786: Mission Santa Bárbara
1787: Mission La Purisima Concepción – *southeast of Lompoc*
1791: Mission Nuestra Señora de la Soledad – *southwest of Soledad*
1791: Mission Santa Cruz – *Santa Cruz*
1797: Mission San Fernando Rey de España – *Los Angeles*
1797: Mission San José – *Fremont*
1797: Mission San Juan Bautista – *San Juan Bautista*
1797: Mission San Miguel Arcángel – *San Miguel*
1798: Mission San Luis Rey de Francia – *Oceanside*
1804: Mission Santa Inés – *Solvang*
1817: Mission San Rafael Arcángel – *San Rafael*
1823: Mission San Francisco Solano – *Sonoma*
1836: Presidio of Sonoma

The first nine of the missions, starting with San Diego in 1769 and ending with San Buenaventura in 1782, were founded by Franciscan missionary Padre Junipero Serra, who died in 1784 at San Carlos Borroméo, where he is buried under the sanctuary floor. Long a patron of vocations and evangelization, and called "Apostle of California," Junipero Serra was beatified by Pope John Paul II in 1988 and canonized by Pope Francis in 2015 at the Basilica of the National Shrine of the Immaculate Conception.

Along with associated *pueblos*, or towns which grew up around the missions for the evangelized Native Americans who were considered to owe various forms of labor service to the Spanish and Mexicans, the Spanish missions effected a reasonably quick and thorough – and controversial in the viewpoint of many today – assimilation of the California natives to Spanish Mexican culture. Many of the missions and pueblos became the kernel around which formed the major cities of coastal California today – including San Diego and San Francisco.

The various missions exhibit many variations in the general style of New World Spanish architecture, which adapted from the Native Americans the use of mud brick and adobe to supplement stone, timber, and tilework. They were typically built around large plazas with adobe walls; individual buildings had patios and courtyards that contained fountains and gardens. Once the people of the local area accepted Christianity, the missionaries who established the mission would move on to a new territory, and the existing mission would become an ordinary parish church for the pueblo or town that had arisen.

While all survive and serve as stops along a pilgrims' way which can take a week and more to complete, visiting just five of the missions can give a good sense of the variety to be found among the California missions: *San Diego de Alcala, San Juan Capistrano, Santa Barbara, La Purisima Concepción*, and *San Carlos Borroméo de Carmelo*. Even that is a 450-mile drive, however, meaning that even for someone already in the area, the Spanish Missions of California are not just an afternoon or even a weekend trip.

Contact information: Given the nature of the missions and *presidios*, two dozen or more sites over 500-plus miles, concise contact information as provided here for most other US pilgrimage destinations is impractical. An excellent alternative is the California Department of Parks and Recreation page, "The California Missions Trail," which provides a great deal of useful information on the group as a whole and on the sites individually [https://www.parks.ca.gov/?page_id=22722].

xtra: *The Spanish Missions of Texas (mainly San Antonio and El Paso regions*

California was not the only area of Spanish colonial activity in what is now the United States. Nearing the end of a century and a half period of establishment (1632-1793) when the California missions had only recently begun (1769), similar outposts numbered in the dozens had spread across much of Texas, founded for much the same reasons as in California, some also serving as foundations for some of the state's most important cities today. Many of the Texas missions were abandoned and forgotten, even lost.

As an aside (within an aside), the "Spanish Missions of Texas" were not confined to the modern state of Texas. Just fourteen miles west of where I sit writing this was the easternmost of the Texas missions, *San Miguel de Linares de los Adaes*. Established in 1716 to evangelize the Caddo Adai Indians and to counter French claims to disputed territory east of the Sabine River (the modern border between Texas and Louisiana) and west of the Red River, represented by Fort St. Jean-Baptiste on the latter and its associated town of Natchitoches (founded 1714), Los Adaes would endure for much of the mid-eighteenth century. When France ceded to Spain all its territories west of the Mississippi in 1762, Los Adaes' secular purpose was rendered obsolete. It was decommissioned in 1772-1773. Sadly, nothing remains of the mission or its presidio, although it is now a thriving archaeological site, Louisiana state park, and National Historic Landmark.

A number of Spanish missions in the state of Texas survived, being still active as Catholic parishes today. Two major clusters of sites allow efficient overviews of two very different styles of building: three around El Paso in the far west, with a decidedly "New Mexican" flavor (*Mission Corpus Christi de la Ysleta, Mission Nuestra Señora de la Limpia Concepción de Los Piros de Socorro del Sur*, and the *San Elizario Presidio Chapel*); and four well-preserved and reconstructed missions in San Antonio (including the iconic Alamo, formally *Mission San Antonio de Valero*; the other three are *Mission Nuestra Señora de la Purísima Concepción de Acuña, Mission San José y San Miguel de Aguayo*, and *Mission San Juan Capistrano*). Either close group can easily be visited in a single day.

Regarding the San Antonio Missions, the Alamo is most famous. This former mission church had been secularized for several decades before the 1836 siege that made it forever after the symbol of the fierce spirit of Texan independence. Those events understandably dominate the presentation as it stands today. The best restored of the missions as a religious foundation is, however, *Mission San José*, which for its beauty is called the "Queen of the Texas Missions."

Contact information: Currently, the best "one-stop" guide to the Texas missions overall appears to be the website, *Texas Mission Guide*, [http://texasmissionguide.com/].

National Shrine of St. Elizabeth Ann Seton (Emmitsburg, Maryland)

In 1975, "Mother" Elizabeth Ann Seton became the first native-born saint of the United States.[121] It is therefore fitting that her shrine should appear in any list such as this.

Born in New York City in 1774 to a prominent doctor and his wife, the first three decades of Elizabeth's life were unsettled as she suffered the loss of her mother in later childbirth, the loss of her subsequent stepmother to divorce and estrangement, and the loss of her father's presence when he left her and her younger siblings with relatives to undertake further medical training in London. She took refuge in reading, especially the Bible, for which she developed a deep love. Hopes for stability in marriage and motherhood seemed fulfilled with the birth of several children but were then dashed when her husband's mercantile fortunes failed along with his health. Then, in 1803, a desperate attempt to restore William Seton's health in the more favorable climate of Italy ended in his death. Elizabeth and their oldest daughter, who had accompanied him, were left in the custody of one of her husband's Italian business friends. It was there in Italy, during several months before returning to America, that the formerly devout Anglican-Episcopalian found herself attracted to Catholicism.

Elizabeth returned to New York as a widow with several young children. She opened a finishing school for young ladies – a common expedient for widows of high society such as she. But she continued her studies of Catholicism and was received into the Catholic Church in 1806. When her conversion became known, her clientele dwindled as Protestant parents pulled their daughters out of her tutelage. In

---

[121] It is fair to say this although she was born before the founding of the United States. She was born in the what would become the United States within two years and lived most of her life as an American citizen. And she is indeed the first of three saints, all women, born in what is now the United States to be canonized (1975). She is not the earliest-born, however. That would be St. Kateri Tekakwitha, born 1656 in what is now New York State, but only canonized in 2012. The third is St. Katherine Drexel, born 1850 in Philadelphia, and canonized in 1980.

1809, she accepted an invitation from the Sulpicians of St. Mary's College in Baltimore to move to Emmitsburg, Maryland, to undertake the establishment of a school for Catholic girls. She and two other young women who joined her in the endeavor formed a new religious community dedicated to the care of the children of the poor; accommodations were made in their rule for Elizabeth to continue raising her children. This first congregation of religious sisters formed in America came to be known as the Sisters of Charity and their foundress as "Mother Seton." By the time she died in 1821, at just 46 years of age, she had furthermore established the first Catholic parochial school in the United States as well as the first Catholic orphanage. The Sisters of Charity eventually expanded their services from education into nursing and health care, with the result that in addition to churches and schools, hospitals bear her name and attest to this first American saint's profound influence.

The campus of Mother Seton's first school and convent there in Emmitsburg, where she is also interred, quickly became a destination for Catholic pilgrims. After her canonization in 1975, the shrine was expanded. The chapel received the status of minor basilica in 1991. As well as the basilica and a museum, the original buildings in which Mother Seton contributed so much to Catholic social services in the United States have been preserved and may be visited.

Contact information:
NATIONAL SHRINE OF ST. ELIZABETH ANN SETON
339 South Seton Avenue
Emmitsburg, MD 21727-9297
301-447-6606
https://setonshrine.org

Shrine of Our Lady of La Leche (St. Augustine, Florida)

On Saturday 08 September 1565, the Feast of the Nativity of the Blessed Virgin Mary, five Spanish ships made landfall in a small cove of Spanish Florida. King Philip II had sent them to establish a colony on the North American mainland, to secure Spanish claims there, and convert the Native Americans to Christianity. Father Francisco López de Mendoza Grajales celebrated what was the first parish Mass in what is now the United States. Chaplains accompanying earlier explorers had celebrated Masses in those lands before, of course, but they did not establish any permanent presence there and specifically where they offered those earlier Masses are unknown. In this spot on the coast of Florida, however, the Holy Sacrifice of the

Mass continues to be offered more than 450 years later. The chapel established there took the name *Mission Nombre de Dios* (Mission Holy Name of God) and is the oldest Spanish mission in the United States, predating the California missions by two hundred years, even the earliest Texas missions by seventy. Around it grew up the oldest city in the territory of the United States, the first European settlement on the North American continent, called St. Augustine after the saint of the day (28 August) when the Spaniards had first sighted land and began sailing the coast in search of a suitable landfall.

Within fifty years of its establishment, there was placed in the chapel a statue of the Blessed Mother smiling with love as she holds the Christ Child in her right arm, offering him to nurse – *Nuestra Señora de La Leche y Buen Parto*. Our Nursing Lady of Happy Delivery is an ancient devotion celebrating the reality of the Incarnation, the humility of God Who became a little child, and the loving Motherhood of Mary. It is attested in the early church by drawings in the Roman catacombs, mentioned approvingly by Pope Gregory the Great, and most recently was in a state of resurgence in sixteenth- and seventeenth-century Spain following the miraculous survival of both mother and child through a dangerous childbirth after the frantic father prayed fervently to Our Lady under this title. Heavily promoted by Philip II's son King Philip III, the devotion and a copy of the original statue in Madrid was brought to *Mission Nombre de Dios*, where by 1620 a shrine to *Nuestra Señora de La Leche* was established – the first Marian shrine in the United States. It quickly became a pilgrimage destination for individuals seeking the intercession of the Blessed Mother for fertility, the health of their children, and for a safe childbirth. The location of the chapel so near the shore, however, left it vulnerable to both manmade and natural threats. The shrine and the statue of Our Nursing Lady were severely damaged by cannon fire from ships offshore attacking the Spanish outpost during later colonial wars; it was ultimately destroyed altogether by a hurricane. The beautiful vine-covered shrine and its statue which stand today on the spot, continuing as a center for pilgrimage, are reconstructions dating from 1915. In a sad irony, Republican forces destroyed the original statue and shrine in Madrid during the Spanish Civil War (1936-1939), leaving St. Augustine, Florida, as the world center for devotion to Our Lady of La Leche.

Contact information:
SHRINE OF OUR LADY OF LA LECHE
101 San Marco Avenue
St. Augustine, Florida 32084

(904) 824-2809
https://missionandshrine.org

National Shrine of St. John Neumann (Philadelphia, Pennsylvania)

Saint John Neumann, of German heritage and born in Bohemia in 1811, immigrated to the United States at age fifteen and became a citizen, was ordained a priest of the Redemptorist Order, and became the fourth bishop of Philadelphia in 1852. Known for his piety, kindness, and generosity, among his accomplishments in eight years as bishop was establishing the first Catholic diocesan school system in the United States. Dying in 1860, he became in 1977 the first (and to date only) male American citizen to be canonized.

Shortly after his canonization, a shrine was established in the crypt of the Redemptorist parish of St. Peter the Apostle, where St. John Neumann's mortal remains had, at his request, rested in the company of his religious brethren. They are now displayed for veneration in an expanded, lower church, in a glass-walled reliquary under the altar. Although he is not among the incorrupt saints such as Padre Pio, the well-preserved nature of his body, vested as a bishop with his face covered by a life-like plaster mask, has led many observers to that mistaken belief. Adjoining the shrine is a small museum.

Miracles have been associated with veneration of St. John Neumann throughout the century and a half since his death. Long known for acts of mercy during his life, those seemed redoubled after his death, drawing pilgrims to his tomb from the beginning. Nevertheless, the most spectacular wonder was the shrine's survival of a fire in 2009. Overnight, while no one was present, an electrical short sparked a fire which could have been a total loss – of the shrine, the lower church, even the upper, main church of St. Peter. But after briefly raging, the fire died out quickly of its own accord. Only the next morning did a sacristan find the pulpit reduced to ash – but nothing else. The altar and the reliquary containing the body, only feet away, were left unscathed despite an abundance of combustible materials in between. One of the shrine's priests called the lack of damage overall "miraculous."[122]

Contact information:
NATIONAL SHRINE OF ST. JOHN NEUMANN

---

[122] Christie L Chicoine, "Fire singes shrine; Relics of St. John Neumann unscathed" (28 May 2009), *Catholic Philly.com* [catholicphilly.com/2009/05/news/fire-singes-shrine/].

1019 North Fifth Street
Philadelphia, PA 19123
(215) 627-3080
sjnoffice@comcast.net
https://stjohnneumann.org

Shrine of Our Lady of Martyrs (Auriesville, New York)

Commemorated together since they were canonized together in 1930 under the rubric "Saint Isaac Jogues and Companions," the North American Martyrs are eight seventeenth-century French Jesuit missionaries who died witnessing to the Faith, mainly to the Hurons of southern Ontario, who were currently fighting against the Mohawks of upstate New York. The conflict, known as the "Beaver Wars," was driven by competition in the fur trade between the Dutch and the English on the one hand (allied with the Iroquois Confederation, which included the Mohawks) and the French on the other (in alliances with the Algonquians and the Hurons). In all, six priests and two lay brothers were killed; five were martyred in Canada in 1648 and 1649 after three had already met their mortal ends between 1642 and 1646 in New York.

The three martyrs in New York state all died in the Mohawk village of Ossernenon. First, in 1642, Father Isaac Jogues and Brother René Goupil were captured by the Mohawks, taken to Ossernenon, and tortured for months; Goupil was killed outright while Jogues survived to be enslaved. Dutch traders eventually ransomed him. Having recuperated in France, he returned to Quebec. Bravely undertaking a 1646 embassy along with Brother Jean de Lalande to the place of his captivity, torture, and enslavement in an attempt to broker peace between the French and the Mohawks, both Jogues and his companion met only martyrdom, and there was no peace. Mohawk raids into Ontario claimed five more Jesuit lives within a few years: Antoine Daniel in 1648; and Jean de Brébeuf, Noël Chabanel, Charles Garnier, and Gabriel Lalemant, all in 1649.

Nevertheless, the bravery and witness of Fr. Jogues in his torture and death arguably brought graces to the Mohawks. No direct influence can be traced, but within a few years (1656), a baby girl would be born in Ossernenon who would - in the face of persecution from her family and tribesmen - convert to Catholicism and hold fast to the Faith despite grievous persecutions. Born Tekakwitha, she took the Christian name Kateri (Catherine). Although she died of natural causes in exile from her people, the severity of the trials she endured for the Faith won her the status of "White Martyrdom" – bloodless martyrdom. St. Kateri Tekakwitha was canonized in 2012.

After a devastating smallpox epidemic, Ossernenon was abandoned and forgotten.

In 1884, however, the pastor of St. Joseph's Church in Troy, New York, Jesuit Fr. Joseph Loyzance oversaw an effort long believed to have found the location of the lost village of Ossernenon in Auriesville, New York, a hamlet of Fultonville. (Twentieth-century archaeologists proved otherwise, determining the correct location to have been several miles to the west.) Buying land in Auriesville, Fr. Loyzance built a chapel and erected a cross, calling it the Shrine of Our Lady of Martyrs. Four thousand pilgrims from Troy and Albany attended the first Mass said there in 1885. Local parishes quickly established a tradition of making pilgrimages to Auriesville. In time, numbers on the critical feasts of the Church year, including the Feast of the Assumption, the date that Isaac Jogues first came to Ossernenon, necessitating building an enormous "Coliseum church" (1931), which can accommodate ten thousand persons – 6,500 seated, with additional standing room for 3,500. Today, there are, besides, chapels and statues of the individual saints, three rough-hewn red wooden crosses bearing the names of the three martyrs of Ossernenon, contemplative walking trails, a museum, and a gift shop.

Contact information:
SHRINE OF OUR LADY OF MARTYRS
136 Shrine Road
Fultonville, NY 12072
(518) 853-3939
https://www.ourladyofmartyrsshrine.org

Walk to Mary Pilgrimage (De Pere to Champion, Wisconsin)
Called a "pilgrimage," this is more of an event – that connects two important pilgrimage sites. So, in addition to being a walk, which is itself fitting considering the mode of transportation employed by most pilgrims before the twentieth century and likewise embodied in the Camino de Santiago, here we get two sites for the price of one....

Taking place on the first weekend of May each year, the route covers approximately 21 miles along the Fox River and the Niagara Escarpment, connecting the National Shrine of St. Joseph with the National Shrine of Our Lady of Good Help. Saint Joseph is, of course, the chaste husband of Our Lady and foster-father of Our Lord; Our

Lady of Good Help is Our Lady herself – under a title bestowed upon her in commemoration of the only approved Marian apparition in the United States.

The National Shrine of St. Joseph. In 1888, Fr. Joseph Durin, SCJ (Priest of the Sacred Heart) began working to have a statue of St. Joseph in the church named for him in DePere, New York, crowned and declared a national shrine. He was possibly inspired in this by his memory of witnessing such a coronation in 1874. Toward this end, he began leading a novena every Wednesday at 15:15 – which has continued every week, ever since. The prayers were answered within four years when the Bishop of Green Bay presided over a solemn coronation. St. Joseph gained a flat mural crown granted to the shrine by Pope Leo XIII; the Christ Child on his right arm received a similar crown; Joseph holds his iconic lily-bloomed staff in his left hand. Father Durin died four years later, and in 1898 the Norbertine Order came to establish St. Norbert Priory and took over operation of the shrine to a principal patron of their order, Saint Joseph. The crowned statue remained in St. Joseph's Church, which was engulfed in the expanding campus of St. Norbert College, until 1969, when renovations necessitated moving it to what was now St. Norbert Abbey. There it would remain until 2015, but the shrine has now been re-established in its rightful place, the church of its namesake.

(Contact information: NATIONAL SHRINE OF ST. JOSEPH, 123 Grant Street, De Pere, Wisconsin 54115; (920) 403-3010; parish@snc.edu; [https://www.snc.edu/parish/shrine.html])

The Walk: Here is the basic information at present (2019): Starting at 07:00 and walking at an average 2.5 miles per hour, it should take about nine hours and end about 16:00. That total estimated time includes a complimentary sandwich lunch for all registered walkers at the half-way point. There are designated join-in points along the way (at fourteen, seven, and two miles from the end) for those unable to make the full walk. There is provision for assistance to be rendered to those pilgrims who experience difficulty along the way. A designated parking area is provided, with shuttle transportation running between the parking area and the starting point. It seems a well-planned event, but please check the official web site at [https://walktomary.com/] for current information.

The National Shrine of Our Lady of Good Help: In 1859, the year after the 1858 appearance of Our Lady of the Immaculate Conception in Lourdes, France, Marie Adele Joseph Brise, a Belgian immigrant in Champion, Wisconsin, aged 28, received several apparitions of a beautiful woman clothed in light, with golden hair and a crown of stars, identifying herself as "the Queen of Heaven, who prays for the conversion of sinners," and bade Adele do the same, giving her the specific mission of teaching the Catholic Faith to children. Adele took that as her vocation and formed a group of women who undertook to live under the rule of Third Order Franciscans, although they never took formal vows. The same year his daughter received the visions, her father built the first chapel for Adele and her companions, and two years later, the second, dedicated to *Notre Dame de Bon Secours*, "Our Lady of Good Help." This latter chapel was eventually expanded into a school (Saint Mary's Boarding School for Children) and a convent dedicated by the Bishop of nearby Green Bay.

Then, disaster threatened. In 1871, the cataclysmic Peshtigo Firestorm devastated a wide area of Wisconsin. Spreading rapidly, it killed two thousand people. As it bore down on Champion, Adele organized a prayer procession begging the Blessed Mother's protection, and although the firestorm destroyed all the surrounding lands, it spared the chapel, the school, the convent, and their grounds, along with all who took refuge there.

Sister Adele died in 1896. After her death, Saint Mary's ministry was regularized under the Franciscan Sisters. Although the boarding school closed in 1929, its mission continued as a home for physically challenged children until the 1950s, when it became a novitiate for high school girls discerning a vocation to the Franciscan sisters. With the collapse in vocations following the Second Vatican Council, however, the novitiate closed. Since then, the mission entrusted to Sister Adele by Our Lady has gone unfulfilled.

Before and after, however, pilgrims made their way to the chapel seeking the intercession of Our Lady of Good Help, necessitating several expansions. The present shrine dates from 1942 when a new chapel and oratory were built, specifically commemorating the apparition. Over time an outdoor Rosary walk and Stations of the Cross were added. Healings occurred, attested mainly by a collection of crutches discarded by their former owners, hanging along one wall of the shrine. Since taking custody in the late 1960s, the Diocese of Green Bay has supported the shrine as a center of pilgrimage. In 2010, after well over a century of *de facto* but unofficial approval by the Church, on 08 December 2010, the Feast of the Immaculate Conception, Green Bay Bishop David Ricken officially declared the apparition "worthy of belief." In so doing, he considered himself merely regularizing an implicit approval rendered by his predecessors. Finally, on the

Feast of the Assumption, 15 August 2016, the shrine was raised to the status of *National* Shrine of Our Lady of Good Help.
(Contact information: NATIONAL SHRINE OF OUR LADY OF GOOD HELP, 4047 Chapel Drive, Champion, Wisconsin 54229; (920) 315-0398; [https://www.shrineofourladyofgoodhelp.com])

Ave Maria Grotto and St. Bernard Abbey (Cullmann, Alabama)

Located almost dead center in the northern half of Alabama, the only Benedictine monastery in the state began as a center of ministry to German Catholics in the area in the 1890s. Since that time, St. Bernard Abbey has been a staple of Catholic education in the region, operating at various times high schools, colleges, and seminaries. At present, the monks concentrate their efforts in St. Bernard Preparatory School, which is a worthwhile endeavor indeed – but not at all what brings the abbey its fame. That would be something entirely different that began as a modest hobby undertaken by one of the Bavarian monks over the half-century he whiled away time in his monastic assignment tending the abbey's power plant. By the time he passed away in 1961, Brother Joseph Zoetle, O.S.B., had adorned the former abbey quarry with over a hundred miniature reproductions of some of the most famous buildings in the world, creating a four-acre landscaped garden pathway of prayer winding among his idiosyncratic renditions of such iconic structures as St. Peter's Square and Basilica, Monte Cassino Abbey, the Alamo, the Leaning Tower of Pisa, assorted castles and cathedrals, memorials and shrines – including miniatures of so many locales in the Holy Land that the whole is sometimes called "Jerusalem in Miniature." Its formal name is, however, Ave Maria Grotto, from an artificial cavern at the bottom of the hillside, which serves as a sort of centerpiece before which the pathway winds and which contains a reproduction of the Apparition Grotto at Lourdes, its ceiling encrusted with stalactites and filled with statues of Our Lady and assorted monks and nuns.

Do not look for historical or architectural accuracy, however. Ave Maria Grotto is a labor of love, a meditation given form based largely upon Brother Joseph's imagination of what the structures he had usually seen only in two dimensions – in a picture or two, often from a postcard or book in the monastery's library – would look like in three dimensions. Of all the buildings he reproduced, he had only seen a handful with his own eyes – those from his home town in Bavaria and those of St. Bernard Abbey itself, including the power plant whose furnace he kept stoked with coal day-in and day-out for most of his monastic life, and which he memorialized in miniature. Some models are entirely figments of his imagination, such as the Temple of the Fairies from the German folk tale, *Hansel und Gretel*. Finally, the reproductions are constructed using whatever discarded materials he might find or scrounge up around the abbey and its grounds – discarded building supplies, tiles, bricks, broken pottery, marble, and the like. The western towers of the model of the Cathedral of the Immaculate Conception in Mobile are capped with domes made from discarded toilet bowl floats.[123] The result is a sometimes bizarre but always captivating vision of Brother Joseph's unique view of the transcendent reality of God's creation.

Contact information:
ST. BERNARD ABBEY AND AVE MARIA GROTTO
1600 St. Bernard Dr. SE
Cullman, Alabama 35055
(256) 734-4110
http://www.avemariagrotto.com

Franciscan Monastery of the Holy Land (Washington, DC)

We end this survey of "top ten" pilgrimage destinations in the United States more or less where we began, just a metaphorical stone's throw from the National Shrine of the Immaculate Conception. Directly across the campus of the Catholic University of America in northeastern Washington, DC, on a hill called Mount Saint Sepulcher, there stands the Franciscan Monastery of the Holy Land in America. Affiliated with the Franciscan Custody of the Holy Land which does so much directly, on the ground, to maintain the holy places and support our brother Christians in the land of Christ's birth, the Franciscan Monastery takes that as its mission from afar, raising money for and awareness of the mission of their brothers in the Holy Land, encouraging vocations and sponsoring pilgrimages but also offering a chance to experience something of a "pilgrimage to the Holy Land" without leaving the United States.

It was the dream of Fr. Charles Vassani and Fr. Godfrey Schilling, O.F.M., to establish a United States Commissariat of the Holy Land in New York City. In 1880, they proposed to create a "Holy Land in America," including a Church of the Holy Sepulcher on Staten Island.

---

[123] *Ave Maria Grotto: Miniature Miracles* (Kansas City, KS: Terrell Publishing, 2016), p. 7.

That did not work out, but a little over a decade later another opportunity presented itself. Acquiring land in the Brookland neighborhood of Washington, Fr. Schiller visited the Holy Land and surveyed the holy sites, taking photographs and measurements. Building commenced in 1898; in 1899, the Memorial Church of the Holy Sepulcher was dedicated, and a quarter-century later, it was consecrated.

Designed by the Roman architect Aristide Leonori along the general lines and dimensions of the Church of the Holy Sepulcher in Jerusalem, the Memorial Church is formally constructed in the Byzantine style reminiscent as well of the Church of Hagia Sophia in Constantinople, modern Istanbul. The impression given by the interior is, in my opinion, that of a "fantasyland" version of the original. It is easy to see the basic layout, but there is a considerable difference between the dark, ancient, cacophony of styles, predominantly Eastern Orthodox, making up the Holy Sepulcher as it stands today in Jerusalem and the open, gold, bright interior of the Memorial Church in Washington. Eastern influences are apparent, but they are much more subtle. At one end, on a higher level just as in the Holy Sepulcher, a Calvary Chapel faces a very different depiction of the Crucifixion, with a small altar below which is even a mock-up of the shaft allowing one to reach down and touch the bare rock of Calvary. It is not a "replica." It is an idealization, perhaps.

Besides the adjacent monastery, built in a Late Romanesque style, there are beautifully maintained gardens, the one before the main entrance to the Memorial Church being enclosed by the Rosary Portico, designed by John Joseph Earley to recall the cloister of the Lateran Basilica in Rome. Fifteen chapels around the periphery focus on fifteen mosaics of the traditional mysteries of the Rosary. Almost two hundred plaques are displayed as well, setting forth the Hail Mary prayer in as many different languages, ancient and modern. There are, finally, replicas of various other shrines, both in the Holy Land and elsewhere – the Grotto of the Nativity from the Basilica in Bethlehem (bearing as much resemblance as does the Calvary Chapel); the Roman Catacombs; the Grotto at Lourdes; and the Portiuncula in the Franciscan Church of St. Mary of the Angels in Assisi. Some of these key buildings and shrines may be viewed in 360° panoramic views that constitute something of a "virtual pilgrimage."[124]

Contact information:
FRANCISCAN MONASTERY OF THE HOLY LAND

---

[124] https://myfranciscan.org/virtual-tour/.

Kent G. Hare

1400 Quincy Street N.E.
Washington, DC 20017
(202) 526-6800
mail@myfranciscan.com
https://myfranciscan.org

Thus far, the list of "top ten" pilgrimage destinations in the United States derived from a comparison of four lists. For informational purposes, here are the 27 other unique items that each appear once in the aggregate of the four lists:

11. National Shrine of St. Frances of Assisi (San Francisco, California)
12. Our Lady of San Juan del Valle National Shrine (San Juan, Texas)
13. St. Peregrine Cancer Shrine (Mesa, Arizona)
14. National Shrine of the Divine Mercy (Stockbridge, Massachusetts)
15. San Antonio Missions (San Antonio, Texas) – *I included them as an "extra" above.*
16. Shrine of St. Katherine Drexel (Bensalem, Pennsylvania)
17. Shrine of Our Lady of Guadalupe (La Cross, Wisconsin)
18. National Shrine of Our Lady of La Salette (Attleboro, Massachusetts)
19. National Shrine of St. Rita of Cascia (Philadelphia, Pennsylvania)
20. National Blue Army Shrine of the Immaculate Heart of Mary (Washington, DC)
21. St. Francis Cabrini Shrine (New York City, New York)
22. National Shrine of St. Kateri Tekakwitha (Fonda, New York)
23. St. Antony's Chapel (Philadelphia, Pennsylvania)
24. Mother Cabrini Shrine (Golden, Colorado)
25. National Shrine of Our Lady of the Snows (Belleville, Illinois)
26. Our Lady of the Sierras (Hereford, Arizona)
27. Shrine of Christ's Passion (St. John, Indiana)
28. Basilica of the National Shrine of the Assumption of the Blessed Virgin Mary (Baltimore, Maryland)
29. Cathedral Basilica of St. Louis (St. Louis, Missouri)

30. Shrine of Our Lady of the Island (Long Island, New York)
31. The Sorrowful Mother Shrine (Bellevue, Ohio)
32. House of Mary Shrine (Yankton, South Dakota)
33. Shrine of the True Cross (Dickenson, Texas)
34. National Shrine of St. Odilia (Onamia, Minnesota)
35. National Shrine of the Cross in the Woods (Indian River, Michigan)
36. Monastery of the Holy Spirit (Conyers, Georgia)
37. Madonna Queen of the Universe Shrine (Boston, Massachusetts)

There are, of course, many, many more that could be added to this list. I will limit myself to mentioning only one: The Shrine of the Most Blessed Sacrament in Hanceville, Alabama, about sixty miles north of Mother Angelica's more famous enterprise, EWTN, the Eternal Word Television Network, in Irondale, Alabama.

Micro pilgrimages

"Micro pilgrimage" is a term I started using regarding an excursion I put together in the spring of 2019. Early in April, a group of twelve parishioners from the basilica in Natchitoches, Louisiana, assembled in Schulenburg, Texas, to visit the Painted Churches in the immediate vicinity, just a few of about thirty such generally small country churches scattered across the state.[125] The Painted Churches of Texas are sadly overlooked jewels that display the rich beauty and cultural heritage of the Catholic Church in the United States. That they appear in none of the Internet lists I consulted, and in only one of the books I cited, is a shame. Culturally, they represent an oft-forgotten secondary port-of-entry for central and eastern European immigrants – Czech, southern German, Silesian Polish – coming to the United States during the late nineteenth and early twentieth centuries. Arriving in Galveston, Texas, many of these settled down in the fertile and open farmland and pasture of the southeast-central regions of Texas, where the coastal plains shade into the Hill Country. Most of these immigrants were Catholic, and, missing the ancient, ornately decorated churches of their homelands, they set out to reproduce those qualities in their new homes. The fruit of their ingenuity is breathtaking. Passing through the doors of what appear from the

---

[125] See Appendix Two for a list and map.

outside as unremarkable, usually white, wood-framed country churches, one enters an enchanting world of incredible beauty. Four Painted Churches near Schulenburg make up an official "Painted Churches Tour" sponsored by the Greater Schulenburg Chamber of Commerce. Together, they exhibit a variety of architectural and artistic styles which were engagingly described, along with their history and cultural significance, by a wonderful Catholic docent who understood and accommodated our wish not just to see the churches as tourists but to experience them prayerfully as well – to make a pilgrimage.[126]

Our visit to the Painted Churches began and ended in a single day, although it was five hours' driving time away from home, thus a three-day excursion. I used the term "micro pilgrimage" to describe it, initially half in jest, to contrast this experience with the five- to ten-day international pilgrimages that I and others on that trip had experienced before. I use the term here to emphasize that not every pilgrimage has to be such a major undertaking. It could be taken to mean a visit to any pilgrimage site that can be effectively taken in during a visit of a day or two – or less. Depending on geographical proximity, any of the preceding US pilgrimage destinations could be a "micro pilgrimage" for someone. It is an intrinsically relative term. Of course, the journey is part of the experience of pilgrimage as well. But does a longer journey make a pilgrimage more of a pilgrimage? Perhaps; I would say it depends largely on one's disposition. There is no reason I can see that someone cannot experience a deeply moving pilgrimage in their own backyard.

Even a family vacation with no overtly religious focus can become something of a micro pilgrimage. Find the Catholic churches and shrines near your destination or lodging. That can be as easy as typing the search argument, "Catholic churches and shrines near [place]," into an Internet search engine. In June of 2016, my wife's non-Catholic niece (the daughter of Kristal, my companion on the pilgrimage to the Holy Land two years later) was getting married at a resort on the Lake of the Ozarks in Missouri. We would be there for several days, staying in a vacation home in Osage Beach. As we have done on more than one occasion, my wife and I decided that we would turn this into

---

[126] Information on booking tours of the churches around Schulenburg can be found at the website for the Greater Schulenburg Chamber of Commerce, [https://www.schulenburgchamber.org/painted-churches-tour]. Ask for a Catholic docent; most of them are not.

I considered putting a full account of this "micro pilgrimage" as a chapter in this book but decided that text, even if supplemented by a few black-and-white pictures, do not do the Painted Churches justice. I do intend to put together a book of color photographs that will, however.

a pilgrimage. Searching for "Catholic churches and shrines near Osage Beach Lake of the Ozarks" yielded three churches and two shrines within about a half-hour drive:

- **Our Lady of the Lake Church**, Lake Ozark, Missouri
- **St. Anthony Church**, Camdenton, Missouri
- **St. Patrick Church**, Laurie, Missouri, with its two associated shrines...
- **The Shrine of Saint Patrick** is fashioned after the Saint Patrick's Memorial Church of Four Masters in Donegal, Ireland. The Shrine is Celtic in design, with semi-circular recessed doorways, a central rose window, Celtic crosses, and a round bell tower that is native to Ireland. [http://saintpatrickshrine.com/]
- **The National Shrine of Mary, Mother of the Church**, was initially constructed in the mid-1980s as a way to honor Mary, the mother of Jesus, and to handle the overflow crowds at St. Patrick's summer services. In 2003, the shrine became the sixteenth National Shrine in the United States. The Mothers' Wall is a tribute to all mothers, living or deceased. Patrons can visit the shrine at any time to view the names of mothers memorialized by their children. Patrons can also purchase space for future engravings. [https://www. mothersshrine.com/]

We, therefore, had several options for Mass each day we were there, as well as a couple of unexpected, and apparently little-known shrines. Although both have existed since well before that date, neither of these shrines appears in the two books I have which were published in 1998-1999 (USCCB and Copp, listed near the beginning of this chapter).

That is just one example based on our own experience. Visiting any city, large or small, may give multiple examples – churches, of course, but shrines as well, some well-known and heavily trafficked, some more like the two near Lake of the Ozarks. Any large city, especially in the northeast, will likely give an abundance of results. A large city in a historically Catholic area can be a bonanza – e.g., New Orleans:[127]

---

[127] Brochure, *Catholic Shrines of New Orleans*, no date or source information given [http://www.seelos.org/NOLA_Shrines_8.5x11_sm.pdf], accessed on 14 September 2019.

- **Mère Henrietta Delille Prayer Room**, a shrine to the Venerable founder of the Sisters of the Holy Family.
- **Catholic Cultural Heritage Center:** The Old Ursuline Convent, "together with the attached St. Mary's Church and St. Louis Cathedral, ... forms a shrine...."[128]
- **International Shrine of Saint Jude**, New Orleans' oldest church building.
- **National Shrine of Blessed Francis Xavier Seelos**, a nineteenth-century mystic to whom are attributed many miracles of healing both in life and after death.
- **National Shrine of Our Lady of Prompt Succor**, the patroness of the State of Louisiana, whose most famous miracles include saving the city first during the disastrous Great Fire of 1812 and three years later during 1815 Battle of New Orleans, the latter of which brought the thanks and lifelong patronage of General - later U.S. President, and thoroughly Protestant - Andrew "Old Hickory" Jackson.
- **Saint Frances Cabrini Shrine**, celebrating the New Orleans founder of the Missionary Sisters of the Sacred Heart and patroness of immigrants.
- **Saint Ann Church and National Shrine**, devoted to the grandmother of God.

The point is that local shrines abound, just waiting to be discovered by a diligent search in preparation for a trip that can be transformed into a pilgrimage - or even accidentally. Always keep your eyes peeled. Before I ever "caught the pilgrimage bug," during my wife's and my first driving tour of England and Scotland, we were visiting numerous old religious sites of historical interest to me in my studies. It was with intention that we visited the ruins of Glastonbury Abbey and that I prayed at the tombs of St. Bede the Venerable and St. Cuthbert of Lindisfarne, both in Durham Cathedral. But it was totally by accident that, while driving along a road in northern England toward the ruins of an old Roman fort along Hadrian's Wall, I spied a large wooden cross beside the road, along with a historical marker with lettering just large enough for the name "Heavenfield" to jump out at me. We stopped, of course, and I was able, however imperfectly

---

[128] Op. cit.

because I had not yet come to the mindset, to venerate the site of one of the most critical events in both the political and religious history of England. The AD 633 Battle of Heavenfield, was described by St. Bede in his *Ecclesiastical History of the English People* as a clash won by the "most Christian king of the Northumbrians"[129] – "a man beloved of God,"[130] the only king whom that sober historian called "saint," even "most saintly"[131] – St. Oswald of Northumbria, with heavenly aid which hallowed that plot of English soil forever.[132]

Similarly, the afternoon before our tour of the Painted Churches, Anne and I, having arrived in Schulenburg earlier than our friends, struck out toward Shiner, Texas, to see a Painted Church that we knew would not be on our tour. Just west of Hallettsville, a small town on the way, we happened upon a roadside shrine, the Pine Grove Apparition Park, commemorating an alleged apparition of Our Lady to a local rancher who had stuck his tractor in a muddy field. His prayer to the Virgin Mary was answered – his tractor was freed – and he built the shrine to honor her. "Our Lady of Hallettsville" – 18 September 1986, to Daniel Jares – "No decision" is the annotation at Michael O'Neill's *The Miracle Hunter* web site, the premier online resource cataloging all known Marian apparitions according to their ecclesiastical status.[133] *Of course*, there has been no decision – and there likely never will be. But Jares claimed no profound messages from the Mother of God to be given to the world. He simply celebrated a prayer sent up and an answer received. Who are we to say that Our Lady did not – *does not* – respond to the fervent prayer of one of her children?

Finally, even if it is not formally designated as a "shrine," any Catholic church may be a fruitful destination for pilgrimage. Each has its own unique history tying it to the local community as well as the Church Universal. Some maintain permanent exhibits or shrines (as those at St. Patrick's Church in Laurie, Missouri) that get little or no attention, as if the local community is jealously guarding it for itself – as one imagines some medieval churches and monasteries doing with their most spiritually valuable relics. Certainly not in that class,

---

[129] "*Christianissimus rex Nordamhymbronum,*" Bede, *Historia Ecclesiastica gentis Anglorum*, 3.9.

[130] "*viri Deo dilecti,*" Op cit., 3.1.

[131] "*sanctum,*" Op cit. 3. 11; "*sanctissimum,*" 3.7.

[132] The story is told in op cit., 3.2, trans. Leo Sherley-Price in Bede, *A History of the English Church and People* (Penguin Books, 1955; repr. Barnes & Noble, 1993), pp. 142-143.

[133] Michael O'Neill, "Unapproved Apparitions Since 1900," *The Miracle* Hunter [http://www.miraclehunter.com/marian_apparitions/unapproved_apparitions/index.html], accessed 14 September 2019.

because it promises to develop into a major public exhibit, is a new Holy Shroud Museum and Research Center being established at the Cathedral of St. John Berchmans in Shreveport, Louisiana. During the middle months of 2019, the cathedral exhibited a small portion of the *third largest collection* of artifacts, research materials, and memorabilia concerning the Holy Shroud of Turin – the *third largest ... in the world.* Late in July, a group from the basilica made an afternoon micro pilgrimage and are waiting to see the full museum once it is completed.[134]

Some churches, such as minor basilicas, are affiliated with other churches – e.g., the four major basilicas in Rome – and from them gain the privilege of bestowing indulgences on those who devoutly visit, pray, and hear Mass there, as if they were attending the mother church itself. The Minor Basilica of the Immaculate Conception in Natchitoches, Louisiana, my own church parish, is affiliated with the magnificent Basilica of St. Mary Major in Rome and enjoys such privilege. As the point was made in the Introduction, however, on every Catholic altar, no matter how great or how humble, the greatest Miracle of God is made present each and every time the priest celebrates Mass – the Incarnation and Sacrifice of our Lord God Himself in the Second Person of the Trinity, by which He won our Salvation. When you attend the Holy Sacrifice of the Mass, you stand at the foot of Calvary itself, where Our Lord, as Priest and Victim, both makes and is the Sacrifice. You are, at that moment, making the most fruitful pilgrimage of all.

---

[134] *The Museum of the Holy Shroud* [https://www.museumoftheholyshroud.net], accessed 06 October 2019.

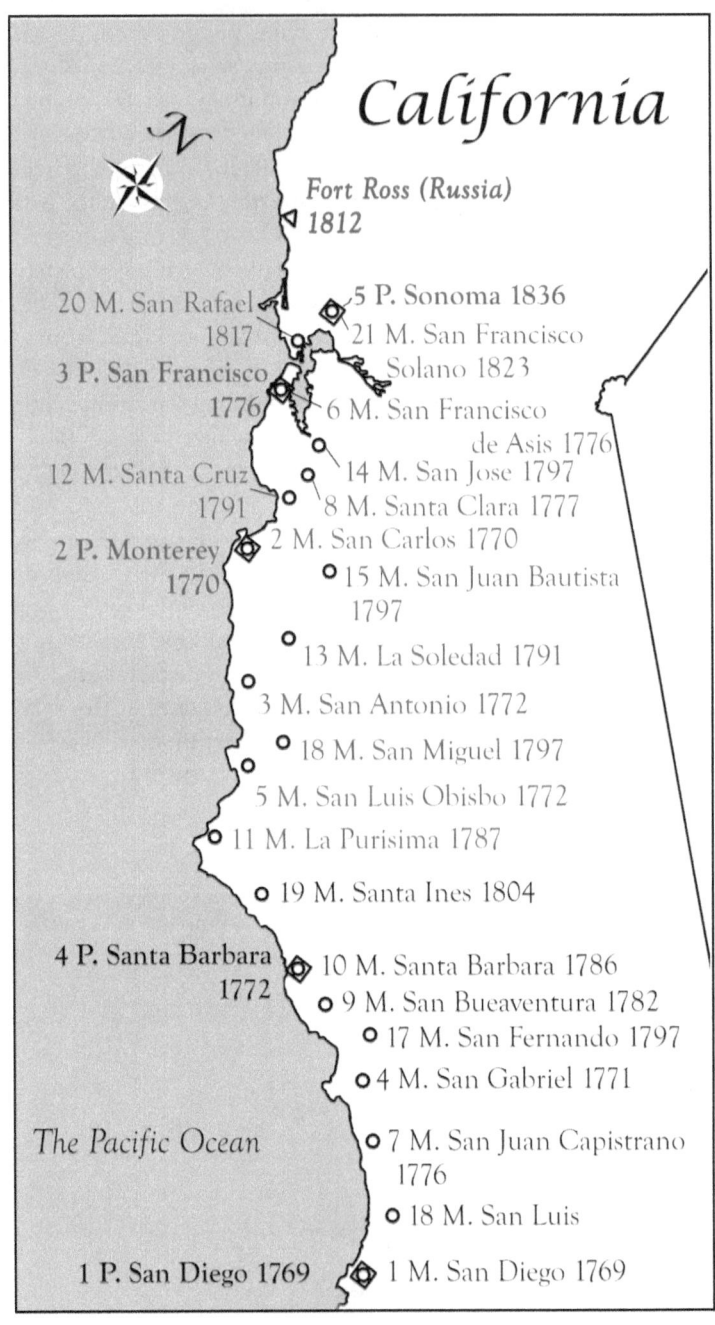

Figure 39: The California Mission Trail (M = Mission; P = Presidio)

CHAPTER SIX

... AND PILGRIMAGES HERE

The primary connotation of the idea of "pilgrimage" is physical, that of a bodily journey usually toward a physical destination having some religious significance. In today's increasingly connected world, however, it is suggested that one need not necessarily make such a physical journey at all to attain at least something of the qualities of a pilgrimage. And it is often overlooked that some of the most stereotypically Catholic devotions may be conceptually considered pilgrimage in their very nature. Different ways are proposed to make what has variously been termed an "armchair pilgrimage" or a "virtual pilgrimage" while remaining "here," i.e., at home. In today's technologically connected world, of course, the latter term evokes a particular activity that is worth discussion in its own right. I will begin, however, with an activity far more fundamental, one grounded not in technology and available to - dare I say? - *virtually* everyone.

Reading Pilgrimages

As touted in countless campaigns promoting literacy, books open whole new worlds to the reader. The spiritual writings of the saints connect us with these allies in heaven in a way that can be, although quite different from, no less profound and much more accessible than making a pilgrimage to their shrines or tombs. The same is obviously true of Holy Scripture, inspired by God as it is, the written word of God through which we encounter the Divine Word of God. This is especially the case when the reading of Scripture takes place against memories gained in a physical pilgrimage to the Holy Land, one's own, or perhaps those of someone else.

Written accounts of pilgrims' travels stand in a tradition that goes back to the beginning of Christian pilgrimage during the heady century following the sudden - and, I would posit, unexpected and shocking - emergence of the Church from the catacombs after three centuries of at best social and legal marginalization and at worse bloody, fiery persecution. Just after the year 300, having attained supremacy in the western half of the Roman Empire, Emperor Constantine the Great legalized Christianity by the 313 Edict of Milan, instantly deflecting the trajectory of church-state relations onto a path that would have the Church socially, legally, and religiously dominant before that fourth century of the Christian era (as it would soon be considered) had passed. What had hitherto been a local practice of venerating the mortal remains of those Christians who had witnessed to the Faith unto death as martyrs and thus became triumphant victims of the Romans' oft-times frantic efforts to stamp out what they considered a plague of anti-Roman, anti-*human*, irreligious, "atheistic," insanity now had an incredible and practical new focus. Rome, the capital of the empire, held the places of martyrdom and the powerful relics of the two most important figures of the first years of the Church: St. Peter, to whom Christ had given the keys to the kingdom of heaven, the first Vicar of Christ, who had been martyred on the Vatican hill just across the Tiber River; and St. Paul, the great Apostle to the Gentiles, who had written more than half of the Christian Scriptures, who had been martyred just "Outside the Walls" along the Appian Way. Not to denigrate the local martyr who was just as surely in heaven with Christ and a powerful intercessor as witnessed by miracles and wonders told and retold and eventually written down, how much *more* powerful must be these foundational heroes of the Faith. So must the thought process have gone as pilgrims from every corner of the empire almost immediately began to descend upon Rome. Then, a mere dozen years later, once Constantine had won control of the eastern half of the Empire as well, word spread that his mother, Helena, had traveled to Jerusalem, the mother city of the Faith, where the Savior had walked the earth as man, and there had miraculously discovered the site of the Crucifixion, the location of the Tomb and the Resurrection, the site of the Ascension, even the True Cross itself. At once, pilgrims started streaming eastward to that Holy Land which by its very nature, as the land where the Savior had been born, had lived, had died and rose again and ascended to heaven, was itself a great and powerful relic capable of imparting enormous graces. At the same time, Helena's transporting many individual relics back to Rome – the Manger from Bethlehem, the Scala Sancta from Jerusalem, even the land itself (embedded in the foundation of the Basilica of Santa Croce in Gerusalemme, Holy Cross in Jerusalem) – reinforced the Eternal City's status as a destination for pilgrims in the west.

    Almost as quickly, pilgrims' accounts of their travels began appearing. There had been pilgrimages earlier. The natural human impulse to see the land of the Savior led the earliest pilgrim of whom we know, St. Melito, Bishop of Sardis in the mid-late second century, in his journey to the Holy Land; Origen traveled there ca. 250; both sought to see for themselves the holy places of the patriarchs and prophets, Jesus and his disciples. Origen found that the locals had the sales pitch already down, being all too ready to show him the exact location where, e.g., Jesus had driven out the Gadarene swine. Neither left systematic accounts of their travels, but close on the heels of Christianity's legalization (and of St. Helena's explorations), in the 330s there appeared the first pilgrim's account, that of the widely distributed *Itinerarium Burdigalense* (Bordeaux Itinerary) which recounts in sometimes excruciating detail every stage of an anonymous pilgrim's journey, where he stopped (*every* stop), for how long, and so forth, from Bordeaux through northern Italy, to Constantinople, across Anatolia and Syria to Jerusalem – and back again by a more southerly route through Macedonia, Otranto, Rome, and Milan. It is generally more a list and notes than a narrative, although it does identify the places in the Holy Land with the Biblical events for which they are known. The anonymous pilgrim of Bordeaux must have run into Origen's locals because he was apparently shown where the Transfiguration took place on the Mount of Olives....

Two interesting documents from the later fourth century attest to a quickly flourishing pilgrimage culture in the Holy Land. There, having joined their spiritual director, St. Jerome, mother and daughter Sts. Paula and Eustochium wrote a letter, probably dated 386, back to a friend in Rome, urging one Marcella to join them in the east. They asserted that pilgrimage was a longstanding custom from Apostolic days to their own, with pilgrims from Armenia, Persia, India, and Ethiopia, from Gaul and Britain – and every place in between – crowding the holy places. We have direct testimony from one of these in the form of the earliest fully narrative account of a Christian pilgrimage that we possess, at least in part. In those same 380s that Paula and Eustochium invited Marcella, one Egeria (formerly rendered Etheria, or Aetheria, or even Sylvia), a nun probably from northern Spain but just possibly from southern Gaul, spent several years on a journey from her home in the west to the holy places in the east, toward the end of which she composed a letter back to her religious sisters describing the places she had been. These included Mount Sinai, Constantinople, Jerusalem (for three years), and Palestine, with excursions to Mount Nebo, Syria, Haran, Asia Minor, and probably many other places. Egeria's *Perigrinatio* (Pilgrimage) only survives in part, but what we have is incredibly informative, with the travelogue being supplemented by detailed descriptions of the various liturgies in Jerusalem, attesting early consolidation of the ecclesiastical calendar. Her description of Holy Week and the commemoration of the Passion and Resurrection make for fruitful reading during that holiest time of the year.

Two centuries later, another anonymous pilgrim, typically called "The Piacenza Pilgrim" from an erroneous attribution to St. Antoninus of Piacenza, provides us with another travelogue of great interest and value for its depth of description, especially of the landscape, and for attesting to probably universal pilgrims' customs such as when he went to Cana and reclined on the very couch Our Lord did – and proceeded to inscribe the names of his parents as a sort of prayer. He describes important relics such as the chalice of onyx already venerated in the Church of the Holy Sepulcher and the Holy Lance in the Basilica of Zion.[135] One importance of the Piacenza Pilgrim's account is its date – in the late sixth century, only a couple of generations before the coming of the double blow of the Persian invasion of 614 and its destruction of Constantine's Church of the Holy Sepulcher, followed by the 638 irruption of Islam into Palestine, shearing off much of the increasingly decrepit Eastern Roman or Byzantine Empire as it then stood – bringing the golden age of Roman-Byzantine Mediterranean Christendom to an end.

Despite the common assumption that the advent of Islam slammed shut the doors to the holy sites for Christian pilgrims, evidence suggests otherwise. Forty or fifty years later, ca. 680, the Frankish Bishop Arculf returned from there, bringing back memories of his pilgrimage that were immortalized when his descriptions to the abbot of Iona Abbey off the coast of western Scotland, St. Adómnan, became the latter's *De Locis Sanctis* (Concerning the Holy Places) – which formed the basis, a further half-century later, for St. Bede the Venerable to compose *his* book of the same name. Arculf/Adómnan/Bede described Jerusalem as being filled with throngs of Christian pilgrims.

Two centuries later, a Carolingian Frankish monk, Bernard the Pilgrim, left a travelogue of his journey around the Mediterranean.

---

[135] Of mysterious origin, with no modern consensus exactly what it comprised, this is most commonly supposed to have been a church going back to a Judaeo-Christian synagogue-church of the late 1st-c., known as the "Church of the Apostles," later rebuilt as a Byzantine basilica under the name *Hagia Sion* ("Holy Zion") and called the "Mother of All Churches." It is said to have "covered the entire area now occupied by the Church of the Dormition, the Cenacle and the Tomb of David" – See *The Holy Land* s.v. "Mount Zion" [https://www.seetheholyland.net/mount-zion/], accessed 26 November 2019. See also Wikipedia, s.v. "Church of Zion, Jerusalem," accessed same date.

And so on.... Many other such accounts appeared as centuries passed. They were obviously of enduring popularity. The article at Wikipedia, "Travelogues of Palestine," cites "more than 3,000 books and other materials detailing accounts of [...] journeys" to the region, giving a select list numbering several dozen, starting in Pre-Ottoman times (pre-sixteenth century) and carrying forward into the twentieth century. Many of the accounts listed are not overtly religious in nature, which does bring up the question of what pertinence they are to one seeking a "pilgrimage account" – but even those "not overtly religious" were obviously written by travelers from a Christian culture attracted to the region for an historical import that is, fundamentally, grounded in that Christian heritage. The nineteenth century, in particular, witnessed an explosion in interest that inspired the creation in England of the Palestine Pilgrims' Text Society to publish a series of editions and translations of medieval texts ranging from the fourth century to the fifteenth, including almost every one of those I have listed above.

Twentieth- and 21st-century travelers have continued the literary tradition, although examples seem harder to run down, and they bear the mark of a post-Enlightenment, increasingly post-Christian world. One notable exception, both in its availability and outlook – the former doubtless because of the current renaissance in Chesterton studies, the latter because of his fundamentally Catholic sensibility even a dozen or more years before his formal conversion, is the famed English essayist G. K. Chesterton's *The New Jerusalem* (1920). Chesterton scholar Dale Ahlquist characterizes this book as recounting "a philosophical travelogue of [Chesterton's] journey across Europe, across the desert, to Palestine."[136] Scholarly works about pilgrimage and the various accounts through the centuries seem more numerous in the modern era, but, usually standing aloof from the Faith, they are generally not spiritually edifying. Although there is a relative abundance of travel guides, both secular and religious, searching Amazon.com for Catholic pilgrimage travelogues to the Holy Land yields only a handful of items from recent years:

M. Basil Pennington, *Journey in a Holy Land: A Spiritual Journal* (Brewster, Massachusetts: Paraclete Press, 2006).

---

[136] Dale Ahlquist, "Chesterton University: Lecture 35: The New Jerusalem," *The Society of Gilbert Keith Chesterton* [https://www.chesterton.org/lecture-35/], accessed 14 September 2019)

George Jerjian, *Seeking God – A Pilgrimage to the Holy Land* (self-published, 2013)

Mitch Pacwa, S.J., *The Holy Land: An Armchair Pilgrimage* (Cincinnati, OH: Franciscan Media – Servant Books, 2013)

James Martin, S.J., *Jesus: A Pilgrimage* (New York: HarperCollins, 2014).

Lawrence R. Farley, *Following Egeria: A Modern Pilgrim in the Holy Land* (Ancient Faith Publishing, 2015)

Of these, I have read only Jerjian, Pacwa, and Farley. The former, by a British Armenian Catholic, attempts to balance travelogue with devotional and includes substantial quotations from his Catholic priest pilgrimage director. Interestingly, I have seen this little self-published book promoted on the bookstore section of the web site for the Notre Dame Centre in Jerusalem. I found Farley's a more polished read, especially his asynchronous interaction with the fourth-century nun while following her extant itinerary. He is an Orthodox priest, so his general outlook is quite compatible with that of Catholics, in most respects. One interesting fact emphasized by his account is the reality that for many of the holy places venerated for specific events, there are competing locations, Catholic and Orthodox. Very late in the writing of this book, after months of finding Fr. Pacwa's volume listed as out-of-stock and available only at greatly inflated used-book prices, I discovered a few copies once more being offered on Amazon at cover price. I seized one of the last copies and am incredibly happy that I did so. It is, in my judgment, the perfect example of what it proclaims itself to be – an "armchair pilgrimage" combining an excellent selection of photographs, description, pertinent scriptural passages, and meditations, presented in the general order that a typical pilgrim encounters the various sites.

Although historically far and away the foremost topic of Catholic religious travelogues has been the Holy Land, the modern explosion of popularity enjoyed by the Camino de Santiago has resulted in the creation of a subgenre, a relative flood of books (as well as movies, although those seem mostly fictional) describing various individuals' experiences on "their" Camino. Of course, one must, as in all things, exercise due caution in weeding through them. Not all are Catholic; some are overtly new-age pantheistic nonsense; some manage to be downright anti-Christian. As with those walking the Camino itself, the recent resurgence of St. James' Way has brought many different types of people into the "Camino literature" fold, as can be seen by merely perusing the list entitled "Camino de Santiago" at GoodReads' Listopia – which currently numbers 91 entries ranging from travel guides to travelogues to pilgrimage accounts to novels.[137] Having done no more than a cursory survey to see what is available, I can make no informed assessments, suggestions, or even first-hand comments on individual items.

Similarly, for all the importance of pilgrimage to Rome through the centuries – and its unique centrality in the Christian Faith of my own particular area of scholarly interest, early Anglo-Saxon England (Bede makes reference to numerous Englishmen visiting Rome during the seventh and early eighth century; we know from his biographer Asser that in the mid-ninth century Alfred the Great as a very young child accompanied his father Athelwulf, king of Wessex, to Rome and, perhaps through a child's misunderstanding, always considered himself to have been anointed by the Pope his father's heir and successor) – there is a dearth of direct accounts of such, until recently. When I first encountered a number of books with some variation of "From Canterbury to Rome" in the title, I first took it to be a euphemism for a small flood of High Church Anglicans and Episcopalians availing themselves of Pope Benedict XVI's establishment of the Anglican Use and Ordinariates as legitimate variants of the Roman Rite to return home to the Catholic Church. The phrase is not, however, a euphemism at all; it refers instead to a literal journey, a modern revival of one of the other great medieval pilgrimage roads across Europe. The *Via Francigena* (Frankish Road) stretches in a relatively straight shot southeastward from Canterbury, across the Channel, thence across France, the Rhineland, and the Alps, through Italy, to Rome. Its traffic, most likely as a knock-on effect from the modern revival of the Camino, has similarly increased in recent years and generated several recent pilgrimage accounts. But, again, I have done no more than survey the available literature to see what is available regarding Catholic pilgrimage to Rome. My impression from that cursory survey is, however, that like the growth in Camino "pilgrimage," some portion of Via Francigena "pilgrimage" is not really.

In the case of all the pilgrimage accounts I did find, both ancient and modern, most are mere records, perhaps enhanced with the writer's observations, even meditations. They may be used to get a

---

[137] https://www.goodreads.com/list/show/35717.Camino_de_Santiago. Accessed 14 September 2019.

"feel" for the pilgrimage, but - and this needs to be clear - I am not suggesting that simply reading about any pilgrimage destination or another individual's pilgrimage has in and of itself in any way the spiritual quality of a pilgrimage. It can, perhaps, but only in so far as it is used prayerfully, as inspiration for meditation on the awesome mysteries of our Salvation. And, even so, creating a "vicarious pilgrimage" with its attendant graces per se may or may not have been the purpose of the various authors in writing. The only one I would say for certain aspires to do so is Fr. Pacwa's *The Holy Land: An Armchair Pilgrimage*.

With one interesting exception: Of particular interest among the editions included in the late nineteenth-century Palestine Pilgrims' Text Society's publication program are the works of Felix Fabri, a fifteenth-century Swiss Dominican friar. In the 1480s, Fabri undertook two pilgrimages to Jerusalem and one to St. Catherine's on Mount Sinai, which he recounted in several versions and different languages for different readerships - first, the *Gereimtes Pilgerbüchlein* (Rhymed Pilgrim Booklet) a rhymed vernacular High German poem in epic form for his noble patron; then, the *Pilgerbuch* (Pilgrim Book) a prose account in the Swabian-German vernacular for other lay benefactors; and, finally, the expansive Latin *Evagatorium* (Wandering Forth) for his fellow clerics. Then, in the 1490s, at the request of cloistered nuns whom Fabri served as spiritual director, he created a fourth vernacular version, *Die Sionpilger* (The Zion Pilgrim), which Kathryne Beebe characterizes as:

> ... a pilgrimage account with a difference: it was meant as a virtual pilgrimage - a work that took its readers on a spiritual journey to the holy land that they could not themselves make in person. Drawing upon both the Pilgerbuch and the Evagatorium, Fabri fashioned the Sionpilger into a meditative text that also incorporated details of a real voyage.[138]

Writing in the *Journal of Religion & Society*, Michael Xiarhos elaborates:

> The nuns' request included detailed travel logs, day to day rituals, description of shrines, and physical challenges so they could fully participate in the pilgrimage in a metaphysical or spiritual way. They wished to be there in the most real way possible, not just read about another pilgrim's experience;

---

[138] Kathryne Beebe, *Pilgrim & Preacher: The Audiences and Observant Spirituality of Friar Felix Fabri (1437/8-1502)* (New York: Oxford University Press, 2014), pp. 3-4.

they wanted to use the experience to help create a different but still authentic pilgrim road. The result of this request was that by 1495, Fabri produced [...] the Sionpilger, which provided what the nuns requested for mental pilgrimages to Jerusalem, Rome, and even Santiago de Compostela.[139]

In contrast to earlier memoirs and descriptive travelogues, *Die Sionpilger* was explicitly intended to create a sense on the part of Fabri's cloistered readers that they were being *included* in the pilgrimage that he had accomplished. Or, putting bluntly what Xiarhos intimates, and Beebe states merely in passing: Fabri conceptually created, in the fifteenth century, a Virtual Pilgrimage.

Virtual Pilgrimage

As a child of the 1960s who came of age in the 1980s, I have experienced how the advent of the personal computer and then the Internet has transformed the world and how we interact with it. What began as fancy adding machines, later becoming fancy typewriters, suddenly became in the 1990s fancy libraries giving fingertip access to a flood of information retrieval and sharing – that by the 2000s with the advent of blogging, vlogging, and social networking have led to ... ... Well, no one really knows, now, do they? The social consequences of the current information revolution thus far have been mixed, to be sure, and are fundamentally unknown and unknowable, *unpredictable*, as the rate of change seems to accelerate. But we do know this, that the information network linking potentially every corner of the world has resulted in an abundance of resources available to any individual anywhere wishing to experience just about any place in the world to one degree of virtual reality or another. Webcams set up in churches from Europe to North America allow one to "attend" Mass in the Extraordinary Form from Fribourg, Warrington, Sarasota, and Guadalajara.[140] Google Earth and Google Street View enable one to "walk" the very streets of Jerusalem from the Lions' Gate to the Holy Sepulcher, following the *Via Dolorosa* Station by Station. The means have arisen for something akin to an authentic, multimedia, virtual pilgrimage to take place from the comfort of one's favorite chair. There are many resources available on the Internet for "virtual" pilgrimage,

---

[139] Michael Xiarhos, "Authenticity and the Cyber Pilgrim," *Journal of Religion & Society* 18 (2016): 1-11; quotation from p. 4.

[140] LiveMass.net.

inspiring a new field of scholarly study and debate regarding the validity of such "pilgrimages."[141]

Predictably, at this point, there is no perfect consensus on what precisely the term "virtual pilgrimage" even means. Can it be, as Beebe and Xiarhos suggest, as simple as any intensely immersive experience, even one gained through reading words on a page as composed by Fabri for his nuns? Conceptually, they obviously believe so. In the fifteenth century – even as late as the nineteenth century – text-based "reading pilgrimage" was all that was available, perhaps supplemented with drawings, maps, and the like. With the advent of photography this became more refined, but it was a difference in quality, not essence. The appearance of motion picture technology by the twentieth century, however, began a convergence toward a certain degree of verisimilitude followed by the advent of the Internet and the real-time information sharing possibilities described above. Ultimately, in the modern context, "reading pilgrimage" is in no way what people think of when the subject of "virtual pilgrimage" is raised.

At present, a range of options are available. Several years ago – from the timing of an Internet article (15 September 2015) describing it as happening "last year," about the same time as my pilgrimage to Italy – a priest in Philadelphia led a pilgrimage to Lourdes, the Camino, and Fatima. For the benefit of parishioners who could not join the rigorous pilgrimage for health or other reasons, he put together what one of those parishioners called a "virtual pilgrimage." To quote the article:

> Our pastor invited everyone who was interested, including those who were not traveling, to a series of prepilgrimage meetings, where he talked about the route and other information about the trip.
>
> He made and distributed pilgrimage guides to each of us. The guides gave a day-by-day explanation of where the tour would go and what was on the agenda. Also included in the guides was space for personal journaling, associated prayers and thoughts about saintly sites and church history, along with resources in case you wanted to learn more.
>
> When the pilgrims embarked on their trip, Father Tom Welbers, our pastor, also provided us all (travelers and

---

[141] Among that scholarship is the aforementioned Michael Xiarhos, "Authenticity and the Cyber Pilgrim," *Journal of Religion & Society* 7 (2016): 1-18; also, Mark W. MacWilliams, "Virtual Pilgrimages on the Internet," *Religion* 32.4 (October 2002): 315-335.

armchair pilgrims) with email addresses for one another. Throughout the pilgrimage, those of us who stayed home exchanged emails with those on the physical journey. On a blog, Father Tom wrote journal-like posts that told of the experiences and insights gleaned along the way.

Although I did not have the "real" experience of site tours, candlelit processions or Masses celebrated in faith-drenched locales, I was blessed by my virtual pilgrimage in many ways that still resonate with me.

For example, I did not know each pilgrim before the event, but got to know many new fellow parishioners throughout the experience – new friends who are still very present in my life. I enjoyed the structure of following along with the journey of faith that accompanied the time-sensitive itinerary. It was a refreshing departure from my usual devotions.[142]

The author goes on to describe how she subsequently made use of "other online sources that provide similar, or even more enhanced, virtual pilgrimage experiences," and gives a few cursory suggestions on how to find those resources.

I took special note of the approximate concurrence of the Philadelphia pilgrimage as a physical pilgrimage with a virtual component via email and blog posts with my pilgrimage to Italy in the fall of 2014 because such is very much what I envisioned for the benefit of my students, albeit for historical rather than religious reasons. As described in Chapter One, the result fell quite short of my intention, at least at the time, as the physical realities of the pilgrim's way, even today, quickly made it clear that full-on, "real-time" (or at least daily) posts of fully fleshed-out narrative and illustrations were beyond me as a simple pilgrim. By the time of my pilgrimage to the Holy Land four years later, I had developed a more manageable tactic of posting "placeholder" entries each day, containing bare description of what places we visited, what sights we saw on that day, accompanied by a few select pictures, that I could then over a couple of weeks after returning home flesh out into a fully narrated and illustrated record. I have continued that blog, which ultimately gave birth to this book, to the present day, and have every intention of adding to it in the future when God willing, I intend

---

[142] Maureen Pratt, "Can't travel to explore your faith? Try a virtual pilgrimage," *Catholic News Service* (15 September 2015), posted at *Catholic Philly.com* under "Commentaries" [http://catholicphilly.com/2015/09/commentaries/cant-travel-to-explore-your-faith-try-a-virtual-pilgrimage/].

to make more pilgrimages. I have, however, come to accept that such placeholder posts are all I am capable of as an individual balancing the realities of travel with the ideal of my ambition.

Although there are myriad travel blogs to be found with a simple Internet search, specifically Catholic, specifically pilgrimage-oriented, blogs seem to be rare. One problem is the metaphor that life in this world is properly a pilgrimage to the next. Just because a website has "Catholic" and "pilgrim" in it does not mean that it is a blog about "Catholic pilgrimage" – e.g., catholicpilgrim.net, where Amy Thomas "get[s] to talk about the beauty and truth of Catholicism" – in general. "We are all on a journey in this life...."[143] Or they turn out to be influenced heavily by eastern forms of spirituality in a general religious enthusiasm that manifests in essential religious indifferentism. Or they are relics of initiatives that barely got going before dying a lingering death of neglect, such as one associated with the Catholic pilgrimage broker, The Catholic Traveler,[144] whose director several years ago set up a shell within his web site to organize and post records of all his past (and implicitly future) pilgrimages, of which only a few ended up populated with more than destination and date. Although his business appears to be a continuing enterprise, even the list of "past pilgrimages" does not extend past 2016. With one exception, I have not found a single active Catholic pilgrimage blog to recommend – besides my own, of course, which probably does not appear in any kind of Internet search because of an ill-chosen, in no way evocative, name surviving from when I first conceived it.[145]

The exception is part of Catholic evangelist Steve Ray's overall website, *Defenders of the Catholic Faith* [https://www.catholic-convert.com]. A former Baptist, Ray has since his conversion in the 1990s maintained a vigorous schedule of event appearances in a wide variety of venues, blogging, posting articles, publishing books of Catholic apologetics, creating high-quality video series, maintaining an extensive online collection of resources – and leading pilgrimages via his associated pilgrimage brokering web site, *Footprints of God Pilgrimages* [https://www.footprintsofgodpilgrimages.com]. He and his wife, Janet, have conducted well over a hundred pilgrimages to the Holy Land, and a good number to just about every other major Catholic pilgrimage destination there is – Italy, France, Ireland, Mexico,

---

[143] Amy Thomas, *Catholic Pilgriim: Living Out Your Catholic Faith* [https://catholicpilgrim.net/]

[144] https://thecatholictraveler.com/

[145] *The Absent-Minded Professor's Travels* [https://www.theprofstravels.blogspot.com].

Poland, Fatima/Santiago/Lourdes, and so forth. Finally, at least for the past few years, he has shared those pilgrimages with the world. From the moment their plane touches down to the day they depart, Ray (and doubtless an excellent production crew) documents almost everything in high-quality ten- to twenty-minute videos, sometimes with a separate video of the homily from the day's Mass celebrated by the priest spiritual director accompanying the current pilgrimage. These appear daily on Ray's blog, enabling anyone to "ride-along" with his pilgrimage from start to finish. I know this from experience. Recall that part of my process of discerning whether I was indeed called to undertake my own August 2018 pilgrimage to the Holy Land was watching Ray's then-current (April 2018) pilgrimage – a nine-day pilgrimage perfectly coinciding with the nine days I was praying a novena for guidance. By day nine, although I did receive the sign from God that I asked for right at the end, I must admit that some part of my final decision was also heavily influenced by the virtual pilgrimage experience I found in Ray's videos.

Such is probably not exactly the way Ray envisioned his blog being used – essentially promoting someone to make a pilgrimage with another broker! – but I would like to believe he would not begrudge me that, either.

At some point after Ray's pilgrimage ends, a compilation video appears as well, usually totaling a couple of hours in length, presumably edited and cleaned up a bit, but allowing someone to watch a completed pilgrimage from start to finish, uninterrupted even by the need to find and start the next day's video. I have watched some of those as well. Clicking on the "Past Pilgrimages" link opens a substantial library of virtual pilgrimages free for the watching. It is probably the next to closest thing an "armchair pilgrim" can experience to accompanying a "real," guided pilgrimage. The closest thing, I would say, would be doing what I did – following the daily videos as they appear, knowing that you are virtually sharing in activities that occurred only a few hours before.

Ray's virtual pilgrimages appear first in the form of a daily blog, then in the library/archive as both the collection of blog posts and videos and the compilation video. They form a record of his pilgrimage leadership. Are there other such resources out there, not blog-based as are Ray's, but affording virtual access to individual sites in a more *á la carte* manner? Of course, there are. Here is a wonderful portal to numerous such virtual pilgrimages:

Catholic Pilgrimage Sites [https://catholicpilgrimagesites.wordpress.com/virtual-tours-e-pilgrimages/]

Besides offering the lists of sites by state and by country for which I referenced this website in the previous chapter, under 'Virtual Tours & Pilgrimages," there appear links to many different sites, mostly around Italy and the United States. In addition, there is a thematic virtual pilgrimage to the sites of Eucharistic miracles around the world and an associated virtual museum. The collection is credited to and stands as a legacy of Carlo Acutis, "a 15-year-old Italian boy who died in 2006 of leukemia and whose cause is under consideration for Sainthood." He was declared Venerable in July 2018. My only *caveat* regarding this site is that I am not sure it is being maintained. Although the link to "Holy Doors of Mercy" maintains the links while noting that the Jubilee Year of Mercy ended on 20 November 2016, it refers to an associated page of "Relics and Events" that appears to have gone without an update since March 2018.

As to specific pilgrimage destinations, the easiest and most obvious thing to do is search for "[LOCATION] virtual tour" or "pilgrimage," e.g., "Holy Land virtual tour." This can be done either in a general Internet search or specifically on YouTube. Either search may produce interesting results. On the Internet, they might be well-indexed and curated pages with multimedia presentations of all the significant sights in 360° panoramic views, inside and outside. The web site for the Franciscan Monastery of the Holy Land in Washington, DC, has such, as noticed in the previous chapter. They may be simple galleries of photographs. They may be anything in between. Some are highly structured, leading the viewer along a set route, with or without narration. Others allow the virtual pilgrim to wander the site at will. Some might be enhanced with nice, soft, meditative music in the background. Others ... well, unfortunately, the music choices can be pretty bad, as well. It is a matter of taste, of course – and that is what the volume control is for. In addition to the virtual walkthroughs "following the blue lines," Google Maps allows users to post photographs and "Photo Spheres," which can be a lot of fun to explore; they are generally marked by blue dots when in "Street View" mode. On YouTube, walkthroughs of important sites posted by individual pilgrims are too many to count, basically just raw smartphone or camcorder footage; there are far fewer genuinely polished videos or collections of videos of the quality exhibited by Steve Ray's.

The best thing to do is just start exploring. The possibilities are so endless and changing, expanding all the time (and, unfortunately, contracting as well, as links go dead – all the time), and the criteria by which to judge them so subjective, that I hesitate to call attention to any specific one. Nevertheless, I do:

Holy Land Virtual Reality Tour & 360 Degree Jerusalem 3D Tour [https://www.p4panorama.com/panos/HOLYLAND/index.html], accessed 16 September 2019.

"Visit Holy Land & Jerusalem online and walk around as if you are actually there. One click to start the virtual tour of Holy Land & 360° Jerusalem 3D tour."[146]

This site offers several dozen high-resolution static panoramic "scenes" in which the viewer can move back and forth, up and down, or just let the page slowly pan around and move to the next. Starting on Mount Nebo overlooking the Holy Land, facing a plaque showing what major sights are visible and in what direction, the sequence then takes you to the Greek Orthodox church at Madaba, to the Dead Sea, to Bethlehem, and so forth. Labeled icons allow you to break off to the next view, the previous view, or to select other views depending on where you are. A dropdown menu at the top allows selection of any site in the sequence (and always indicates the current view), which can also be accomplished by accessing a still photo gallery at the top left. Controls at the bottom allow entry into "VR mode" if you are viewing on a mobile phone (and presumably if you have the VR headset), volume control, access to a map, sharing, full screen, and an informational popup describing the scene. Occasional icons pop up short YouTube videos affording that type of controlled panoramic view of given scenes. You can even frame and take photos, which you can then share to Facebook, etc. – "Wish you were here! (Wish *I* was there!);" I do not think there is any way to download that photo, however – and it has a prominent "Holy Land 360°" watermark on it anyway. This site has its quirks – the Shepherds' Field scene has what I presume to be gently falling snow on a bright, sunny day!; and the music throughout is ... well, this is the one I was thinking of a couple of paragraphs ago! Also, a bit annoying is that I can figure out no way to remove the labeled icon allowing you to jump to the next scene, and it often appears in a very distracting location. But the main control bar

---

[146] Google Search snippet, accessed 16 September 2019.

can be hidden (and easily retrieved) at the bottom of the screen. All in all, this is a very nice virtual tour.

Is it a pilgrimage, however? Is even the most immersive multimedia Virtual Reality "cyber pilgrimage" really that? Michael Xiarhos considers that question in his article, "Authenticity and the Cyber pilgrim," cited here a couple of times already. His formal conclusion is a tentative, "Virtual faith practice is an evolving and hugely complex issue."[147] For sure. His clear intimation is, however, "Yes!" I base that inference on the general tone of the latter half of his eleven-page article, the centerpiece of which is an account of "Pope John Paul II: The Virtual Pilgrim," which bears quotation in full:

> Pope John Paul II's 2000 Holy Land pilgrimage is a prime example of the validity of online-virtual pilgrimage. Rather than seeing virtual pilgrimage as the easy way or a mere convenience to the somewhat partially committed pilgrim, Pope John Paull II illustrated that the virtual pilgrim may operate from a place of deep devotion and desire for spiritual connection and ultimately hopes for a chance at a transcendent experience.
>
> Originally, the Pope intended on making a chronological biblical pilgrimage, starting with the holy city of Ur, considered by many biblical experts to be the city mentioned in the book of Genesis as the birth place of the patriarch Abraham. The Pope, recognizing the importance of Abraham as the "model of unconditional submission to the will of God," (Stanley)[[148]] and as a shared prophet and source of unity between Jews, Christians, and Muslims, wanted his journey to begin at the beginning. From there the Holy Father would travel to Egypt to pray atop Mount Sinai where the Bible says God delivered the Ten Commandments to Moses, then he would move on to Israel and Palestine. As devout as his intentions were, secular realities and complex international politics trumped his desire for spiritual transcendence.
>
> Lengthy discussions between the Pope and the President of Iraq, Saddam Hussein, eventually broke down and the

---

[147] Xiarhos, "Authenticity," p. 10.
[148] Alexandria Stanley, "Pope Makes Virtual Visit to Iraqi Site He Must Skip," *New York Times* (24 February 2000) [http://www.nytimes.com/2000/02/24/world/pope-makes-virtual-visit-to-iraqi-site-he-must-skip.html]. – Citation defined on Xiarhos, "Authenticity," p. 11.

Pope was denied admission into the country. So strong was the Pope's desire to begin his pilgrimage in Ur that he organized a virtual visit in an effort to make his biblical chronology more authentic. Using large screens, the Vatican broadcast images of various holy sites creating a virtual travelogue which included desert scenes, paintings, and churches. The Pope ritualized the virtual pilgrimage by offering prayer and incense poured in a copper pot signifying the sacrifice of Isaac. The Pope may not have been physically there in Turner and Turner's understanding, [149] but the spiritual meaning and power of this constructed event offered an experience the Pope identified as "pilgrimage." It would be difficult to argue that the Pope's virtual pilgrimage was any less an act of devotion because it took a stationary form; he was focused, present, and engaged in the experience, separated from the profane distractions of normality. This mentality continued as he then made his way physically to other significant locations.[150]

I certainly would not argue that the now sainted Pope's "virtual pilgrimage" was *not* "an act of devotion," but I *would* argue that, regardless of the degree to which he was "focused, present, and engaged in the experience, separated from the profane distractions of normality," or even if the Holy Father himself referred to the experience as a "pilgrimage," he was not truly on a "pilgrimage," or at least on the same kind of "pilgrimage" as he would have experienced had not the international situation precluded his going to Ur – which was, it must be recalled, his first intention.

The mere fact that we feel the need to qualify such experiences as "virtual" – or Xiarhos' "cyber" – indicates to me an instinctive recognition of these "pilgrimages" as qualitatively different. I am not just being reactionary here. In the Introduction of this book, I set out to define "pilgrimage" and what it means for Catholics. Central to my definition was what I called "the power of place" in the distinctive, incarnational, sacramental world view of Catholicism. I used the Holy Eucharist as an example. It is in that Most Blessed Sacrament that I

---

[149] Victor Turner and Edith Turner, *Image and Pilgrimage in Christian Culture* (New York: Columbia University Press, 1978). Kindle edition. Citation defined at Xiarhos, p. 11. Xiarhos had opened his article with a brief discussion of Turner and Turner's conception of pilgrimage as a physical act (pp. 1-2).

[150] Xiarhos, "Authenticity," pp. 6-7.

find support for my position regarding pilgrimage. From Pope Benedict XVI's Apostolic Exhortation of 22 February 2007:

> [W]ith regard to the value of taking part in Mass via the communications media, those who hear or view these broadcasts should be aware that, under normal circumstances, they do not fulfil the obligation of attending Mass. Visual images can represent reality, but they do not actually reproduce it. While it is most praiseworthy that the elderly and the sick participate in Sunday Mass through radio and television, the same cannot be said of those who think that such broadcasts dispense them from going to church and sharing in the eucharistic assembly in the living Church.[151]

And even if there might be *extraordinary* circumstances under which an individual might fulfill the obligation of attending Mass via synchronous audio or video broadcast, one would hardly say that they would or could by such means receive the actual Body and Blood of Our Lord in the Eucharist. They might make a Spiritual Communion. But it is not the same. Ours is an Incarnational Faith. Matter matters. "Visual images" – and by extension, any other type of sensory input – "can represent reality, but they do not actually reproduce it."

Along the same lines, to my knowledge (and this might change at any time, of course, as Holy Mother Church considers, in her mercy, the intersection of "virtual reality" and pilgrimage), only one so-called "virtual pilgrimage" carries with it any sort of indulgence. Briefly, as per the Catechism of the Catholic Church:

> An indulgence is a remission before God of the temporal punishment due to sins of a person whose guilt has already been forgiven, which the faithful Christian who is duly disposed gains under certain prescribed conditions through the action of the Church which, as the minister of redemption, dispenses and applies with authority the treasury of the satisfactions of Christ and the saints.[152]

---

[151] Benedict XVI, *Sacramentum Caritatis* (The Sacrament of Charity, Apostolic Exhortation on the Eucharist as the Source and Summit of the Church's Life and Mission) (22 February 2007), 57 [http://w2.vatican.va/content/benedict-xvi/en/apost_exhortations/documents/hf_ben-xvi_exh_20070222_sacramentum-caritatis.html] Accessed 20 September 2019.

[152] *Catechism of the Catholic Church* § 1471.

Although certain pilgrimage destinations, through the mercy of the Church, have been offered to the faithful as "indulgenced," meaning a devout visit by a faithful Christian of due disposition carries with it an indulgence (as, for instance, passing through a designated Holy Door at any cathedral or basilica during the recent Jubilee Year of Mercy 2016), the act of pilgrimage in and of itself does not. And, in fact, the "virtual pilgrimage" that *does* (at the time of this writing) carry with it an indulgence is not what I would typically even consider an act of "pilgrimage" of any sort.

According to another link at the aforementioned index of Catholic Pilgrimage Sites [https://catholicpilgrimagesites.wordpress.com/indulgences/], in addition to a pilgrimage to the Sanctuary of Our Lady of Lourdes in Lourdes France before 15 July 2020 gaining an indulgence, experiencing what is known as a Lourdes Virtual Pilgrimage with the North American Lourdes Volunteers *also* gains an indulgence. According to the informational page of their website [https://lourdesvolunteers.org/what-is-a-virtual-pilgrimage/], "Virtual Pilgrimage Experience™ re-creates a pilgrimage to Lourdes without ever leaving home. This prayerful experience draws pilgrims nearer to God in the company of Our Lady as they are guided through a prayerful visit to the Grotto, the experience of the water, prayer in a Rosary procession and a Eucharistic blessing." An on-line article describing the program at one host church gives more information on specifics. It includes a presentation on the apparitions to St. Bernadette and the opportunity to touch a rock from the grotto where Our Lady appeared in addition to blessing with water from the spring that she revealed to the saint. In itself, that sounds much more like a relic tour or perhaps a home visit from one of the Pilgrim Statues of Our Lady of Fatima than a "pilgrimage," although I can easily see the conceptual connection of any of these with the idea of "pilgrimage." Any of these can be a blessing to the properly disposed.

Nevertheless, just as "it is most praiseworthy that the elderly and the sick participate in [virtual] Sunday Mass through radio and television," it stands to reason that the devotional use of "virtual pilgrimage" through all means discussed so far in this chapter, and doubtless through means that I cannot even imagine at present, by those who are correctly disposed can be a deeply spiritual experience. In drawing the distinction, I do not mean to discourage someone from utilizing any such resources they have available that enhance their connection with God, especially if a virtual pilgrimage is the only pilgrimage they can manage. But I also believe the distinction must be made. A "virtual" pilgrimage is not a "real" pilgrimage.

Devotional Pilgrimages

Besides reading about pilgrimage destinations and other pilgrims' experiences, besides vicariously participating in virtual pilgrimage, two common Catholic devotions are intrinsically quasi-pilgrimage in nature – and arguably attain a higher level of spiritual equivalence to pilgrimage than either reading *or* virtual pilgrimage. One explicitly has its origin in perhaps the most common activity undertaken by almost every Christian pilgrim to Jerusalem, from the very beginning – walking the *Via Dolorosa*, the Way of the Cross.

According to tradition and mystics, the Blessed Mother would, after Jesus' Ascension, devotionally follow the path he had walked from his condemnation to his death. According to visionary Blessed Anne Catherine Emmerich, when the Beloved Disciple to whom Jesus had entrusted his Mother from the Cross took her with him to live near Ephesus, she set up a garden path, setting up stones on which she inscribed markings to represent the various important stages of the Way.[153] It is unknown if there is any continuity between the putative practices of the Virgin Mary and those of later ages. We do know that public processions to the various spots identified, rightly or wrongly, with the various events of the Passion were in practice very soon after the Emperor Constantine's legalization of Christianity and establishment of churches in Jerusalem, as attested for the fourth century by early pilgrims such as Egeria as well as by the Church Father St. Jerome. Nevertheless, the Stations of the Cross that we all know today are a product of much later, during the centuries after the Franciscans established their presence in the Holy Land and began managing the visits of European pilgrims to Jerusalem. In the seventeenth century the practice arose of erecting memorials of those Franciscan Stations from Jerusalem in churches outside the Holy Land, and the Pope extended the indulgences attendant on making the pilgrimage to Jerusalem and walking the *Via Dolorosa* to those memorials, making them available to the faithful who use them to devoutly meditate on Our Lord's Passion. So, praying the Stations of the Cross is quite literally participation in the Pilgrimage to Jerusalem. The indulgence

---

[153] Blessed Anne Catherine Emmerich, *The Life of the Blessed Virgin Mary*, trans. Sir Michael Pelairet (London: Catholic Way Publishing, 2013), 18: 3, Kindle edition at 75%.

attached to the pious exercise of the Way of the Cross has been maintained in the 1968 revision to the *Enchiridion of Indulgences* (n. 63).[154]

Although its origin is less explicitly grounded in the place of the events it commemorates than are the Stations of the Cross, the Holy Rosary can easily be considered a pilgrimage following the Life of Christ. To make a long story short, the Rosary, in its traditional form, originated in the ancient ascetical practice of reciting the 150 Psalms in order. From memory. Which is an amazing feat that says a lot about the ability of our pre-literate ancestors to retain information in a way and to a degree that more literate ages such as our own have sadly lost. Such a prodigious feat of memorization was, nevertheless, beyond the ability of many or most persons even then. Early on, therefore, the practice arose of substituting 150 Paters, and later 150 Ave Marias, prayed on 150 pebbles or beads – in a bag, or more conveniently strung together. One-hundred-fifty Ave Marias prayed in such manner in place of the psalms came to be called "Our Lady's Psalter." Over time, the traditional form of the Rosary appeared (associated with St. Dominic, who reportedly received it directly from Our Lady herself in the thirteenth century), with fifteen groups of ten Ave Marias punctuated by a Pater, during which were meditated one of fifteen crucial events in the Incarnation, the Passion, and the Exaltation of Our Lord, considered from the perspective of Our Lady – Fifteen "Mysteries": Five Joyous, Five Sorrowful, and Five Glorious. Pope John Paul II's addition of Five "Luminous" Mysteries late in his pontificate broke the connection with the Psalter by adding fifty additional Ave Marias but not the connection with the events of Our Lord's life as considered by Our Lady. With a single exception, each can be associated with one of the Holy Places:

The Five Joyous Mysteries
The Annunciation – *The Basilica of the Annunciation, Nazareth*
The Visitation – *The Church of the Visitation, Ein Karem*
The Nativity – *The Basilica of the Nativity, Bethlehem*
The Presentation – *The Temple Mount, Jerusalem*
The Finding in the Temple – *The Temple Mount, Jerusalem*

---

[154] *The Enchiridion of Indulgences: Norms and Practices.* Authorized English Edition. Issued by the Sacred Apostolic Penitentiary, 1968. Formatted into electronic text 02 June 1998 [https://www.freecatholicbooks.com/books/indulgences.pdf], accessed 20 September 2019.

The Five Luminous Mysteries
The Baptism in the Jordan – *The Jordan River*
The Wedding at Cana – *The Catholic Wedding Chapel, Cana*
The Preaching of the Kingdom – *The Church of the Beatitudes, Galilee*
The Transfiguration – *The Church of the Transfiguration on Mount Tabor, Galilee*
The Gift of the Eucharist – *The Cenacle on Mount Zion, Jerusalem*

The Five Sorrowful Mysteries
The Agony in the Garden – *The Basilica of the Agony, i.e., the Church of All Nations, the Mount of Olives*
The Scourging at the Pillar – *The Temple Mount, Jerusalem*
The Crowning with Thorns – *The Temple Mount, Jerusalem*
The Carrying of the Cross – *The Via Dolorosa, Jerusalem*
The Crucifixion and Death of Our Lord – *The Golgotha Chapel in the Church of the Holy Sepulcher, Jerusalem*

The Five Glorious Mysteries
The Resurrection – *The Edicule in the Church of the Holy Sepulcher, Jerusalem*
The Ascension – *The Chapel of the Ascension, the Mount of Olives, Jerusalem*
The Sending of the Holy Spirit – *The Cenacle on Mount Zion, Jerusalem*
The Assumption of Our Lady into Heaven – *The Church of the Dormition on Mount Zion, Jerusalem*
The Crowning of Our Lady as Queen of Heaven – *The Empyrean Heaven*[155]....

I can say that being able to recall these places from personal experience, to visualize and put myself back in them, dramatically enhances my meditations on the associated Mysteries of the Rosary – which are also powerfully indulgenced.[156] So do my memories of walking the *Via Dolorosa* in Jerusalem whenever I pray the Stations of the Cross in my home parish. A semblance of those experiences for the Holy Land as

---

[155] The Highest Heaven. Originating in ancient cosmology for the place of the pure and eternal fire or *aether* in Aristotle's natural philosophy, medieval Christian philosophers used the term of the dwelling place of God and the highest of the angels. See Wikipedia s.v. "Empyrean." It is the Presence of God, the place of the Beatific Vision which is the goal of every believer, the ultimate destination of every Christian pilgrim.

[156] *Enchiridion of Indulgences*, n. 48.

well as other destinations might well be gained through media unavailable to our fathers' generations; that semblance is, however, merely a semblance. The most polished, realistic, networked media by themselves create no more than a "reality" that remains merely "virtual," which only imperfectly if at all conveys the actual graces of pilgrimage. Such graces are, on the other hand, available to all through these simple, sacramental devotionals bearing indulgences bestowed by the Church through the Authority of the Vicar of Christ out of her Treasury of Merits. I would go so far as to say that a devoutly prayed Rosary or Way of the Cross is more virtually a pilgrimage than any "virtual pilgrimage."

CHAPTER SEVEN

CONCLUDING THOUGHTS AND ADVICE FOR PILGRIMS

Through nearly two thousand years, Christians have sought to experience the places graced by the presence of Our Lord and his saints, most notably his Blessed Mother. At no time in that long history has doing so been easier than it is today. I hope that this book, based mostly on my own experience, conveys some sense of how spiritually rewarding being in those places can be when approached with the proper disposition – which I admittedly did not possess in the beginning. Beyond the undeniable power of place that draws tourists to a variety of locales of historical, literary, cultural, personal, or natural significance, the supernatural power of place imparted by the sacramental world view inherent in the Incarnational nature of the Catholic Faith makes certain places the loci of tremendous spiritual power where one can stand in the presence of God. Much as the sacramental world view acknowledges and hallows the physical nature of man as a material creature by God's use of matter as a conduit for grace – which He could admittedly impart in an instant, by *fiat*, but does not because that is not how He made us – so does, psychologically at least, the physical journey taking us outside our normal environs open us to graces outside our normal experience.

I hope that readers who may have made pilgrimages to one or more of the three major destinations I describe in detail in Chapters One through Three have enjoyed reliving that experience from another perspective. Likewise, I hope readers who have not been on pilgrimage have benefited from the detailed accounts I have provided and see in them a window into the wonderful experiences to be had, perhaps even to the point of considering embarking on a pilgrimage of their own – to one of those locations or to one of the other destinations I explored in the subsequent Chapters Four through Six, pilgrimages far (international), near (national or local), or even "here" ("virtual").

This concluding chapter is directed toward those intrepid souls, primarily toward those seeking to visit one of the "far" pilgrimage sites. Destinations "near" and "here" (literal or figurative) are much more accessible, and in both cases the primary importance is to approach them in an attitude of prayer, seeing them not as simple tourist sites or - in the case of "devotional pilgrimages" such as the Rosary or the Stations of the Cross - mere religious "exercises." In the case of bodily pilgrimage, the logistics of the journey itself, whether across the country or across town to a local shrine, is not significantly different than any other trip for any other reason, including pure tourism.

In many ways, the same is true for "far" pilgrimages, which are, as I have defined them here, international travel for readers in the United States. Depending on the circumstances, much of the practical planning and preparation will be identical for religious pilgrimage and secular tourism. Nevertheless, for the same reason that I included rather detailed accounts of the planning and preparation phases for each of my big pilgrimages, I want to attempt to pass on here some general suggestions based on my own, admittedly limited, experience - to provide a general overview of things you should consider, pray about, and do in preparation before, during, and after for Your Big Pilgrimage.

Before

The first and most important preparation is to discern whether the pilgrimage you are contemplating accords with the will of God for your life. *"Is God calling me to this pilgrimage?"* is a very personal question, but it is an important question. Unless your pilgrimage is born of an authentic call by God, I question whether there would be any spiritual fruits to be had. Fortunately, I believe, God is always calling us into His presence, which is another way to define what a pilgrimage is - a journey into the presence of God, directly in the places He walked as a man or indirectly through the places graced by the presence of His Blessed Mother or His saints. But it remains the case that there are doubtless, individually, times to pilgrimage and times not to pilgrimage - and one must discern these individually. I always tell people, "If you get a chance to go to (you fill in the blank - I most often fill it in with 'the Holy Land'), *do not let that chance pass you by.*" I consider just about any opportunity to go on a pilgrimage to originate with God. And yet even I do not jump at every opportunity I come across. There are practical matters of timing, family and work responsibilities, and finances, that must be considered individually. The best way to do so is, of course, through prayer. At the beginning of my account of my pilgrimage to the Holy Land, I relate Taylor Marshall's admonition when I expressed doubt about finances, to "Pray a novena!" – and how, over two years later, I remembered and followed that advice. I firmly believe that God answered me, first through a financial windfall, an unexpected tax refund that eased concerns on that score, and then in response to one final appeal for a clear sign – I can be rather thick-headed and self-doubting – giving me one in the actual voice of the spiritual director for the pilgrimage.

I freely admit that my response to the opportunity arising to make the pilgrimage to Italy in 2014 was less perfect than it should have been, more about the historical, cultural, and artistic significance of Rome than anything else. One theme through this book has been how I consider my understanding of pilgrimage to have grown over the past few years. At the time, I considered the "pilgrimage" basically a tour with a strong religious theme to it. The realization that there is something more, that there is a fundamental difference that I was hopefully able to enunciate in the Introduction, was slow to develop – did I say that I can be rather thick-headed? – although it began early on, when we formally signed on at that first pilgrims' meeting in October 2013 and Fr. Ryan Humphries urged us to consider something that I will repeat below, that key to the *spiritual* preparation for a pilgrimage is prayer. Nevertheless, although I did not embrace his advice as deeply as I should have, and do not believe my reasons for answering the call to that pilgrimage were entirely right, I do believe I was answering a call sent by God in part to begin that process of spiritual growth.

If you have discerned a call from God to undertake a pilgrimage, the next question is, "*Where should I go?*" Realistically, that question is probably already answered for you, in that you probably are responding to an opportunity to join a pilgrimage group to a specific destination. Or, the call to pilgrimage to which you are responding already has some focus, a longing to see, e.g., the Holy Land or Lourdes or the miraculous image of Our Lady of Guadalupe. If not, if you have discerned a call to pilgrimage in the abstract and are searching for a destination, I would suggest skimming back over Chapters One through Five of this book. Then, check out websites for major pilgrimage brokers for what pilgrimages they are offering.

Implicit in that answer is my answer to this next question: "*Should I go 'individual or group?'*" It is entirely possible to make a pilgrimage as an individual, although most laypeople today do not. Most join up with a group of pilgrims. I have never made an individual pilgrimage, so I have little to say about it. First, however, by "individual or group,"

I include a family trip for which you are responsible to be "individual" and accompanying a group where you are *not* responsible as "group." By that definition, I have traveled "individually" to the United Kingdom, twice, once accompanied by my wife, once accompanied by my wife and my son. I had never visited the UK before, but had no trouble and would not hesitate to do so again. But I was (and am) very hesitant to travel "individually" to just about anywhere else.

The primary deciding factor for me is language. My main facility with another language is Latin ... which is not particularly useful in any pilgrimage destination of which I am aware. Not even the Vatican these days. Besides which, my facility is reading rather than "conversational." Although I know intellectually that English is a *lingua franca* just about anywhere in the world, I also know experientially that fact to mean different things in different places. Without belaboring the point because I address it to varying degrees in the respective chapters, having experienced Italy, Mexico, and Israel as part of groups, I still would hesitate to travel individually in either of the first two but would have little or no hesitation returning literally by myself to Israel, where English seemed very widely spoken and understood. I hope to do so sooner rather than later.

In my mind, the language issue is related to safety by the sense of security a common language affords. I have discussed safety mainly in the context of the Holy Land. Today's world is increasingly unstable all around, and vigilance is necessary, so what I am about to say about Israel holds elsewhere as well. Regarding Israel, while I believe that the widely held misperception of a people under siege is just that, a *misper-ception*, I do not want to give the wrong impression by that statement. Concern is warranted, although that would not keep me away. If - when! - I return there by myself, I would stay in well-traveled areas, mainly Tel Aviv and Jerusalem, maybe Tiberias. I would be cautious everywhere, to be sure, and even within Jerusalem, there are hot spots I would most likely stay clear of on my own - most notably the Temple Mount. Any ventures beyond those cities, however, even for a day trip, I would make sure to be with a well-vetted group that I would check out thoroughly beforehand, and I would stay tuned-in obsessively with US State Department bulletins and other news sources. Just in case.

Taking the language and safety issues out of the equation, but still based primarily on tourism as opposed to pilgrimage, I would still say that there are advantages and disadvantages to both individual and group travel.

The advantage of traveling as an individual is primarily the freedom it affords both in the overall structure of the trip and in adaptability on the ground – the ability to linger for a time in a spot that you find particularly attractive for whatever reason, even one you knew nothing about and happened upon unexpectedly. The big disadvantage is that you are responsible for *everything* – travel, lodging, meals, knowing what sites are open when and not, safety, *everything*. If there is a language barrier, it is on you to figure out a way to communicate. If you get sick or injured, depending on how "individual" we are talking about, you may be absolutely on your own.

The advantage of traveling in a group is the security of knowing that practically everything is taken care of for you – travel, lodging, admission to sites, meals (for the most part, usually). You show up and follow the group. And that is indeed the disadvantage. There is little or no freedom. There is an itinerary that must be maintained (although it may change; but if it does, it does so for everyone). You will always leave any given site feeling as if you have barely scratched the surface – because you have indeed barely scratched the surface. I quoted my wife elsewhere that guided tours mainly just show you things that you then want to come back to see and absorb at your leisure. And you will always be tired, as the group flits (is flitted) from site to site to get in as much as possible.

On the other hand, as I discussed in Chapter Three, the fact that you are entirely subject to another's direction can be a blessing, a lesson in humility, a lesson in docility. Another advantage is that you are with a group who all speak a common language. If you get sick or injured, you have a ready network of support. From a spiritual standpoint, almost every organized Catholic pilgrimage has a priest spiritual adviser accompanying it. Individually, you will not have that. Depending on your self-discipline, being with a good group who are of a like mind that this is a pilgrimage with a spiritual as opposed to "sight-seeing" purpose can help you keep your focus when you are surrounded by sights and experiences that are constantly distracting.

All things considered, my advice for a first-time pilgrim would be to join a group. For at least the first visit to any particular overseas destination, the advantages far outweigh the disadvantages.

Most pilgrimages, especially when undertaken by a group, are contracted with a broker whose business is putting together, overseeing, making all the travel and lodging arrangements, etc., for the group. There are many such brokers out there – many of them dealing exclusively in Catholic pilgrimages. *How does one choose a pilgrimage broker?* I have never really "chosen" a broker, in that I have never set out in search of a pilgrimage to sign on to "cold," so to speak. In each case, the decision was made for me. The pilgrimage to Italy was sponsored by my parish, who worked with Magnificat Travel in Lafayette, Louisiana, in putting it together; I learned of and signed on to the one to Mexico because of Taylor Marshall, who chose 206 Tours; and I found the pilgrimage to the Holy Land through Radio Maria and a poster at my parish hall, and Nativity Pilgrimage was the choice of Fr. Emilio based on his own experience with them. Which is to say that I had some preexisting relationship with the sponsors of each pilgrimage that was more a determining factor than who the broker was, albeit the relationship with Radio Maria was somewhat tenuous, that of a listener and financial supporter. Were I to set out "cold" in search of a pilgrimage broker, I imagine the process of "due diligence" would apply much as it would in search of a travel agent for any other type of tour. I would seek out reviews and recommendations, try to talk to others that had used them as to how their experience was, and employ other such obvious means of evaluation.

As to my own experience, I consider myself three for three with pilgrimage brokers, although each had its strengths, and each had its weaknesses. All three of them oversaw trips that went smoothly and efficiently from beginning to end. Nevertheless, allow me to identify some strengths and weaknesses that come to mind for each, bearing in mind that my experience is in each case based on one trip alone, which can always be anomalous:

As far as Magnificat Travel goes, the primary strength was that there was a sense of security in having not just the guide with us the whole time, but in also having a representative of the broker along with us the whole time, with her avowed responsibility being as an immediately available liaison between us and the broker. That was incredibly comforting.

On the other hand – and perhaps this cannot be laid at Magnificat's feet per se, but if this was not the first time that they used our guide in Italy, then they must accept some responsibility. Although Debra was personable and knowledgeable, she never shut up! Never. With only a couple of notable exceptions, she was always talking – often repeating the same information again and again. As we passed Castel Sant'Angelo near the Vatican for the dozenth time, she said for the dozenth time, "There *is* no 'Saint Angelo'! It's named for the Archangel Saint *Michael*, you see! – the holy *angel* St Michael, you see!" Her constant chatter – and the relative inexperience of our two priests, Fr. Humphries and Fr. Decker, leading their first pilgrimage, making them hesitant to assert themselves (Fr. Humphries, hesitant to assert himself ... imagine that. But there you go...) – resulted in planned religious devotions falling almost entirely by the wayside, making this trip, overall, feel the least like what I now consider a true pilgrimage than any of the three. That was a definite weakness that I hope *was* anomalous.

To be sure, Alexis, the Magnificat representative on the ground, tried to oversee "caring and sharing" sessions. That is not what we were interested in. Rosaries – Divine Mercy Chaplets – *Catholic* devotions – opportunities for spiritual direction and Confession – *that* is what we wanted.

I have less of a strong feeling about 206 Tours' service – strengths or weaknesses – than either of the others. Everything went splendidly. The guides – two, both native Mexicans – were terrific. The religious character of the pilgrimage was fostered by the pilgrimage packet we received upon arrival including a copy of the monthly liturgical and devotional magazine, *Magnificat* (no relation to the pilgrimage broker), allowing us to pray morning and evening prayers together as a group, as well as everyone having the propers and readings for our daily Masses readily at hand. Time was taken for other prayers as well, primarily the Rosary. How much that was due to Taylor Marshall's insistence, I cannot say – but it was part of the overall experience and, especially after the Italy experience, I will give 206 Tours credit for that.

The main weakness I would identify was that a certain impersonalness in dealing with 206 Tours itself balanced the efficiency and smoothness of the entire experience. Unlike the other two pilgrimages, at no time did we meet anyone from 206 Tours itself. The guides apparently worked with them regularly, but they contract with other brokers as well.[157] As I have described it elsewhere, 206 Tours, born in the late 1980s out of the Medjugorje movement, is now a major player in the Catholic pilgrimage industry. It appears on just about every list of pilgrimage brokers you will find; if you do a Google search of the same, for just about any destination, it comes up within the first few results. Google search for "Catholic pilgrimage travel agents," it comes up first. It is obviously highly regarded, and based on my experience

---

[157] Having "liked" Nativity Pilgrimage's Facebook page, I see regular posts of short videos from their pilgrimages. Sometime after the Holy Land trip, I saw a Nativity Pilgrimage YouTube post about Our Lady of Guadalupe. I opened it – and there was Roberto!

deservedly so, so I would not count this as a critical weakness at all. The better word would probably be "professional" ... but it did seem a bit impersonal.

Finally, Nativity Pilgrimage: I am basing what I say here in part on what I am told, not on objectively verified information, but the testimony of our guide in Israel, Tony, as well as their representative in the Holy Land, Hatem. Tony throughout - although he admittedly would contract with other brokers - and Hatem during that "farewell dinner" near the end of the trip, both passionately promoted Nativity Pilgrimage as an apostolate as much as a business. They insisted that Nativity Pilgrimage is the pilgrimage broker most closely connected to our Catholic brethren in the Holy Land, that it uses only Catholic guides and bus drivers. The founder, Jakoub Khaled, is a native of Bethlehem and keeps an office there although he is based now in Houston, which I am unaware of any other pilgrimage company doing. Nativity Pilgrimage's web site [https://www.nativitypilgrimage.com] confirms their heavy involvement in the lives of Bethlehemite Christians, working in partnership with the Church of the Nativity and the Terra Sancta schools, for which Khaled funds scholarships. A more direct advantage that I perceive in using Nativity Pilgrimage is that, based on several surveys of pilgrimage costs that I have done over several months, they consistently seem to offer packages at or near the lowest cost. Based again on my (somewhat limited experience), I perceived no diminution in service. We stayed in the very same hotel in Tiberias that Steve Ray uses - and paid almost half the package cost!

Although I really could not find any overt "weakness" with Nativity Pilgrimage, my perception is that they are a relatively small and unknown company, which may explain a couple of things. I had certainly never heard of Nativity before I began discerning the pilgrimage opportunity, and my search for information about it produced little beyond their own website. I cannot say except as speculation, but perhaps that lack of information dissuaded some Radio Maria listeners from signing on to the pilgrimage, leading (along with some sort of misunderstanding surrounding one pilgrim's registration status) to the trip being in danger of falling through entirely. But even that worked out for the best, at least from my perspective, as detailed in Chapter Three. The smallness of the group was nice; it fostered a certain intimacy - but it did have consequences. It impacted our access to certain things, such as our Mass in the chapel at Dominus Flevit. That is the only specific example of which I am aware, but were there others? Nevertheless, as far as the pilgrimage experience itself goes, everything went smoothly and efficiently, and I would not hesitate to use them again and recommend them to anyone.

Really, I would use any of these again and would have little hesitance in using just about any Catholic broker unless "due diligence" threw up some kind of major red flag. Ultimately, however, for either international tourism or pilgrimage, little of what I have discussed thus far addresses what is, to my mind, the primary concern of most potential travelers – cost.

International travel is expensive. There is no way of getting around it. "*Can I financially afford to go on this pilgrimage?*" is, of course, another entirely personal question. While I would not counsel going into debt to pay for a pilgrimage, there are ways for even individuals of modest means to do so. I base the following on an excellent online article at *Consumer Catholic*, entitled "How to Afford a Catholic Pilgrimage,"[158] that I will abstract here just in case it vanishes.

The unsigned article begins with the most obvious admonition, which says much more concisely what I was trying to say above:

> Pray: Have a discussion with God about your desire to go on a pilgrimage. Tell Him why you want to go and where you're thinking about going. Pray, sleep on it and don't rush into it.
>
> Spend time in Adoration, pray the Rosary, talk with your spiritual director – use your spiritual tools of choice to discern if this is where God is calling you. But don't obsess over this decision or overcomplicate it. If you have the time, the means, and the desire to go on a pilgrimage, it's likely that when you pray about it, you will feel a peace about it.
>
> Don't forget to talk to people who've been on pilgrimages. They can give you the low-down on which tour companies are the best and what they wish they'd known before.

There follows a discussion of logistics: Should you opt for the "land only" portion of the pilgrimage – i.e., the pilgrimage itself, per se – and make your own air travel arrangements? That is usually offered as an option, although if you avail yourself of it, you assume the responsibility of managing the logistics of meeting up with the group at the destination. Know what is included in the package and what is

---

[158] "How to Afford a Catholic Pilgrimage," *Consumer Catholic* (updated 29 August 2019) [https://www.consumercatholic.com/how-to-afford-a-catholic-pilgrimage/].

not. Investigate discounts and cheaper options, which may be offered by the broker even if not advertised as such. The article gives advice on how to save up for a pilgrimage – mostly utterly practical, but including the idea, rather repugnant in today's world but historically integral to the experience of pilgrimage, of *sacrifice*. It is possible to save money before and during the trip in many small ways that add up, including packing lightly to save on checked-bag fees and packing snacks for layover periods in airports to avoid the significantly inflated prices they demand of their basically captive customers (which are just shy of those in movie theaters!). And it admonishes, "Don't Go Into Debt: I highly discourage going into debt to go on a pilgrimage. If you have to go into debt to travel, then it's probably not the right time to go." The writer qualifies that, however, with the admission, "[t]hat said, God works in His own ways, so it's entirely possible that He may call you to go even when you're not in a good financial position." In which case, as I have repeated from Taylor Marshall several times already, "Pray a novena!" It works.

Then: You have decided to go. You have paid your money. And it is still (usually) going to be several months before the pilgrimage begins. It is time to "prep." I will try to keep this reasonably brief, but it is essential. You should prepare yourself mentally, physically, *and spiritually*:

Mentally: Educate yourself on the destination as a tourist destination in general and as a religious destination in particular. Your pilgrimage broker will likely provide you with some information along these lines, but it will not be nearly enough. The more you learn about the destination, the more you will get out of the whole experience while you are there, both as a living, breathing culture and as a vital part of our Universal Catholic Faith, the latter being the whole reason you have chosen – or been called – to go there on pilgrimage. Any decent guide will give you a tremendous amount of useful information about both while you are there – so much information that you will not retain a tenth of what you hear. Take it from the professor in me: The more you know about a subject going in, the more you are going to retain any subsequent information you are given. It is the way the human mind works. Every bit of data received is sifted and sorted to be tucked away into an existing matrix, which, if not present, must be created on the fly, in the process of which a lot is going to be lost. Set up the matrix beforehand. I would suggest, at minimum, reading at least one general history of the country you are visiting and one about the primary pilgrimage destination you are visiting. At minimum. If there are pertinent movies or documentaries, watch them. You will not regret it.

As an aside, this is where I see the real value of the multimedia, Internet-based "Virtual Pilgrimages" to be. They are an excellent way to scout out the destinations you are preparing to experience for yourself. But they are *not* the experience itself.

As a tourist destination, there are guidebooks for just about any locale in the world. There are several well-known series: I personally love and keep going back to the DK (Dorling-Kindersley) travel books [https://www.dk.com/us/category/travel/]. They are stuffed with useful maps, charts, diagrams, cutaways of the most significant buildings and monuments giving you a three-dimensional perspective, generally good historical information and practical advice for how to best take in a site, and loads of good (albeit typically small) full-color photographs. Useful information is provided about essential cultural, legal, social issues – all from a strictly secular viewpoint, of course. An attempt is made to give lodging and culinary advice, but it is cursory and impersonal. For that kind of information (essential if you are planning a trip on your own), my series of choice is Rick Steves' [https://store.ricksteves.com/shop/guidebooks]. Other decent series are Fodor's [https://www.fodors.com/guidebooks] and Lonely Planet [https://shop.lonelyplanet.com]. Although if you are traveling with a pilgrimage group, you might think you do not need the practical travel information to be found in those books, I cannot help but believe it is useful to have read through it at least (build that matrix!). Specific areas meriting close attention: Be familiar with the monetary situation and the exchange rate; learn the numerals; what kind of electrical adapters do you need?; if you intend to purchase clothing, know how that clothing is sized; be aware of cultural oddities that might trip you up – or give offense.

In a similar vein, learn at least the most essential phrases, especially having to do with making a purchase. As a friend of mine says, "*Always* know how to say, 'Where is the bathroom?' and 'Take me to the US Embassy!'" in the local language. Of course, English is omnipresent in the modern world, especially where there is a thriving pilgrimage travel industry – but better safe than sorry. The more of the local language you can master, even as little as being able to sound out street signs and interpret menus, the more you will feel you are truly engaging in the experience of the land and the people. I never feel that I have done this adequately, but every little bit that I *have* done, I have found to come in useful.

Do not overlook preparation for likely religious exercises you might engage in while on pilgrimage. If you are going to be at St. Peter's Square during the Pope's regular Sunday Angelus, learn the Angelus in Latin. It is not difficult. Likewise, if you are going to visit the Shrine of Our Lady of Guadalupe, find the words and a recording of *La Guadalupana*. It is a bit more difficult than the Angelus in Latin, mainly because it is generally sung at a fast pace. It is peppy and fun. And you can thank me later for it being stuck in your head for days.

In addition to books and movies about the destination in its general significance, and here I include fictional accounts in addition to historical non-fiction, I would add Catholic pilgrimage guidebooks, of which many are available, especially for the Holy Land. But if you get away from the prominent international destinations, they get harder to come by. The Internet, however, gives access to what are usually very good websites for just about any shrine or destination. Most countries put a fair amount of resources into maintaining very prominent tourism websites, which may well include sections on the Catholic pilgrimage sites even if they emphasize the cultural rather than the religious importance. In this respect, although I discovered it far too late to use in 2018, before I go back to the Holy Land I will be scouring Israel's "Holy Land Pilgrimage" web site,[159] which contains an index/guide to pilgrimage brokers, sample itineraries, maps, and virtual visits to the major sites.

Physically: Pilgrimages are strenuous, especially the intensive, see-as-many-sites-as-possible-in-the-least-amount-of-time pilgrimages such as to the Holy Land. Although my pilgrimages have been fortunate in that accommodations could be made on the fly for those who were either intrinsically (because of age) or briefly (because of an injury) mobility impaired, they are not set up for people who have trouble getting around. And if you lead a generally sedentary life (as I do), the near-constant walking that a pilgrimage entails, even with the generally-advertised "air-conditioned coach" taking you from site to site, could potentially prove a bit much without adequate preparation.

So, walk! Try to work yourself up to five miles a day, but even just a couple of miles a day at a brisk pace will help once you get there. Brokers always tell their pilgrims to be prepared to walk that five miles a day I just suggested, but rarely will you actually walk that far in a single day, and it will be spaced out over the entire day. During my pilgrimage to the Holy Land, only on the first day, when we visited

---

[159] www.holyland-pilgrimage.org

several places around the Sea of Galilee *and* I joined in the walk a good distance up the street in Tiberias, from the Ron Beach Hotel to the Scots Hotel for the wine-tasting, did my Fitbit register more than five miles, and that not by much (5.33 miles for the day); even on the last day, walking down the Mount of Olives then across the Old City of Jerusalem from the Lions' Gate to the Jaffa Gate, the total distance walked was just shy of five miles (4.99, to be exact). At no time did I feel overly stressed from walking on those days, even in the heat of August, even being considerably overweight and having a brand-new pacemaker – but then, I *had* been walking pretty much two miles a day during the preceding months, albeit sometimes on a treadmill, at a brisk pace.

Do that preparatory walking in the shoes you intend to wear on the pilgrimage. Make sure they are well broken in.

The other health-related advice that I would give concerns the risk of getting sick. Be extra careful, in the weeks leading up to departure, to avoid (as much as possible) exposure to any contagions that might manifest at the worst possible time. There is, of course, no way to eliminate that possibility, but do what you can to minimize it. For my part, I start boosting Vitamin C, apple cider vinegar, and similar homeopathic preventatives of dubious effectiveness at least a couple of weeks early and keep them up as best as I can during the trip. And I seem to have been lucky so far. Apart from a minor head-cold that struck me during our trip to the UK in 2010, I have generally been healthy during my various travels. Before and after? – that is a different story, of course. But I did put off having my heart attack until I was landing back in Houston at the end of the aforementioned UK 2010 trip (*sure...* "put off" ... it was a conscious *choice!* – on *God's* part!) – and by the grace of God (working through my cardiologists) the implantation of a pacemaker *six days* before leaving for the Holy Land in 2018 did not keep me from going. Really, it was by the grace of God that I had the medical crisis necessitating the pacemaker while I was still at home, there was time to deal with it, and that I had good doctors who in their charity made sure I was fit to go.

Spiritual: Finally, pilgrimage is a religious exercise. Self-education on the destination as a pilgrimage site, especially if done by reading (and praying over), e.g., the Gospels in preparation for a pilgrimage to the Holy Land or a biography of or writing by the saint whose shrine you are going to visit, can be spiritually rewarding in itself. Beyond that, my advice is simple and merely echoes that given by Fr. Humphries during that first pilgrimage meeting a year in advance of our pilgrimage to Italy that I mentioned earlier. Prepare yourself by praying and fasting for a spiritually rewarding pilgrimage.

As I have said, I did not take Father seriously enough prior to that pilgrimage to Italy, which might be one reason that in retrospect, while I look back on it as an important and fulfilling experience, I do not believe I received all of the graces that I could have out of it. I had not spiritually prepared as I should have done. My prayer was half-hearted and sporadic. My fasting was non-existent. Fasting is not my strong suit and never has been. But I could have done better. Fasting need not mean going without food for an entire day. Just skipping a meal as I sometimes do now (not that you would know it from looking at me – but that is not the point) *can* be a spiritually fruitful fast.

I did take the intention of spiritual preparation by prayer and fasting more seriously for later pilgrimages, and I believe it made a difference. As I described at the beginning of Chapter Two, I preceded the pilgrimage to the Shrine of Our Lady of Guadalupe by making the 33-Day Total Consecration to Mary culminating on Candlemas 2016, which I believe brought powerful graces to my aid and helped make that pilgrimage perhaps the most consistently focused on the Faith of any of the three, maybe even more so than the pilgrimage to the Holy Land.

A final suggestion, although I did not pick it up until late in the writing of this book and thus incorporated little of it into my own recommendations, wife and husband María Ruiz and Michael Scaperlanda's *The Journey: A Guide for the Modern Pilgrim* is in many ways a book-length version of this final chapter, especially the last few paragraphs, albeit from a very different perspective – or perspectives, since they write in alternating sections. But, in common with a strong autobiographical thread drawing on much longer experience as a *family* of pilgrims from their response to Pope John Paul II's universal invitation to celebrate Jubilee Year 2000 in Rome, theirs is a more spiritually-directed treatment with chapter titles such as "Developing a Pilgrim Heart," "Learning from Pilgrims of the Bible," "Getting Help for the Interior Journey," and "Facing Our Obstacles." You could do worse than prayerfully reading their book in the months leading up to your own pilgrimage.

In summation: Spiritually prepare yourself by prayer, fasting, reading, and other appropriate religious exercises, to orient your heart toward heaven before setting forth on your pilgrimage. This is as or more important than mentally and physically preparing.

The rest of the preparatory phase that I would suggest for any trip abroad, secular or religious. Put together personal information packets of two types. The first, to leave with a family member or a close friend, would consist of a photocopy of your passport and ID; an itinerary with contact information for the travel agent or pilgrimage broker as well as all of the hotels or other type of lodging and the dates that you will be based at each; include, and this is *just in case*, the contact information for the US embassy and consulates in the destination country. Just in case. Seal this in an envelope and give it to the family member or close friend a couple of days before departure. Second, for a fellow pilgrim, the sponsor or pilgrimage director, and the guide who will be with you, a sealed envelope each containing a photocopy of your passport and ID, contact information for the friend or family member back home with whom you left the aforementioned packets, plus any relevant medical information including a list of any medications you are on and the reasons you are taking them, preferably on the letterhead of your personal doctor bearing their contact information. Include your medical insurance, travel insurance, and so forth in both packets as well.

Finally, make sure you have essential supplies, necessary toiletries in air travel-compliant packaging, and so forth. If you wear glasses or contact lenses, take an extra pair. Paying attention to baggage regulations, pack some AA and AAA batteries in your checked luggage, for the Whisper radio sets. Also, pack some good earbuds; the ones supplied by the travel agents and pilgrimage brokers are typically cheap, disposable ones that just do not work that well.

During

While on the pilgrimage be sure you do the following: 1) Continue praying for a spiritually rewarding pilgrimage, for the safety of all your companions and their safe return home, and for your family and friends back home – especially for those who have asked you to do so in the spiritually powerful places you will be visited. 2) Be flexible, especially if on a group tour. Changes always occur. You just have to go with it. Humility. Docility. 3) Make notes as often as you can, as soon after each event or site as you can. Use a voice recording app on your smartphone if necessary. Get the information down. You will not regret it. You *will* regret not doing so. 4) Do take pictures, but do not let obsession over taking pictures take over the experience. At each site, take your pictures, then put the camera or smartphone away and focus on the spiritual presence that you have truly come to experience. 5) And take time to pray – wait. Did I say that already? It does not matter. It is worth saying again: Take time to pray. If you are not on pilgrimage to draw nearer to God, you are not on pilgrimage. You are on a sightseeing tour.

Along the same lines, I would encourage you to stay focused – on the pilgrimage, on God. Writing this book has forced me to consider at length the three major pilgrimages I have undertaken and why, for all my fond memories of it, I place the 2014 Pilgrimage to Italy a close third as a religious experience. I touched on this in concluding that chapter, but I would like to repeat here that, besides my admitted lack of spiritual preparation, the distractions made possible by modern technology were very detrimental to my first pilgrimage experience. The Internet is a wonderful thing! – But it is also a curse. The more we give attention to the wider world, the less attention we give to the here and now – and the hereafter and forever. Pilgrimage is all about the hereafter and forever – through the here and now – and the wider world can wait. Based on my experience, my advice is ... Well, I am not so naïve as to think anyone in this day and age is going to go without their smartphone for a week! But do 6) Consider putting the smartphone and the computer away as much as possible, turn them off entirely if possible. Limit yourself very strictly in checking phone messages and emails. Impress on your loved ones back home that you are essentially on a religious retreat and that they should not expect to hear from you often, but that you will be praying for them. If you *must* post a few pictures to social media – or put up a blog – do so as quickly and efficiently as possible; as far as a blog goes, limit yourself to simple, daily placeholder posts while on pilgrimage. *Stay focused.*

After

Once you have returned home: 1) Continue to pray and meditate on the experiences you have had. Ask God to deepen your understanding of their importance and role in our Faith. An excellent way to do that is 2) Organize the notes and pictures you took into some sort of coherent form, as soon as you can. I do that by finishing off blog entries I have posted in rudimentary, "placeholder" form along the way, reliving the experience as I do so. Do so however you want to – but *do so*. Or you will be amazed how much you forget and how quickly. 3) Let others know how wonderful the experience was. Perhaps you, or God acting through you, will inspire them to undertake their own pilgrimage. 4) And, if you are anything like me, you will be looking forward to *your* next pilgrimage. Start praying about and saving up to be able to seize that opportunity when it comes.

Conclusion

My pilgrimage experience is admittedly limited, but for what it is worth, the above are the points of advice that I would give based upon that experience. I do not believe it is complete, nor will it ever be. But there is one last piece of advice that I would give, upon which everything given above is contingent. It is advice that I have given many times in the past year since my pilgrimage to the Holy Land, usually regarding specifically the Holy Land but, in reality, applicable to any pilgrimage destination whatsoever. If you feel that God is calling you, answer; if you think that God is calling you to pilgrimage, go; and if you have doubts whether you should go or how you can afford it – *Pray a novena.*

God will answer.

APPENDIX ONE

ITINERARIES

Ideal and Reality: Israel 2018

Day	Itinerary – The Ideal	Reality
13 Aug	Fly out of Houston	Fly out of Houston
14 Aug	Land in Israel Drive to Tiberias	Land in Israel Drive to Tiberias
15 Aug	Mt. Tabor Cana Nazareth	Capernaum Tabgha Peter's Primacy Galilee boat trip Magdala
16 Aug	Capernaum Tabgha Peter's Primacy Galilee boat trip	Cana Nazareth Mt. Tabor
17 Aug	Bethlehem Ein Karem	Depart Tiberias Haifa-Carmel Jaffa Arrive Bethlehem
18 Aug	Mount of Olives Mount Zion	Bethlehem Mount Zion
19 Aug	Jerusalem Old City *Via Dolorosa* Holy Sepulcher Western Wall *Free time*	Ein Karim Jericho (Qumran) Dead Sea
20 Aug	Jordan River Jericho Qumran Dead Sea	Mount of Olives *Via Dolorosa* Holy Sepulcher
21 Aug	Flight home	Flight home

APPENDIX TWO

A REGIONAL LIST OF THE PAINTED CHURCHES OF TEXAS

In my research, various citations as to the number of Painted Churches in Texas ranged from "twenty" to "a couple of dozen," but I never found a comprehensive list. On the day of our tour mentioned in Chapter Five, however, I asked for and received an official list from the Schulenburg Chamber of Commerce, totaling thirty and ranging further away from the epicenter around Schulenburg than I expected. Rather than list them here in alphabetical order by city, town, or community (the latter of which can be pretty obscure, especially in a vast state such as Texas, which is at least as big as "a whole 'nother country"), I am here grouping them together regionally as best as I can, starting with the area around Schulenburg, and including the name of the church, the community in which it is located, its physical address and contact information where available, the URL web address, and any other information that might be useful, particularly if it is a mission parish of some other church in the area, with some contact information for that church.

Schulenburg

1. **The Nativity of the Blessed Virgin Mary Church (St. Mary's), High Hill.** 2833 FM 2672, Schulenburg, Texas 78956, (979) 561-8455. [www.stmary-highhill.com] A mission of St. Rose of Lima, Schulenburg, Texas. *St. Mary's – High Hill is regarded as the "Queen of the Painted Churches."*
2. **Saints Cyril and Methodius Church, Dubina.** FM Road 1383, Dubina, Texas 78956. [https://stmichael-weimar.org/stscyril-methodius] A mission of St. Michael the Archangel Church, Weimar, Texas, (979) 725-6714.
3. **Saint John the Baptist Church, Ammannsville.** 7745 Mensik Road, Schulenburg, Texas 78956, (979) 743-

3117. A mission of St. Rose of Lima, Schulenburg, Texas. *"The Pink Church."*
4. **The Assumption of the Blessed Virgin Mary Church (St. Mary's), Praha.** 821 FM 1295, Flatonia, Texas 78941, (361) 865-3560. [stmaryspraha.org].
5. **Saint John the Baptist, St. John.** 7026 FM 957, Schulenburg, Texas 78956, (979) 798-5888. [https://discovermass.com/church/st-john-the-baptist-saint-john-tx/]. A mission of Sacred Heart Church, Hallettsville, Texas. [https://www.shcatholicchurch.org/sacred-heart-missions/].
6. **The Ascension of Our Lord, Moravia.** Hallettsville, Texas, 77964. [http://www.gcatholic.org/churches/usa-10/34212.htm]. A mission of Sacred Heart Church, Hallettsville, Texas. [https://www.shcatholicchurch.org/sacred-heart-missions/].
7. **Saint Mary's, St. Mary.** 1648 FM 340, Hallettsville, Texas 77964, (361) 798-2128.
8. **Saint Mary's Church, Ellinger.** 815 St. Mary's Church Road, Fayetteville, Texas 78940. [www.stmaryellinger.com] A mission of St. John the Baptist, Fayetteville. [www.stjohnfayetteville.com]
9. **Saints Cyril and Methodius, Shiner.** 306 South Avenue F, Shiner, Texas 77984, (361) 594-3836. [http://sscm-shiner.org/]
10. **Saint John the Baptist, Koerth.** 13202 FM 531, Hallettsville, Texas 77964. A mission of Queen of Peace Church, P. O. Box 201, Sweet Home, Texas 77987, (361) 741-3206. [https://qpcatholicchurch.com/contact-us-1]
11. **Wesley Brethren Church, Wesley.** 9643 Wesley Church Lane, Brenham, Texas 77833, (979) 836-0672. *I include this and the next church, even though they are not Catholic, both because they are frequently referenced as the couple of Painted Churches that are not Catholic and because they do appear on the official list provided by the Greater Schulenburg Chamber of Commerce.*
12. **Saint Paul Lutheran Church, Serbin.** 1572 County Road 211, Giddings, Texas 78942. [http://www.stpauls-erbin.org/].

Houston
13. **Church of the Annunciation, Houston.** 1618 Texas Avenue, Houston, Texas 77003, (713) 222-2289. [www.annunciationcc.org]
14. **Saint Joseph's, Galveston.** 2202 Avenue K, Galveston, Texas 77550, (409) 765-3402. [http://www.galvestonhistory.org/]
15. **Guardian Angel, Wallis.** 5610 Demel Street, Wallis, Texas 77485, (979) 478-6532. [http://www.archgh.org/]
16. **Saint Mary's, Plantersville.** 8227 County Road 205, Plantersville, Texas 77485, (936) 894-2223. [http://www.smsj.org/]
17. **Saint Anthony Cathedral Basilica, Beaumont.** 700 Jefferson Street, Beaumont, Texas 77701, (409) 833-6433. [http://www.stanthonycathedralbasilica.org/]

San Antonio
18. **Saint Mary's, San Antonio.** 202 North St. Mary's Street, San Antonio, Texas 78205, (210) 226-8381. [http://www.archsa.org/]
19. **Immaculate Heart of Mary, San Antonio.** 617 South Santa Rosa Avenue, San Antonio, Texas 78204, (210) 226 8268. [http://www.ihmsatx.org/]
20. **Annunciation, St. Hedwig.** 14011 FM 1346, St. Hedwig, Texas 78152, (210) 667-1232. [http://www.sthcc.org/]
21. **Our Lady of Grace, LaCoste.** 15825 Bexar Street, LaCoste, TX 78039, (830) 985-3357. [olglacostetexas.org]
22. **Saint Stanislaus, Bandera.** 602 7th Street, Bandera, TX 78003, (830) 460-4712. [http://www.ststanislausbandera.com/]

Outliers South of San Antonio
23. **Our Lady of Loreto Chapel (*Presidio La Bahia*), Goliad.** 217 S-183, Goliad, Texas 77963, (361) 645-3752. [https://presidiolabahia.org/history-of-chapel] *I include this one because it is on the official list, but I do not consider it one of the "Painted Churches." It is definitely important – historically, architecturally, artistically – but not in the Central European tradition.*

24. **Immaculate Conception of the Blessed Virgin Mary, Panna Maria.** 13879 FM 81 / P.O. Box 25, Panna Maria, Texas 78144. (830) 780-2748. [www.pannamariatexas.com]

Outliers North of San Antonio
25. **Saint Mary's, Fredericksburg.** 304 West San Antonio Street, Fredericksburg, Texas 78624, (830) 997-9523. [Church.stmarysfbg.com]
26. **Saint Joseph, Mason.** 210 South Avenue B, Mason, Texas 76856, (325) 347-6932.
27. **Saint Boniface, Offen.** 1118 County Road 234, Rowena, Texas 76875, (325) 442-2893. [Sanangelodiocese.org]

Extreme Outliers
28. **Sacred Heart, Palestine.** 503 North Queen Street, Palestine, Texas 75801, (903) 729-2463. *Palestine is located in the eastern part of the state.*
29. **Saint Peter's, Lindsay.** 424 Main Street, Lindsay, Texas 76250, (940) 668-7609. [https://stpeterlindsay.org/org] *Lindsay is located in the northeastern part of the state, north of Dallas.*
30. **Saint Mary's, Umbarger.** 22830 Pondseta Road, Umbarger, TX 79091, (806) 499-3531 [https://stmarysumbarger.com] *Umbarger is located in the northwestern part of the state, south of Amarillo, far outside the expected orbit of the Painted Churches.*

Figure 40: The Painted Churches of Texas – see text for number references

Figure 41: Inside St. John the Baptist Church, Ammannsville, Texas – "The Pink Church." Photo taken by the author.

REFERENCES

Many more articles, books, and commentaries were consulted at various stages in my research than are explicitly cited.

General and Encyclopedic References

Catechism of the Catholic Church with Modifications from the Editio Typica. 2nd ed. New York: Doubleday, 2003.

Goodreads [https://www.goodreads.com/]

Google Books [https://books.google.com/]

Magnificat Holy Land Companion: A Spiritual Guide for Pilgrims. 2nd ed. Yonkers, NY: Magnificat in Cooperation with the Franciscan Custody of the Holy Land, 2019.

O'Neill, Michael. *The Miracle Hunter* [http://www.miraclehunter.com/]

See the Holy Land [https://www.seetheholyland.net/]

The Catholic Encyclopedia. 15 vols. New York: Robert Appleton Company, 1907-1912 [http://home.newadvent.org/cathen/index.html]

Wikipedia. [https://en.wikipedia.org/wiki/Main_Page]

General Websites and Blogs

Catholic Pilgrimage Sites. [https://catholicpilgrimage sites.wordpress.com/]

Hare, Kent G. *The Absent-Minded Professor's Travels.* [https://www.theprofstravels .blogspot.com]

Holy Land Pilgrimage. [www.holyland-pilgrimage.org]

Holy Land Virtual Reality Tour & 360 Degree Jerusalem 3D Tour. [https://www.p4panorama.com/panos/HOLYLAND/index.html]

LiveMass.net. [LiveMass.net]

Marshall, Taylor R. *The Taylor Marshall Catholic Show.* [https://taylormarshall.com]

Ray, Stephen. *Defenders of the Catholic Faith.* [https://www.catholicconvert.com/]

Religious Planning Travel Guide. [http://religioustravelplanningguide.com/]

The Catholic Travel Guide. [https://thecatholictravelguide .com/]

Thomas, Amy, *Catholic Pilgrim: Living Out Your Catholic Faith.* [https://catholicpilgrim.net/]

Articles, Books, Videos

"10 Top Catholic Shrines in the U.S." *Religious Planning Travel Guide*. [http://religioustravelplanningguide.com/10-top-catholic-shrines-in-the-u-s/]

"20 Pilgrimage Sites Across the United States Worth Visiting" (2018 edition). *Religious Travel Planning Guide* [http://religioustravelplanningguide.com/20-pilgrimage-sites-across-united-states-worth-visiting/]

Ahlquist, Dale. "Chesterton University: Lecture 35: The New Jerusalem," *The Society of Gilbert Keith Chesterton*. [https://www.chesterton.org/lecture-35/]

Alessio, Mark. "Where did the Assumption take place?" *The Angelus* (July 2003). Reprinted by the Society of Saint Pius X, *News & Events* (14 August 2014). [https://sspx.org/en/news-events/news/where-did-assumption-take-place-4650]

Arthington, Madeline. "Holy Ground: Catholic Pilgrimages to Rome," *International Mission Board* (IMB) (09 November 2018). [https://www.imb.org/2018/11/09/catholic-pilgrimages-to-rome/]

Ave Maria Grotto: Miniature Miracles. Kansas City, KS: Terrell Publishing, 2016.

Badde, Paul. *Maria of Guadalupe: Shaper of History, Shaper of Hearts*. Trans. Carol Cowgil. San Francisco: Ignatius Press, 2008.

Baldwin, David. *Why Pilgrimage?* London: Catholic Truth Society, 2015.

Beck, John A. *The Holy Land for Christian Travelers: An Illustrated Guide to Israel*. Grand Rapids, MI: Baker Books, 2017.

Bede. *Ecclesiastical History of the English People*. Ed. and trans. Bertram Colgrave and R. A. B. Mynors. Oxford: Clarendon Press,1969; Trans. Leo Shirley Price (Penguin Books, 1955; repr. Barnes & Noble, 1993).

Beebe, Kathryne. *Pilgrim & Preacher: The Audiences and Observant Spirituality of Friar Felix Fabri (1437/8-1502)*. New York: Oxford University Press, 2014.

Benedict XVI, Pope. *Sacramentum Caritatis* (The Sacrament of Charity, Apostolic Exhortation on the Eucharist as the Source and Summit of the Church's Life and Mission) (22 February 2007). [http://w2.vatican.va/content/benedict-xvi/en/apost_exhortations/documents/hf_ben-xvi_exh_20070222_sacramentum-caritatis.html]

Booth, William, and Taylor Luck. "Pope picks one of dueling baptism sites in visit to Holy Land," *The Washington Post* (20 May 2014). [https://www.washingtonpost.com/world/middle_east/pope-picks-one-of-dueling-baptism-sites-in-visit-to-holy-land/2014/05/20/7cd22336-e00a-11e3-9442-54189bf1a809_story.html]

Bradley, Ian. *Pilgrimage: A Spiritual and Cultural Journey*. Oxford: Lion Hudson, 2009.

Brockman, Norbert D. "Marian Pilgrimage and Shrines." *Marian Studies* 51 (2000): 96-111.

Brown, Peter. *The Cult of the Saints*. Chicago: University of Chicago, 1981.

Caridi, Cathy. "Are Catholics Supposed to Abstain from Meat Every Friday?" *Canon Law Made Easy*. (05 March 2009). [http://canonlawmadeeasy.com/2009/03/05/are-catholics-supposed-to-abstain-from-meat-every-friday/]

Carroll, Warren. *Our Lady of Guadalupe and the Conquest of Darkness*. Front Royal, VA: Christendom Publications, 1983.

Cast a Giant Shadow. Directed by Melville Shavelson. Beverly Hills, CA: MGM, 1966.

"Catholic Shrines of New Orleans" Brochure, no date or source information given. [Accessed at http://www.seelos.org/NOLA_Shrines_8.5x11_sm.pdf]

"Catholic Shrines, Pilgrimage Sites & Places of Interest in the United States." *The Catholic Travel Guide*. [https://thecatholictravelguide .com/destinations/u-s-a/]

Chesterton, G. K. *The New Jerusalem*. 1920. Project Gutenberg eBook #13468, 2014; updated 2018. [http://www.gutenberg.org/ebooks/]

Chiara e Francesco (a.k.a. *Clara e Francesco*, a.k.a. *Clare and Francis*. Directed by Fabrizio Costa. Rome: Lux Vide and Rai Fiction, 2007.

"Christian evangelicals from the US flock to Holy Land in Israeli Tourism Boom," *The Independent* (06 April 2018). [https://www.independent.co.uk/news/world/middle-east/us-christian-evangelicals-israel-tourism-holy-land-jerusalem-a8290521.html]

Collins, Larry, and Dominique Lapierre. *O Jerusalem!* New York: Simon & Schuster, 1972; ebook: Beverly Hills, California: Renaissance Literary & Talent, 2015. Kindle edition.

Copp, Jay. *The Liguori Guide to Catholic U.S.A: A Treasury of Churches, Schools, Monuments, Shrines, and Monasteries*. Liguori, Missouri: Liguori Publications, 1999.

Cragon, Julie Dortch. *Visiting Mary: Her U.S. Shrines and Their Graces*. Cincinnati, Ohio: Servant, 2014.

Craughwell, Thomas J. *101 Places to Pray Before You Die: A Roamin' Catholic's Guide*. Cincinnati, Ohio: Franciscan Media, 2017.

Czarnopys, Theresa Santa, and Thomas M. Santa. *Marian Shrines of the United States: A Pilgrim's Travel Guide*. Liguori, Missouri: Liguori Publications, 1998.

de Montfort, St. Louis. *True Devotion to Mary with Preparation for Total Consecration*. London: Catholic Way Publication, 2013. Kindle edition.

Dietz, Maribel. *Wandering Monks, Virgins, and Pilgrims: Ascetic Travel in the Mediterranean World, A.D. 300-800*. University Park, PA: Penn State Press, 2005.

DK Eyewitness Travel. *Italy 2014*. London: Dorling Kindersley Limited, 1997-2013.

DK Eyewitness Travel. *Jerusalem, Israel, Petra, & Sinai 2014*. London: Dorling Kindersley Limited, 2000-2014.

Dreher, Rod. *The Little Way of Ruthie Leming: A Southern Girl, a Small Town, and the Secret of a Good Life*. New York: Grand Central Publishing, 2013. Kindle edition.

Emmerich, Blessed Anne Catherine. *The Life of the Blessed Virgin Mary*. Trans. Sir Michael Palairet. London: Catholic Way Publishing, 2013. Kindle edition

Erdmann, Carl. *Die Enstehung des Kreuzzugsgedanken*. Stuttgart, 1935. Trans. M. W. Baldwin and Walter Goffart as *The Origin of the Idea of Crusade*. Princeton, 1977.

Eubanks, Larry. "Bethlehem: City of David?" *Larry Eubanks* (02 December 2015). [larryeubanks.com/bethlehem-city-david/]

Farley, Lawrence R. *Following Egeria: A Visit to the Holy Land through Time and Space*. Chesterton, Indiana: Ancient Faith Publishing, 2014. Kindle edition.

Foley, Stephanie. "7 Pilgrimages You Can Make in the United States." *Relevant Radio* (19 April 2018). [https://relevantradio.com/2018/04/7-pilgrimages-you-can-make-in-the-united-states/]

For Greater Glory (a.k.a. *Cristiada*). Directed by Dean Wright. Eynsham, UK: NewLand Films, 2012.

Franciscan Friars. "How the Sun Danced at Noon at Fatima!" *Fatima* (17 June 2016). [http://livingfatima.com/how-the-sun-danced-at-noon-in-fatima/]

"Frequently Asked Questions regarding The Most Visited Catholic Sites," *Catholic Doors Ministry* [https://www.catholicdoors.com/faq/1000/qu1222.htm]

Frost, Robert. "When did John Wayne first use the word 'pilgrim' in his movies? – Answered 02 August 2015." *Quora*. [https://www.quora.com/When-did-John-Wayne-first-use-the-word-pilgrim-in-his-movies]

"Fundamental Differences Between Catholics' and Other Christians' Worldviews." *Fish Eaters*. [https://www.fisheaters.com/differences.html]

Gartman, Eric. *Return to Zion: The History of Modern Israel*. Lincoln: University of Nebraska Press – Jewish Publication Society, 2015. Kindle edition.

Geary, Patrick J. *Furta Sacra: Thefts of Relics in the Central Middle Ages*. Princeton: Princeton University Press, 1978. Revised edition 1991.

Gitlitz, David M., and Linda Kay Davidson, *The Pilgrimage Road to Santiago: The Complete Cultural Handbook*. New York: St. Martin's Griffin, 2000.

Gordon, Nehemia, and Keith Johnson. *A Prayer to Our Father: Hebrew Origins of the Lord's Prayer*. Atascosa, Texas: Hilkiah Press, 2010.

Gray, Richard. "Could we soon drink the same wine as Jesus? DNA from ancient seeds is being used to resurrect 2,000-year-old drinks," *Daily Mail.com* (01 December 2015, updated 04 December 2015). [http://www.dailymail.co.uk/sciencetech/article-3341187/Could-soon-drink-wine-Jesus-DNA-ancient-seeds-used-resurrect-2-000-year-old-drinks.html]

Hammad, Shatha. "Israeli settlers target Christian Palestinians in West Bank town." *Middle East Eye* (29 November 2019). [https://www.middleeasteye.net/news/israeli-settlers-target-christian-palestinians-west-bank-town].

Hare, Kent Gregory. "Christian Heroism and Holy War in Anglo-Saxon England." Ph.D. Dissertation, Louisiana State University (1997). [Abstract: https://digitalcommons.lsu.edu/gradschool_disstheses/6485/]

Hare, Kent Gregory. "Religion, Warfare, and the *Gens Anglorum*: Aspects of Holy War and its Development in Anglo-Saxon England." M.A. Thesis, Louisiana State University (1992).

Harpur, James. *Pilgrim Journey: A History of Pilgrimage in the Western World*. Oxford: Lion Hudson, 2016.

Hesemann, Michael. *Mary of Nazareth: History, Archaeology, Legends*. Trans. Michael J. Miller. San Jose, California: Ignatius Press, 2016. Kindle edition.

Hilliard, Alison, and Betty Jane Bailey. *Living Stones Pilgrimage with the Christians of the Holy Land*. London: Cassell, 1999.

Hoefer, Nancy. "A land of calm and chaos: 'There's a militarized wall around Bethlehem?' and other Holy Land pilgrimage observations," *Archdiocese of Indianapolis: The Criterion Online Edition* (13 March 2015). [http://www.archindy.org/criterion/local/2015/03-13/holyland.html].

Hoefer, Nancy. "A land of calm, chaos and other Holy Land observations," *Diocese of Oakland: The Catholic Voice Online Edition* (06 April 2015). [https://www.catholicvoiceoakland.org/2015/04-06/inthisissue15.htm]

Hoefer, Nancy. "How Catholics in central and southern Indiana can help keep a Christian presence in the Holy Land," *Archdiocese of Indianapolis: The Criterion Online Edition* (13 March 2015). [http://www.archindy.org/criterion/local/2015/03-13/holyland-sidebar.html]

Hoefer, Nancy. "Life for Catholics in Holy Land involves persecution and economic hardship," *Archdiocese of Indianapolis: The Criterion Online Edition* (20 March 2015). [http://www.archindy.org/criterion/local/2015/03-20/holyland.html]

Hoefer, Nancy. "Tour guide gives cultural, historical and archaeological insight," *Diocese of Oakland: The Catholic Voice Online Edition* (18 May 2015). [http://www.catholicvoiceoakland.org/2015/05-18/inthisissue11.htm]

"How many Tourists visited Medjugorje last Year?" *Sarajevo Times* (19 April 2018). [https://www.sarajevotimes.com/how-many-tourists-visited-medjugorje-last-year/]

"How to Afford a Catholic Pilgrimage." *Consumer Catholic* (Updated 29 August 2019). [https://www.consumercatholic.com/how-to-afford-a-catholic-pilgrimage/]

Israeli Ministry of Foreign Affairs. "Christian Tourism to Israel." *About Israel: Spotlight* (23 December 2014). [https://mfa.gov.il/MFA/AboutIsrael/ Spotlight/Pages/Christian-tourism-to-Israel.aspx]

Jerjian, George. *Seeking God – A Pilgrimage to the Holy Land*. Self-published, 2013. Kindle edition.

"Jesus manger: Relic returns to Bethlehem in time for Christmas." *BBC News*. (30 November 2019) [https://www.bbc.com/news/world-middle-east-50600025].

Just, Felix, S.J. "Biblical Geography: The Galilee," *Catholic Resources.org*. [http://catholic-resources.org/Bible/Geography-Galilee.htm]

Levine, Art. "Ki Tissa: Moses' Horns: Not a Mistranslation." *Yerushatenu: Our Heritage* (08 March 2012). [http://rabbiartlevine.com/Home/tabid/2652/ID/840/Ki-Tissa-Moses-Horns-Not-a-Mistranslation.aspx]

Lichtman, Steven John. "Catholic Retreats." *Institute for Traditional Medicine: Body Theology*. [http://www.itmonline.org/bodytheology/part1.htm]

Luomanen, Petri. *Recovering Jewish-Christian Sects and Gospels*. Leiden: Brill, 2011. [https://books.google.com/books]

MacWilliams, Mark W. "Virtual Pilgrimages on the Internet," *Religion* 32.4 (October 2002): 315-335.

Martin, James, S.J. *Jesus: A Pilgrimage*. New York: HarperCollins, 2014.

McAfee, Shaun. "These +100 Catholic Pilgrimage Sites in the US are Completely Out of this World." *epicPew* (15 May 2016). [https://epicpew.com/100-catholic-pilgrimage-sites-in-united-states/]

McGowan, Anne, and Paul F. Bradshaw. *The Pilgrimage of Egeria: A New Translation of the Itinerarium Egeriae with Introduction and Commentary*. Collegeville, MN: Liturgical Press Academic, 2018. Kindle edition.

Medjuck, Bena Elisha. "Exodus 34:29-35 : Moses' 'horns' in early Bible translations and interpretations." M.A. Thesis, McGill University (1988). [Abstract: http://digitool.library.mcgill.ca/R/-?func=dbin-jump-full&current_base=GEN01&object_id=20 449]

"Medjugorje: All the Statistics," *Medjugorje: Le Cri du Ciel vers La Terre* (20 August 2014). [http://marie-oasis.eklablog.com/medjugorje-all-the-statistics-a109071380]

Meyer, Jan. *La Cristiada: The Mexican People's War for Religious Liberty*. Garden City Park, New York: Square One Publishers, 2013.

Michener, James A. *The Source: A Novel*. New York: Random House, 1965. Reprinted Random House-Dial Press Trade Paperbacks, 2014. Kindle edition.

Miravalle, Mark. "Clarifications on Pope Francis' Guadalupe Homily Concerning 'Co-redemptrix'." *Mother of All Peoples – The Marian Library* (13 December 2019). [https://www.motherofallpeoples.com/blog/clarifications-on-pope-francis-guadalupe-homily-concerning-co-redemptrix]).

Montefiore, Simon Sebag. *Jerusalem: The Biography*. New York: Knopf, 2011.

Murphy-O'Connor, Jerome, O.P. *The Holy Land: An Oxford Archaeological Guide from Earliest times to 1700*. Oxford: Oxford University Press, 1998.

Murphy-O'Connor, Jerome, O.P. "Tracing the Via Dolorosa." Chapter 5 in *Jesus: The Last Day – A Collection of Essays Published by the Biblical Archaeology Society*. Ed. Molly Dewsnap Meinhardt. Washington: Biblical Archaeology Society, 2003. Pp. 71-89.

Nalbandian, Garo, and Fred Strickert. *The Church of the Nativity*. Bethlehem: Diyar Publisher, 2013.

National Conference of Catholic Bishops. *Catholic Shrines and Places of Pilgrimage in the United States, Jubilee 2000 Edition*. United States Conference of Catholic Bishops, 1998.

Nolan, Mary Lee, and Sidney Nolan. *Christian Pilgrimage in Modern Western Europe*. Chapel Hill, NC, and London: University of North Carolina Press, 1989.

O Jerusalem (a.k.a. *Beyond Friendship*). Directed by Élie Chouraqui. Culver City, CA: Samuel Goldwyn Films – IDP Distribution, 2006.

O'Brien, Michael D. *Father Elijah: An Apocalypse*. San Francisco, CA: Ignatius Press, 1996. Kindle edition.

Pacwa, Mitch, S.J. *The Holy Land: An Armchair Pilgrimage*. Cincinnati, OH: Franciscan Media – Servant Books, 2013.

Pangle, Teresa M. "Medjugorje's Effects: A History of Local, State, and Church Response to the Medjugorje Phenomenon." M.A. Thesis, Bowling Green State University (2011). [Abstract: http://rave.ohiolink.edu/etdc/view?acc_num=bgsu1300755377]

Pennington, M. Basil. *Journey in a Holy Land: A Spiritual Journal*. Brewster, MA: Paraclete Press, 2006.

"Pilgrimage Sites in the United States and Canada." *Servants of the Lord and the Virgin of Matara*. [https://ssvmusa.org/index.php/catholic-culture/pilgrimage-sites-in-the-united-states/]

"The Pilgrims." *History.com*. [https://www.history.com/ topics/colonial-america/pilgrims; updated 4 October 2018].

Pratt, Maureen. "Can't travel to explore your faith? Try a virtual pilgrimage," *Catholic Philly.com: Commentaries* (15 September 2015). [http://catholicphilly.com/2015/09/commentaries/cant-travel-to-explore-your-faith-try-a-virtual-pilgrimage/]

Ray, Steve. "Holy Land with Fr. Scott Courtney April 2018 (SOLD OUT)." *Footprints of God Pilgrimages*. 04 April to 13 April 2018. [https://www.footprintsofgodpilgrimages.com/pilgrimage/holy-land-with-fr-scott-courtney-april-2017/]

Ray, Steve. "Why Do Catholics Go on Pilgrimages?" YouTube: *The Coming Home Network International* (04 January 2019). [https://www.YouTube.com/watch?v=3gu0HJ5Yxo0].

Regalbuto, Robert J., *Monastery Guest Houses of North America: A Visitor's Guide*. 5th ed. Woodstock, Vermont: Countryman Press, 2010.

Riley-Smith, Jonathan. *The First Crusade and the Idea of Crusading*. 1986. Reprinted London: Continuum Press, 2003.

Sacred Apostolic Penitentiary. *The Enchiridion of Indulgences: Norms and Practices*. Authorized English Edition (1968). [https://www.freecatholicbooks.com/books/indulgences.pdf]

Samson, Charles. *Come and See: A Catholic Guide to the Holy Land.* Steubenville, OH: Emmaus Road, 2017.

San Martin, Inéz. "Pope calls idea of declaring Mary co-redemptrix 'foolishness'." *Crux* (13 December 2019). [https://cruxnow.com/vatican/2019/12/pope-calls-idea-of-declaring-mary-co-redemptrix-foolishness/]

Scaperlanda, María Ruiz and Michael Scaperlanda. *The Journey: A Guide for the Modern Pilgrim.* Chicago: Loyola Press, 2004.

"Shrines, Basilicas, Cathedrals, Monasteries." *Catholic Shrines and Holy Places.* [catholicplaces.org]

"Sites by State." *Catholic Pilgrimage Sites.* [https://catholicpilgrimagesites.wordpress.com/sites-by-state-2/]

Smith, Jody Brant. *The Image of Guadalupe: Myth or Miracle?* New York: Doubleday, 1983.

Spitzer, Robert J. "Science and the Shroud of Turin." *Magis Center of Reason and Faith* (May 2015). [https://2i7i0l43ftgic4pas6ndtk6b-wpengine.netdna-ssl.com/wp-content/uploads/2017/07/Science_and_the_Shroud_of_Turin.pdf]

Stanley, Alexandria. "Pope Makes Virtual Visit to Iraqi Site He Must Skip," *New York Times* (24 February 2000). [http://www.nytimes.com/2000/02/24/world/pope-makes-virtual-visit-to-iraqi-site-he-must-skip.html]

Sumption, Jonathan. *The Age of Pilgrimage: The Medieval Journey to God.* 1975. Reprinted Mahwah, NJ: Paulist Press – Hidden Spring, 2003.

"Pope authorizes pilgrimages to Medjugorje." *Vatican News* (12 May 2019). [https://www.vaticannews.va/en/pope/news/2019-05/pope-authorizes-pilgrimages-to-medjugorje.html]

Wright, Kevin J. *Catholic Shrines of Central and Eastern Europe: A Pilgrim's Travel Guide.* Liguori, MO: Liguori, 1999.

Wright, Kevin J. *Catholic Shrines of Western Europe: A Pilgrim's Travel Guide.* Liguori, MO: Liguori, 1997.

Xiarhos, Michael. "Authenticity and the Cyber Pilgrim," *Journal of Religion & Society* 18 (2016): 1-18.

www.ingramcontent.com/pod-product-compliance
Lightning Source LLC
Chambersburg PA
CBHW020938180426

43194CB00038B/224